Thus Far on My Journey

by
E. Raymond Wilson

RICHMOND
INDIANA

Published by
Friends United Press
Richmond, Indiana

Library of Congress Cataloging in Publication Data

Wilson, Edward Raymond, 1896-
   Thus far on my journey.

1. Wilson, Edward Raymond, 1896- 2. Pacifists — United States —
Biography. I. Title. JX1962.W54A37   327'.172'0924 (B) 76-42308
ISBN 0-913408-26-3

Printed in the United States of America
by
R.R. Donnelley & Sons Co.

To my parents —

Anna Jane Willson Wilson
and
Charles Brown Wilson

whose love and example
inspired my journey

Preface

"There is a destiny that shapes our ends, rough hew them as we will," observed Shakespeare in the play *Hamlet*. As I looked backward on my spiritual journey the following glimpses of my past recount some of the decisions that profoundly influenced the course of events and shaped my life.

One major decision was to give up plans to return to the farm on which I had been born, and for which I had trained during my earlier years, including earning a degree in animal husbandry at Iowa State College. This leading was to embark on an uncharted course in which I expressed my willingness to offer myself for Christian life service in some other country. However, this eventually led to more than three decades of legislative activity in the foreign mission field of Washington, D.C.!

Another crucial decision grew out of the challenge by Kirby Page at the International Student Volunteer Convention at Indianapolis during the Christmas holidays in 1923. Kirby Page insisted that war was innately contrary to the life and teachings of Jesus, that one ought to withhold support of, and participation in, it, and that our religious duty was to do all we could to abolish war. This pilgrimage was intensified by the invitation to help launch the National Committee on Militarism in Education. Working against compulsory military training started my half century's involvement in the struggle for world peace and drove me to the personal pacifist position.

Only part of that effort for peace is recounted in this book. More of the story of my involvement is portrayed in *Uphill for Peace* which tells the highlights of more than thirty years of the history of the Friends Committee on National Legislation and which is compressed into chapter 9 of *Thus Far on My Journey*.

I believe in dreaming dreams and then attempting to have some part in bringing them to realization. Miriam and I were among those dreaming of a productive community life in the country. We were among the charter members of the remarkable and successful cooperative venture, the Bryn Gweled Homesteads near Southampton, Pennsylvania.

Ray Newton and I dreamed of a vigorous Quaker lobby in Washington to work in Congress for peace, freedom and justice. The Friends Committee on National Legislation was launched in 1943 as the first full-time religious lobby.

Some of us dreamed that the FCNL might have an office on Capitol Hill. The office now is located just across the street from where the addition to the Dirksen Senate Office Building is under construction.

Three things coalesced to bring into realization our hope for an educational center which would bring in people from around the country for seminars and strategy meetings and other opportunities to get acquainted with official Washington. An appropriate site was found just east of the Capitol, some funds were promised, Robert and Sally Cory became available as co-directors, and in 1965 William Penn House began its unique function as window on Washington.

This somewhat unvarnished story of some of the episodes in my life was undertaken at the urging of my friends. In part this is the record of a career spent largely in the still unachieved search for international peace and justice, with time out to pick up hitchhikers or listen to the crocus spoof the human race.

We believe that peace is the will of God and that man will ultimately develop the global will and the global institutions to establish it. Peace will have to be founded on justice under law. We need to challenge the supposedly divine right of governments and peoples to undertake and carry on war or to hold on to practices that lead to war.

Since within not too many more years my generation will be laying its burdens down, let us hope and pray and expect that increasing numbers of men and women around the world will dedicate their lives to working for the principles and programs that will abolish war.

With finite resources and burgeoning population there will be more and more conflicts in the future. These should be settled without violence under law. That should be agenda item number 1 for the future.

E. RAYMOND WILSON
SANDY SPRING, MARYLAND
JULY 1976

Acknowledgments

The labors of many people go into the preparation and publication of even a modest-sized book like this. Lynn Bowling worked closely with me on research, editing and typing most of the manuscript until her husband, Arthur Bowling, transferred his college teaching from Swarthmore to Ohio. Jan Gager finished the typing. Jere Knight constructively criticized the first draft of my chapter recounting my year as a student in Japan.

A much too laudatory introduction was written by Samuel R. Levering. He and his wife, Miriam, have been life-long workers for peace. During the last three years they have worked incessantly for a fair and honorable treaty to emerge from the United Nations Conferences on the Law of the Seas toward utilizing the "last great heritage of mankind" for the benefit of the world's people rather than profits for multinational corporations.

At the Friends United Press Vickey Short has done the composition on this volume while Carol Beals has been the editorial and copy reader. Ethel Prignitz has set up the page proof. Friends United Press has been represented by Earl Prignitz with whom I have dealt in working out arrangements for the preparation and publication of *Thus Far on My Journey*.

The Swarthmore College Peace Collection is the depository of what I facetiously call the "E. Raymond Wilson Inconsequentialities" — the accumulation of personal and historical materials, including correspondence, picture albums, diaries and other personal records without which this volume could not have been written. The Peace Collection houses a unique and comprehensive range of archives relating to peace organizations and peace leaders around the world. Bernice Nichols and her colleagues have been unfailing in their cooperation and help in this enterprise.

My heartfelt thanks go to my friends and relatives who have contributed to the printing of this life story so that the price would not be prohibitive. Marie Stefan in the business office of Haverford

College has handled the accounts for my two literary efforts — my prior book on Quaker lobbying and the work of the Friends Committee on National Legislation *Uphill for Peace*, and for this one.

— E. RAYMOND WILSON

Contents

Introduction

How was an Iowa farm boy turned into a conscience of the National Council of Churches?

How did a lad raised as a strict Presbyterian become the ablest Quaker voice in Washington for twenty-five years?

What were the personal experiences and decisions which molded this person so widely loved and respected, even by those who most differed with him?

How could anyone absorb so much frustration and disappointment and yet always have a joke and a laugh ready?

Since 1900, three American Quakers have had the greatest impact on the Society of Friends and the wider world. All came from deeply Christian homes, and their lives and work expressed their commitment and faith.

Rufus Jones articulated the Quaker faith beautifully in speech and writing, helped Friends to appreciate and work with each other, and guided the early years of the American Friends Service Committee. Clarence Pickett was the moving spirit as the American Friends Service Committee became an outstanding worldwide expression of Quaker compassion. Raymond Wilson, from the founding of the Friends Committee on National Legislation in 1943 (and before), has represented the best in Quakerism to decision-makers in the United States government, and inspired an increasingly effective involvement of Friends in the great issues of peace and justice in our time.

In his book, *Uphill for Peace*, Raymond Wilson has described some of the outstanding accomplishments of the Friends Committee on National Legislation, as well as the great present challenges. In this book we see more clearly the person, which, of course, largely explains the accomplishments. This book is in the tradition of Quaker journals and of the Rufus Jones autobiographical writings. Here we have a current warm and human model from which many persons may find inspiration and goals for their own lives.

But no autobiography could quite portray the spirit and character of Raymond Wilson. There are inklings of it in his description of hitchhikers, and especially in his tribute to his wife, Miriam Wilson. But he says nothing about his unfailing affection for everyone he worked with, expressed by his going out of his way to help, especially the humblest. Nor is anything said of his ancient Chevrolet, symbol of his modest personal wants and expenditures.

Characteristically, this autobiography gives only a slight indication of Raymond Wilson's abilities and accomplishments. Here are only two examples: He is in demand as speaker, as chairman of meetings, and of drafting committees because of a remarkable ability to sift the verbiage and clearly organize the essentials, and his willingness to toil long and well.

One can only surmise from a Japanese incident in the book that Raymond Wilson helped save millions from malnutrition or starvation by thinking of an idea (and getting it enacted) whereby U.S. government food surpluses would be given (and freight paid) for distribution to the neediest through committed private agencies such as Church World Service, the AFSC and CARE.

It has been my privilege to know Rufus Jones well, Clarence Pickett somewhat, and Raymond Wilson intimately, as a co-founder of FCNL and Chairman of its Executive Committee for sixteen years. Douglas Southall Freeman, after completing a thorough biography of Robert E. Lee, said that in that work he felt that he had always been in the presence of a gentleman. As one who has been close to Raymond Wilson for 33 years, I gladly report that he has always been a deeply committed and effective Christian.

SAMUEL R. LEVERING

CHAPTER 1

Early Influences on My Life

When people ask me about my early life, I tell them I was raised on a farmer's eight-hour day — eight hours before lunch, eight hours after lunch, and a couple of hours of chores night and morning to keep me in shape for the eight-hour day. Our eighty acres, bought from the government at $1.25 an acre, have been in the Wilson family for more than 130 years.

GROWING UP ON THE FARM

There are many advantages to growing up on a farm. One is independence. You're your own boss or else your father is. The environment wasn't much polluted at that time — we could see the sun and the moon and the stars clearly. Another advantage is self-reliance: I drove a horse and buggy to town by myself to get the groceries when I was seven years old. Time never hung heavy on our hands because there was always something to be done. We learned to undertake any kind of work in any kind of weather. If it was hot or cold, wet or dry, we kept right on going. If the windmill wheel got out of order and the weather was below zero, we climbed up the forty feet to try to get the windmill going again. The stock must have water whatever the temperature.

I shiver even now when I think of husking corn in the snow with a husking peg, moving along with the team and wagon, trying to keep the ears of corn banging with a nice rhythm against the bang boards of the wagon. A good husker could husk a hundred bushels a day, but I never was that good. My mittens would get wet, the wind was blowing and my fingers were freezing. There was no opportunity to stop and feel sorry for myself, so I went right ahead. Fifty bushels an acre was supposed to be a pretty good yield in those days. Now with all the advances of hybrid seeds and fertilizer a farmer would feel that 125 bushels an acre would be a modest crop.

In those days many things which we now take for granted were nonexistent or were just being adopted. Six weeks after my birth on September 20, 1896, near Morning Sun, Iowa, the first rural free delivery system was inaugurated in Iowa following the precedent set six weeks earlier in West Virginia. The R.F.D. ran right by Cloverdale Farm where I was born. The businessmen didn't want R.F.D. because they wanted the farmers to come to town to trade, but the farmers figured if they took a day a week to go in for their mail, they'd loose fifty cents, the value of a day's work. So the R.F.D. was started with Bert McKinley as the carrier on our particular twenty-five-mile route. He was to be paid $250 a year and furnish his own horse. Bert rode a horse with a couple of saddle bags. When it got too cold to ride, he'd get off and lead the horse. And he did that until May when he was able to use a buggy. The dirt roads were graded only once a year. When there was a heavy rain, or when the frost went out in the spring, the roads became almost bottomless.

The first mail boxes were made out of anything available — old boots, upended drain pipes, cigar boxes, discarded stove pipes, milk cans and old wash basins. The mail carrier would have to deposit the letters wherever the farmer had nailed up the container — on a tree in the back yard or up on the back porch. Senator John Gear of Burlington recommended our village of Morning Sun, Iowa, as the place to start rural free delivery, because this community of 850 people was the "readingest people" he knew.

On the farm we lived close to nature — I used to get out in the spring to see if I could find the first wild flowers which we called Easter lilies or trillium. Then along would come the hepaticas, anemones, lamb's tongues and Dutchman's breeches. Columbines finished the spring season.

Rattlesnakes were rather common on our farm. While cutting oats one morning my father stopped his four-horse team to oil the binder only to find there was a rattlesnake wrapped around the hub of the bull wheel, joy riding. My father killed it with a stick.

I remember once my mother was walking with a teacher from the grade school in town down along Honey Creek on our farm, enjoying the trees and wild flowers. This teacher saw something peculiar on the foundation of an old house. She went up and was just about to kick it, saying, "What kind of a queer rock formation is this?" My mother saw her and screamed at her to be careful because it was a coiled rattlesnake. They came home and told me about it. I called up our neighbor about a quarter of a mile away and he went down and found the snake still there. He took a string from his shoe, tied the end of it to a long stick, made a loose loop from the string, slipped it over the rattlesnake's head and led it up home where he tied it to the fence. Later he thought that a little dangerous for children and finally killed it.

You learn all kinds of things on a farm: how to drive a sixteen-foot harrow through a twelve-foot gate, how to take care of livestock, how to look after baby pigs or calves or colts, how to repair machinery.

My younger brother and I would take turns each week helping father outside or mother inside. My oldest sister lived just a few days, so I was the oldest girl in my family most of the time. I made some progress in home economics, but I never reached the domestic heights of casseroles, custards and angel food cakes.

The house was heated by a big potbellied wood stove in the living room. Part of the chores was splitting wood for the range in the kitchen. We studied our lessons under a kerosene lamp. The Saturday night special was a bath in a big round tub in the kitchen with water heated on the range. Since our family always went to church rain or shine, wet or dry, hot or cold, this was when cleanliness got closest to godliness. A Montgomery Ward catalog served as toilet paper in our outdoor amenities.

There are also disadvantages to growing up on a farm. In those days we didn't see very much money. After my father died in 1927, my brother and I tried to hold the farm together in the depression. In one year he bought one pair of overalls and his wife bought one pair of hose. If I'm a pacifist today, as I am, I am partially an agricultural pacifist because of what I saw of the effects of the First World War on agriculture in the Midwest. Our farm depression started in 1921. In that next decade one farmer in seven lost his farm in Iowa, and one farmer in four lost his in South Dakota, largely because of the inflationary and other economic effects of the war.

We were in the path of storms and tornadoes which unroofed each of our two barns at different times. During the spring of my sophomore year in high school I came home at noon to help my father get the crops in. One stormy day I had just reached home and was lying across the bed looking out the window when I saw lightning strike the cattle barn. A high wind swept the fire through the foot of straw in the haymow and the barn burned down in a few minutes. The livestock ran out to safety. The neighbors rallied around and were able to save some of the ear corn in a corner crib in the barn basement, but the wind carried the burning shingles and embers for more than a quarter of a mile missing our house by only forty feet. Luckily the wind didn't blow the shingles onto the house or we might have lost it too.

Tragedy Strikes Twice

We lived not only with disadvantages but also with tragedy. On the farm we had two fatal accidents and various minor ones. My sixteen-year-old brother, Russell, a year and a half younger than I, was hauling rock with me from our stone quarry to the highway that was being surfaced about a mile away. He had a rather spirited team which ran away and pulled him under the wagon. A wheel ran over his head, and he never regained consciousness. Though we took him up to our house and called the doctor who came as quickly as possible, his skull was crushed and he lived for only a few hours.

Some years later when the only son of my brother, Ralph, was missing at supper time, Ralph went out to look for him. He found the son at the bottom of the haychute, dead. The boy had gone over to the cattle barn to throw down some hay from the haymow for the cattle and somehow he had slipped down the haychute and hit his head on the stone foundation. Apparently he was instantly killed.

When I was in college at Ames, my younger sister died from scarlet fever and pneumonia, diseases which today are usually overcome with modern medicine. My father died at the age of sixty-six, partly because of physical overwork. In those days you had to shovel corn, shovel manure, pitch hay — most farm work was done by hand. Life was pretty rugged. Yet my mother, who was always frail, lived to be ninety-three.

Happy Memories of Honey Creek Country School

I went eight years to the Honey Creek one-room country school. That's an open education, because you hear everybody's recitation. I think I read more books when I was in country school than I have ever done in the same amount of time since. We had good teachers and although the country school may have had some disadvantages, I felt it was a great experience. The first schoolhouse had been built in 1845 and burned down in 1856. The schoolhouse which my brother and I attended was built in 1857.

I think back nostalgically about the personal attention by the teacher in the small classes, and the joy of learning about a world which I hadn't experienced firsthand. My memories of the details of the particular studies, including the struggle to learn the multiplication tables, have pretty well faded, but some incidents were indelibly painted on my mind as I look back fondly to those early years. The total effect of country school on me was wholesome and stimulating.

We walked three-quarters of a mile to school in every kind of weather except the most inclement when our parents would take us by buggy or bobsled. We crossed Honey Creek every day on the way to school. One spring, for variety, I tried to cross at a different place each morning, and one time I either stumbled or stepped in a hole and went clear under. I climbed out, pressed the water out of my clothes the best that I could, and went on to school. At morning recess I was sitting out in the sun shivering, and friends asked what was the matter. During the day my clothes finally did dry out. But that night my cousin, Marion, who lived on a farm half a mile away, told my mother and I had an encounter with the discipline of the lilac bush. There was a lilac bush pretty close to our kitchen door and it never really thrived very well as long as I was a boy. I guess my family went on the theory that if you spare the rod you spoil the child. I wasn't over-spoiled and I was glad when the time came that I outgrew the applications of the lilac bush.

One Christmas when I was in country school I was given a pair of skates and learned to skate a little bit forward on Honey Creek. I figured if I could skate very fast forward, then jump up and turn around in the air, I would be able to start skating backwards. Well, I tried it but just as I turned around, the ice came up and hit me very fast. I cracked open my forehead above one eyebrow and had to be sent to town to the doctor to be stitched back together.

Going to country school I saw the trees leafing out in spring and the vivid coloring in fall with oaks and sumac and maples making a great range of color. In the center of the schoolroom was a potbellied stove that burned wood or coal. A hole had been burned in the floor where coals dropped out of the stove. One morning a garter snake crawled up through that hole and wrapped itself around the foot of a desk. We had to encourage him to leave. There seemed to be no class where a garter snake would fit in.

One time I took a couple of young screech owls to school in my pocket to show my classmates. The screech owls had a nest in the maple tree in our yard at home. I used to go out in the evening and tease them. The older birds would fly down snapping their beaks. One night after I had been teasing them, an owl plowed his talons through my hair and furrowed the top of my head.

Some of the boys would trap during the winter. There's nothing quite like the sweet, ripe smell of skunk on a classmate's clothing, another vivid impression of country school.

Country children lost something in 1921 when the schools were consolidated. I had a good teacher every year. Camaraderie between students and teachers was close, bred in part by our common struggle to get to school through rain and snow and ice, and built up in part by the informality, friendliness and lack of ostentation which characterized our country school.

High School

In the fall of 1909 I started high school in Morning Sun which was about two-and-a-half miles from my home. During those years I drove a horse and buggy to school. I remember once the old gray mare was frightened by a motorcycle and ran wild with me down the main street of town, but fortunately I had no major accidents in my horse-and-buggy days. My routine was to get up with the chickens every morning, feed a couple of carloads of cattle, hitch up the horse and drive to school, unhitch, put the horse in the stable and be in school at nine o'clock. There were nineteen in my graduating class of 1914. Fifty years later sixteen of the class were still alive, and thirteen of them gathered for a reunion on the farm, coming all the way from as far as California.

Among the classes I took were English, history, math, German and Latin. Now I wish that high school classes might have been more relevant to what I have tried to do since then. For example, I took four years of Latin which I would gladly trade for typing or some other useful skill.

Most of my classes I enjoyed. One vivid memory is of a debate in high school history class with Helen Campbell whether the Revolutionary War was necessary and justified. I took the position that the problems separating the colonies and the mother country could have been solved without war, and that Canada now has substantially the same freedoms which the United States enjoys.

We had many high school parties at the farm. The students would come out and we'd crank up the freezer and make a batch of rich ice cream. Once in a while we had a school fight between our class and another class, but usually the parties were times of good fun. One night somebody started "the follow the leader" and the line of about twenty went right through the watermelon patch, so that next morning the patch was a complete ruin. On that same night one boy got caught in the barbed wire fence and practically tore off his clothes, requiring a tailor to put him back together. In one encounter in the yard a boy ran hard against the clothesline which caught him right below the chin. The line became taut and dropped him flat on his back on the ground, knocking the breath out of him.

Life was pretty hard, but we had many good times. Neighborhood socials were rollicking fun where people of all ages would come for a good time. We played spin the platter, post office, charades, and other games where everyone would join in. How much is lost today when people of different generations fail to play together and when so much emphasis is on spectator sports or theaters or other entertainment where people watch and listen rather than participate.

In 1914 when our class graduated we had a varied program in which the graduates all took part. I gave an oration on "The Future of Electricity." Sixty years later, everything I predicted has been realized except one idea, the transmission of power without wires over long distances. And even that has been partly accomplished by the development of satellites, voyages to the moon and spaceships. The *New York Times* of October 10, 1975, carried a story of the transmission in California by radio beam of a limited amount of electric power a distance of one mile. But prediction is always risky. How far wrong I was on one forecast is indicated by the following paragraph:

> Because of its many advantages, electricity is destined to almost entirely supplant steam, compressed air, or other forms of power in all manufacturing industries. The smoke nuisance will be an item of history. Electricity will thus be supplied from central stations displacing the open fires in homes or factories for heat, light and power. This will bring us closer to the model we find in nature, which needs no flame for the production of light, heat, or power. The rays of the sun are the one inexhaustible force.

Boys' Camp at the Iowa State Fair

As an enthusiastic farm boy in high school, expecting eventually to return to the farm, I had written an article entitled, "Farming in Iowa, Its Possibilities Compared with Other Vocations." I claimed that Iowa raised more corn than South America, Africa, Australia and Hungary combined, and more oats than all Africa, Asia and Australia. "There never has been nor probably ever will be a total failure of crops in Iowa," I wrote, "Life on the farm is indeed the ideal one. . . ."

My anticipation of farming was reflected by the essay which I wrote later on "The Ideal Farm" which won a contest to represent Louisa County at the Iowa State Fair Boys' Camp. There were ninety-nine counties in Iowa and I think virtually every one of them was represented. We were housed in two large tents and supposed to work half the day and have the other half for recreation, taking notes and so forth. I was, of course, terrifically impressed by what I saw. There were livestock of all kinds, the grand champion dairy cow and the cow that had been offered to President Wilson as a gift. In one of the horse barns was the stallion that won the International Championship in 1910, and close to the draft horses weighing nearly a ton each, were the Shetland ponies ranging in size down to little colts which we could carry in our arms. We saw something of the preparation and care necessary for the show ring. Acres were covered with different kinds of farm machinery. Countless varieties of fruits and vegetables were exhibited in another large building. The fruit exhibit convinced me that with proper culture Iowa could raise many fruits as good as those produced anywhere in the United States.

We heard a number of speakers including the governor and other prominent leaders in the State of Iowa. Those speakers emphasized uprightness in living, thorough preparation for life's work, and invariably extolled the calling of the farmer. Some of the events I remember are the boys' livestock judging contest and a number of horse shows. One night in the horse show four of us dressed in white served as pivots for horses to be ridden or driven around. One girl who was driving two horses in tandem tried to see how close she could come to us as she went around while we stood there like posts. The sulky missed us by inches. I guess she felt that one less boy camper wouldn't make too much difference since they were sprouting all over the place.

The Iowa State Fair of 1914 was a foreshadowing of much of the coming revolution in American agriculture. The fifty years since 1921, when I finished at Iowa State College, have brought artificial insemination, hybrid seeds, power of all kinds, fertilizers, pesticides, new and improved machinery, and paved roads — more changes than there had been in the previous five hundred years of farming. At the 1914 State Fair I saw the beginnings of many of these advances. I considered it the most profitable week I had spent up to that time.

INFLUENCE OF MY PARENTS

My paternal grandfather, James X. Wilson, homesteaded the family farm in 1844. There, near what was to become Morning Sun, Iowa, he built a one-room brick house and fathered ten children of whom eight lived. My father was the youngest of the family. His sister, Cynthia, spent forty years in India, and his sister, Rosa, spent thirty years there, as missionaries under the United Presbyterian Board. My early background emphasized that people should try to serve where they could, at home or abroad.

My parents were God-fearing, conscientious, hard-working, public-spirited citizens. I owe more than I can say to the religious influence of my home and church while I was a boy. My father was a good farmer and manager. He spent his entire life on that one farm which has been in the family for 130 years and which now belongs to my brother Ralph and his wife Martha.

My father was assessor for Morning Sun Township for twelve years. I never knew him to violate any confidences about who had what, but I do remember his calling me down very strongly for making noise at home when he was adding up long columns of figures before we had an adding machine.

He was elected Republican representative to the Iowa General Assembly in 1915 and 1917 from Louisa County and took his responsibilities very seriously. He was involved in the debates over establishing the state primary road system, over the enactment of prohibition and Sunday closing laws, over taxes and appropriations.

I had a few opportunities of visiting him there at the state capitol and hearing some of the debates. I remember one time there was a bill introduced to require that the width of the bobsled which is about two-and-a-half to three feet wide be made the same width as wagon wheels and buggy wheels so it would make the same width track in the snow. This went to a committee and there was a wag on the committee who wrote a long poem. This poem dealt at some length with the disadvantages of widening the bobsled to the sleigh width because when John took Jane out riding they wouldn't be nearly as cozy as they would be in the narrower track. And then he proposed an amendment that all bobsleds should be painted green. Ridicule was his way of ending this proposition.

Another time when I was at the House of Representatives to visit my father one of the representatives' children was playing in the aisle. The speaker rapped his gavel and said, "Are you ready for the question?" and the boy piped up, "Mr. Speaker, what is the question?"

My parents were quite religious; they were never too busy for family worship. Morning and evening we had Bible readings and singing of psalms. The singing wasn't too melodious; I couldn't carry a tune in a gunny sack; but at least we went through the psalm book and through the Bible. Bible reading proved to have practical as well as spiritual value. My younger brother, Russell, for example, began to pick up various words in family worship — "and," "the" and other simple words — and began recognizing them in the readings. When he first went to country school at seven the teacher started him in the fourth grade reader because at family worship he had learned not to hesitate on "Nebuchadnezzar, Belshazzar, Beelzebub, Shadrach, Meshach, or Abednego." The reading at family worship was educational as well as devotional.

An Ecumenical Family

I was raised in an ecumenical atmosphere, because my mother belonged to the Reformed Presbyterian Church or Covenanter Church, and my father to the United Presbyterian Church. I was raised on the two church papers, the Covenanter's *The Christian Nation* and *The United Presbyterian.* I went to the Covenanter Church with my mother and brothers. Father attended the United Presbyterian Church. We would drive uptown and separate.

The American Covenanters took the position of political dissent, because they believed that the United States had refused to acknowledge God in the Constitution as the source of all authority, and refused to submit to Jesus Christ as King and to the Bible as the rule of law. So they did not vote nor hold governmental office. Only recently have they changed their position on voting. The United Presbyterians did vote so this was one of the differences between the two denominations.

The other difference was that the Covenanters believed that instrumental music was not prescribed by Jesus, and that what was not commanded by Him was forbidden. Both churches used the psalms at that time and the United Presbyterians used organs or pianos in their worship. The doctrinal differences were not substantial and were never a matter of conflict in our family. Mother and father respected each other's views. As children we enjoyed the benefits of both churches and the privilege of entertaining many visiting clergymen and missionaries from both denominations.

The first five dollars I ever earned was for reading the Bible through from Genesis I to Revelation XXII, all sixty-six books of the Bible. I suppose it took some months, I don't remember exactly. It went pretty fast. On Sunday afternoon we would have serious reading or learn verses or do things that were in harmony with our parents' idea of the Sabbath. It was never too hot, cold or rainy to go to church and Sabbath school. We drove a team of draft horses and a surrey with a fringe on top a long time before that mode of transport was popularized in the musical, *Oklahoma*. Side curtains were put up in rain or cold weather. If it was cold we'd wrap ourselves up in horse blankets and travel either in the surrey or in a bobsled.

One of my dominant early impressions was of the continuity of the leadership in the local church to which I belonged. Dr. D.D. Trumbull was pastor for forty years. He was succeeded by the Reverend H.G. Patterson who was minister then for thirty-five years. The two of them spanned the seventy-five years between 1874 and 1949. When Dr. Patterson retired and reviewed his ministerial career, he found he'd preached 3003 sermons, three more than the proverbs of Solomon, conducted 146 funerals, baptized 91 people, wed 27 couples and received 249 people into the church. His salary when he started was twelve hundred dollars and thirty-five years later it was twenty-one hundred dollars.

When I joined the staff of the American Friends Service Committee and started traveling among the Society of Friends in 1931, my travel was mostly among the pastoral Friends. It was a shock to me to find many of these men at that time had not had much formal education, and that after one or two years they would reach the bottom of the barrel of sermons and would move on. After having had only two ministers in my home church, to see churches where ministers change so often or are shifted nearly every year like the Methodists did then was a surprising contrast to my early background.

I was a rebel very early concerning certain doctrines. In grade school I made up my mind not to spend my life arguing theology. I appreciated my religious background, was active religiously in high school and college, but I didn't like the rigid dogma of the church I grew up in.

I worked some though not enough after I became a pacifist to encourage the Covenanter Church to take a pacifist position; I felt if they were a church dissenting against the government, they should dissent on some central issues, not just on formulation of doctrine. I wrote a letter on November 8, 1939, to the ministers and correspondents of the Reformed Presbyterian Church, sending them copies of two pamphlets, *How To Keep America Out of War*, and the

Pacifist Handbook, urging them to put copies of them in the hands of every young man of military age. In my appeal to them I quoted Clyde Allee of the University of Chicago who said, "I know of no Christian way to kill a man." "Every young man of military age," I wrote, "faces the question of his relation to supporting the destruction and demoralization of war in case our country should become involved. . . . Can we raise our united voices against the pagan method of war and use our influence in seeking peace and justice?"

While the church did not act immediately upon my suggestion, the Synod sometime later did affirm its support of the rights of conscience of its young men of military age. It never, however, categorically renounced war as evil and unchristian.

For me it was a long and tortuous journey from a theological position based largely on belief in certain doctrines to a Quaker view of religion based largely on experience applicable to all of life and subject to continuing revelation. However I started with a solid and rich background to begin the religious journey in which I am still engaged.

CHAPTER 2

Spiritual Crossroads in College

College is chiefly important because of the opportunities it affords, in addition to formal classes, and because of the things it makes possible afterwards. It is not a goal, but a road. I am supremely grateful for the many wholesome and uplifting influences which enriched my college life — inspiring faculty and courses, student activities including leadership training in the YMCA at Iowa State College and Columbia University, the challenge of student conferences, marvelous group experiences, and the joy and fellowship of living at International House.

The humbling experience of graduate work in New York City prompted this reflection in a letter which I wrote home in 1923:

> When I graduated from high school, I thought I knew most of the important things to be learned. Four or five years in college create a strong question whether one knows very much or not. A year's or two years' work along a special line strengthens the suspicion that perhaps you don't know anything at all. Finally, contact with the specialists in a given field creates the suspicion that, practically speaking, you know nothing.

Iowa State College

My collegiate track record was more of a marathon than a hundred-yard dash because it started in 1915 and ended in 1926. After a year's hard work on the farm after high school, I went to Monmouth College for one year beginning a liberal arts course. Then I transferred to Iowa State College at Ames. The first year was interrupted by the United States entering the war in April 1917, and

I left school almost immediately. For over a year I helped my father on the farm, responding to the call for more food, and in June 1918, enlisted in the Navy.

Returning to college when the war was over, I finished the course in animal husbandry. One of my most unused courses since that time was entitled "Soundness and Shoeing of Horses." The horse age, so far as horsepower in the flesh was concerned, began rapidly to disappear with the automobile, the tractor and other power machinery. There are still a large number of horses in the United States — race horses, riding horses and ponies — but I don't drive them, ride them, race them, shoe them or bet on them.

My chief extracurricular activity as an undergraduate was in the student YMCA under the magnificent leadership of Fred Hansen, the dynamic secretary of the Iowa State College Association. Fred was seldom at a loss for an appropriate word or a sparkling quip. He once described a sourfaced gentleman as so long-faced that he could eat oats out of a churn. Maybe since the eclipse of the horse and the tall churn with the up-and-down beaters, this reference may not sound as funny to you as it always has to me.

One of the many inspiring experiences was the opportunity of serving as president of the large Sunday school class taught by Fred Hansen at the Collegiate Presbyterian Church. Fred Hansen was a very inspiring teacher. One year "All Out to Church Sunday" brought an attendance of a hundred and forty men.

In my junior year I was on the Y Cabinet and was elected president in my senior year. For the next two years, I served half time as Fred Hansen's assistant while completing a Master's degree in Vocational Education. The Y outreach was indicated by the organization in one year alone of an average of forty-one discussion groups, usually led by faculty, which met in dormitories, rooming houses and fraternities.

One of my activities while working in the student YMCA was to put a one-line cryptic quotation under the title, "The Daily Dribble," on a blackboard. These were quotations which I had gleaned, or which had been passed on to me by some other student. Among my favorites were the following:

When you get to the end of your rope, tie a knot in it and hang on.

Better to remain silent and be thought a fool, than to speak and remove all doubt.

When a man is wrapped up in himself, he makes a mighty small parcel.

There are no statues erected to those who thought it best to leave well enough alone.

Some men grow under responsibility; others just swell.

When you kill time remember it has no resurrection.

The face of the world looks as though it had shaved itself with a broken beer bottle while standing on a barrel in a cyclone.

Civilization is just a slow process of getting rid of our prejudices.

The measure of a man is the friends he keeps in the guest chamber of the heart.

No man's thinking is better than his information.

The worth of existence depends on success in a game infinitely more complicated than that of chess, in which no mistake is ever overlooked and no move ever taken back and where knowledge from one's own experience often comes too late for use.

Some so-called open minds should be closed for repairs.

There are no free scholarships in the school of experience.

We make a living by what we get; but a life by what we give.

The chief difficulty with the harmony of the nations is that every power wants to beat the war drum and none is willing to play second fiddle.

Many a man has the eyesight of a hawk and the vision of a clam.

Jumping at conclusions is about the only mental exercise some folks take.

Life is not a goblet to be drained; it is a measure to be filled.

About the time you think you make both ends meet, somebody moves the ends.

Most of the shadows that cross our path through life are caused by our standing in our own light.

Following the paths of least resistance is what makes rivers and men crooked.

Ames was usually represented by the largest or second largest delegation to the regional summer YMCA student conference for the central region, held in June at Lake Geneva, Wisconsin. I went to five of these summer conferences which were immeasurably enriching experiences to me with the challenging speakers and warm fellowship I always found there.

One of the major turning points of my life was a beautiful moonlit night when I walked the shores of the lake a long time alone and finally decided to sign the Student Volunteer Movement pledge to offer myself for Christian service abroad, if the way opened. I gave up my agricultural training and my plan to return to the farm for an uncertain and uncharted future. This was much to the disappointment of my father who was feeling the burden of his years, but he soon gave me his wholehearted blessing. The decision came down, in part, to the question of whether I wanted to work with animals or people, whether running a farm was the best contribution I could make toward a better world, using whatever talents God had endowed me.

It was ten long years after graduation before I found a cause into which I could throw myself with genuine and unrestrained enthusiasm — working among the Society of Friends in peace education for the American Friends Service Committee.

TEACHERS COLLEGE, COLUMBIA UNIVERSITY

In search of a way to make my contribution to a better world I enrolled as a religious education major at Teachers College, Columbia University, my studies financed by a three-year Lydia C. Roberts Fellowship (for a student born in Iowa and a graduate of an Iowa college). I didn't intend to be a professional minister or religious educator, but that seemed to be the nearest line of study to what I was groping for.

For a green country boy, with a technical agricultural education, life in New York with its myriad challenges was an explosive experience. It meant a tremendous widening of religious, social and political outlook. The one-hour course on Ethical Interpretations of Current Events, taught by Dr. Harry Ward across Broadway in Union Theological Seminary, opened up wide and new vistas to a boy just out of the corn rows. Professor William Heard Kilpatrick's course on the Philosophy of Education was a great eye-opener. It was my good fortune to have many, many fine professors in college to whom I am ever in debt, but I would rank Dr. Kilpatrick at the top of the list. When I met Dr. Kilpatrick later in Tokyo during his long round-the-world trip, I asked him whether he was going to write a book about his experiences. "No," he replied, "I am just acquiring a point of view." His answer reflected much of what college is all about.

The two major professors in my field, Dr. George A. Coe and Miss Adelaide Case, were very helpful in expanding my religious outlook and understanding from the rather dogmatic religious framework in which I grew up.

At Iowa State College I had written my Master's thesis on the need for vocational guidance, based on a study of the transfers which students had made from one department to another. When I asked about guidance courses at Columbia, I was told the only one being offered was a major course for Deans of Women! So I called on Miss Sarah Sturtevant and told her of my interest in the guidance field — she laughed and said she wouldn't admit one man to her course, but she might admit two.

That evening when a young man whom I did not know walked into my room at International House, my greeting to him was: "How would you like to take a major course for Deans of Women?" He smiled and said that he might do that. So the two of us enrolled in a heavy course that met three hours a day — Monday, Wednesday and Friday. He left at the end of the first semester, but I continued during the rest of the academic year. As a man, before the days of women's equality and liberation, I was only discriminated against once, and that was when they left me behind when the class made a tour of women's colleges. I never became a dean of women — but years later, I married one — Miriam Davidson who was dean of freshman girls at Monmouth College. When it fell to her lot, as a former country girl, to care for some sick pigs for our pig cooperative at the Bryn Gweled Homestead during the wartime meat shortage, she twitted me that I had the training in agriculture and deaning, but that she was the one who had the practical experience in both.

In my last year at Teachers College I became involved in helping to launch the Committee on Militarism in Education to fight compulsory military training in schools and colleges, so I never finished a dissertation for a Ph.D. and have had to content myself as a partially finished product of the academic system.

In a somewhat long, crowded and stimulating college career, some events stand out because of their intensity of human fellowship, or because of deep, shared religious experiences, or because they opened up new and wide vistas for contemplation and action. Only a very few times of such deep fellowship can be touched upon here, but I remember five which were especially meaningful: the meetings of seven of us at Ames hoping to work together in Christian service abroad; the eager undergraduates at Ames seeking ways to get the most out of college; the Indianapolis Student Volunteer Convention,

which confronted seven thousand students in a very dynamic way
with the issues of war and racial and economic injustice; the ensuing
Pawling Retreat which was a deep experience of fellowship; and life
at International House in New York with students from all over the
world.

GROUP OF SEVEN

A group of seven students at Ames met together frequently over a
period of more than a year, exploring the possibility of going
together to some foreign country in Christian service. We defined our
goal at an early meeting:

> The purpose of the group is to go out as a unit, consisting of men
> who have specialized in agriculture, engineering, medicine,
> theology and education, to some strategic point in the
> underdeveloped world, in order to establish an institution where
> natives can be trained to help in developing and Christianizing
> their country.
>
> It is the further purpose of this group to make the proposed
> undertaking self-supporting as far as possible, through the
> development of the natural resources of the country. It is our
> expectation to become affiliated with some organization which
> shall give support in launching and maintaining this enterprise.
> We hope to complete the personnel by the enlistment of
> physicians, nurses, ministers, or other such specially trained
> persons which an enterprise of this kind might demand.

In the group, which was later augmented, were students from
various major courses of study — including farm crops and soils,
farm management, dairy husbandry, mechanical engineering,
electrical engineering and animal husbandry.

We talked with, or corresponded with, several executives of
different mission boards. All were favorably impressed with the
earnestness and seriousness of the group, but all were convinced that
the project, as outlined, was not feasible, because the enterprise
would probably not be self-supporting. So the idea of going as a unit,
possibly to some place in Africa, was given up. However, each
member later found some important field for useful service.

Charles Smith and his wife Viola spent their lives, until
retirement, in the Belgian Congo. Rush Wagner headed for
Rhodesia, where he later died. We lost track of dairy husbandman,
Carl Schmolke, after he returned to South Africa. Kirk Dewey added

a theological education to his training in chemical engineering and became minister of a church in Butte, Montana, and was a leader in the Montana Council of Churches. Elmer Erickson devoted his energies to agricultural extension and rural development in the South. I went to the foreign missions field of Washington, D.C., to serve as a lobbyist for peace and justice and other unachieved goals with the Friends Committee on National Legislation.

Even though the project as originally outlined did not materialize, each of us went on his own way greatly blessed by the fellowship in searching out God's will for us and experiencing something of the Divine Community.

Morning Seminar on Getting the Most Out of College

As an eager freshman at Ames, I met a senior for whom I had a very high regard who was riding on the same train. I asked him: "What advice would you give to a freshman who wanted to get the most out of college and out of life?" His reply was: "Get into something bigger than you are and forget yourself in it."

Not until I had spent nearly four years in college, did I try to define for myself just what college should have done for me or helped me do. It seemed to be generally conceded that a college education was a good thing. But at that time, I had never heard or read much about specifically what it should do for one. Reviewing my college days, it seemed that I had missed ten times as many opportunities as I had embraced — often because I lacked a definite objective and a clear conception of the function of higher education.

Because Wallace McKee, one of my closest friends, and I had made so many mistakes in school, it seemed regrettable to us that every freshman should come to college and make many of them all over again. Gathering together a small select group of freshmen, we endeavored to challenge them to think through some of the questions they must face in college, to profit by the mistakes of their predecessors, and to make the most of their opportunities. For most of us, classes began at eight o'clock. We selected freshmen of promise and initiative who were willing to meet at 6:30 in the morning at the YMCA Alumni Hall each Wednesday for discussion.

Some ten lessons were outlined. The format was a series of questions and supplementary references — quotation, suggested books to read, and information that would be stimulating and enlightening. We were flying completely blind, because we had never had such a course ourselves. We had to rely on our own experience and material which we knew about or could find. Out of working with this and similar groups evolved an eighty-page compilation entitled "I'm in College, But What For?" of which six hundred copies were printed so that for a time it was available not only for group members, but for others who might benefit from it.

We structured the course largely around Harrington Emerson's correspondence course, *Thirteen Principles of Personal Efficiency*. Usually there was a page of questions for each topic, some apt quotations and references to books and magazine articles.

These morning meetings were usually discussion sessions, based on questions, quotations, and references to books and magazine articles. They included a consideration of goals in college, note taking and records and methods of study, self-discipline, religious and personal ideals, and responsibilities of leadership. Students were urged to think out what were the most important things to get out of college and out of life. One of the many quotations used was "It has been well said that the ability to see great things large and little things small is the final test of education."

I think it was four out of five of the top elective positions in student activities in a student body of three thousand which were filled by members of this group when they were seniors. I don't know how much I stimulated them, but I know these men were a great stimulus to me. I conducted three of these groups, each numbering between fifteen and twenty men, and I wish every freshman could have been offered such a course of searching questions at the beginning of his college career.

In 1921 more than forty groups on the campus, in a wide-ranging series of discussions, spent one period on the question, "How can I become more efficient in study?" and another week on the subject, "What should my four years in college give me besides my technical training?" This was to be followed by a discussion of the utilization of time in order to accomplish these things. As resource material, on behalf of the YMCA, I wrote to quite a number of faculty including the president and some of the deans, asking for their comments to be used to enrich the discussion.

President R.A. Pearson replied:

The future of our country and of the world depends upon education supplemented by and supported by right ideals and a strong spirit of service. Many students come to college with these collateral phases more or less well developed. Every student should leave

college with them much better developed. If that is not done, the
student and the college have failed.

In spite of heavy concentration on studies and campus
responsibilities, there was, of course, a much lighter side of college
life which was reflected in a bit of doggerel which I wrote:

Is It Campus-itis?

Say teacher I don't have the flu
I think that I have something new
I'm not quite sure what I should do
So that is why I'm asking you
  If it's Campus-itis?

I've no desire to go to class
I do not care my work to pass
I'd rather sit out on the grass
And talk to some fair college lass
  Is it Campus-itis?

It's not because the grass is soft
It's not because clouds float aloft
It must be something in the air
Because it's spreading everywhere
  Can it be Campus-itis?

At one o'clock you call the roll
My body's here but not my soul
I'm in no mood for algebra
I guess I'll cut my class today
  I've got Campus-itis.

INDIANAPOLIS STUDENT VOLUNTEER CONVENTION, DECEMBER 1923

For a great many of us college students in the early twenties,
perhaps the most inspiring and challenging single event was the
Ninth International Student Volunteer Convention at Christmas
time in 1923. Among the array of some twenty-five speakers from
around the world, for this quadrennial convention, there were five
who especially shook the student world of that decade and whom I
had the privilege of getting to know somewhat personally —
Sherwood Eddy, in whose seminar I went to Russia in 1930 and
1938; John R. Mott, general secretary of the International
Committee of the YMCA; Kirby Page, whose speaking and writing
on war and peace moved thousands; Robert E. Speer, chairman of

the Federal Council of Churches of Christ in America and senior secretary of the Presbyterian Board of Foreign Missions; and Robert P. Wilder, who was founder and general secretary of the Student Volunteer Movement and with whom I became better acquainted when I later served on the National Council of the SVM.

The triple thrust of the convention on war and racial and economic injustice was well expressed by Dr. Joseph C. Robbins, chairman of the executive committee of the Student Volunteer Movement:

> The world is one, and we must in some way internationalize the thinking of our people. . . . The utter futility, cruelty, destructiveness and awful waste and wickedness of war together with the absolute incompatibility of the war spirit with the missionary spirit and the Christian ideal is becoming more and more apparent to thoughtful leaders of Church and State.

> The very life of the race is being threatened by great systems, institutions and movements — war, economic selfishness and exploitation, race hatreds and materialistic philosophies.

The Council of the Student Fellowship for Christian Life Service met on the morning prior to the opening of the convention and issued a call to commitment on the part of the seven thousand students from the four corners of the globe. This call, which characterized the spirit and drive of the conference, said in part:

> Because we recognize the domination of pagan principles and motives in present-day human relationships, especially as shown in the flagrant disregard for human values in industry, the widespread denial of brotherhood between the white and colored races and the devastation of the greatest values in life by war — we are confronted with the need of men and women with the spirit of Christ who will, at any cost, strive to make the principles of love and service effective in all these relationships throughout the world, and we cannot do less than to give our lives to this task; and we solemnly covenant with God that we will earnestly seek until we find where we can be most effectively used by Him.

Sometimes in huge conventions, smaller rump sessions have a profound influence on the students involved. During the convention about four hundred students held an informal meeting at the Shortridge High School to discuss pacifism. Those at the meeting expressed a variety of views on pacifism, including some defense of the Reserve Officer Training Corps in many American colleges. Finally the students there adopted, by a close vote, the following statement: "Believing that Jesus Christ was right in his teaching of non-resistance, we, the students of America, pledge ourselves not to aid directly or indirectly in the prosecution of war after November 11, 1924." Two of those who were active leaders in this student drive against war were Alexander and Annalee Stewart with whom I was later associated in the campaign against universal military training as well as many other peace issues.

Later I was at a luncheon arranged by the Union Seminary students where Kirby Page made an eloquent plea for total opposition to war based on the life and principles of Jesus. His talk was the first detailed and closely reasoned argument against war that I had squarely faced, and it started me on a two-year struggle to reach the pacifist position.

The student agitation for pacifism was countered the same week by the Service Club luncheon of ex-servicemen who deplored the pacifism expressed by some of the delegates. James D. Quinn, national commander of the American Legion, declared: "It is well for the men who served during the World War to rededicate their lives to the cause for which they fought. We shall not have performed our full duty until we teach that lesson of preparedness which we and soldiers of our allies learned on Flanders' fields."

In reply to this argument that military preparedness prevents war Canon Woods, from England, made a strong plea on the convention floor for Anglo-American cooperation: "If your and my countries came together in thinking of God's way of dealing with war, we could deal a lasting blow to war and bring about everlasting peace."

That the race issue and war gripped the convention was indicated by the fact that forty-one of the forty-nine discussion groups wrestled with the problem of race in detail and thirty-five of the forty-nine groups discussed what should be done about war — support it fully, oppose war completely, uphold only wars of defense or seek the abolition of war by means of international cooperation through the League of Nations, the World Court, and other international institutions.

An untabulated straw vote in the last session showed a heavy majority favoring the abolition of war through such instruments as the League and the World Court, with a distinct minority upholding the all-out pacifist position, and an even smaller number relying wholly on outright military preparedness. Allan Hunter, a lifelong friend of mine, upheld the pacifist position, asserting that "wars have not served their purpose, except to increase the number of orphans and widows and the crop of cripples and dead. War does not end war, but sets in motion new potential forces that cause more war." Allan Hunter was later minister of the Hollywood, California, Congregational Church, and an outstanding writer and speaker on peace and nonviolence.

RETREAT AT PAWLING, NEW YORK, SEPTEMBER 1924

There may be some experiences in life so rich in spiritual fellowship, so full of meaning, so intimate as to defy adequate description in words. For most of us who were there, the retreat at Quaker Hill Inn, Pawling, New York, in the beautiful rolling countryside of Duchess County, was such a time.

Three or four of us, at the suggestion of Chet Hartlett, took the initiative right after the Indianapolis convention to call together on September 2-15 a group of men and women students for an unhurried fortnight of worship and discussion. There were about two dozen of us from some sixteen colleges and seminaries, plus part-time participants from the national staffs of the YWCA, YMCA and the Student Volunteer Movement.

In the midst of an old Quaker community with its great houses and apple orchards, its rivers and tiny waterfalls, its wooded slopes dipping down to the valleys and sliding up again on to the hills, in countryside checkered with small pastures and fields of corn, set against the purple-blue mist of the distant mountains, we met in a common search for God, for what the Christian *way of life* should mean in our own lives and in our student generation.

In the mornings Howard Thurman, with his deep voice and expressive eyes, would read a chapter of the gospel of Mark and open up a probing discussion. One night we sat around the blazing fireplace — it was already chilly in that part of New York — and listened to Hugh MacMillan read aloud the whole gospel of Mark. When he had finished we were all conscious of the very close presence of Christ among us, so vividly had we seen Him walking among His disciples. As we finally shared our own thoughts with each other, and not just things that we had read or heard sometime, we really got deeper down to the things that matter than we ever had before while working alone. We were reminded that faith is not belief in spite of evidence, but life in scorn of consequences.

We studied the first eight chapters of Mark in some detail the first week, giving special attention to our own conceptions and those of Jesus, about the Kingdom of God, of faith, of love and of prayer. We also discussed His method of reaching people and of meeting opposition.

After supper we sat around the fire and sang until we got into the spirit of the evening. We discussed specific questions such as racial relations, our attitude toward war, relations between men and women, functions and cooperation of various religious organizations on our campuses. To all of these we tried to apply the principles which we had been thinking about in our morning discussions. After these sessions formally ended, came intimate personal talks, extending far into the night. We attempted to carry out Hugh MacMillan's definition of true friendship — "a relationship in which folks care so intensely about each other that they lose their own personalities."

Quiet walks and talks in the afternoon left us with the vivid impression of our inadequacy and the realization of the problems right on our own campuses which we were not only failing to meet, but even to consider. We were challenged again and again to begin living for God.

This mountain-top experience was a resting place and not a journey's end. If only we could have lived out the implications of the insights and the visions we saw there! We never could be quite the same. Mountain-top experiences make possible the life of the spirit in the valley.

Mike Dillingham telegraphed from Raleigh, North Carolina: "I feel I got something from Quaker Hill which I am unable to explain. I intend to give the Jesus Way a chance in my life." Another participant expressed his feelings: "Pawling gave me a glimpse of reality. Something got under my skin and has been pricking me ever since. Things plastered on the outside are shed like an overcoat, but when an experience is woven into us it becomes vital and is valuable in proportion to its power to make us see further, feel more truly, act more nobly."

Marvin Harper wrote: "None of us may be led to become famous because of our experience there, but I am sure that not one of us is the same person for having been there. And Esther Smucker, who returned to an exceedingly difficult school situation, after struggling two months there, commented: "I am convinced more than ever that we draw nigh to God only as we draw nigh to men; there's no other way to do it."

Three or four of us in the New York area were able to get together a few times afterward. But the group scattered over the world and I soon lost track of most of them. Howard Thurman wrote many devotional books. He has inspired tens of thousands of people with his penetrating sermons and addresses and devotional services.

Henry P. Van Dusen is dead now, but for many years was president of Union Theological Seminary in New York. Ralph Bridgeman served as president of Hampton Institute. Dorothy Dunning, who helped plan the retreat, finished her medical training, went to India, married an Indian professor of international relations, Joseph Chacko. She served as conference physician at the Third World Assembly of the World Council of Churches in New Delhi in 1961, where she assured me I was going to live awhile longer after a mild heart attack following a strenuous and exhausting day. The Chackos are now in Chester, Pennsylvania, where he is teaching at Widener College and Dorothy is continuing her medical service to the community.

I visited Hugh and Donalda MacMillan in 1927 in Tansui, Formosa, where they shared their lives with the Chinese for so long under the auspices of the Presbyterian Church. I believe Lynda Goodsell went to Iran. Miriam Hastings Rowe became dean of women at Hanover College in Indiana, until her marriage and assumption of family responsibilities. We have been scattered but bound together with an invisible web woven by a common search for truth, for the meaning of life and our responsibility to our fellow men.

INTERNATIONAL HOUSE

International House in New York City opened in 1924. But the idea began in 1908 when Harry Edmonds said good morning to a Chinese student on the steps of the Columbia University Library — the student had been in the United States for three weeks and nobody had spoken to him. This led to the formation of the Intercollegiate Cosmopolitan Club by Mr. and Mrs. Edmonds, which brought together American and foreign students over the years. By March 1, 1924, the Intercollegiate Cosmopolitan Club had a membership of 784 students from sixty-four different lands studying in fifty-three colleges, universities and professional schools in the greater New York City area. Religions represented were Brahminism, Islam and Zoroastrianism. Christianity was professed by Catholics — Roman, Greek, Gregorian and Nestorian — and other groups including Christian Scientists and the various Protestant denominations ranging from the Quakers to the Orthodox bodies. How's that for ecumenism?

International House was the first building of its kind in the world, erected to gather a considerable number of nationalities into one community for the purpose of furthering peace through the fellowship of living together. It was my high privilege to live there the first two years after it opened, with over five hundred students from some fifty-five countries under one roof. The membership of International House during the winter term (1925-1926) — resident and nonresident, totaled 1035 students from sixty-six different countries. Goals which were largely achieved in this diverse community were reflected in two captions used around International House: "That Brotherhood May Prevail" and "Above All Nations Is Humanity."

Life at International House was always exciting because of the variety of students you became acquainted with and the great number of activities that were always going on. The most colorful event of the year was the annual Candlelight Ceremony. One representative of each nation, in the costume of his or her country, lighted his neighbor's candle, saying as he passed the light, "I represent (giving the name of his country)." When all the candles were lighted, the service concluded with these words: "As light begets light, so Love, Service and Goodwill are passed on to others." Frequently a National Night for some country was observed. Students from that country dressed in their native costumes, sang their favorite songs, and a meal characteristic of the country was prepared.

The weekly Sunday night suppers at International House brought a glittering array of speakers. One night Nicholas Murray Butler, president of Columbia University who was later awarded the Nobel Peace Prize, spoke on the effects of the First World War, an event still fresh in most people's memories. "Government always uses the instrument of force," he asserted.

> One of the great objects of civilization is to suppress the use of force and to exalt the rule of reason. One of the sad things in the world today is that we are so very far from the accomplishments of those noble ends that were declared to be the purpose of the Great War, which rocked the structure of civilization to its foundations. Rarely, if ever, has a great historic event been interpreted in terms so exalted, so exhilarating and so thrilling. We were to make the world safe for democracy, we were to wage a war to end war. The sacrifice was stupendous, unbelievable. A hundred years to come will see the damage unrepaired in its entirety.

It is now fifty years since that speech. We can see more clearly how we were deceived by those noble words about saving democracy and ending war, and how much of the damage is unrepaired. What we get out of one war is usually another one. The First World War laid the ground for the Second World War. The settlements of the Second World War were in part responsible for the Korean War. The United States, with a huge conscript army, got involved in a civil war in South Vietnam. Almost nothing has been done by the United States for reconstruction in either North or South Vietnam, which was so devastated by American firepower. When will the damage of these wars be repaired?

The most provocative speech during my two years' residence at International House was by Scott Nearing on "The Crumbling British Empire." The House buzzed for days — particularly the British and Canadian students. It was a brilliant analysis and forecast of what has happened to the British Empire in its dissolution from what was at that time the Empire on which the sun never set. He portrayed the weakness of the colonial system and foretold its break-up with prophetic clarity.

One night in the washroom a man approached me, held out his hand warmly, and said, "Rockefeller is my name." It was John D. Rockefeller, Jr., whose generosity had made International House possible. He went on to endow International Houses at student centers in Chicago, Berkeley, Paris, and a somewhat different type International House in Tokyo — a very farsighted and beneficial philanthropy. There were numerous anniversary celebrations in 1974, honoring his pioneering benefaction half a century ago.

Among the former residents of International House are very distinguished leaders occupying important positions in almost every country in the world. Many have been sending back their sons and daughters to study in the United States and to live at International House. One German student observed, "To really get an international point of view, one must know intimately and personally people from other nations."

International House is a world in miniature. Unhappily, world peace hasn't yet been achieved, but one of the real forces building toward it are the thousands of alumni of the various Houses working in more than a hundred countries, "That Brotherhood May Prevail."

At a dinner on November 19, 1937, celebrating the first organization of the Alumni Association of International House, New York City, its donor, John D. Rockefeller, Jr., said in part:

> Every individual who is honest, fearless, peace-loving, who is imbued with the spirit of brotherhood and of service to his fellowmen, is an influence for good in any group or party or nation

of which he is a member and helps to insure the wise use of its power.

And so, instead of holding out to you the challenge of service in conspicuous places and in connection with vital world problems, I am saying to you, as I am saying to myself, let us tonight highly resolve to be the masters of our own souls and to make our inner life and its outward manifestation a positive influence for good in the world. In this way, if we have access to those hidden sources of power that earnest seeking and right living will make available to us, we shall make the most of our lives whether they are lived high or low.

If then, in the development of the individual lies the hope of raising the level of organized groups and mass action, how doubly important it is that brotherhood should prevail. . . .

You have lighted a great light — Guard it jealously that it not be extinguished, hold it ever aloft that it may shine far. Pass it on to others who will cherish it and in turn pass it on until, as you have so often circled this room with the light, it may some day circle the globe and *brotherhood may prevail* throughout the world.

CHAPTER 3

From Gob in the Dry Land Navy to Ardent Pacifist

My eight-year spiritual climb from blind and uncritical acceptance of the First World War to vigorous and ardent pacifism in 1926 was a long and involved journey. I confronted no outright challenges to my conventional thinking during the war or immediately after. Although I had grown up as a somewhat idealistic young man not too far from several Quaker churches within fifty miles from my home, no Quaker or other antiwar individual crossed my path or shook the rafters of my thinking. I had spent nearly two years in college, one at Monmouth College and almost a year at Iowa State College at Ames. My father wrote home from the Iowa Legislature on March 31, 1917, while I was at Ames: "I am very much afraid we are going to declare war with Germany when Congress meets. I do hope and pray we may be kept out of this terrible conflict. I hope you will discourage Raymond if he thinks anything about enlisting from such an idea. I see there is quite a military spirit being fostered in the schools."

I had done squads right and squads left in ROTC during my freshman year at Ames. A few days after the United States declared war on Germany on April 7, 1917, I went to the Junior Dean, W.H. Stanton, and told him that I wanted to leave school and return to the farm. He tried to persuade me to finish out the school year. There was a great cry at that time for more food production and this seemed a useful part of the war effort for I was young and strong and eager. The Junior Dean wrote to my father, "I was sorry to have your son leave college. . . . I hope he will return at some future time to finish his college course, and if he does, we will help him as much as possible to make up his back work."

As the war went on and on and more and more of my buddies had entered military service, I decided to enlist in the Navy. I went to the recruiting office at Burlington, Iowa, twenty-three miles from home. They weighed in my six foot frame at a scant 127 pounds (shades of my present silhouette). So they took a dim view of my naval suitability. (How could you stop a bullet if there was nothing there to stop it or hoist an anchor if you were as thin as a razorback hog?) They said in effect that I had enough longitude but not enough latitude. The recruiting officer saw that salt-water gleam in my eye and ventured the suggestion that if I tried to enlist at Great Lakes just north of Chicago and about two hundred miles away, that the recruiters might take a more lenient view of my lack of avoirdupois. They did enlist me and I arrived at Great Lakes on July 27, 1918, as green as cabbage just off the farm. The war, of course, was pretty much out of sight and out of mind. Looking back now I see my military experience was totally inconsequential and hardly worth mentioning when measured by that of tens of millions of veterans who did see combat and death.

During the first few days I was excited by navy life. I was really thrilled to see the boys in their white suits and black ties sitting in the Ravine row above row singing the "Missouri Waltz" and alternately swaying right and left in rows to the music. John Philip Sousa was the Great Lakes bandmaster. It was a great day when some thirty or forty bands converged on the huge drill field playing such exhilarating tunes as "The Stars and Stripes Forever." For several days thousands of us sailors dressed in blue and white spent hours forming huge pictures spelling out the navy symbol or "America Answers" or "Great Lakes" or the British or American flags. On August 2, they took a picture of the entire personnel of the Great Lakes station exceeding 40,000.

My first jolt occurred a few days after I arrived and while I was still in detention. A bunch of us had been building a fence around one of the camps. When we knocked off for chow at noon I asked the captain, who was really a very nice guy, "What are we going to be doing this afternoon?" He shrugged his shoulders and replied, "Hell, you're in the Navy now."

I was just off the farm which was a family enterprise where we candidly talked over what we were doing, what we might be doing, and where it was no crime to ask questions. This was my first brush with military authority and frankly I didn't like it. Authority comes down from the top. You are supposed to do what you are told. You don't ask unnecessary questions and you don't talk back to your superiors.

Another jolt was the uncertainty. I had been in service less than a week when I wrote home:

> We expect to move to another camp today or tomorrow. You never know here what is in store for you more than a minute ahead. They call, "Company fall in," and you don't know whether you are going for another shot or vaccination, to pick up matches, drill, or what not. Maybe you get called out and marched down to the Ravine to sing. Great life to be in the Navy and not see any water except what comes out of the faucet. The only time I saw the lake (Michigan) was just a glimpse through the trees as we passed through Highland Park on the way up here.

By August 9 this was a familiar refrain:

> I am about 98 percent broke and if nothing happens we will get 12 hours of liberty about next Saturday. If you could spare it, I would like to have at least ten dollars by the middle or last of next week.

A couple of days later:

> All sorts of stories flying since the Navy stopped recruiting. I have quit believing anything till I get it straight, so won't repeat anything.

Later my Aunt Lois wrote:

> Yesterday we called on Mary and Will E. (Willson). She said there were fourteen of our Morning Sun boys in the service. I think Grandfather Willson, your great-grandfather who fought in the War of 1812, would be proud of you.

My brother Ralph wrote from Morning Sun on August 8:

> The flag from the *Christian Herald* came a few days ago. It's sure a big one and it hangs on the front porch east of the parlor window. In the parlor window hangs a silk service flag which we are proud of.

Mother told of the two war sermons in my home church in her letter of August 13:

> Delber (Elliott) preached two sermons Sabbath. Both war sermons. In the morning the taking of Jericho — Joshua a great leader trained for forty years. Under direct command of the "Captain of the Lord's hosts" Jesus Christ, Seasoned troops. Righteous Cause, Obedience, Victory. In the evening — "Is War

Justified and When?" Is this war justified? When does God give
victory to the Righteous Cause? His view when there is
Repentence and Prayer and a Willingness to give up sin by his
people. Delber is a fine preacher. There was no other preacher in
town that eve and we had a good house.

Late in August I was transferred a few miles north to the rifle
range at Camp Logan near Zion City, Illinois. Here we often fired an
army rifle all day. One exercise was to fire five shots prone at 500
yards, run to 400 yards and squat and fire, and then to 300 and kneel
and finally to 200 and fire standing. You have to hold the rifle close
to your shoulder or it will kick like a mule. Next to me one day was a
little fellow from the city who was afraid of his rifle and held it too far
away from his shoulder. It kicked, hit him in the face and his lips
looked as if he had been kissed by a brick.

At the entrance to Zion City, which was unpaved and had rough
roads like a young roller coaster, were signs, "No drug stores, no
apothecaries, no doctors, no tobacco" and so forth. It was the
headquarters of the Deweyites, a rather strange religious cult. I went
to one of their big meetings in the tabernacle one Sabbath afternoon.

The huge organ in Shiloh Tabernacle weighed twenty-eight tons
and contained 5,124 pipes. There were hundreds of people there, a
great many of them with their open Bibles reading along in the
service. On the rostrum sat the apostles and several took part. I
thought the sermon was a strange mixture of what seemed to me
truth and error, but it was a long and deadly earnest meeting.

On either side of the stage there were huge backdrops covered with
crutches, braces and other evidences of healing of the faithful. High
up in the background were two large letters, S on one side and P on
the other. When I asked someone if they stood for St. Peter, or St.
Paul, the answer was, "No, for spittoons," because of the leader's
great antipathy to the use of tobacco.

While there was much emphasis on faith healing among the
Deweyites, I later heard rumors that some of the residents of Zion
City, where doctors and drugs were forbidden, would come over at
night to Camp Logan to see the doctors there.

I sometimes say that I am probably one of two fellows who quit
smoking in the Navy. I am not sure about the other one. I smoked
perhaps a pack or two of cigarettes, but so many many sailors said to
me that they wished they had never started that I said to myself,
"O.K. that's the end," and swore off completely.

By late September a real epidemic of Spanish influenza hit the
camp. The morning paper on September 26, when I was in the

hospital with influenza myself, reported that in nearby Waukegan there were over a thousand cases, and that the total down at the Great Lakes Naval Training Station was over eighty-seven hundred, with seventy-seven deaths in twenty-four hours. At that time at Camp Logan all the wooden barracks, several of the concrete ones, and the YMCA were full of men, most of whom were not very sick, but who were kept in bed until the orderlies registered two or three normal temperatures. There had been only two deaths at Camp Logan up to that time, and those from other causes. But the high incidence of influenza that fall and the high mortality rate certainly made some of us think seriously about the frailty of human life, life which shouldn't be wasted.

On October 15 I attended the memorial service for the men of Camp Logan at Zion City who had died while members of the Camp. The sailors wore dress blues and the service was held near the YMCA building. The flag was lowered to half mast, and then a couple of hymns were sung and prayers said before the address and the dedication of a service flag with forty gold stars. All but two or three had died of influenza. After the address, prayers were offered and each man was remembered by name. The firing squad fired a three-round salute and the bugler blew taps. Then the flag was lowered and then raised with the service flag flying below it. The band concluded the ceremony by playing "The Star Spangled Banner."

The last star on the service flag was the result of a very sad accident a few days before. The chaplain's orderly had just driven the chaplain from Zion City and had started to fill the tank with gasoline. Somehow the gasoline exploded and he was covered with flames. In agony he ran until someone tripped him and smothered the fire. But he was fatally burned and died at 5 a.m.

This memorial service was a very sorrowful occasion because all of these men had died in the prime of life.

While the medical care for those of us who had influenza was excellent, the invalid diet left me constantly hungry. I wrote home:

> Oh, they certainly feed us great here. Three crackers or one slice of toast with three or four tablespoons of soup on it and a couple of spoonfulls of apricots or half an orange. I am going to rate a good meal when I get out of here if I have to go to Iowa after it. . . . Couldn't you fill up one of those cracker boxes with a fried chicken, a cake, some cookies, candy and a half dozen apples; and everything else that is good to eat and can be mailed?

I did receive several boxes of food and candy during my navy days which I shared with my buddies, but unfortunately the chicken I had asked for spoiled before it reached me. My parents were unduly thoughtful and concerned about my welfare, particularly when I was sick, and were generous in mailing me goodies from home.

Apparently I absorbed the current war fever, for on October 4, I wrote my family: "The paper this morning says that Germany will accede to all of President Wilson's terms but that the offer will be rejected. Now that we have the dog on the run, we don't want to stop till we twist his tail a few times."

Men were being shipped out of Camp Logan in every direction and soon I was sent back to Great Lakes. Every day I thought I might be shipped to Norfolk or New York or somewhere else for sea duty, but in November I was telling my family:

> It looks now as if the war is virtually over. The Armistice terms with Austria given out in last night's paper were certainly sweeping, and it's surely goodbye Germany before long. It looks as if most of us will put in the period of the war on the battleship Great Lakes.

Four days before Armistice Day, November 11, I was transferred to the receiving ship, the *U.S.S. Commodore,* which was permanently docked on the edge of Grant Park at the foot of Randolph Street, Chicago. We designated it at various times as the *U.S.S. Nevermove,* the *U.S.S. Standstill,* and the *Battleship Stationary.*

"Your being on a boat on dry land does seem fishy," was the comment from my cousin Arnetta Wilson:

> I am thankful you are well and able for duty. I am hoping you may soon be home. We as a people have not realized the horribleness of this war. Leland Scott has made the supreme sacrifice on October 15 and word may come yet of others. There are lots of broken hearts. Parents who will mourn for sons who will never return. But we rejoice that it is all over.

America went wild on Armistice Day. In the morning I was on truck detail hauling officers' furniture, and in the afternoon at one time I led a snake dance down Michigan Avenue. I wrote my brother:

> It was worth seven hundred dollars to be in Chicago Monday. We were hauling baggage in the morning to several depots. Of all the

crowds you ever saw — they would climb on the truck or anything
that moved, as many as could hang on. We were going and coming
all forenoon and it was certainly great. Then in the afternoon we
all had liberty till midnight. Tin horns, ticklers by the thousand,
cow bells, anything under the sun to make noise. Most of the autos
had dish pans, old tubs, barrels or something tied behind them and
loaded with about seventeen more people than capacity. If a few
gobs came along with a bugle or drum there would soon be a
parade. I'd like to have a dollar a mile for the distance I went
either afoot or on a truck that afternoon and evening.

Everyone was after everyone else's hat. I was lucky to keep mine,
but it was knocked off a hundred times. There were many who
came back hatless.

And the crowds! I thought I had seen crowds before. I'd seen State
Street at 5 p.m. rush hour, the streets packed for the Columbus
Day parade and the crowds at the War Exposition, but nothing
like this. All the stores were closed and about everybody was
downtown having the time of their lives. I never expect to see such
a time again if I live to be a hundred.

My next job to make the world safe for democracy after hauling
luggage and swabbing decks for awhile was out in Southwest
Chicago collecting nickels and dimes on the street or in a department
store or taking collections in theaters and movie houses for the
United War Work Campaign, organized to aid men in uniform who
needed help. I collected thirty-two dollars in front of Oppenheimer's
store on Saturday night and about twenty dollars on a Monday
afternoon. The 29th ward contributed a little more than its quota.
The Peoples Stock Yards State Bank, which administered the fund,
paid our expenses and we stayed at the Stock Yards Inn, the finest
hotel in the community.

My one wartime naval cruise occurred a few days later when a
sub-chaser came alongside and asked for men to go across Lake
Michigan to a spot near Benton Harbor, Michigan, to raise a
thirty-ton boat that had been beached. It was supposed to be a one-
day trip, but actually we were gone about a week. I had only the
clothes I was wearing — dungarees and rubber boots — and ten
cents in my pocket. It turned out to be a difficult job to raise the
boat, pump her out and tow her to the harbor with various mishaps
on the way — with cables slipping off or the boat going aground
again.

There was a little interurban that ran from the House of David, a
religious community outside the city, to Benton Harbor past the

canal where we finally towed the boat. The House of David won great fame for its baseball teams. Usually there were only two men on the trolley, the engineer in the front and the conductor in the rear, both wearing long beards. The interurban had an underslung carriage so it would bob up and down, the men's beards flopping up and down with it, and it made one of the funniest silhouettes or pantomimes I had ever seen.

I think I got back to Chicago with the ten cents I had when I left, but money never lasted very long in the Navy.

"Join the Navy and see the Loop" was a favorite wisecrack around Chicago. One night I was walking in the Loop in Chicago when an usher stopped me in front of a theater. He asked me if I would like to see the show going on. A gentleman had given him a ticket to give to a sailor in uniform. I gladly accepted. The play had already begun and to my surprise I was ushered down to a center aisle seat on the second row. The man in the seat next to mine asked me where I was from and welcomed me warmly.

My benefactor turned out to be Mr. Loeb of Sears and Roebuck. Apparently he was the father of young Loeb who, some years later, conspired with Richard Leopold to commit the perfect murder. Their case attracted world-wide attention when Clarence Darrow defended them. They were sentenced to prison and sent to the penitentiary at Joliet, Illinois. Loeb was murdered in prison, but Leopold was later paroled and for a time worked with a Church of the Brethren camp in Puerto Rico.

When the intermission began, a famous actress made quite an appeal for buying Liberty Bonds. I really pricked up my ears when my neighbor, referring to the previous Liberty Bond drive, said to the man in front of him, who was J. Ogden Armour, the meat packer, "I was sorry that we gave them that last million." That was the first time I ever had heard anyone speak casually about a million dollars and I thought maybe that for once I was really in the big time. These men displayed the power and advantage of great wealth. One man said to the other "measured in the lives of ordinary men, we have lived ten thousand years."

Some years later I visited the Lake Forest estate of the Armour family. The superintendent showed us around the seven-million-dollar grounds with their beautiful plantings and large artificial lakes and pointed out the three-million-dollar house. I thought of the hundreds of bushels of corn I had shoveled into cattle and hogs and felt that somewhere there must be a couple of blades of grass in which I could claim a proprietary interest.

My insignificant naval career ended in time to spend Christmas 1918 with my family in Morning Sun, Iowa. I hadn't seen one drop of salt water, and no more military action than several weeks on the rifle range shooting at inanimate targets. Hauling furniture all over greater Chicago for officers and picking up cigarette butts around camp didn't heighten my love for the military caste system. The waste of time, manpower and materials didn't impress me with the ideals and the efficiency of the military. But if I did any really serious thinking about the great issues of war and peace while in uniform, that recollection escapes me. I was one more pawn in the power game who didn't much ask the reason why.

I returned to Iowa State College at Ames to complete the course in animal husbandry in 1921 and a Master's degree in Vocational Education in 1923. It was at Teachers College at Columbia University that my social and political education began in earnest.

Kirby Page Calls Modern War Unchristian

During the Christmas vacation in 1923 I was a delegate from Teachers College to the huge Student Volunteer Convention at Indianapolis, Indiana. This convention was a soul-searching experience for hundreds of the students who were there from all over the United States. At one of the small informal luncheons arranged by the Union Seminary delegates Kirby Page was the speaker. His theme, vigorously argued, was that modern war was contrary to the life and teachings and example of Jesus. It was a powerful address and really shook me, although it didn't entirely convince me. It takes a good deal to shake a dyed-in-the-wool Scotch-Irish Calvinist out of his earlier convictions and prejudices. This appeal was reinforced by several dynamic addresses to the whole convention by other speakers who stressed the responsibility of the individual student to make his religious faith relevant to the great problems of war and race and justice in the contemporary world. I am inclined to think that this convention was the most challenging student conference during the period between the two World Wars in confronting students with the issues of war and peace.

Living in International House in New York City during the first two years of its operation, 1924-1926, with students from fifty-five countries under one roof, helped me feel how much more alike than different the human race was. Why should I want to kill any of my fellow students or their countrymen? In the fall of 1925 I was asked to help organize the Committee on Militarism in Education.

The CME was directed against compulsory military training in schools and colleges and against all military training in high schools. I threw myself into that crusade on a part-time basis, along with my studies. Troublesome questions began to arise. If one is opposed to compulsory military training why not all military training? I wrestled with that question. Then if one is opposed to training young men in school in the arts of war and murder, what about the military establishment? Isn't the purpose of the Army to train men to kill? Why be squeamish about the ultimate purpose of a military establishment: if peace fails, then slaughter the enemy by the most efficient and deadly means possible.

I kept getting pushed back farther and farther until I decided that somewhere I had to stand on firm convictions and solid ground. I finally came to the conviction that my purpose would be to refuse all forms of military service or noncombatant service, no matter under what auspices, and to take the consequences. In so doing I would neither court martyrdom nor publicity, but would try to maintain a conscience against war and conscription which no mere words could ever sufficiently express. So long as men will submit, the state will maintain its perogative to conscript. The problem then of getting rid of war is partly, but only partly, a problem of getting rid of conscription, and the brunt of this must be carried by men who are subject to it.

So in a sense I really backed into the pacifist position, in spite of its various dilemmas, and decided to give up support of the military system, and to dedicate the rest of my life to the quest for international peace and the effort to build the conditions and institutions which would make peace possible. It's a long climb yet for the human race, but peace has become imperative for decent life on earth.

CHAPTER 4

"When You Are in Japan, Do as the Japans Do"

(written by a Japanese student in my college memory book)

The year I was in Japan was a watershed year with ominous portents. In March 1927, the liberal Shidehara government fell and was succeeded by the Tanaka regime which led the nation on toward the seizure of Manchuria, the war with China and then the attack on the United States at Pearl Harbor.

The prompt and generous outpouring of food and relief by the United States in helping the victims of the devastating 1923 earthquake created a warm feeling in Japan toward the American people. This disaster had leveled a large part of Tokyo and Yokohama, and had resulted in the loss of more than a hundred thousand lives. However this friendly feeling toward the United States was largely nullified by the rash of anti-alien land laws and other discriminations against the Japanese over the years and by the passage of the Japanese Exclusion Act by Congress in 1924 which restricted the immigration of Japanese to 100 per year. It was not until 1965, forty-one years after the Exclusion Act was enacted, and twenty-one years after the Friends Committee on National Legislation had called for the liberalization of our immigration laws, that the national origins provisions were modified and the Japanese Exclusion Act was changed.

THE JAPANESE BROTHERHOOD SCHOLARSHIP

Robert Kamide from Japan was studying in New York City. He was much distressed by the passage of the Japanese Exclusion Act. During the summer of 1924 Kamide had hitchhiked fifteen hundred miles through New England and had found the people there friendly and open-hearted. He carried only a pup tent, a blanket and a few necessities. Never once during the entire trip did he meet with harsh treatment. This young man came to sense a depth of common feeling between Japan and the United States that transcended race or creed.

Kamide wanted in some way to express to the American people his appreciation to them and his belief that the passage of the Exclusion Act did not really represent the innate friendliness of most Americans. So, with the help of other students from Japan who were in the United States, he started the idea of sending an American student to see Japan as it really was and to get acquainted with the Japanese people. They raised enough money to put on some old Japanese No dramas at New York City's International House from which sufficient funds were realized to launch a $1500 Japanese Brotherhood Scholarship — the first and only one of its kind. The money was put into the hands of a distinguished committee including the Japanese consul-general in New York City and Nicholas Murray Butler, president of Columbia University. This scholarship was instituted long before the great procession of American students who now have the opportunity of a semester or a year abroad.

I was in my second year at International House at the time. Harry E. Edmonds, founder and director of International House, urged me to apply. I was pleasantly surprised when the committee chose me for the award which was presented at a ceremony in May 1926, at International House.

Dr. Sidney L. Gulick, who had lived many years in Japan and who was secretary for international relations of the Federal Council of Churches, made the presentation. He had fought hard against the Exclusion Act and had been the prime mover in the Dolls for Friendship Project, a program in which hundreds of American children sent dolls to Japan as a gesture of good will. In his extended remarks, he said in part:

> (The scholarship) is not a gift of wealth, but comes from students of whom not a few are themselves struggling for an education. It is not a scholarship founded by Americans for Americans, nor by Japanese for Japanese, but by Japanese in America. And it is given at a time when strain and irritation vex the multitudes in both lands. . . . It is to promote friendship through personal contacts and real understanding. . . .

From his close association with Japan he sketched many of the characteristics of the Japanese people and culture which I should seek to understand. "Live if you can in Japanese houses, be much

with Japanese youth, tramp with them, eat with them, get into their
social life," he admonished. "Learn their intellectual interests, their
personal, social and national aspirations." He urged me to study
their huge experiments in political, social, economic, industrial,
scientific, philosophical and religious adjustments and development.
He hoped I would mingle with the common people, the industrial
workers, artisans, artists, day laborers, farmers and fisher folk. It
was a tall order for a green country boy from Iowa with three years of
life and study in the melting pot of New York. But in my response I
expressed the hope that I could radiate some of the earnestness and
concern which marked many of the youth in the various student
movements and churches in this country with which I had been
associated, and that I could transplant in miniature the spirit that
motivated International House. Parenthetically, the story in the
Literary Digest about the Japanese Brotherhood Scholarship went
half way round the world and was read by Miriam Davidson who was
teaching in a mission school in Assiut, Egypt, and whóm I was to
marry in 1932.

For two months I lived with the Kiyooka family, whose son, Eiichi
was a student at Cornell University, and for about seven months
with some forty students from Tokyo Imperial University who were
living in the YMCA dormitory near the gate of the University.
Tokyo Imperial University was ranked by some as the number one
university in Japan. I did not take formal classes because I did not
know the langauge, but spent my time busily seeing and learning
and reading what I could.

I had an earnest talk in Tokyo one night with a Chinese student
who was inclined to feel that the only course for China was to prepare
to fight Japan because of Japan's possible imperialist adventures. I
urged him to do all he could to see if such conflicts between the two
nations could be settled peacefully. Just before he left to return to
China he wrote me a letter in which he said: "Many thanks for your
kindness of the other day. I was glad that I could (hear) a voice of
justice and goodwill from you. I shall never forget the day we talked. . .Face to face, there is no east and west. Both come from the end
of each side." I never heard from him again and often wondered what
happened to him back in his country during all the warfare between
Japan and China.

What a rich and rewarding year it was! I was impressed by the
innate courtesy and thoughtfulness of the Japanese who seemed to
anticipate my needs before I had expressed them. I found the
Japanese on the whole somewhat reserved, but very friendly and

considerate. The only exception was when they were trying to get into the crowded subway and elevated trains. Then it was everybody for himself and the hindmost left on the train station platform for the next mob rush!

TRANSPORTATION IN JAPAN

Japan at that period did not have widespread use of automobiles and trucks. On the streets of Tokyo I empathized with men pulling carts piled high with lumber or stone or an amazing variety of cargo as I trudged about on foot or took public conveyances. Bicycles swarmed the streets like mosquitoes, many of them with two-wheeled carriers attached either in front or behind. One heard the melodious sound of the horn of the tofu or bean curd peddler, or the fish peddler carrying his supplies in tubs suspended from the two ends of a pole carried on his shoulders. Now Tokyo like most cities is choked with automobile and trucks. The new bullet trains carry passengers from Tokyo to Osaka at lightning speed.

Motorcycles were beginning to displace bicycles and hand carts. Most country roads were little more than trails where the farmer and his wife, with his horse or ox if they had one, would wind their way from the tiny field back to the farmhouse with their burden of rice sheaves or soybeans or other farm crops.

One vivid memory was when I accompanied Gurney Binford, a Quaker doing religious work at Shimotsuma, on a visit to an elementary school whose principal was a good friend of his. We traveled by motorcycle with me in the sidecar. I was intrigued to see that they had built a small shelter of brick on the school grounds in which was displayed the Emperor's picture which was not to be left unguarded in a building which might burn down. After touring the school the principal asked us if we would like to go firefly viewing. I said I had been raised among the fireflies on the farm, but that I had never gone "firefly viewing." So he took us to a little valley on whose banks was a teahouse from which we could look out at dusk at a cloud of flickering fireflies in the valley below. It was one more evidence to me of how the Japanese took pleasure in rather simple but aesthetically beautiful experiences.

Our road home was over very narrow lanes on dikes separating rice paddy fields. The acetylene lights on Gurney's motorcycle went out, so I sat in the sidecar shielding a candle as we inched over the treacherous road where a little mishap might have landed us several feet below in the mire of a flooded rice field.

Population Pressure and Competition for Jobs

The Japanese in the 1920's were just becoming aware of the population problem which was to become so acute in succeeding years. The Japanese press kept saying that the population question was an internal one and that they would solve it. Meanwhile the papers reported an estimated increase in 1925 of a million people, although they were at pains to explain that the increase over the former average of around 750,000 a year was due to the fact that sanitary and medical conditions were rapidly improving and therefore not so many people died. I wrote my brother Ralph that

> If the military idea that many people made a strong nation —
> regardless of whether they have a decent chance or not — could be
> pushed into the ocean, then modern nations might intelligently
> and dispassionately discuss the question of birth control and
> limitation of population. Until some nation is willing to break the
> vicious circle of competitive armaments and massed force, the
> upper crust must strive madly for the all too few influential
> openings while the lower strata is ground into poverty and
> suffering, as if such an increase of people were an inexorable law of
> nature.

Living in a dormitory at the Imperial University with some boys whose families held high positions in business or government made me conscious of the intense competition for entrance to universities and after that for good jobs. Graduates of the Imperial University and of Hitotsubashi, the leading university for business and commercial training, generally were able to obtain good positions after graduation. Students finishing high school often took examinations several times in trying to get into higher institutions. One of the recommendations which General MacArthur made during the American military occupation of Japan was the establishment of universities in each prefecture where there were none, so that higher education would be more accessible. But Tokyo still holds a predominant place in Japanese higher education in prestige and in the number of colleges and universities.

The Changing Missionary Enterprise

As one who became a student volunteer for possible Christian service abroad, I was concerned in Japan about the changing tides in the missionary enterprise. A shift was under way from early paternalism toward greater initiative and responsibility on the part of the indigenous churches until they would become independent and the relationship would become reciprocal and more of a real partnership.

The small group of Christians in Japan numbering about one per cent of the population have had an impact far greater than the statistics might indicate.

Fifty years later some significant changes have taken place. Asian Christians take effective leadership in regional religious organizations and in the World Council of Churches. It is becoming more true that missionaries and teachers from the West come and serve at the invitation of the native churches. In 1927 the Canadian Presbyterians were active in the northern part of the Island of Formosa and the English Presbyterians in the south in a commendable polity division of territory in which to work. When I visited Formosa in 1957, there were about fifty different missionary groups including many small fundamentalist bodies who were not very cooperative with other denominations and with too much emphasis on sectarianism and not much on ecumenical fellowship and outlook. The Christian church should lead in cultivating unity and cooperation, not on divisiveness and separateness.

Missionaries were working on translations and dictionaries. They had founded many of the leading schools and universities. Gilbert Bowles, for example, was the confidant of many men of influence in Japan and introduced me to a number of leading Japanese. I was entertained in forty-two missionary homes all the way from the northernmost station in Hokkaido to the southernmost one in Taiwan. These and other contacts enabled me to be entertained in many homes, both Japanese and those of residents of other countries, to meet so many men and women in the Diet and some major figures in government and in business and to have earnest talks with the leaders of thought in Japan, including such men as Viscount Shibusawa and Viscount Kaneko who expressed their views on Japanese-American relations.

INTERVIEW WITH VISCOUNT SHIBUSAWA

Viscount Eiichi Shibusawa was nearly ninety years old, but was still quite active, although he had given up direct control of most of his interests. He was often called the Rockefeller of Japan because of his age and the variety of his business connections.

Few, if any Japanese, were more interested than the Viscount in cultivating friendship between America and Japan, and I felt genuinely so. He worked for better understanding constantly. He welcomed me on behalf of the Japan American Relations Committee which was composed of more than thirty statesmen, scholars and businessmen of Japan.

Shibusawa admired the United States greatly. He said that one outstanding trait of the American people was their sense of justice, and he believed this trait was prominent among the Japanese. Japan was a mixture of the old and new. In spite of our differences he thought the road to mutual understanding between America and Japan lay in recognizing the similarities in the moral traits of the two peoples.

Control of the economy of Japan at that time was heavily concentrated in the Zaibatsu, an oligarchy of leading firms and families who wielded tremendous power in the business world and in the government of Japan. This concentration of economic power was considerably broken up by the American occupation but the tendency now is to coalesce again although perhaps not yet with the stranglehold of the nineteen twenties and thirties.

VISIT WITH VISCOUNT KANEKO

Viscount Kentaro Kaneko was another great friend of the United States and looked upon the honorary LL.D. from Harvard University as the greatest honor of his life. He reviewed for us some of the efforts he had made to improve U.S.-Japanese relations on the touchy question of Japanese immigration into the United States.

Kaneko was a great admirer of Theodore Roosevelt. During the Russo-Japanese War in 1904 he had been sent by the Japanese government to approach Roosevelt and then again a year later. While at the White House he and the President talked about the relative roles of their two nations in the Pacific and about the developments on the West Coast which were disturbing the Japanese, including discrimination in various ways and the passage of anti-alien land laws.

Roosevelt asked Kaneko to tell his government not to send laborers, but to send businessmen, merchants and similar people as immigrants in order to avoid anti-Japanese feelings.

Kaneko agreed with this and told us that as early as 1884 or 1885 when he was private secretary to Prince Ito he had argued strongly in a Japanese Cabinet meeting against the proposed policy of sending laborers to America. This was right after the Chinese Exclusion Act of 1882, and he felt the time would come when the

Americans would want to kick the Japanese out also.

But the Cabinet had letters from California fruit and vegetable growers and from the American Secretary of State asking for laborers to harvest these perishable crops. Kaneko emphasized to us that the first sizeable number of Japanese to come to the United States were at the request of the American capitalists and not as trespassers.

The conversation with the Viscount turned to the current scene of Japanese immigration in 1927 following the Exclusion Act. Thirteen states had passed anti-alien land laws. When the problem first became acute in California, Kaneko proposed a joint commission of seven men from each country — high-minded and impartial — which might meet in Washington to thrash out all the questions which were causing trouble. The Japanese government proposed this to Washington, but Washington refused on the grounds that the country was on the eve of a presidential election and the appointment of such a commission would arouse widespread antagonism. After the election when Kaneko again proposed the commission, it still wasn't accepted. In the Mexican land dispute a joint commission had been appointed, had gone to Mexico for several weeks and had successfully settled that issue. But the United States refused to use the same method with Japan.

When asked what the Japanese would consider a satisfactory solution to the immigration question, Mr. Kaneko proposed cancelling the racially discriminatory clause in the Exclusion Act and substituting something like the following: "No laborers or undesirable class of people from Oriental countries may be permitted to enter the United States." He didn't favor the quota system because that would open up the question of Koreans, Indians and Chinese. Such a program could enable the United States to keep out immigrants that they did not want, and he believed it could be worked out in a way to satisfy Japan. If something like that could be done, he said, he would go all over Japan to encourage its acceptance.

After the close of the Russo-Japanese war President Roosevelt said to Mr. Kaneko in effect:

> Japan now has a career. You have beaten Russia. Japan is the only country that can look after all Asia. If Japan will educate and elevate Asia, then Asia will equal the rest of the world. You can have Asia from Suez to Kamchatka as your special sphere of influence. You can proclaim a Monroe Doctrine for Asia, provided you recognize the territory controlled by European nations, such

as India, Hong Kong and the Philippines. While I live, America
will never protest.

And so when Japan annexed Korea, not an American statesman
nor an American newspaper spoke against the annexation, according
to the Viscount.

I have not ceased to be appalled by this story of an American
president urging what amounted to a blank check for Japanese
imperialism over as much of Asia as possible. Extension of reciprocal
trade and development, yes, but not expansion of military, economic
and political control first over Korea, then over Manchuria and later
over China. This military imperialism finally culminated in the
attack on Pearl Harbor on December 7, 1941. I doubt if Roosevelt
had this amount of imperialism in mind. American imperialism was a
major factor in entangling the United States in the Vietnam War.
The Japanese have had their great problems of population pressure,
of scarcity of raw materials, of discrimination in immigration, and
other difficulties to surmount, but the Japanese chauvinists, and I
don't think Kaneko was really one, didn't need the encouragement of
an American president for their military adventures.

When the U.S. passed the Exclusion Act, Kaneko resigned as
president of the American-Japan Society and said he didn't want to
go to America again as long as his race was discriminated against.
But he hoped he would be able to visit the United States again, and
to feel as welcome as he did while a student at Harvard University.

As we rose to bid our host farewell, Viscount Kaneko asked, "Why
does the U.S. talk peace and fortify Pearl Harbor so much and build
huge oil tanks and appropriate money for new cruisers, and disturb
the peace of the Pacific?

"I envy you as Americans, because America will set the whole
world to play on the American flute to the tune of 'Yankee Doodle'!
You have the resources, the power, the education, the initiative. You
are isolated and can dictate to the world and no man can reach you.
Goodbye."

In less than five short years, it was the Japanese military who
took its turn in disturbing the peace of the Pacific by its seizure of
Mukden and its actions in Manchukuo. It was an unjustified act and
led down the bloody trail to war with China and then with the United
States. Some of its roots were in the Exclusion Act, trade and other
policies by the United States. Men of goodwill in both countries, like
Shibusawa and Kaneko and Sidney L. Gulick in the United States,
were not powerful enough to halt the drift toward war. In spite of the

enormous difficulties it is our task to build toward a warless world of cooperation and peace under law.

THE IMPERIAL FUNERAL PROCESSION

On a warm and cloudless winter day, February 7, 1927, more than a million people from all levels of Japanese life waited for more than four hours to view the imperial funeral procession of Emperor Taisho. From where I sat in the second row in front of the foreign office, I faced a hundred-foot broad street covered with fresh sand and lined with two columns of soldiers erect in their dress uniforms.

The silence of the crowd was impressive as at six o'clock the first minute gun sounded and the first company of soldiers passed by. They were followed by a varied and colorful array of people and objects — the traditions of the past reaching back more than a thousand years as they marched along in the semi-darkness. After forty-five minutes the hearse went by drawn by four sacred oxen and the creaking wheels produced strange harmonies as the hearse glided by on the carpet of sand. Not far behind in solitude strode Prince Chichibu, representative of the Imperial Family. It had been an hour and fifty minutes when the last bugle corps swung by and the procession was over.

Weeks later I could close my eyes and see the procession still flitting by, the hundred and twenty-third emperor in an unbroken line, a solemn and almost unbroken stream of mourners passing the million people bowed in silence along the route of the procession. For most of his life Emperor Taisho had been unable to rule effectively because of mental and physical ill health. His elaborate funeral observance was an expression of the Japanese respect for the authority of the Emperor, and a moving tribute to their affection for the Imperial family.

A VISIT TO FORMOSA

During the year I had the opportunity of traveling more than six thousand miles, all the way from Saghalien or Karafuto which is now under Russian control, to the southern tip of Formosa or Taiwan as it is now officially called.

Formosa is less than a quarter of the size of my native state, Iowa. Its population, which has nearly quadrupled since I was there in 1927, was estimated as 15.7 million in 1974.

Gordon Bowles and I who initiated the trip around the island had two main objectives in mind. Gordon was specializing in anthropology and wanted to visit the former headhunting aborigines. I wanted to see something of Japanese colonization since Japan had governed Formosa since the end of the war with China in 1895, which they were to control until the end of World War II in 1945.

Our first stop was at Tansui to visit Hugh and Donalda MacMillan who had been at the Pawling retreat in 1924. They represented the Canadian Presbyterian Church and were becoming well established in working with the Chinese. Hugh was warm-hearted, deep-souled, just like a breeze from the Canadian Rockies.

One day Hugh MacMillan and I climbed the high hill behind his house which gave us a fine view of the Tansui River where it flows into the ocean. He told me that one of his dreams was to take a series of pictures in that area which he believed would make the New Testament really come alive, because of the resemblance to Biblical scenes, like fishermen letting down their nets, or mending their nets or walking near the Sea of Galilee.

High up on the mountain we came upon a patch of blazing red azaleas. We stopped enthralled at their beauty. I wondered if it might have been a bush like that in which Moses saw the glory of God, and took off his shoes to worship. It was a great spiritual uplift to stop and gaze at this unusual sight. The Chinese call it "the whole mountain red flower."

JAPANESE RULE IN FORMOSA

The Japanese numbered about two hundred thousand out of a total population of around four million. As was the case with much of colonialism, the Japanese ran the island with a fairly heavy hand — filling most of the governmental offices, running the railways and the postal system, requiring Japanese as the language of education, and enforcing monopolies on camphor, salt and some other commodities. At Anping we saw something of the salt extraction process where brine from the evaporating fields was filtered and pumped through bamboo pipes into huge vats to be evaporated dry before being shipped to Kobe to be refined for commercial use.

It seemed to me the military had a quiet but nonetheless final and almost complete control of Formosa, and information was usually given at their sufferance. The statistics one got about many things in Formosa were either obsolete or incomplete or juggled or all three, so they had to be carefully checked. Getting accurate information is difficult when conversations have to be translated both ways.

I did not find any significant move for independence in Formosa, but one example of a plea for more self-determination was related in a letter I received from Tansui which seemed to be a beautiful example of diplomatic diversionary tactics:

> A plea for a separate Diet for Taiwan was made last year by some of the Chinese. The delegates went to Tokyo, but were denied a hearing. But the premier said in part, "To give the power of making laws or of formulating a budget to any separate diet is against the constitution. No petition against or aimed at alteration of the constitution can be introduced into, or accepted by the Imperial Diet. The Government does not, of course, intend to prevent the submission in a proper manner of petitions representing any political views which are constitutional.

After conferring with the British consul who had just returned from a circuit of the island, we decided to undertake a visit to six of the former headhunting tribes and go all the way around Formosa. Our diverse group which finally assembled had a variety of interests and backgrounds.

Gordon Bowles had been born in Japan, spoke Japanese fluently, and could tell from what part of Japan the girls in the inns came from their dialects. Arthur Rinden had been a missionary in China in Foochow, but came to Formosa when the very unsettled conditions in China caused most Americans to leave. Sam Grathwell was an American lecturer who was gathering material for Chautauqua and other appearances. Clarence Griffin was an energetic Irishman with a huge walrus moustache who moved and talked faster than any man I have ever seen. He had been teaching English in several schools in Taihoku. Mr. Koshimura, official greeter for the Taiwanese government, was our guide, mentor and friend. He had chaperoned many distinguished visitors down the more accessible west side of Formosa, but had never been back among the headhunters in the east side of the island. We asked him to cancel the four alternative plans he had prepared for the west side of Formosa usually shown visitors, and he joined our round-the-island trip with enthusiasm.

As we went down the west side of the island we took an interesting side trip up Mt. Ari, one of the higher peaks of Formosa. One of the major foothills was entirely covered with bamboo. The shoots are dug when only a few inches high and are widely used for food. Bamboo is used in myriad ways — in buildings, for utensils or ornaments or picture frames, by aborigines for carrying water and as clothes poles for hanging out wash to dry. There are about fifty varieties of bamboo in Formosa and small groves dot the landscape or frequently surround homes. Higher up we passed large forests of other trees highly prized for their commercial value, since the Japanese empire was short of quality lumber.

The train ride to the top of the mountain was about the most unusual one I can remember. We started at seven in the morning and reached the top of the 7258-foot mountain at three in the afternoon. The track was forty-seven miles long with many horseshoe bends and switchbacks, going over seventy-three bridges and through eighty-six tunnels. Here was a worthy rival to the slow train through Arkansas.

AMONG THE HEADHUNTERS OF FORMOSA

In our seventeen-day trip around the island we visited villages of the Taiyal, Ami, Saisett, Paiwan, Tsuou and Payuma aborigine tribes, and a few of the Bununs. For the most part these tribes had given up headhunting, although some of the Tsuou were still kept behind an electric fence as some protection against their activities and to force them to come to selected gates to barter for salt or other necessities. This account will include visits to three aborigine villages. And how it could rain in that climate! We saw the sun only three times in those seventeen days.

VISIT TO A TSUOU VILLAGE

The day after our trip up Mt. Ari we visited Tappan, a Tsuou village where we spent the afternoon. The Tsuou houses had roofs thatched like haystacks, the straw reaching almost to the ground, bamboo or wooden walls, and a fireplace in the center of the house. The men wore skin skullcaps with two feathers, capes over their backs made from deer or wild boar skins, tight bamboo belts, loin cloths, square pieces of cloth hung by the four corners over the chest, usually a pocketbook or pouch suspended by two straps from the neck and covered with shells or buttons, and large two-foot-long knives hung from woven straps decorated with shells.

The women wore skirts of black cloth with a border of brighter color about an inch wide, and a waist of striped flannel with a square cloth in front decorated with stripes of bright embroidery. Their heads were wrapped with either a towel or a black cloth tied so it looked very huge and box-like. Some of them wore bright fans in their hair. Despite their colorful clothes, I was saddened by what seemed so little beauty in their lives. These women lived in houses with few ornaments and spent most of their days at hard labor in the fields or in their homes.

One of the few diversions these people had was music. They had a few primitive musical instruments such as a small bow harp, a sort of reed flute, and an instrument that looked like a double recorder. Later at Lake Candidius we saw Bunun women singing to the accompaniment of wooden pestles of various lengths as they pounded grain into flour.

Each Tsuou dwelling had a trophy house near it and in one we counted over four hundred wild boar skulls, seven skins drying, birds' claws, antlers, jawbones of other animals, bow and arrows, and a gun. The floor of these trophy houses was about three to five feet off the ground and was reached by climbing up notches cut in a post.

The assembly hall where the young men slept had a board and bamboo floor from three to six feet off the ground and a fireplace in the center. On the east side was a bamboo enclosure with 365 old weather-worn human skulls. If these were actually headhunting trophies, they were the only ones I saw.

The houses in which the people lived had doors in the north and south ends. The floor was earth except where they slept on a shelf of woven bamboo. Most of the people were out on their little farms on the hillside where they raised sweet potatoes, millet and other crops, in little patches scratched out of the mountainside.

The Taiyals — The Most Numerous Tribe

We visited villages of the Taiyals on both sides of the central mountain range. To get to one of the Taiyal villages we wound around a path up a very steep gorge and crossed twenty-two suspension bridges that day and passed more than twenty beautiful waterfalls.

Most of these people were fair-skinned, almost as white as Caucasians. They wove their clothes out of China grass fiber, which is much like heavy linen, and no doubt very long wearing. The cloth is woven in strips about ten inches wide and then sewn together for skirts or a kind of slip-on dress. One ingenious device that women wore which I have never seen anywhere else, was demountable sleeves. One China grass fiber strip was sewn into sleeves at each end with the wide part of the cloth passing over the shoulders. So this part of the costume would come off by itself. The main dress was made out of two strips looped over the shoulders and sewn down the back and below the sleeves, but open in front. The skirts were each about three feet square, often decorated with red wool designs woven into the cloth, and made of three strips sewn together. A woven belt of some design would be tied securely around the waist to hold up the two-piece skirt. Some of the men wore clothing heavily decorated with white pearl buttons sewn in geometric designs.

Women's liberation seemed to have reached the Taiyals more than fifty years ago, for often we would see the women carrying very heavy loads of firewood or farm produce on their backs suspended from a strap around their foreheads.

In the Taiyal villages we visited the granaries were set up on poles three to six feet high covered with mushroom-shaped circular pieces of wood or slate to prevent rats or other rodents from getting into the stock of grain. This was rather common in the various parts of Formosa which we saw. Another common way of preserving food or other possessions was in large earthenware urns.

One of the striking things about the Taiyals was their custom of tatooing. When a boy attained the age of five or six, a series of horizontal lines were tattooed across his forehead. The usual method was to insert needles into a block of wood, drive this through the skin, wipe the blood away, and rub in soot from the bottom of a pan from the fireplace. Girls were tattooed at the same age, and when they reached womenhood another set of marks was made on both cheeks running from their mouths in an upward curve to their ears. In the good old headhunting days, when a man had been successful in headhunting, he had another set of tattoos on his chin. The successful headhunter would enjoy the further distinction of wearing shell ornaments and a red coat on the occasion of a grand festival.

Historically, headhunting was about the only crime which these people practiced. That would be done on three occasions:

1. When a boy attained his majority.
2. To settle a dispute or clear themselves of false charges.
3. In revenge for the murder of a male relative.

Aborigines took heads for trophies, but they never ate human flesh. Headhunting had at that time recently been given up. The Japanese police claimed that they had suffered nearly ten thousand casualties in their thirty-year campaign to stamp out the practice of headhunting between 1895 and the time we were there.

It was maintained by visitors who had made a detailed study of Taiyal customs, that other than headhunting, the moral character of the Taiyals was very high and compared favorably with most of the civilized world. They didn't steal each other's property, they kept their promises, they were faithful to their friends, they respected their parents and elders, they loved their wives and children, and morality between the sexes was very high.[1] One wonders how increasing contact with the evils of Eastern and Western civilization has affected them over the fifty years since we were there. When it comes to taking human heads or human lives, the so-called civilized world outranks the savagery of the headhunters a thousand times. Tens of millions of lives have been lost in the bloodshed of the Second World War, the Korean War, four wars in the Middle East, two brief wars between India and Pakistan, and more than a decade of active fighting in Southeast Asia.

A PAIWAN VILLAGE IN SOUTHERN FORMOSA

There was no railroad or even a decent road, only a footpath over the southern ridge of Formosa from the west side to the east side. It was a hard hot climb, although the coolies with us carried our nondescript baggage.

After we passed over the ridge at 3700 feet and started downward, we soon came in view of the village of Rikiriki. All the school children were lined up military fashion standing out along the road in the sun in their white uniforms to greet this man Wilson and his party. Some seemed to enjoy it but most looked as if they were about to be shot at sunrise. Griffin saved the day. He waltzed up to the group, and began passing out tiny Japanese umbrellas to the girls, or little ducks on a string, and amusing all the children with his plush monkey puppet over his hand with which he did all kinds of tricks. I would have felt much safer with Griffin and his little toys and cloth monkey among the headhunting tribes the next ten days than with the Japanese armed policemen who were our constant companions for that part of the trip.

After the usual greetings, exchange of cards, and the inevitable but delicious tea at the police station, we started to explore the Paiwan village further. The Paiwanese were very dark-skinned in contrast to the Taiyals. The chief and his daughter welcomed us very heartily. He put on two different ceremonial costumes so we could take his picture in them. One striking tunic was made out of a leopard skin.

---

[1]Shingi Ishii, *The Island of Formosa and Its Primitive Inhabitants*, vol. XIV: *Transactions of the Japan Society of London* (Claxton Hall, London, Feb. 24, 1916).

The houses in this village were all made of slate. The front door of the chief's house was about three feet high so one would have to get down on hands and knees to enter. The interior was almost as dark as night since these houses only had one or two small windows. On the back wall millet heads hung drying, and the shelves around the room were filled with bowls and baskets. At one end of the room was a fire on the floor for cooking.

We went outside to visit further with the policeman as interpreter. We were told that the daughter would be married later to some man who would be adopted into the family. This was an example of the matriarchal system which seemed to be common among some of the tribes. As we stood there talking I was really quite touched when an old man came up and told us that he had never seen a white man before. He seemed quite old and his toes ran out in three directions like a duck's foot.

We were entertained at the home of the chief policeman of that district. Such a supper we had! Probably some of it had been carried the thirty miles we traversed that day from the west side of Formosa near Tainan. Rinden and Grathwell proclaimed loudly that they had never eaten such a good meal. The policeman's wife served us graciously. Then she got up at three a.m. to prepare our breakfast. If I live to be as old as Methuselah I won't be able to repay the thousands of courtesies and kindnesses I have received in my life, among them the gracious entertainment we received in that remote policeman's home.

And such a climate! The air was invigorating. The full moon shone just over the edge of the mountains through a palm tree as we crawled under the futons to sleep like hardwood logs. At this village it never frosted and the thermometer never got much above 75 degrees.

Traveling in eastern Formosa, in the headhunting district, an armed policeman would meet us half way between police stations, escort us through his district, and pass us on to the next armed policeman, so we were under police protection for ten days. The terrain here was so rocky and uneven that it was perfectly obvious that no railroad could be built along the east coast in that area except at prohibitive cost.

THE AMI TRIBE

Our next tribal stop was at an Ami village. Here we saw a family sitting on their haunches eating with their fingers out of three wooden bowls on the floor. In another house we saw a woman polishing rice, beating it with a wooden pestle.

The young, unmarried men of the village all slept in the men's assembly hall on beds made out of split bamboo raised about two feet above the floor. Instead of the black slate roofs which we saw among the Paiwans, here the roofs were thatched. The men of the village were all out in the fields so we didn't see many of them.

This group of Ami villages had five men who kept watch all the time, acting as sentinels, fire guards or messengers, or to warn against war, catastrophe or any emergency. They made the assembly hall their headquarters, but were always ready to rush out to meet any emergency.

It was only a short distance from the Ami village to a Payuma village — a tribe that was almost extinct. There we visited one house where there was a cocoanut hanging — a memento that the proprietor of the house had taken a head. The Japanese government took the skull away, but would let people keep cocoanuts as tokens of their prowess.

The Ami people were changing rather rapidly. They were the most progressive, the most advanced, of the savage tribes. However only about six hundred of the Ami people had really finished four years of schooling and had begun to value education. Some three hundred had continued some study, but only a handful had received an education worth speaking of. At that time the Japanese government tried to restrict education and did not provide schools for these aborigines sufficiently advanced so they could go on to middle schools unless the student was very insistent on more education.

The parents built the aborigine village schools and the dormitories for the pupils, and the government furnished the teachers. The Ami did not have any theory about the origin of man or the origin of the universe. Previous to the Chinese coming to the island, they had thought Formosa was the only land anywhere. Then China was added, and then Japan. Many Ami had never seen a foreigner. At that time the Ami had no written language. Aborigine children were taught in virtually unfurnished school rooms, and more and more of them were learning to speak and read Japanese. I don't think that there was any emphasis by the Japanese on helping the Ami keep their tribal culture, a situation similar to that of the American Indian children in the United States at that time.

As yet there were no Ami dictionaries, but first and second readers had been printed in Japanese syllabary with Ami notations. Eighty-two boys and seventy-two girls lived in separate dormitories, but they brought rice from home and ate in family groups. Food included rice, fish and vegetables. The children had their own truck garden which worked something like an experimental agricultural course, so they could go back home and teach their families what they had learned.

Because the Ami lived simply and mostly off the land, they kept practically all the money they earned, and saved until they got several hundred or a few thousand yen to invest in land — usually rice paddies. This put them in serious competition with the Chinese for whatever rice land might be available for sale. Japan allowed them to have quite a bit of farmland from the outset. If they had been living in the forests when Japan took over the island, the government required them to stake out the land they wanted, and would register it so they could keep it, up to a certain limit. They could keep all the land which they had under cultivation, but that was usually very steep hillside ground subject to serious erosion because of the heavy rains in Formosa.

We walked about two hundred and fifty miles on this expedition. I had seen the aborigines in their native haunts, and something of the way they lived. Although there was not much opportunity to converse with them at length regarding their ideas and customs and convictions, I had acquired two headhunting knives, typical clothes from the Taiyal, Paiwan, Bunun and Tsuou, and a bow and arrow which we carried seventy-two miles. We went over almost every mile of government railways. We ate rice and bamboo and fish and chicken and beef and pork and wild boar meat, eggs raw and boiled and in omelettes and otherwise disguised, seaweed, pressed fish, bananas, oranges, tangerines, kirisa, papaya, pineapple, mulberries, pomelo, rivers and waterfalls of tea, cakes and food I couldn't begin to identify, let alone describe.

We waded streams, climbed mountains, inched along lonely and narrow trails in green hillsides, bathed in mist and fog most of the time. We passed sugar cane and rice fields, millet, wheat, sweet potatoes, peanuts, rushes, water hyacinths and elephant ear, wild hydrangeas and viburnums, beautiful Japanese cherry trees in bloom, camphor and cryptomeria and banyan and golden acacia trees, vines and palms and tree ferns higher than your head (Bowles counted more than twenty-eight different varieties of ferns). We rode in rickshas and trains and pushcars and motorbuses and oxcarts and autos. We walked through rain that would moisten the Sahara, and saw moonlight that would make an Egyptian mummy want to go strolling. We looked up at fog and down at mist, out at rocks and

gorges and suspension bridges, and seawater at Soisui so blue that
you wouldn't believe it if you saw a colored photograph. After you
walked twenty or thirty miles in the tropical heat, the futons looked
mighty good to crawl under for a night's sleep. It was a once in a
lifetime trip — at any rate something different from the silk hat tour
which Koshimura had originally planned for us.

Arthur Rinden blistered one foot soon after we started out on our
hiking trip on the eastern side of the island, but he still could
outwalk me most of the time. On the last leg of our journey as we
were coming down a mountain to the railway line that would take us
back to the capital city, Taihoku, I yelled to Arthur who was quite a
ways in front of me, "Art, how come that you are not limping
today?" He turned back to me with an anguished face and remarked,
"Gosh, a man can't limp on both feet, can he?"

CLIMBING MT. ASAMA

Twenty of us climbed Mt. Asama one night in August 1927. It is
the largest active volcano in Japan and quite a tourist attraction.
The height is 8,340 feet, but the actual climb from where we started
was about 4,000 feet. We began climbing about midnight. It was a
beautiful starlit night, and as we climbed higher and higher we saw a
wider panorama of twinkling lights in the valley below. I got to the
top too late to see the fiery lava since the crater was filled with steam
when I arrived. When I reached the mouth of the volcano, there were
about two hundred people silhouetted against the sky, waiting for
the sunrise, while they shivered and huddled together or walked
along the crater rim. Then the heavens gradually became lighter,
snuffing out the stars one by one. The mists gathered in the valley
below us while the sun struggled to shine through. Several times just
a bit of the sun like a tip of fire peeked above the edge of the banks of
clouds, only to be hidden again when the clouds reached up to veil
the sun. But finally for an instant the sun climbed out of the mist
and shone on the valley of snowy and billowy clouds. It painted the
whole scene with rose as it had been just tinting the eastern sky for
an hour. It was one of the most beautiful sights I have ever seen and
worth the climb a hundred times over.

I had other delightful hiking trips in various parts of Japan as
well. But along with the joys of hiking there were sometimes certain
discomforts. On one of the trips the joys were offset by the attention
I received from the mosquitoes. I wrote home on July 21, 1927:

The mosquitoes that come into my room are the most affectionate
brutes I ever played with. They caress you on one cheek and then

flit to your forehead and kiss you above the eyebrows and then
stop for blood and tea on your other cheek. Their favorite time is
between ten p.m. and before daylight. They haven't been
numerous, but they certainly have been attentive. They don't
fight in companies — I think these are snipers and work best
alone. I'm burning some kind of incense tonight — it is supposed to
paralyze their insomnia and sufficiently intoxicate them so that
they fall to the floor in a twilight sleep for a time. These
night-biting varieties were evidently designed to take a man's
mind off the weather and make him scratch for a living.

TRIP TO HOKKAIDO AND SAGHALIEN

After having circled Japan's southernmost and tropical island, it
seemed inviting to visit the extreme north end of the Japanese
empire, Hokkaido and Saghalien. Eiichi Kiyooka, in whose home I
had lived when first in Japan, and who had returned to Japan after
several years' study at Cornell University; Mr. Ehlers, the
commercial attache in the U.S. Embassy in Tokyo, and I planned to
spend a month getting acquainted with these northern regions of
Japan.

Hokkaido, like most of Japan, is rough and mountainous with
about five per cent of the land under cultivation, and about fifteen
percent suitable for cultivation. With a latitude about that of Maine,
the country was just beginning to shift from raising largely rice to
raising corn for silage, clover, potatoes and other crops. The farmers
were also beginning to establish a few beef herds, but chiefly they
were expanding dairy production to provide milk which is generally
in short supply in Japan. We circled the entire island by train. One of
our visits was to the very eastern tip of Hokkaido, at Nemuro, made
famous because of the stopover flight of Wiley Post and his
companion on a pioneer flight across the Pacific from west to east.
Chief among the industries at Nemuro was a whale cannery — one of
the delectable foods of which the Japanese are fond. It tasted a good
deal like beef, but I never worked up a huge appetite for it. Here, too,
huge quantities of seaweed were harvested and baled for shipment to
other parts of Japan. Seaweed of different kinds was a staple of the
Japanese diet and I developed quite a taste for it while I was living in
Japan. Nemuro also exported huge crabs nearly a yard across from
claw to claw.

In the southern part of Hokkaido there were a few of the Ainu left
— a friendly and peaceable group which antedated the Japanese on
the island. These people were generally white-skinned and the men

wore beards. The clothing of men and women alike was quite striking, the underlying color being overlaid and appliqued with a contrasting shade in large, abstract designs. Their outdoor clothing was quilted for warmth in a climate that gets quite cold in the winter. Again, unfortunately, I was unable to sit down with these people for any long talk about their history, ideals and hopes.

In some of the seacoast villages in Hokkaido, there were long lines of fish hung up to dry in the sunshine. Elaborate systems of raised poles stretched for hundreds of square yards. This was in days before refrigeration or canning on shipboard or on the seacoast became common. The smell of the drying fish must nearly have reached high heaven. Fish and shellfish have been the principle source of animal protein for a large proportion of the Japanese.

In the port city of Odomari in Saghalien where we landed (now in Russian possession) the streets were not paved, the roadways were very rough and bumpy, and I imagine this looked like a frontier town in Alaska. But proudly displayed in front of the only movie theater was a sign featuring Charlie Chaplin in *The Gold Rush*. The biggest industry there was a large pulp mill making paper and cardboard, and the manager entertained us graciously. We had the opportunity to drive clear across the peninsula in an antique Chevrolet, mostly through virgin forest. We saw logging operations, smoldering mounds of charcoal, fields of oats and hay, and we passed several fox farms. We didn't get up to the demarcation line between that part of the island held by the Russians in the north and the Japanese in the south, but that we were far north was indicated by one small island we saw dotted with seals and penguins.

When I got as far back as Sapparo, twelve hundred miles north of Tokyo, I was called home by my father's last illness. So I took the first train to Tokyo, the first boat to Vancouver and arrived in Morning Sun, Iowa, in twelve days.

During 1927, Japanese businessmen generously offered to extend the scholarship another year in order for me to get better acquainted with Japan, and hopefully to visit Korea, Manchuria and the mainland of China. But because of my father's illness, my Hokkaido trip was cut short, and I did not get to the Asian mainland at that time.

During a school year of living among students one felt the intense competition of students to get an education. I was alarmed by the rising tide of militarism, particularly as it affected the schools, and the pressure for conformity exerted by the government over the thinking of the college and university students. I glimpsed how the

Japanese perceived themselves to be in the pinchers between American and Russian economic and military power which was a factor in the developing of right wing nationalism and their own form of imperialism.

As I look back on this unparalled year, I realize how fortunate I was in being given the opportunity to visit with people and study events firsthand. I was able to enjoy the unusual privilege of living in a very hospitable Japanese home, of associating with Japanese students and of meeting so many Japanese people in my widespread travels.

This year in Japan was filled with opportunities to share the innate sense of beauty and courtesy of the Japanese people and to absorb something of the richness of their art, their architecture, their history and their culture. I left Japan in great haste and with regret, but twice again I was to be fortunate enough to enjoy the privilege of living for a time in this fascinating and challenging country.

CHAPTER 5

The Orient Revisited

My appointment by the American Friends Service Committee as Quaker International Affairs Representative from July 1956 to May 1957, gave my wife, Miriam, our eleven-year-old son, Lee, and me a year of fascinating experiences. For me this was just thirty years after my student year under the Japanese Brotherhood Scholarship, and though some of the changes were startling, much of rural Japan went on as it had before. This year gave me a chance not only to visit Hokkaido twice, but to go to Okinawa, Taiwan, the Philippines, Hong Kong and Korea.

Miriam rounded out her teaching experience by giving English lessons four days a week at the nearby Friends Girls School, but was able in spring vacation to join me in a week's visit to both Hong Kong and Taiwan.

The first assignments for Miriam and me were to participate in two AFSC International Service Seminars lasting nearly two weeks each. The subject of the first one at Kobe College was "Sources of Tension and Ways of Peace." Each had between forty and fifty participants with about half from the United States and the rest widely scattered from many countries in Asia. While everyone was expected to be able to understand and speak English, the language barrier was real for some of those attending. The formal lectures were often penetrating and provocative, but the great value of the seminars lay in the informal conversations at meal time, in free time, while worshiping together, or playing together.

At Kobe College one fine afternoon we sat around informally on the grass for a wide-ranging discussion on the problems of a hungry world, and on the political relations between India and other major countries led by B.R. Sen, Indian Ambassador to Japan, who was

later Director of the United Nations Food and Agriculture
Organization. An extra session was held with a Japanese physicist
on the peaceful uses of atomic energy and on some of the Japanese
reactions to the United States hydrogen bomb tests in the Pacific.
This was seven years before the treaty was ratified outlawing
atmospheric bomb tests.

The second seminar which lasted a fortnight and dealt with the
"Place of Youth in World Peace" was held on the new International
Christian University campus on the outskirts of Tokyo. This
institution was a serious attempt to develop a bilingual university so
that graduates could assume positions of leadership in business and
the professions where ability to speak both English and Japanese
would be a great asset. Located on what had been an airplane factory
grounds, it had about the largest campus in Japan. There the leading
universities are usually crowded into center city locations in cities
like Tokyo. Numerically Tokyo was not only the center of
government and of much of Japanese business, but, with more than
fifty universities, colleges and technical schools, it was the mecca for
education as well. One thing which General MacArthur and his staff
did during the American occupation after the war, was to encourage
the establishment of a government university in each of the
forty-five prefectures of Japan, where there was not one already, in
order to decentralize higher education.

THE SECOND WORLD CONFERENCE
AGAINST ATOMIC AND HYDROGEN BOMBS

During the first afternoon prior to the opening of the big
conference on A and H bombs, foreign delegates from many
countries were entertained at the Prince Hotel. They were received
by the Governor of Tokyo, Senchiro Yasui, to whose welcoming
speech I was asked to give a response. Here too I had an opportunity
for brief visits with three of the Soviet Union representatives and
with Madame Hsu Kuan-pin, who seemed to be heading the
delegates from the People's Republic of China.

The program of the conference which lasted from 5:30 p.m. until
after 10 p.m. was held in a big indoor wrestling stadium seating a
noisy and demonstrative audience of some twenty thousand people.
This huge circular stadium had three galleries, besides the huge
floor, and it was packed to the rafters.

The program started off with the introduction of delegates, and a
sheaf of greetings including a message from the Japanese Prime

Minister, Ichiro Hatoyama, and one from Prime Minister Nehru of India. His message concluded, "Not only must atomic war be ruled out but even test explosions must be ended, for it is feared now that even such explosions cause injury to the human race."

The secretary-general of the committee which planned the conference gave an impassioned speech in which he reported that 33,556,308 people in Japan had signed petitions asking that atomic bomb tests be stopped, and that the world total was nearly seven hundred million. Both Houses of the Japanese Diet had passed resolutions asking for an end to bomb tests.

I was asked to speak as a member of the U.S. delegation. I concluded my brief remarks with these comments:

> I speak here tonight as an individual citizen and not as an official representative of the government under which I live. As Americans we prize the liberties we enjoy and long and work for the day when these liberties may be more widely shared, not only in our country but throughout the world. As a visitor this year to the country where the atomic bomb was first used, one stands here humbled by that fact, and I am doubly determined to try to see that the vast power of atomic energy is only used in the future for peaceful purposes and for the betterment of human life. I believe God calls our generation to seek to abolish war and the fear of war. That means that each of us has a responsibility as a citizen of his country to do his part to see that his nation acts so that peace is possible. Let us seek not only to ban A and H bombs, but abolish war itself.

I wasn't free to go on to the rest of the conference which was held in Hiroshima and Nagasaki because of the Tokyo seminar, but this meeting gave me a vivid picture of the feelings of almost every Japanese. During the program a group of children trooped to the platform and presented each delegate with a huge bouquet of flowers amid thunderous applause. That was one part of the conference which did not have to be translated. There was great popular enthusiasm for the conference. People lining the hallway as the foreigners came in clapped enthusiastically and as we came out reached out to shake our hands. Several mothers brought their children to meet us. It was to be seven long years before the treaty this conference was calling for was finally signed and ratified.

This Japanese movement to ban A and H bombs had a somewhat checkered career with limited participation from organizations in the United States, because some people felt that the communist influence was so strong that most of the resolutions condemned the

American tests but were not equally severe about the Russian tests. The movement in Japan even split for a time. But it was a major factor in the continued opposition to bomb testing, in keeping alive in Japan a strong antiwar sentiment, and in urging steps toward general disarmament.

One of the big dangers of the tests was illustrated by the radioactive ash from one of the Bikini tests which in 1954 showered the *Lucky Dragon*, a Japanese fishing boat over eighty miles from the test site and well beyond the restricted area, causing radiation sickness in the twenty-three man crew and the death of one of the sailors. A few weeks after this conference I tried unsuccessfully, along with others, to get visas for two women, one the wife of the radio operator on the ship who had died after exposure to radioactive fallout. She should have had the right to tell her story to American audiences. There is no excuse for Americans to shield themselves from learning the results of their unfortunate policies and actions.

THE TOKYO FRIENDS CENTER

During this year Miriam, Lee and I stayed at the Friends Center in Tokyo which was a large western-style residence which had withstood both the 1923 earthquake and the war. The site was a small irregularly-shaped piece of land with the Friends Meeting House nearby. The center was perched on one of the highest spots in the area — once called Temple Hill — and was crowded closely on all sides by houses, a large elementary school, temples, shrines and burial grounds. I have no idea how many temples and burial grounds were in that one huge block.

In the morning a medley of unaccustomed sounds awakened the new arrival, the temple bell, the priest beating his drums or clapping wooden sticks while at prayer, the grating of sliding doors as houses opened to greet the day, the incessant honking of cars and buses, the melodious toot of the bean curd man, and even the crowing rooster, for several of the neighbors and the center itself kept a few chickens. A few times on very clear mornings we could see Mt. Fuji from our bedroom window.

A great range of activities went on at the center. Miriam Wilson and Jane Rittenhouse would walk to the Friends Girls School about a quarter of a mile away. The center served at that time as the headquarters for many AFSC activities, arranging a variety of meetings and the preparation of numerous reports to Philadelphia and London. There were many visitors including Lucille Nixon from

Palo Alto, California, who received very widespread publicity because she was the first non-Japanese to be awarded a place among the fifteen poets who were honored at the annual Imperial Poetry Contest. Wolf Mendl from England and Tayeko Yamanouchi worked on plans for seminars, lecture series, and other related AFSC enterprises. Joy Povolny helped me prepare material for the *Japan Journey*, a series of reports I made on various topics, some of which were reprinted in Philadelphia as Quaker International Affairs Reports (QIAR).

At the center were luncheons, teas and receptions, a Friday night discussion group in English, a Tuesday afternoon women's group, and committee meetings of all kinds, so we were at the hub of Quaker activities. Esther Rhoads also lived there, who among her myriad duties was tutoring the Empress in English. At Christmas we had a day of real excitement when a representative from the Imperial Household arrived at the center with a beautifully wrapped package. It turned out to be two ducks from the moat around the Imperial Palace, ready for roasting — so we had quite a feast on Imperial duck which greatly outranked the customary Christmas turkey.

A VISIT TO NORTHERN JAPAN AND HOKKAIDO

One of the main features of the year was two trips to Hokkaido. The first was in company with energetic eighty-three-year-old Henry C. Taylor, dean of American agricultural economists, and his wife. Dr. Taylor was gathering materials for a book on the agricultural developments in Great Britain, Germany and Japan.

Henry Taylor had taught many years at the University of Wisconsin, had founded the Bureau of Agricultural Economics in the U.S. Department of Agriculture, and more recently had been the U.S. representative at the Agricultural Institute in Rome which was the predecessor to the U.N. Food and Agricultural Organization. So he was well known among the agriculturalists in Japan, and a number of them had been his students.

He invited me to accompany him and his wife on a ten-day trip to the three northern prefectures in Honshu, the main island, and Hokkaido. We were to visit agricultural experimental stations, and view agricultural changes and developments in northern Japan, winding up with a visit to the agricultural university at Sapporo in Hokkaido. At each place we were met by the prefectural governor or one or more of his staff in a Buick car, given the royal treatment, and taken to see the main points of new farming methods in each prefecture. The major shift in northern Japan was from open field crops to more corn for silage, clover and other meadow crops for hay. These crops were to support the increase in the raising of livestock, beef cattle, horses, and particularly dairy cattle.

Traveling in October one doesn't see the early crops of wheat, rye, barley, or early vegetables, but still there was a great variety of agricultural products in the fields. Even though the climate is northern and the season is short, it is hard for the Japanese to give up growing rice. We saw farmers beginning to plant winter wheat or barley in rows between the upland rice plants which were not yet ready to harvest. Rice is cut just before it has entirely turned yellow to prevent the rice grains from cracking, but these huge waving fields of rice just before harvest were a shimmering sea of golden grain interspersed by still-green soybeans.

These farmers also grew some darker colored rice that is pounded into a rather tough dough called mocha which is used for most of the festivals and holidays. It was one of the very few things in the Japanese diet that I didn't enjoy. To me it had all the taste and crispness of a worn-out rubber tire, but the Japanese make it quite a feature of celebrations.

On this trip in addition to paddy rice and upland rice we saw soybeans in profusion particularly along the narrow dikes between rice fields, sweet corn, field corn, edible burdock (which I had never eaten before), onions and leeks, cabbage and Chinese cabbage, broad-leafed lotus growing in water, the large-leafed taro that grows on dry land, sweet potatoes as a major crop, bush beans, pole beans, turnips, carrots, yams, eggplants, peanuts, mulberry for raising silkworms, tomatoes on stakes or trellises, tea, pumpkins, squash, cucumbers, buckwheat, tobacco, daikon (the huge white radish often four inches in diameter and two feet long eaten either fresh or often pickled), apples, grapes, bamboo, chestnuts, and persimmons beginning to color.

Among all the crops we saw a few flowers. Dahlias were common with a variety of beautiful colors lighting up a drab background in city or country. There were gay cosmos, here and there the flaming red of salvia, moonflowers rambling over a fence or trellis, and now and then a few chrysanthemums promising a brilliant autumn very soon.

One of the never ending delights of traveling in Japan is the infinite variety of silhouettes of pines against the sea, or racing across mountain tops, or straggling along a winding road or gracing the grounds of temples and shrines or spreading their arms over the hedges and walls and roof tops even in the crowded city. I was so fond of these irregular pines that I collected a whole album of pictures of them.

October's varied landscape defies adequate description. As we traveled north the beautiful waving fields of rice were being cut and tied into small bundles. Either they are hung upside down on long ricks to dry or built into cylindrical stacks. Later on they are carted or carried on horseback or on the farmer's burdened shoulders back to the farmstead where the rice is threshed in small machines and then the grain is spread out to dry before being stored in bags made of rice straw.

In the busy season farmers toil from sunup until dark in the fields, often trudging home after dark with a huge load of rice sheaves or soybeans to be hung up in the farm yard. In one respect equality has gone pretty far in rural Japan; the women have an equal or more than equal chance to wield the huge mattock-like hoe, or cut and stack the rice, or share in every other part of farm labor.

But the prospect for this 1956 rice crop in Hokkaido was particularly ominous. There had been a cold snap during the time the rice would normally fertilize. A head which usually would contain nearly a hundred grains might have three or four or five. So when I returned to Tokyo I went straight to see W.D. Termohlen, the American agricultural attache in the U.S. Embassy. I said to him that all the indications were that Hokkaido was in for really serious trouble and that the United States should be importing and storing rice for relief. He told me that the U.S. government could do nothing without a formal request from the Japanese government and that none had been received. "You," he said, referring to the American Friends Service Committee and other voluntary agencies, "are in a much better position to move effectively and I would encourage you to do so."

The rice harvest in Hokkaido did turn out to be disastrously short. Hallam Shorrock was representing Church World Service and he was forehanded enough to stock a large supply of American relief rice in warehouses in Yokohama.

DISTRIBUTION OF RELIEF IN HOKKAIDO, FEBRUARY 1957

As a representative of the American Friends Service Committee it was my privilege to return to Hokkaido in February 1957 with representatives of Church World Service and Catholic Relief Services, all of which were working as a unit on the Hokkaido relief program, to witness something of the value of American aid.

When we reached the northern island we divided into three groups so we could go to nine different areas and then gather in Sapporo to review our experiences and assess the situation.

The snow was nine feet deep when I reached Kuromatsunai. Our small party was taken by bobsled out to some "pioneer" villages — settlements that had been created by the return of repatriates from Saghalien, Manchuria, Korea and Taiwan after the close of the war. It would have been uphill farming under the best of circumstances starting all over again, living on marginal land without much capital, equipment or assistance. On the way we stopped at a schoolhouse where there was a kettle of milk warming for the school lunch made from American dried milk.

We were welcomed in the village community building by about a dozen pioneer farmers ranging in age from twenty-four to forty-five with the average age around twenty-eight. We ate our lunch of sandwiches which we had brought along and they ate their simple lunch of rice or potatoes or whatever they had brought with them.

The main crop in this particular area was potatoes. This region was on the narrow southern peninsula of Hokkaido and was subject to cold winds, so field crops were a hazard. Some barley, wheat and beans were grown. Wheat was usually used for hay. No rice was grown here so it had to be brought in from some distance if they were to have any to eat.

The settlers had one horse apiece. Some had cows and two sold milk. The four hundred chickens in the community laid some eggs, but these were sold instead of eaten, because of the scarcity of money. When I asked them how often they had meat, fish or eggs, they merely smiled and replied, "Practically never." They got tiny dried fish in soup from time to time, but what protein they got came largely from beans and soybeans. Fourteen farmers had a total of thirty-four pigs. The one thing they were not short of was fresh air because this village lay four miles from the Japan Sea between Japan and Siberia, and not far from the Pacific Ocean.

According to these farmers, their future depended on changing from open field crops to livestock, but a horse cost from $110 to $135, a milk cow twice that much. They figured that it would take about fourteen-hundred dollars capital investment, which is a lot of money if you don't have any, and about twenty-five acres of land to make a go of farming. The government furnished a little work relief on the roads or in the forests, but at $1.15 a day for a man or $3.00 a day for a man and horse, one can see how difficult it was to get started in farming. We did see quite a number of silos on our two northern trips so that dairying based on hay and silage was making some headway in this inhospitable climate.

This group of men expressed in heartfelt words what the American relief program had meant to them. I was overwhelmed all over Hokkaido by the outpouring of gratitude for American aid. When I asked one farmer from what country he thought the rice was, he replied, "California."

I was especially interested in this visitation because I had led a five-day blitz in Congress in March of that year to get an increased variety of relief supplies, to extend the number of countries to which aid might go, and to obtain ocean freight for the supplies to the port of entry. Here I was witnessing the end result. No man is good enough to be the arbiter of who should eat and who should starve, and I was humbled by the warm expressions of gratitude for having done something to help make these supplies available. I enjoyed visiting with the farmers about the size of their farms, the livestock they were trying to raise, and the problems they were running up against in their attempts to get re-established in what I felt was a very inhospitable situation for farming.

Another village some of us went to was Oshamambe, whose activity was mainly fishing and where the snow was only two feet deep. These people had not had a good crop year since the settlement was started in 1947. There were twenty-two families in the community. The farmers had around twelve-and-a-half acres each. Some of the settlers were repatriates from Saghalien, others had grown up near Osaka and had come to Hokkaido only to find the land too swampy for rice paddy. They tried to raise beans, soybeans, corn, barley and vegetables like cabbage and daikon, a long white radish, but only with moderate success. They got fish every three days, but never saw beef although Hokkaido was a growing beef country. If they had chickens, they sold the eggs to get cash. The nurse, who served five villages, said that there was a serious lack of vitamins A and D, so that rickets and deformity of the back among children were common. Apparently they had been getting some relief rice, but none was in evidence that day.

The men of the community had had a very poor fish catch that year and most of them were out working on the roads for a little relief money, but we were welcomed by the women and children in their tiny little community hall. After a lively visit with them and the community nurse, it became lunch time. I took out my Japanese lunch box or bento which had been beautifully packed by the

Japanese inn where we had stayed the night before. But viewing this hungry group of women and children, I couldn't eat a bite. So I passed my bento to one of the women who immediately shared it with some of the children.

I had noticed one or two women flitting in and out of the room and soon one came back with the only thing which they had raised that year — a simple bowl of white potatoes, and passed them to us as their way of sharing what they had. I've participated in many communion services before I joined the nonsacramental Quakers, and in some moving ecumenical services since, but this was the most sacramental experience I have ever had, and nearly twenty years afterward I cannot think of this incident without tears — the grace and dignity of sharing their only food with total strangers.

At Iwagame, near Sapporo, we met with the children and the farmers of the community as we sat in a circle on the schoolroom floor. First each of the three relief agencies was presented with a beautifully handwritten scroll of thanks for the relief rice which had gone to each of the fourteen families. This presentation was made by the leading county official present. Three of us made very brief acknowledgments.

I said my grandfathers on both sides had been pioneer farmers in Iowa more than a hundred years ago, and that my brother was living on the same farm now. The school reminded me of eight years' attendance in a one-room country school, and I told some of the pleasant and interesting experiences of life in school and on the farm. I also said that the farmers in Iowa had gone through a very serious depression after the First World War when they hardly saw a dollar from one year's end to the other. The tiny part I had had in the rice program was working on the legislation making government surplus available, so that this was in a real sense a gift from all the American people. Our visit wound up with about an hour-and-a-half of informal discussion about their life and problems.

At Iwagame there had been two distributions of rice — for fifty days if they had received none before, and for thirty days for the four families that had previously received some. They knew that the rice came from California. They said it was excellent quality, and that they were very grateful. To make it go further it was mixed sixty percent rice and forty percent barnyard millet.

Most of the countryside through which we traveled on the three days before reaching Sapporo should never have been taken from God and the Ainu. It really wasn't suitable for profitable farming. We journeyed between rolling hills and steep mountains. Even the trees provided no income for the people living there for they were straggling white birch and other deciduous trees with low lumber yield.

BENEFITS OF THE RELIEF PROGRAM

In the northern part of Japan the relief rice from the United States was distributed on the basis of the Japanese daily ration of 365 grams per person per day to fifty-three thousand farm families who had suffered a seventy percent or more crop loss. The amount of relief was for a period of thirty to sixty days depending on the supplies available which were shipped up from Yokohama by train. The internal freight costs had been largely raised by subscription by the English language newspaper, the *Japan Times,* or by local or prefectural governments. Some relief was also going to about three thousand fisherman families who were suffering acute depression because of poor fishing returns that year. Distribution for the most part was under the Social Affairs section of the Hokkaido Prefectural Government. Relief supplies were signed over to the National Council of Social Welfare, but the actual distribution was done through government channels.

So far as we could learn, the distribution was meticulously carried out on the basis of need described without discrimination and with careful records kept down to the receipt stamped with the personal stamp of the individual recipient. A receipt was made out for every item donated and carried the stamp of the owner's name on it. In all of Japan we found no evidence of fraud or diversion of supplies — somewhat different from the story in Korea and Hong Kong where there was some diversion to the black market.

The relief was greatly appreciated. We had very warm and hearty expressions of appreciation from the recipients themselves, from local, district and prefectural officials and from Hokkaido Governor Tanaka. The numerous individual letters received bore tribute to their gratitude to the American people for this gift and to the voluntary agencies for seeing that it reached them.

Our evaluation was that there were still unmet distress needs in the school lunch program which even with UNICEF help reached only 160,000 out of one million primary and middle school children, not counting preschool children. A major concern of ours was that most of the relief supplies would be used up by March 15 or soon thereafter, and little domestic food could be available until about July 15 when early vegetables might be ready. Looking further ahead there was the consideration that while this year had seen the worst crop failure in forty years, the island was subject to serious frost or weather damage about once every four years. It was obvious that the shift from open field crops to dairying, fruits and nuts, and lumber needed to be accelerated. That would mean more cows; better forage, meadow and silage crops; better barns and houses; more machinery adapted to small-scale livestock agriculture; and better farm-to-market roads. More research was evidently needed to develop cold resistant varieties of crops adapted to that climate.

We spent our last day in Hokkaido as guests of the Governor and various village, county and prefectural officials who talked quite frankly about their hopes and plans and the difficulties involved in the future development of the island. The expressions of appreciation for American aid and that from other countries was very warm and genuine. The Governor said in effect:

> Relief was received first from your organizations. For this we are grateful. But it was spiritual aid also, for it gave us new courage, and helped to make possible the large expression of aid within Japan and some also from Burma and Thailand. Certainly the response of your agencies and of the people abroad has been of immeasurable significance in encouraging our whole nation to answer these basic needs of this island of Hokkaido.

Land Reform

After World War II the American occupation forces with the help of Japanese agricultural economists had carried through a massive land reform program. With some exceptions larger land holdings were divided up and made available to the tenant farmers so that the rate of tenancy dwindled from nearly fifty percent to about nine percent, although the tendency afterwards was to consolidate holdings into large areas. I did not have the opportunity to study this transition as thoroughly as I wanted to. One question I had was whether the small size of farms averaging two-and-a-half acres could provide enough income for the farmer to erect the buildings he needed, or to build a comfortable house, or to send his children to college.

I would think that it was a distinct advantage that the occupation officials helped organize the farmers into hundreds of cooperatives for the purchase or sale of seeds, farm machinery, and products needed or made on the farm. Cooperatives are also a prime source of modest loans at low interest, and a way to avoid financial exploitation of the farmer.

Discontent among the farmers in the twenties and thirties was much exploited by the militarists and expansionists in obtaining support for the seizure of Manchuria, and the aggressive actions against China and eventually against the United States. Let us hope that land reform and progress in Japanese agriculture will prevent any such attitudes in the future.

JAPANESE AGRICULTURE IN 1957

While effort over the years had been made to extend the area under cultivation, that process was slow and very costly, so basically the food produced in Japan had to be grown on the land already under cultivation. Acreage had been increased by forty percent by double cropping. One striking comparison with American agriculture was that in 1953 the rural population of Japan was nearly forty-four percent of the total number of people, while in the United States the number was 13.5 percent. With the rapid consolidation of farms in the United States, farm population now is reduced to around 4.5 percent.

It is the intensiveness of Japanese agriculture that provides the greatest contrast with the United States where the average size farm is over one hundred and twenty times the size of the average Japanese farm. Of the 6,105,049 farm households in Japan on February 1, 1954, the distribution of land under management, which was defined as "all cultivated lands, residential site, meadow, pasture, grazing, forest land, waste land, waterway, water reservoir, and permanent farm road" was roughly as follows: one farmer in six had less than three-fourths of an acre; one in six had between three-fourths of an acre and one-and-one-fourth acres; nearly two in six managed areas between one-and-one-fourth and two-and-one-half acres;only one in six had between two-and-a-half and three-and-three-fourths acres; and a few more than one in six had farms above three-and-three-fourths acres in size.

While there have been some changes in Japan in twenty years, Japanese farming is still done heavily by hand or light machinery in intensive small-size plots. A very large proportion of rural Japanese households has at least one member of the household working off the farm in some other vocation to earn additional money. Some of the principal side jobs for farmers are cutting lumber or making charcoal. Certainly to me one of the most impressive things I saw in Japan was the large areas of reforestation, particularly various kinds of pines, cryptomeria, larch and other trees of the evergreen family.

For extra income some farmers also raised silkworms. As an Iowa corn and hog farmer, it was quite a novel event to visit country houses where silkworms were being raised. Silkworm culture is very carefully supervised by the Ministry of Agriculture to prevent disease. Eggs are laid on small cardboard squares by the silk moths, and kept under refrigeration or low temperature until they are ready for hatching. When hatched, the little silkworms are placed on heavy cardboard trays on top of woven bamboo trays stacked one above another on racks seven or eight inches apart until they fill the room or even the house. The trays are about two-and-a-half by four feet and the cardboard is changed once or twice a day.

Mulberries are trimmed back near the ground and a bunch of branches like whips allowed to grow to six or eight feet before being cut off again. The leaves are pulled off as needed and taken into the house when the silkworms are feeding. The sound of the worms eating is much like a gentle rain on a tin roof.

The worms moult and rest a day about once a week and then the trays are cleaned. As the silkworms grow they are given more room. In something less than a month, I believe, they complete their growth and spin their silk cocoons. Apparently the practice was to raise one batch in the spring and one in the fall. During the season they take a lot of intensive care.

In one house we visited, the silkworms were about two inches long, grayish white and taking their fourth rest, being twenty-three days old that day. When they rest they moult by biting through their skins and crawling out much as a snake does. I guessed there were about a thousand worms on each tray, feeding on the mulberry leaves brought to them. And then begins the process which produced the magnificent variety of silks which are made in Japan.

We saw the next step in the process later in another village where several women were seated in front of pans of almost boiling water in which the silk cocoons were immersed. Several filaments at a time would be taken and twisted together, run through an eyelet overhead and rapidly wound on a reel. Pay for work like these jobs which required considerable skill probably would run between a hundred and fifty and two hundred yen daily, with the yen at that time worth about 365 to the dollar. How much of the world slaves that others may revel in clothes and other beautiful things whose cost to the affluent is a trifle of their income.

Although more meat is being imported into Japan now because of rising income, I figured in 1957 that if evenly distributed, the average Japanese could have beef twice a year, pork for breakfast and lunch once, one small serving of horsemeat, chicken at Easter, whale meat two or three servings a year, with fish and shellfish nearly one pound per week. With twice as many people as chickens, people on the average could look forward to one egg apiece every four days. With one dairy cow for every 220 people, they had little milk, butter or cheese. The most striking change in diet that I witnessed was the increasing use of wheat for bread and much of that wheat has to be imported. The soybean is really the cow of Asia, which along with beans and other pulses provides much of the protein of the East.

While again the situation has improved, during my visits to Japanese farms because of the shortage of draft animals and machinery it was the farmer and his wife who were the main burden bearers and motive power for agricultural machinery. One farmer in three had a draft or beef animal, one in seven a horse, one in eleven one or more sheep or goats, one in ten a pig, one in thirty a dairy cow, and two out of three owned chickens.

While riding across Missouri in a bus some years ago, I thought many times that you could put all the Japanese farmers on the land not used in the United States, or only slightly used, and they would probably make it bloom like the proverbial rose and yield fifty or a hundredfold. This merely points up the great disparity of opportunity in this world and the necessity of making it possible to get food to where people live, if they can't move to where the food can be produced.

HONG KONG — 1957

Hong Kong, which Miriam and I were able to visit in March 1957, was an area of sharp contrasts. Up in the hills were the palatial homes once restricted to the British to whom Hong Kong was ceded in 1841 after the infamous Opium War. Until recently the Chinese, however wealthy, had not been allowed to live with the British but had been forced into crowded conditions in Hong Kong and Kowloon. The larger area in the New Territories had been leased by the British in 1898 for ninety-nine years.

In 1957 downtown Hong Kong and Kowloon were in the midst of a feverish building boom. But essentially Hong Kong was a teeming refugee colony — some from Nationalist China in Formosa, but mostly from mainland China. Miriam and I spent two afternoons in Kowloon visiting some of these areas where refugees numbered well toward a million, and seeing what was being done by religious and voluntary agencies for them.

Many were being housed in four huge areas with forty H-shaped buildings six and seven stories high. Each floor contained sixty-four rooms ten by twelve feet. In each room were supposed to be a minimum of five adults. Children under ten years of age counted as half an adult.

The roofs of these buildings were flat and surrounded by a fence. It was on these roofs that various agencies had formed "clubs" for children to give them a beginning in education and to provide supervised recreation. If they had been called "schools" they would have had to meet certain government standards for staff, equipment and teaching. These were the "well housed refugees."

Festooned up the ravines and hillsides were ramshackle huts of tin, cardboard, plywood, burlap — anything that could be bought, begged or stolen for a semblance of shelter. Water had to be carried a long distance in vessels suspended from poles over the shoulders. Charcoal was the usual fuel and there was very little of that. Some of these people got work in town or started little ingenious cottage industries — weaving, carpentry or needlework. By 1953 there were 300,000 of these squatters. Add to this misery upwards of 75,000 people crowded into shacks built on rooftops or along the streets or under arcades. I heard of people who actually had no floor space of their own and slept above other people on a swinging board, hammock or other support, precariously suspended from some ceiling.

The two big dangers of such crowding were disease and fire. On Christmas night in 1953 more than 50,000 had lost their homes and forty-five acres were cleared of human habitation by the most intensive fire in the colony's history. It was after that that the Hong Kong government really started to house these miserable victims. They had done a lot in four years, but there was a long and expensive job still to be accomplished.

If the United States had absorbed proportionally as many of the homeless victims of war or political revolution as Hong Kong did, there would have been somewhat between forty million to one hundred million to resettle. I can only pay tribute to what Hong Kong had done already and was planning to do to rehouse people. The one bright spot was the sight of the eager faces of the children who played with abandon in the streets and turned friendly inquisitive eyes to wandering visitors.

Church World Service, Catholic Relief Services, CARE and other relief agencies were distributing supplies from surplus American food and doing what they could to alleviate the worst distress. The Children's Nursery, aided by Church World Service, was a model of activity and sunlight and cleanliness. An old China hand, Reverend Dunithorne, as he visited the rooftop in K block or walked the streets, would be surrounded by children crowding around to shake his hand and to look up to him with affection. The personal interest in people and their welfare and their future exhibited by the Chinese churches or by the flood of former missionaries in China provided the invaluable personal ingredient to programs of resettlement far beyond the capacity of any private or religious agency. For many, many people the price of freedom comes awfully high.

Visit to the Philippines — 1957

With no streetcars in Manila, people traveled in buses, cars, jeeps and jeepneys. It looked as if Detroit was doing very well. Jeeps and jeepneys, the latter converted jeeps with gaily decorated open bodies that carried eight passengers in the rear and two in front beside the driver, swarmed the streets like locusts picking up and discharging passengers in helter-skelter abandon.

I was impressed by the spaciousness of Manila after crowded Hong Kong, the variety of modern architecture in hotels and apartment houses, by the six-lane width of the main streets, by the high price level at the official rate of exchange, and by the destructiveness of the war as evidenced by the stark walls of the old city which had been left standing with no buildings inside.

There was severe criticism there of the politicians for feathering their own nests at the expense of the people. The night I visited the House of Representatives in session, there was a lively debate on the division of the Japanese reparations between the government and the "private sector." In plain language it seemed to me a debate on how much of, for example, the cement to be provided by the Japanese in war reparations would go to each representative for allocation or construction in his district, and what his personal cut in the profits might be.

Since the war and up to the end of fiscal year June 30, 1956, U.S. help, not counting direct military aid, including military construction assistance in commodities, technical assistance and other U.S. aid, had amounted to $96,400,000. This went to the development of agriculture, roads, ports, industry, mining, health, education, public administration and community development. Reforestation had hardly started particularly compared with Japan.

The International Rice Research Institute in the Philippines, established by the Rockefeller Foundation and the Ford Foundation, had helped usher in the so-called "Green Revolution" in Asia with the introduction of miracle rice beginning with the variety IR-8 which has increased the yield of rice so much when supplied with adequate fertilizer and irrigation water.

The program for eliminating the disfiguring disease of yaws by injections of penicillin was making good progress. UNICEF had donated drugs and equipment for fighting leprosy and was furnishing skim milk to 200,000 children and mothers through public schools, health centers and child care institutions.

With seven thousand islands and ninety-seven dialects, and at that time only about forty percent literacy, the Philippines faced an uphill task of achieving universal education.

English was widely used and the influence of nearly fifty years of American control could be seen all around the capital city of Manila. The Philippines were given their independence on July 4, 1946, by an act of the American Congress.

During the past few years there has been considerable criticism of the measures taken by President Ferdinand Marcos in repression of civil liberties. When I entered the city hall there was a sign near the door, "Park your guns outside."

When I asked various Filipinos what was bothering them about relations with the U.S., they listed three things. Sugar was a big industry and had gone to the U.S. free, but the U.S. was scheduled to raise the tariff over the ensuing ten years to that charged other countries. A second complaint was that they bought most of their cotton from the United States, but that they had to pay fairly high tariffs to sell back to the United States the blouses, sheets, and other cotton goods woven in the Philippines. The third objection voiced to me was about the American military bases in the Philippines which were causing some friction.

TOKYO REVISITED — 1972

It was a sudden invitation from the revered Korean Quaker, Ham Sok Han, to speak at a peace conference near Seoul in January 1972, that took me on a flying trip to Korea, Okinawa and Japan under the auspices of the American Friends Service Committee. Martin Cobin, AFSC representative in the Far East, went with me on most of the crowded three weeks' round of interviews.

The major question which Martin and I discussed in Korea,

Okinawa and Japan was at what stage the relations among the Americans, Russians, Japanese and Communist Chinese were and how they could be improved.

When we had a leisurely lunch with three members of the Soviet Embassy in Tokyo, I asked them what were the difficult issues between the U.S. and the U.S.S.R. They listed the conflict between capitalism and Marxism-Leninism, the war in Vietnam, the Middle East conflict and the question of wars of liberation. While they denied that the Soviet Union was exporting revolution, they did believe in supporting peoples under dictatorships who were struggling for their freedoms. We didn't have the opportunity to bring up the differences of views on freedom and dissent, on opposition newspapers and on the Soviet invasion of Czechoslovakia.

Between the Soviet Union and the People's Republic of China, they said, the main problem, and a serious one, was ideological. Mao was a revisionist, or deviationist, and the gap was wide. The territorial problems of river boundaries and border disputes, according to our guests, were relatively insignificant compared with the ideological differences. One of the questions we discussed was that of protecting endangered species — certain varieties of whales, herring and even salmon in some places.

I spoke about my disappointment at not finding more books in English on politics, economics and current topics in the big bookstores in Moscow which I had visited in 1971 as I had found in Budapest in Hungary for example. While acknowledging that there was not a great variety of English language books in Moscow bookstores, they replied that Russian translations of many English titles were being published in the Soviet Union. This informal luncheon was an example of the kind of frank, friendly, straightforward discussion that I have had not only with the Russians, but with the nationals of many countries.

Martin and I had a very illuminating afternoon with two staff members of the American Embassy in Tokyo discussing their views on the political conditions in the Far East. I argued that American troops should be withdrawn from Japan and Okinawa, but while reductions were envisaged I got no assurance of any timetable or plans for their ultimate withdrawal in view of the uncertain future of the relations with China and the Soviet Union. In my opinion they did not view Japanese rearmament and the threat of Japanese militarism seriously enough.

I had the privilege of speaking to men from fourteen countries on some of the crosscurrents in American policies toward other countries at a diplomats' luncheon arranged by the American Friends Service Committee. While I dealt briefly with the domestic scene, this was before the full story of Watergate broke.

One of the many interesting interviews on this trip was with Shinsaku Hegan, Deputy Vice-Minister for Foreign Affairs, in his office in the Foreign Ministry. The Japanese were working on a treaty with the Soviet Union and we discussed some of the issues involved. One of the sticky points was their request to the Russians for the return of some of the small Kurile Islands near the Hokkaido coast which they had seized. Another thorny problem was fishing rights in the Japan Sea. Herring had been pretty well fished out and there was intense competition for the available fish near Japan.

We also discussed the relations between Japan, China and the United States. The Vice-Minister indicated that restoring full diplomatic relations with the People's Republic of China was quite a way off for at least two reasons — they didn't want to cut off their diplomatic ties with Taiwan with which Japan carried on heavy trade, and they didn't want to extend full diplomatic recognition too far ahead of the United States, which was making its first move toward softening its hostile relations through the projected visit of President Nixon. Japan was recovering from what was called the two "Nixon shocks," actions which had been taken without consultation with Japan — the devaluation of the dollar and the ten percent surtax on Japanese goods, and Nixon's planned visit to China. Part of the motivation for the surtax looked like an effort to protect the American automakers against the competition of German and Japanese small automobiles which were making quite an inroad into the American market.

IMPERIAL UNIVERSITY DORMITORY REUNION

One evening five of us from the group of about forty-two boys who had lived together in the Imperial University YMCA dormitory forty-five years earlier got together for a very nostalgic evening reunion at the Nippon Club. Atsushi Suzuki had been with the Mitsubishi-Reynolds Aluminum Company in Tokyo and helped arrange the merger between the Mitsubishi and the Reynolds companies. At the time of my visit he was with the Mitsubishi Metal and Mining Company which dealt with nonferrous metals — gold, silver, copper, lead, zinc, and so on. He was active on the committee that was planning to build a new YMCA dormitory.

Ko Oiwa has been an editor of the *Silk Digest* and each year has sent me a very beautiful calendar book full of pictures of Japanese flowers and flower arrangements. Koichi Inomata was teaching two classes at International Christian University — one on Japanese government and politics in Japanese and a course on administrative law in English. For many years he was a judge in one of the higher courts in Tokyo. Paul M. Sekiya came all the way down from Sendai on the train — at least two hundred miles — to join the party and was expecting to sit up all night on the way back. He used to be secretary of the Fellowship of Reconciliation in Japan when I was there before, but now was serving as a priest in the Episcopal Cathedral at Sendai. How precious friendships are that have continued for nearly fifty years, even though we lived on opposite sides of the globe. They roll up the streets early in Tokyo and since public transportation stops soon after 10 p.m. and the Nippon Club closes at 8 p.m., our party broke up its reminiscing then. It would have been instructive and fun to have talked all night.

THE KIYOOKA FAMILY

Another very pleasant reunion was with Eiichi and Chiyono Kiyooka at their home near the site where I had lived with his parents in 1926 during the first two months of my stay in Japan. It was Eiichi who had traveled around Hokkaido and Saghalien with me in the summer of 1927. He had spent his life working on American-Japanese friendship. For the previous eight summers he and Chiyono had taken about forty Japanese students from Keio high school classes to Hawaii to live in American homes and improve their English. If they could find the funds they would like to make it reciprocal and bring American students to Japan.

Eiichi Kiyooka retired from teaching in Keio University in a deserved blaze of glory. The Kiyookas were given a magnificent party in the Tokyo Prince Hotel with six ambassadors and some of the Imperial Family and a distinguished list of guests present. He was awarded a Professor Emeritus status given, I believe, only 115 times in the entire history of the university. The living room was full of awards of different kinds. His wife, Chiyono, had filled several beautiful albums with pictures, clippings and letters.

Chiyono is the daughter of Mrs. Sugimoto who wrote the delightful book, *A Daughter of the Samurai*, which was the first book I read on Japan. Both the Kiyookas were authors. They presented me with a copy of a book Chiyono had written based largely on Eiichi's life. Eiichi had translated the autobiography of his grandfather, Y. Fukusawa, who had founded Keio University where Eiichi taught for some forty years.

On this trip to Japan Roberta Levenbach and I had an all-too-brief visit with Reverend John M. Nakajima, secretary of the Japan National Christian Council. Christians number less than one percent of the population of Japan, although their influence in the Diet and elsewhere is much greater than their numbers might indicate. The Christian churches of Japan are mostly small, and spend much of their time in a struggle for survival, so there isn't much attention paid to national and international affairs. Their Committee on International Affairs is made up of very busy people who are seldom able to get together, so this program is small.

I pressed pretty hard with Mr. Nakajima for the churches in Japan to get behind a crusade for disarmament and international security, political settlements and reconciliation as perhaps the best way to counter the current push for Japanese rearmament and the projected buildup of the Self-Defense Forces. Miss Helen Post of the Japan National Council of Churches staff was wondering what was being done in the churches of America on the Okinawan reversion treaty and Japanese rearmament. She told me that my testimony before the Senate Foreign Relations Committee against the reversion treaty had been translated into Japanese for circulation by the Christian Council.

KOREA 1972

Nineteen seventy-two was a difficult time to hold public meetings that would in any way criticize the Park government. On this trip to the Far East I had been asked to speak on the "Politics of Peace" and the "Future of American Foreign Policy in Asia" to a peace conference near Seoul. I told the conference that I had come primarily to stand with them in their defense of the basic civil liberties of the right of free speech, freedom of petition and freedom of assembly which were so much denied in Korea under the repressive regime of President Park Chung Hee.

In the ensuing three years more than 203 people have been jailed and some of them threatened with execution because of their criticism of the Park government. My very able interpreter at the peace conference, Kim Don Kil, professor at Yonsei University, was one of those imprisoned for many months, and according to the *New York Times* was only released February 15, 1975, along with some of the other liberal critics of the Park government.

Martin Cobin and I had long talks with several members of the

National Assembly and were entertained for our last breakfast at the home of an Assembly member and his wife, the only woman lawyer at that time in South Korea. This breakfast gave us a glimpse of what the liberals in South Korea faced in trying to uphold their civil and political rights.

One group came to see us because of their interest in a type of United Nations Peace Corps which had started on a small scale, but which they hoped to expand. I had a lively hour with a group of journalists for the religious press. They seemed particularly interested in religious lobbying and church activities in the United States — the kind of activities which were not permitted in Korea.

My first and last visits in Seoul were to the American Embassy to express my deep concern about either explicit or implicit support of the Park regime by the United States government. The U.S. has spent more than nine billion dollars in economic and military aid in Korea since the armistice in 1953.

The economic aid has gone for food, for restoring railways, bridges and roads destroyed by the Korean War, and in other ways to rebuild a shattered country. But some of the American aid was invested in huge cement and glass plants which needed more expertise for management than the Koreans yet possessed. Smaller plants could have trained Korean management and would have distributed employment more widely. The large plants seemed to me an unwise expenditure of American aid.

Almost twenty years after the end of the Korean War there were still nearly forty thousand American troops stationed in South Korea, ostensibly to deter any aggression from the North. With very little to do, alcoholism, drugs, prostitution and corruption were affecting many of them, and it seemed to me that in the moral sense they were a blight on the country. They were assisting in modernizing the South Korean Army which was being given great quantities of military supplies from the United States. The large South Korean Army was a heavy drain on the Korean economy, but we saw pictures in the Korean CIA of the thorough and frightening way North Korea was indoctrinating its youth in military ideas, and this made South Korea continue to fear invasion from the North.

This division of Korea grew in part out of the American invitation to Stalin to join the war in the Far East in 1945 and to the arrangement that the Russians would demobilize the Japanese forces north of the 38th parallel while the U.S. would occupy South Korea during the demobilization and reconstruction period after World War II.

The situation in South Korea is complicated and difficult with no easy answers. Martin and I visited with the cabinet minister and others who were working very slowly on opening up relations with North Korea, toward exchange of mail, reunion of families, and perhaps the eventual reunification of the two Koreas in some unforseeable future. In these talks to date very little progress has been made. I think the talks with North Korea ought to continue with the object of facilitating mail and visits and the reunion of families. Countries have to develop the philosophy of live and let live and seek increasing cooperation. The FCNL has advocated the total withdrawal of American troops from South Korea within a reasonable time. Detente has to be worked out eventually with North Korea as has been done to some degree by the United States with the Soviet Union and the People's Republic of China.

OKINAWA — AMERICA'S MILITARY COLONY

Okinawa is a tragic island some 876 miles southwest of Tokyo. It is only sixty-five miles long and the width varies from two to seventeen miles. Though it comprises only 454 square miles of territory, it has historically been caught in a political and military tug of war first with China, and then between Japan and the United States. Okinawa was bitterly contested toward the end of the Second World War with the loss of 122,000 American and Japanese troops and 24,000 civilians. The island then became one of the staging grounds for the final assaults on Japan. Later it was a huge repair base for military vehicles and the primary military center for amassing supplies and launching bombers for carrying on the U.S. war against Vietnam until aerial bombardment ceased.

Abraham Lincoln was fond of saying that no man was good enough to rule another man without his consent. When arbitrary rule is fortified by the doctrine of military necessity to which there is usually no effective appeal, coupled with military secrecy and far removed from civilian control or adequate civilian visitation, it can be arbitrary and impersonal indeed. While the small Okinawan Diet or legislature had been restored, still, in 1957, the final decisions on many matters still rested with the United States Military Commissioner. As an inveterate lobbyist I had visits with members of the Diet on both my trips to Okinawa, but they felt their powers were severely limited.

Okinawa is a living lesson in the price of liberty paid by unfortunate people caught in the middle of major armament races, and ought to be another prime reason for beating the world's swords into plowshares. In 1957 I spent an afternoon driving past U.S. installations stocked with planes, jeeps, trucks, weapons carriers, past huge warehouses full of military supplies in order to visit villages in which the displaced Okinawans lived in crowded shacks. The population density outside the bases is approximately 2400 per square mile, about the greatest population density in the world.

My visits in 1957 and 1972 were short but focused mainly on the character and effects of United States military occupation. On the positive side, sanitation had been improved, hundreds of schools had been built, and roads near military installations had been paved. When we talked to the U.S. officials in charge of civil affairs they were quite proud of their achievements in building up the country which had been almost completely devastated during the Second World War. One notable advance was the establishment, with some American help, of the University of the Ryukyus. Thousands of jobs have been temporarily created by the U.S. military occupation. In 1955 it was estimated that more than 51,000 Ryukyuans were employed, including nearly 10,000 domestics. Service workers and farmers got an average income of $15.37 with an average monthly wage of all workers averaging about $21.80. American workers made considerably more.

Still, the presence of any foreign troops in another country, no matter how benevolently inclined, is apt to be a source of irritation and I would say in Okinawa and South Korea, a cancer in the body politic. The moral influence around military installations is usually bad. Sex is about the biggest business in the island. If you drive down the main street of Koza, near the huge Kadena airbase, an area on one side of the street is the red light district for white soldiers and on the other side is the one for black G.I.'s. I also drove past innumerable houses scattered around the country where a G.I. lives off-base with a "honey" as opposed to a "wife."

Roberta Levenbach, staff member at that time of the Tokyo Office of the American Friends Service Committee, made a special study in May and June 1972, for circulation by the AFSC in Philadelphia of the "Bi-Racial (International) Children in Okinawa." In this report she reviewed some of the psychological, educational, occupational and legal problems of abandoned mothers and children which has been one of the unfortunate legacies of U.S. military occupation.

A conservative estimate is that the number of mixed blood children is around three thousand, of whom about ninety percent have been abandoned by their fathers — either American or Filipino soldiers. The military doesn't keep figures on children fathered and abandoned by the servicemen and takes no responsibility for their support.

In 1972 G.I.'s were implicated in seventy-eight percent of all crimes involving drugs in Okinawa. The amount of heroin confiscated in 1971 was 450 kilograms, which was more than two hundred times as much as that found in all mainland Japan.

Another major cause of trouble was the belief on the part of the Okinawans that there was one kind of justice for the Americans and another for the natives. There were, for example, many accidents caused by soldiers driving huge military trucks down the narrow winding streets, and often a soldier who had caused a death or accident would get a very light sentence when tried in a military court run by Americans. While the average G.I. tended personally to be friendly, the total weight of the military machine was usually insensitive and impersonal.

One of my major interests in visiting Okinawa and other countries in 1957 was to observe the distribution of American relief supplies under legislation which I had worked for in the spring of 1957. Church World Service and Catholic Relief Services were doing a commendable job of distributing relief in cooperation with the civil government. It was extremely difficult because of the erratic shipments received and the uncertainty of what or when further supplies might be available. This area is very susceptible to quite destructive typhoons. Some not-too-distant day we hope the human race will put its ingenuity to feeding disadvantaged hungry people instead of on producing mortars and cannon and rifles.

On my first trip to Okinawa I was particularly concerned about the question of land acquisition. The Okinawans claimed that fifty thousand farm families, comprising about two hundred thousand people out of the 675,000 people on the island, had been dispossessed of their holdings to provide the forty thousand acres then held by the American military. In addition there had been a request for twelve thousand more acres partly for grounds for maneuvers for the Marines in the northern part of this small island, but this request had been refused.

Most disheartening was to see villages of little hovels made out of strips of corrugated iron in which people were crowded who had been moved off their land in order to make a golf course for the American military. On the top of the hill above was the plush and large officers' clubhouse. I visited an embittered, one-armed farmer who had been moved from his good farm and was chopping away with a kind of mattock on rocky ground so poor that it looked as if nothing would grow on it. None of his new land was suitable for rice paddy, and even drinking water was hard to get. It was about the most depressing farm land I can remember seeing. Nearby was the little group of huts huddled together. All were without any livestock except one family which had a sow and a few pigs.

The U.S. military claimed that they owed the farmers nothing for the period between 1945 and 1952 when the first treaty with Japan was signed, and after that they paid only a very nominal and inadequate rent — not enough for a farmer to live on or to buy additional ground. And even if a lump sum payment were made, where would the Okinawan farmer find comparable land for sale? This was a question I worked on some in Congress after I returned to the United States, trying to get adequate compensation for these displaced farmers. Some of their land could never be farmed again, having been covered with concrete for buildings or runways, or the top soil all bulldozed off, or the land otherwise ruined for agricultural purposes. Finally a partial settlement was worked out, which seemed to me totally inadequate. Like the American Indian in the United States, land to these Okinawans was sacred, especially after it had been in the family for generations. To the Okinawans the land "contains the soul of our ancestors in the long course of historical background." The land was lost and the money paid for the land would soon be gone. This was just one of the high-handed injustices of the situation after the Second World War.

The Americans claimed that they were only in the islands for defensive purposes in order to develop a bastion against any further Soviet or Chinese expansion in the Far East, that they did not want title to a single acre of land, but that they would stay as long as necessary for their concept of military security. That argument was stretched to cover a prodigious amount of activity in the Vietnam War.

During the first hearings on the 1952 U.S.-Japan security treaty, Esther Rhoads, who had lived in Japan for more than forty years, and I were the only two witnesses before the congressional committee opposing the treaty on the grounds that it was a moral and political mistake to keep American troops in Japan and Okinawa any longer because they would create constant friction and trouble. American troops had been stationed in Japan and Okinawa for more than twenty-five years. Our prophecies were amply borne out because over the years there have been frequent demonstrations by labor unions or other groups in Japan and Okinawa against U.S.

military occupation. Finally the Nixon-Tanaka agreement allowed for reversion of Okinawa to the political sovereignty of Japan on May 15, 1972, with the promise that no more nuclear weapons would be stored on Okinawa, a staging ground for so many huge B-52 bombers. The agreement improved but did not solve the situation.

One unfortunate provision in the reversion treaty was that the United States would be paid $320 million by Japan in spite of the fact that the U.S. virtually controlled the island from 1945 to 1972. This sum would be in payment for such civilian developments as water systems, electric power, schools, roads, and other expenditures of the United States Civil Administration in Okinawa.

Former U.S. Ambassador to Japan, Edwin O. Reischauer, proposed that at least a large share of this money be used for an educational and cultural interchange to train Okinawan students in the United States, Japan and other countries, something like the use of the Boxer indemnity money in China earlier in this century. But no move was made by the United States to carry out such an excellent idea.

There was no explicit promise in the reversion agreement that the United States bases will be reduced or phased out in the near future. The United States has retained one hundred and twenty-five military bases in Japan and Okinawa now more than thirty years after the end of the war. American troop numbers are now being reduced, but there is a long way to go before true reversion occurs.

I was one of the few witnesses in 1971 against the terms of the reversion which allowed tens of thousands of troops to remain in Japan and eighty-eight U.S. installations and military facilities to remain in Okinawa. This was a treaty of retention instead of reversion I claimed. Again there have been many protests by the Okinawans. One of the ironies is that Okinawa, now restored as a prefecture, but the poorest of the Japanese prefectures, is witnessing the Japanese Self-Defense Force moving into some of the military installations evacuated by the Americans. So these hapless people are the victims of two kinds of military occupation — American and now, increasingly, Japanese. The Okinawan people realize that the presence of troops and military installations may, as Pearl Harbor did, serve as targets of enemy action and thus invite attack.

Okinawa longs to become a tourist attraction like Guam or Hawaii are now to the Japanese, particularly to honeymooners. But its beaches are threatened by pollution from oil refineries. Already the oil tanks have polluted the sea and damaged the fishing industry. The island has very few natural resources. It will for some time to come be a kind of a stepchild to Japan which can't afford to furnish the amount of money that is needed for capital investment. The Okinawans are holding a 1975 oceanographic exposition which they hope will attract many visitors. But when and if the American military forces withdraw is totally unpredictable at this point.

In 1972 I spent an afternoon with a half dozen professors who were mildly optimistic about the future of the island. I hope I am dead wrong in my apprehensions about the future economic and social development of Okinawa, but I do think they will have a hard time ahead in reaching a fair standard of living or freedom from the unfortunate effects of American and Japanese militarism and capitalism.

CHAPTER 6

Shall We Train Our Students for War or for Peace? The Committee on Militarism in Education

In the early fall of 1925, while studying at Teachers College, Columbia University, and living at International House, I was approached by John Nevin Sayre and Norman Thomas and asked to help launch the Committee on Militarism in Education (CME). The goal of the Committee was the abolition of *compulsory* military training in colleges and universities, and *all* military training in public high schools.

The suggested arrangement at the first CME meeting on November 6, 1925, was that I should serve as executive secretary and spend approximately one-quarter time in helping initiate this crusade. I was to be paid $900 for a year's service. Actually I wound up spending about four-fifths of my time on this project during the school year, and full time in June and July 1926, until I left in August for a year's study in Japan. Consequently I never finished writing a dissertation, the last requirement for a Ph.D.

The CME was comprised of a National Council of prestigious men and women and a small executive committee which met frequently and made the administrative and financial decisions. The first year's budget was $6,000, and the budget never exceeded $22,000 during its fifteen years' intensive work. The office was closed down in November 1940, when the oncoming involvement of the United States in the Second World War made such operations nearly impossible.

The major job during the first few months of the CME's existence was the final editing, printing and distribution of a thirty-two-page pamphlet by Winthrop D. Lane entitled *Military Training in Schools and Colleges of the United States — The Facts and an Interpretation.* In his pamphlet Lane challenged the assumption that the Morrill Land Grant Act of 1862, which established the land grant college system, required military training be compulsory. He asserted instead that in those sixty-nine land grant colleges such training only had to be offered.

Up to that time little had been said about the great anomaly that a "war to end war" and "crush militarism" and "make the world safe for democracy" had been followed by a manifold increase in the number of schools having compulsory or optional military training.

Lane summarized the extent of the War Department involvement in the schools in 1925 as follows:

> During the last school year, that of 1924-25, military instruction was given in *more* than 226 educational institutions in the United States. The exact number is difficult to obtain. Two hundred and twenty-six institutions maintained units of the ROTC (Reserve Officers Training Corps), but. . .the Secretary of War encourages military training in schools which do not establish ROTC. For the schools with ROTC Congress appropriated $3,818,020 and the number of students taking military instruction was 125,504. To these schools the War Department assigned 768 officers and 1,064 enlisted men to carry on training; it paid their salaries. Before 1916 there were no ROTC units and the number of officers engaged in military (training) in schools was only 119.
>
> Of the 226 ROTC institutions in 1925, 124 were of college or university rank, 63 were high schools and 39 were what are known as "essentially military schools." [1]

In at least eighty-three colleges and universities military training was compulsory.

In addition, the War Department had established Citizens' Military Training Corps, or the CMTC as they were called, for lads who had left school and gone to work. In the summer of 1925 there were twenty-eight camps and Congress appropriated $2,100,000 for their support.

---

[1] Winthrop D. Lane, *Military Training in Schools and Colleges of the United States* (Committee on Militarism in Education, New York City, 1925), p. 10. Lane's facts and those used in conjunction with the rest of the Lane section were taken from the published *Hearings before the Subcommittee of the House Committee on Appropriations* in charge of the War Department Appropriation Bill for 1926, pp. 600-621. DG 9, Box 35, SCPC (Swarthmore College Peace Collection).

Lane warned of the determination of the War Department to extend military training to other educational institutions, and of the negative influence this would have on academic freedom. Students conscientiously opposed to military drill were, in many institutions, denied the right to be excused from this requirement. "Never yet," Lane argued, "has progress come by institutions putting such ban on individual dissent":

> New truth for mankind, new social advance, is perceived and acted on first by lone individuals and small groups, and never, in the beginning, by majorities or institutions. When they crush inconvenient dissent they crush their own chance of growth. For twenty-five centuries, from Socrates on, by trial and error, at great cost and pain, the proof has accumulated that social interest is served by the man who reverences conscience as his King. [2]

Lane's main argument was that military training went against the best interests of the schools and the highest ideals of democracy. He did not assert that military training produced a desire for war or glory, but that it created a mentality receptive to war as the ultimate "sanction" to be used by patriots, the one process which in some circumstances national honor and necessity must employ. In other words, it tends to make men accept war and does little or nothing to help men understand how to solve conflicts any other way. How can we have peace when people know little or nothing of the ways to achieve it?

More than 150,000 copies of Lane's pamphlet were printed and distributed to educators, clergy, editors, and other leaders of public opinion. This pamphlet received wide publicity in the daily and religious press, and drew many attacks from the military and from patriotic societies. It was my first experience of being under fire as subversive or unpatriotic or as a tool of Moscow because I had advocated the elimination of the compulsory feature of college military drill and was working to end all military indoctrination in the public high schools.

Sadly enough today, more than fifty years later, there seems to be a concerted drive by the Defense Department to expand the number of high school or Junior ROTC units. Between 1936 and 1963 only three schools had been added to the roster. The Pentagon itself seemed willing to let the program die a natural death. But the outspoken opposition to this idea by the American Legion led

---

[2]Ibid., pp. 29-30.

Representatives Hébert and Bray to introduce a bill in Congress calling for an increase in JROTC units to two thousand, and making drill compulsory in those schools. Congress cut back the authorization to twelve hundred high schools and a ceiling of 240,000 boys to be reached over a five-year period, and the bill became law as the ROTC Vitalization Act of 1964.[3]

In 1963, before the bill passed, there were 67,568 enrolled in JROTC at a cost of eighty dollars per student.[4] By 1973, Army cadets alone numbered 107,000. During 1972 there was a forty percent increase in Navy units, a twenty-five percent increase in Marine Corps units, and a fifteen percent increase in Air Corps units.[5] It is ironic that our disastrous involvement in the Vietnam War is being followed by an expansion of military training in our nation's high schools.

In 1926 I left the Committee on Militarism in Education to study for a year in Japan. In 1929, about two years after I had returned from Japan, I worked with the Pennsylvania CME for a short time, and then moved to New York City as Tucker P. Smith's associate in the national CME office. Altogether I spent approximately three years in campaigns against compulsory drill, as opposition erupted on campuses all over the United States. This chapter recounts only a few highlights of those years — the fight for the Welsh optional training bill; the Fellowship of Youth For Peace Conference at Concord, Massachusetts; the spread of compulsory drill and military camps, partly because of the U.S. example, to Japan, the Soviet Union and Mexico; the battle against compulsory military training in the Iowa legislature in 1931; and the peace literature study I did with Elsie Lowenberg during a short leave of absence from the CME.

THE WELSH OPTIONAL TRAINING BILL, 1926

At least twice in its history, the Committee on Militarism in Education made a determined effort to get legislation through Congress to make military training in civilian schools and colleges optional instead of compulsory. The first effort was the Welsh bill, H.R. 8538, in 1926. The second was the Nye-Kvale bill in 1936 and 1937, some years after I had left the Committee.

---

[3]Craig Karpel, "The Teenie Militarists," *Ramparts* VII (September 28, 1968), pp. 43-50.

[4]Ibid.

[5]Bob Seeley, "High School ROTC: From Books to Bazookas," *Friends Journal* XIX (September 15, 1973), p. 452.

The hearings on the Welsh bill on April 29 and 30, and June 15, 1926, before the House Military Affairs Committee were lively confrontations between the proponents and opponents of optional drill, and drew a series of personal attacks on supporters of the bill by opposition witnesses and by some of the committee members themselves.

Congressman Welsh, in opening the case for optional training, defined its purpose:

> To democratize the educational institutions of the country by taking from the present law the provision which makes military training compulsory in schools and colleges. . . . Each one who is here speaks for a large group of people, in some instances running into hundreds of thousands. . . . Every group that is represented here is an essential American group, who respect the flag, respect our institutions, but who want to carry out into the future certain ideals which we think the world is striving for today. . . . [6]

These assertions on his part were to be severely challenged during the hearings.

Speaking for the bill, Major Kenneth Walser, who served in France in the First World War, argued that "you will make better reserve officers if they are not compelled to take a course in military training in schools and colleges than you will if they are compelled to do so." A man, he said, "must want to be an officer before he can command troops successfully." And a boy trained against his will "is no better for the defense of the United States when he gets through than he was when he started."

Professor William Bradley Otis of the College of the City of New York said that while he spoke for himself, he felt that he reflected the "majority educational opinion in this country" in opposing compulsory military training. He quoted President Coolidge as having told the American Legion in Omaha the previous fall that: "Whenever the military power starts dictating to the civil authority, by whatsoever means adopted, the liberties of the country are beginning to end." Otis went on to say, "the freedom of faculties to determine their own curriculum has been invaded for the first time in the history of the country. This compulsory military training is a

---

[6]Except where otherwise indicated, testimony quoted throughout this section is taken from *Abolishment of Compulsory Military Training at Schools and Colleges, Hearings before the Committee on Military Affairs, House of Representatives,* Sixty-ninth Congress on H.R. 8538, Washington, Government Printing Office, 1926.

prerequisite for graduation, and its courses, both civil and military, are determined by the bureaucrats at Washington."

Opponents of the bill were firm in their belief that ROTC would make a valuable contribution to military security. Dr. Henry S. Drinker, former president of Lehigh University, speaking against the bill said, "I come from Quaker descent, and all my antecedents are for peace, but I am heart and soul for this military training because I am a man of peace and wish to maintain peace."

But while some of the testimony against the bill dealt with the military desire for trained officers with a civilian background as a supplement to the regular military establishment, the extensive remarks of Representatives Hill and James on the Military Affairs Committee and of some of the proponents of compulsory military training were mainly attempts to cloud the issue and discredit the supporters of the Welsh bill. Repeatedly Representatives Hill and James questioned the bill's proponents about their military service records, and implied that those who had not served in the armed forces had not earned the right to testify on such legislation. Hill said to Walter Longstreth, a soft-spoken Quaker lawyer, "I can understand your point of view on this bill and it is the point of view of a man who never gave an iota of service to his country in its hour of need."

One of Representative Hill's attempts to discredit a witness did backfire, however, when he spotted and called to the attention of the committee what he took to be a military decoration on the coat of Frederick Lynch, a Secretary of the Church Peace Union who was testifying for the bill. "It is not a military decoration," Lynch corrected Hill, "It is a decoration (from Greece) for feeding hungry children, not killing them."

There were repeated attempts to link supporters of the bill to communist and subversive organizations. Mrs. Cornelia Ross Potts, president of the National Patriotic Council, Washington, D.C., filed with the committee "a list of the organizations affiliated with these so-called peace organizations; and you will see," she declared, "that they are lined up as the Civil Liberties Union is, with communistic orders, taking their instructions from Moscow. . . . Has there been a single man or woman who has testified here yesterday in favor of this bill that has ever done anything for his/her country?"

John Nevin Sayre, testifying on June 15 for the bill, responded to Mrs. Potts' accusations about some of the signers of the introduction to the Lane pamphlet, by pointing out that:

Forty of those fifty-eight signers are mentioned in *Who's Who*, which gives the people who are in leading positions in this country. This Lane pamphlet list includes four United States Senators, two honorable members of the House of Representatives, an ex-governor of Colorado, three bishops, two well-known Jewish rabbis, the founder of the Society of Christian Endeavor, a general secretary of the Federal Council of Churches, four university presidents, six eminent university professors, nine editors, three heads of powerful women's organizations, and businessmen, ministers, social workers, labor leaders, Y.M.C.A. and Y.W.C.A. secretaries, etc.

Interestingly enough during the hearings on the Welsh bill, President Coolidge, himself, commander-in-chief of the Army and Navy, spoke out against compulsory military training. On June 15 in one of his semi-weekly news conferences he told reporters that while he had found the physical exercise that military training involved personally helpful while he was a student at Amherst, he opposed the cultivation of a military spirit and he stressed that military training should not be made the price of a college education.[7] The President's position so incensed the editors of the *Army and Navy Register* that they attacked him for giving "aid and comfort" to those who wished to put the government in a position where it could not "take care of its increasing responsibilities as a world power."[8]

But Coolidge's position on this bill should have been no surprise to them. In October 1925, in a speech before the American Legion in Omaha, Coolidge had said:

> In spite of all the arguments in favor of great military forces, no nation ever had an army large enough to guarantee it against attacks in time of peace or to insure its victory in war. No nation ever will. Peace and security are more likely to result from fair and honorable dealings, and mutual agreements for a limitation of armaments among nations, than by any attempt at competition in squadrons and battalions. [9]

The members of the House Committee on Military Affairs were on the whole very promilitary, so the Welsh bill was never voted out of committee, and the House of Representatives was never given an opportunity to debate this measure.

But while the Welsh bill did not pass, the philosophy behind it gathered support on a number of campuses throughout the country.

---

[7]*New York Times,* June 16, 1926.

[8]*Army and Navy Register,* June 26, 1926.

[9]*New York Times,* October 7, 1925.

In early 1935 the CME published a flier listing seventeen significant victories against militarism in education and named the colleges or universities which had shifted from a compulsory to a voluntary basis. Five institutions discontinued military drill entirely — De-Pauw, Denison, California Institute of Technology, Northwestern and Emory Universities.

This same publication quoted an editorial published in the *New York World-Telegram* of December 6, 1934, and in other Scripps-Howard newspapers which said in part:

> We condemn, and an increasing body of American citizens condemn, compulsory military training as unwise, illiberal and unfair. Moreover, we condemn it as inefficient and wasteful of the taxpayer's money. . . .
>
> The battle against compulsory militarizing of the students of State Universities should go on. . . The fight will have to be made in Congress. . .and the fight will have to be continued in the states.

Forty years later this editorial is still timely and true!

DISCORD IN CONCORD

On the edge of Concord, Massachusetts, is a boulder to commemorate the first British soldiers who died in the Revolutionary War. As I recall, the inscription on this memorial reads:

> They came three thousand miles and died
> To keep the past upon the throne.

Some of us who journeyed to that historic town in June 1926, wondered if some of the residents of Concord were still determined "to keep the past upon the throne." The New England Fellowship of Youth for Peace had called a nine-day student conference to discuss the abolition of war. This interracial, interreligious and international organization in part grew out of the Student Volunteer Convention at Indianapolis between Christmas and New Year's in 1923. These young people believed that their generation should face up to the challenge to eliminate war.

The application for membership in the Fellowship of Youth for Peace read:

> It is my purpose to strive for the removal of the causes of war, *economic* and *racial* as well as *political*, and to work for methods

based upon international justice and goodwill in place of the method of war. Frankness, sincerity, trust, reverence for personality will be the relationship with all men. Working with other youth throughout the world, I am determined to devote every effort toward the abolition of war in my generation. In so doing I seek the fellowship of the Youth of the World.

I went to the conference as one of the speakers in part because of my activities against compulsory military training, a subject on the conference agenda. I arrived a day or so after the conference had started to learn that the delegates had been harassed by a rowdy group of young men who threw stones and rotten eggs for two or three nights. They broke up one meeting with a stink bomb, and disrupted still others. Some women were reported to have drawn their skirts around themselves and crossed to the other side of the street at the sight of the young pacifists.

The local post of the American Legion did everything within its power to prevent the conference from being held in Concord. It set up two indignation meetings prior to the conference and imported sensational orators from Boston who charged every offense in the patriotic decalogue against the approaching conference and its speakers. The post circulated printed propaganda and extravagantly untrue gossip about the meeting throughout the city. It accused a dozen different educational, political and religious organizations in the United States, such as the Fellowship for a Christian Social Order, the Fellowship of Reconciliation, and the Women's Trade Union League, of being destructive, degrading, un-American and unchristian.

The Legion sent communications to churches and to the owners of public halls in Concord asking them not to rent any space to the conference. It warned the selectmen of the village not to permit the conference to rent the assembly hall in the courthouse for a public meeting at which the Rev. Harold Speight of King's Chapel, Boston, was slated to speak on "Our Debt to Two Patriots — John Adams and Thomas Jefferson — Who Kept Us Out of War."

This campaign of vilification led the Wright Tavern and then the Unitarian Church to deny the use of their facilities to the conference. The Episcopal vestry and the minister, the Rev. Smith O. Dexter, however, defended the right of freedom of discussion in the tradition of two earlier Concord residents in this cradle of liberty, Thoreau and Emerson, and permitted the use of their parish hall. The local Episcopal church thus placed itself squarely across the path of intolerance and intimidation in defense of truth and freedom.

In addition to the Rev. Speight, the speakers at the conference included Dr. Harry Elmer Barnes, who discussed the origins of the First World War and why America entered that war, and Professor H.L. Harley on the question, "Is War an Instinct or a Habit?" I led a discussion on the significance of the large increase of military training in the United States. Other speakers dealt with imperialism, nationalism, and with developments in Europe, Russia, China and Latin America. Particular fire was directed by the American Legion against Brent Dow Allinson, chairman of the general committee which organized the program. He had been a conscientious objector in the First World War and had spent two years in prison in Leavenworth. He spoke on disarmament and participated in a symposium on the duty and power of the individual in the quest for peace. There were no communists on the program, but in the eyes of the patriots this was all a communist plot.

I had never before run into quite such intensity of feeling, such outright distortion of facts and motives, and such mendacious propaganda directed against young pacifists.

After three nights of disturbance, egg-throwing and increasing violence, the chairman of the conference went to the chief of police and asked for adequate protection.

Toward the end of the conference, a town crier went through the city to summon citizens to a packed town meeting in the city hall whose purpose was to purge the community of the unwholesome influence of the visiting students. The mayor warned that he would not be responsible for our lives and welfare if we delegates attended, but several of us went anyway. The speakers included Dr. Herbert S. Johnson, a chaplain in the Reserve Officers Corps; Colonel John Thomas Axton, Chief of Chaplains, United States Army; Mrs. Margaret C. Robinson, president of the Massachusetts Public Interest League; and Fred R. Marvin, editor-in-chief of the *New York Commercial*. The last two were the principal sources of the propaganda circulated against the conference.

The conference weathered this community disapproval and completed the program as scheduled. Later the local Legion officials repudiated the acts of violence. Sometime afterwards, the Fellowship for Peace merged with the Fellowship of Reconciliation which is still continuing its crusade against war undiminished.

SCHWIMMER SINKS PROFESSIONAL PATRIOT

Fred Marvin, who had caused us so much trouble at the Fellowship of Youth for Peace Conference, was head of the Key Men of America, and wrote "Searchlight," a daily column in the *Commercial* denouncing pacifists, socialists and communists as one and the same thing, philosophies dedicated to undermining all that was great and good in the land of the free and the home of the brave.

Three years after the Concord Conference Fred Marvin's vicious campaign of vilification, which was also directed against the Committee on Militarism in Education, was pretty well terminated when he lost a libel suit filed by the noted peace leader, Rosika Schwimmer. When Marvin called Madame Schwimmer a German spy, a Bolshevik agent and a communist, she sued the *New York Commercial* for $100,000, and Fred Marvin for $45,000 for libel. The case finally went to the New York State Supreme Court which awarded a verdict of $17,000 in a decision directed against both defendants.[10]

Rosika Schwimmer received world-wide publicity in 1929 when the United States Supreme Court, in one of its much criticized decisions, denied by a six to three vote, her application for United States citizenship. Ironically, this woman who was more than fifty years old at the time and would not have been liable for military service in any case, was denied citizenship on the grounds that she refused to bear arms and kill for her country.

Justice Butler, in the majority decision denying her citizenship, said such a ruling was not so much a result of her unwillingness to bear arms as it was a fear of the influence she would have had in speaking and writing as a citizen. In his decision he argued that:

> The influence of the conscientious objectors against the use of military force in defense of the principle of our government is likely to be more detrimental than their mere refusal to bear arms. The fact that, by reason of sex, age or other cause, they may be unfit to serve does not lessen their purpose or power to influence others. [11]

Justice Holmes in his memorable dissent said in part:

> If there is any principle of the Constitution that more imperatively calls for attachment than any other it is the principle of free thought — not free thought for those who agree with us but freedom for the thought we hate. . . .

---

[10]Clippings and other materials from which this section is taken may be found in Rosika Schwimmer box, CDG-A, Box 135, SCPC.

[11]The Case of Rosika Schwimmer, Alien Pacifists Not Wanted," (American Civil Liberties Union, June, 1929), p. 6.

And recurring to the opinion that bars this applicant's way I would
suggest that the Quakers have done their share to make the
country what it is, that many citizens agree with the applicant's
belief, and that I had not supposed hitherto that we regretted our
inability to expel them because they believe more than some of us
do in the teachings of the Sermon on the Mount. [12]

If Justice Butler thought that denying Rosika Schwimmer
citizenship would stop her peace activities, he was mistaken. She
kept right on as evangelistically as before. Years later, in 1948,
Rosika Schwimmer was nominated for, but did not receive, the
Nobel Peace Prize. Later she was awarded the World Peace Prize of
$8,500 by a distinguished international committee, while she was
working for the formulation of an all-inclusive, democratic,
nonmilitary federation of nations.

Compulsory Military Training Spreads to Japan

We have studied how the American authorities are, through
military discipline, trying to keep the spirit of the nation vigorous,
steady, and energetic, and we have found their system so clever
that we intend to copy it. To impute to us any intention of making
preparation for war is absurd.

This quotation from Baron General Giichi Tanaka, later premier,
was printed in the *New York World* on January 30, 1925, and reveals
one of the sinister overseas results, in part at least, of the American
ROTC system. [13]
Soon after the Concord conference I went to Japan for a year,
where I saw firsthand some of the international effects of American
ROTC influence.
In the early twenties, the Japanese government sent a delegation
to study military training in the schools of the United States. Their
report recommended that compulsory military training be required
in Japanese schools, and in April 1925, the Diet passed the Student's
Preliminary Military Training Act. This law made military training
compulsory in public middle schools above the sixth grade, technical
schools, colleges and universities.
This move was coupled with the Army Reform Act which

---

[12]Ibid., pp. 8, 9.

[13]Much of the information in this section on military training in Japan is found in
DG 70, Series C, Box 1, Folder, "Military Training in Japan, 1925-34," and in
scrapbooks in the Committee on Militarism files, DG 9, SCPC.

abolished four regular divisions and released the funds and the officers to administer the training in the schools. Japan had previously been reducing her military establishment following the Washington Limitation of Arms Conference in 1922. The effect of the Army Reform Act was to shorten the term of service for the conscripts, the approximately one in seven boys inducted into the army. This heightened the desire of the Japanese military to have boys in schools and colleges under their control for training and indoctrination. These boys were to be potential officers in case the army was expanded.

Less than a year later, there was one military officer in nearly all of the 1134 schools which instituted such training.

The introduction of compulsory military training in Japan aroused a wave of student opposition in spite of strict regulations requiring the disbandment of any student organization proposing to discuss social problems. The Otaru Higher Commercial School authorities expelled sixteen student leaders from the school in mid-November. About the same time, a campus daily published by the students of St. Paul's University, Tokyo, was suppressed on the ground that it contained an editorial favoring the combined student antimilitary-training movement sponsored by the newspaper unions of Tokyo Imperial University, Waseda University and St. Paul's University. Tokyo Imperial University put its academic halls at the disposal of protesting students at least for a time. Some members of the faculty were involved in the demonstrations, and several of the professors threatened to resign because of the attitude of the authorities toward a strictly military course.[14]

In one of the high schools in Tokyo, four students were discharged for rather vigorous expression of radicalism, followed by hissing of one of the speakers who tried to convince them that American students were eager for military training. The students organized a National Federation Opposed to Military Training in the Colleges, and sent a delegation representing six universities to call upon the Minister of Education who, in conjunction with the army, was responsible for introducing military training into the school curriculum. Instead of the minister, however, they were met by the police and a riot ensued.

In Kyoto more than twenty students of Kyoto Imperial University and Doshisha University were arrested for propagandizing against military training. The university authorities and even the Governor

---

[14]Dispatch to the *Philadelphia Inquirer*, June 9, 1925.

of the prefecture, however, objected to the illegal invasion of the student dormitories. In one of the roundups of the students by the police, an amusing incident occurred. One of the students was found to be of royal blood.[15]

The *Missionary Herald* of April 1926, in a story about the opposition of Japanese students and of the press, reported that, "some of the editors say military drill is required in American schools as preparation for the war that American papers assert must sooner or later be waged with Japan; therefore Japan, though hoping that no such conflict will arise, must not be found unprepared if it is thrust upon her."

In addition to its push for compulsory military training in schools, the army wanted to distribute officers throughout the country to impart military training to the members of the various associations which were organized for young men from eighteen to twenty-five in every community in the empire. These associations elected their own leaders and had their own democratic rules of procedure. They assisted the police on occasions when crowds assembled, helped the people in case of fires, floods and other calamities and did other good deeds.

The spokesman for this loosely knit national organization in 1925 was H. Tazawa, former vice-mayor of Tokyo. The National Committee adopted a vigorous resolution of protest to present to the department of education, which said in part:

> The fundamental aim of this association is the furtherance of the spirit of self-government among the people which is essentially inconsistent with the idea of military training based on compulsion and blind obedience. Our motto has always been "self government" and we are firmly resolved to tolerate nothing that is calculated to destroy our fundamental aim. [16]

I was in Japan on the Japanese Brotherhood Scholarship from late September 1926 to early October 1927, the year after compulsory military training was introduced. For eight months I lived with forty Japanese students at the Imperial University YMCA and had the opportunity to travel some six thousand miles from one end of the empire to the other.

I was appalled at the repression of ideas and the amount of

15*Japanese Students' Bulletin,* March 1926, and the *Christian Science Monitor,* January 26, 1926.

16Roderick Matheson, "Real Military Training Hits Nippon Snag," *Buffalo* (N.Y.) *Express,* December 13, 1925. Found in CME Scrapbook, DG 9, SCPC.

thought control attempted by the Ministry of Education in the colleges and universities. Some students were still being jailed for "dangerous thoughts," although outspoken opposition to compulsory military drill had somewhat subsided.

When I visited Saghalien, the northernmost part of the Japanese empire, an area which is now Russian territory, I took pictures of middle school students drilling with wooden guns as part of their indoctrination.

Earlier that year I had spent a lively evening with the Canadian faculty members at the Canadian Academy in Osaka. The government was pressuring this private school to introduce military training. I described in considerable detail the struggle against compulsory military training in the United States, expressing strong hope that they would not copy our unfortunate example. The Canadian faculty members seemed opposed to adding military training to the curriculum, but wanted to avoid an outright split with their Japanese counterparts who might be more inclined to accede to the government's request. Since I left Japan a few months later I never heard what the final decision was.

In a letter to my brother on May 25, 1927, I wondered:

> Why shouldn't the agenda of some of these disarmament conferences include an international agreement to do away with compulsory military training? As long as one nation parades with a brass band, there will always be an echo. It is more contagious than measles and it will need international vaccination before the world is immune.

It is impossible to assess accurately the total effect of military training in Japanese schools. In March 1927, the liberal Shidehara government fell and was succeeded by the Tanaka regime which started a deliberate trend toward war with China. When the Manchurian incident occurred in September 1931, only four years later, the only groups that could have put up strong resistance were the schools and colleges. But by that time they were all in the grip of the military establishment. Students had been trained to accept military obedience and war if necessary. Faculty had been intimidated or silenced. Certainly the Japanese system of military training in the schools, copied from the American example but more widely applied, was an important factor in conditioning the minds of the Japanese to accept the onslaught of Japan against Manchuria, then China, and finally the surprise attack on Pearl Harbor, December 7, 1941.

In 1924 and 1925 the Japanese people were in general very friendly

to the United States because of the prompt assistance given them
after the devastating earthquake of 1923. But the passage of the
Japanese Exclusion Act by the U.S. Congress in 1924 was a terrible
blow to the Japanese pride, and the passage of the Smoot-Hawley
Tariff Act of 1930 was a mortal wound in Japanese-American
relations. The Japanese Navy wanted access to the oil of the
southern Pacific; the Japanese Army wanted security from Russian
expansion on the Asian mainland. Japan depended on trade and
access to markets for its economic survival. The damage of military
training on both sides of the Pacific was such that it created a totally
false sense of security and in part distracted each educational system
from a serious study of the complex issues that had to be resolved if
international peace was to be assured.

In a very prophetic book, *The Price of Peace,* published in 1935,
Frank H. Simonds and Brooks Emeny wrote this portentious
comment:

> It is not the munitions-makers, but the masses, who by their votes
> elect and support governments and administrations committed to
> the pursuit of policies of economic nationalism who are the real
> "merchants of death." Italian Fascism, German National
> Socialism, and Japanese Imperialism, despite their common
> doctrine of violence, have done no more to make future wars
> inevitable than has the American Democracy by means of the
> Hawley-Smoot Tariff, the war-debt policy, and its performance at
> the London Economic Conference. [17]

MEXICO AND RUSSIA ALSO COPY U.S. MILITARY TRAINING

Another international repercussion of American military training
policy was contained in a Universal Service dispatch from Mexico
City on December 23, 1925, which reported that President Callas had
asked the Mexican Congress to grant the State power to enforce
compulsory military physical training for all Mexican youths. The
dispatch continued:

> The plan presented for the approval of the Congress is based
> largely on the American Plattsburg plan as to periods of service,
> but every year youths will be required to report to the various
> camps for a period of intensive training instead of voluntary
> attendance [18]

---

[17]Frank H. Simonds and Brooks Emeny, *The Price of Peace* (New York and
London: Harper and Bros., 1935), p. 343.

[18]*New York City American*, December 24, 1925. In CME Scrapbook DG9, SCPC.

The *New York Times* and the *New York World* in an Associated Press dispatch from Moscow reported on January 30, 1926, that:

> Compulsory military training in colleges is the latest means adopted for the development of its (Russia's) national defense machinery. The Commissariat of Education has issued a decree requiring students in the higher classes to take two hours' instruction weekly in the science of war and to spend a part of each summer in military camps. The system in many ways resembles the ones in the United States. Economy makes it impossible for the Soviet to maintain a standing army of more than 600,000 men and so the Government has adopted these supplementary measures.

The *Pittsburgh Express* on July 17, 1926, carried a story that Lauri Pih Kula, a reserve captain in the Finnish Army, and his friend had been visiting our Citizens Military Training Camps and were most enthusiastic about the training. Kula planned to recommend to the Finnish government that they send a delegation of officers to the U.S. to study the program with the hope of starting a Finnish Plattsburg.

The programs in Mexico and Russia, and the proposed program in Finland, do not seem to have fostered a war spirit as Japan's did, but I am convinced that this emphasis on military indoctrination was an important element in the failure to put sufficient mental and political effort into eradicating the war system itself. I came back from Japan even more convinced than before I had left that compulsory military training was a misguided policy for meeting world problems.

CAMPAIGN LOST IN THE IOWA LEGISLATURE:
COWS, CORN AND COMPULSION

On my return to the United States from Japan, I found that opposition to compulsory drill in American colleges had intensified, and after two years on the farm with my brother I returned to the CME. I worked first in Pennsylvania against compulsory military training at Pennsylvania State College, but I later transferred my energies to a major campaign on my home ground in Iowa as the CME fought to abolish compulsory military training in two Iowa state institutions.

Our campaign against compulsory drill in Iowa took place at the same time the agriculture and health authorities in the state were pushing a program to stamp out bovine tuberculosis, and the juxtaposition of the public interest in the two campaigns led me to question just how seriously many people really want to end American militarism, and made me realize how low a priority the search for peace has in the minds of most American citizens.

During the seven hours of spirited debate over the Torgeson-Pattison bill to make military training optional at Iowa State College at Ames and at the State University of Iowa in Iowa City, the House galleries in the state legislature at Des Moines were only partly occupied. When the Torgeson-Pattison bill was voted down in a sixty-three to forty-three vote on March 13, 1931, public reaction was, at best, mild disappointment.

In contrast, just a few days later, three thousand farmers, some in overalls and carrying pitchforks or scoop shovels, stormed the Capitol building in Des Moines, broke up the session of the legislature, and harangued all who would listen in their frenzied opposition to compulsory testing of cattle for tuberculosis. The threat by the health authorities to kill cattle affected with bovine tuberculosis in hopes of lessening the incidence of t.b. in humans literally had these farmers up in arms even though they were to be at least partially reimbursed for their losses.

I remember a similar incident years later when, during a campaign in Congress in the forties against universal military training, I told Representative Leslie Arends of Illinois, House Republican Whip, that I thought a large percentage of his constituents were concerned about, and opposed to, universal military training for their boys. "Oh, no," he replied, "What they are most interested in is the price of corn."

This sort of provincialism was only part of the problem we faced in the campaign to abolish compulsory military training in Iowa. Even though the struggle in Iowa was probably the best organized of any that year by the National Committee on Militarism in Education, we found just how difficult it was to change to optional training by legislation because of the fears and the narrow patriotic fervor such a campaign aroused. Then too, our campaign took place in 1929 and 1930, in the middle of depression, and while we managed to stir up some lively debate around the state, we lacked the funds to carry the campaign far enough to reach and convince enough people.

The proponents of retaining compulsory military training were led by the American Legion (of which I was a member at that time), the Legion Auxiliary, the D.A.R. and their allies, who put on a bitter campaign of vilification of their opponents as mistaken, misled tools of Red Russia who were lacking in patriotism and were not willing to face the realities of our cruel world. The large and vigorous Legion lobby with Legion posts in nearly every community, and the appointive job holders around the Capitol who were mostly wounded Legionnaires, played a large part in defeating the measure. The editor of the *Iowa Legionnaire* wrote that "all of the County legislative chairmen were directed to open fire from all angles, and every conceivable kind of pressure was exerted."

The opponents of compulsory drill who were pushing the Torgeson-Pattison bill were led by the Iowa Committee on Militarism in Education. Their very able and respected chairman was Rev. Stoddard Lane, minister of the Plymouth Congregational Church in Des Moines. He was a World War I veteran and had been awarded the Croix de Guerre.

The strong Iowa Committee was made up of individuals drawn from leadership positions all over the state. Other organizations behind the drive for optional training were many Protestant churches, the State Board of the Iowa Federation of Women's Clubs, twenty-two County Farm Bureaus and at least two local Legion posts, the Iowa Congress of Parents and Teachers, the State Federation of Labor, the State Teachers Association, the Iowa Farmers Union and the Grange, the State Encampment of Sons of Union Veterans of the Civil War, and large groups of students from both Ames and Iowa City who petitioned for the bill.

Frank Miles, editor of the *Iowa Legionnaire*, was quoted in the *Fort Dodge Messenger* for January 27, 1931, as having said about the Iowa Committee on Militarism in Education:

> Some of the Committee members, though misguided are sincere; some are not and are treacherous enemies of our country. . . . Iowa mothers opposed to required military training are working hand in hand with revolutionary groups that believe in the standards accepted by Soviet Russia, standards or rather lack of them, that if given a chance would destroy our homes and churches.

This Iowa Committee at the time of its establishment included the presidents or secretaries of ten state organizations, three college presidents, two college deans and eleven men who either had been or were in the state legislature — including the present Speaker of the House.

Although I had been born and had lived for thirty years in Iowa, graduated from Iowa State College, and my father had served two terms in the Iowa legislature, I was denounced as an outsider, as exerting evil eastern influence and as playing the communist game, because I had returned to Iowa to work on this issue as associate secretary of the National Committee on Militarism in Education in New York City. Frank Miles refused to appear anywhere at the same time in open debate, as one of the luncheon clubs in Burlington had tried to arrange, to allow me to answer his charges.

In reporting what Miles had said, I wrote the Iowa committee that:

> Mr. Miles' geography is slightly scrambled. The peace movement in this country derives much of its inspiration and dynamics — not from Moscow, as he infers, but a little farther to the south in a tiny country called Palestine, where Hebrew prophets talked of the day when "swords shall be beaten into plowshares" and where Jesus staked his life on the principle of "Peace on Earth, good will toward men."

Later Frank Miles was appointed by Governor Turner to the Iowa State Board of Education for a six-year term. To me this seemed quite contrary to most of the ideals which a state board of education should stand for. It was one more example of the Legion being used as a steppingstone to political preference. It was unfortunate that Frank Miles' appointment was made before the Iowa CME had placed any nominations before the governor. In fact the CME was discussing possible nominees the very day of the announcement of Miles' appointment.

When some of the students at Ames invited me to speak at my alma mater against compulsory drill, Harold Pride, director of the Memorial Union which had been erected to commemorate my schoolmates who lost their lives in the First World War, and who was a personal friend of mine, refused to allow that building to be used for such purpose. I took the matter up with Iowa State College President Hughes who said he had no jurisdiction over the Memorial Union, but that he would grant use of any other campus facility. So he designated Agricultural Assembly, one of the largest meeting places at the college for the anti-ROTC meeting. In my address I stressed that the ROTC unit paid as much money for hay and feed for the eighty-four horses in its unit as the college, an institution with more than three thousand students, paid for the time spent by all professors teaching courses on international relations, world organization, the history and lessons of the Great War and similar courses which might train students to think intelligently on the problems of achieving world peace.

In the House debate on the Torgeson-Pattison bill, the supporters of retaining compulsory military training argued in part that if they could be assured that there would never be another war, and that the world would disarm, then they would support the change. They claimed that the army was always for peace until war broke out. The legislature should not listen to the soothing syrup of policies that would wreck or destroy us. The farmer prepares against famine, the doctor against disease and plague. The First World War found us as unprepared as children. Thousands of lives were slaughtered on the altar of our indifference. The ROTC provides a cheaper skeleton army than can be provided in any other way.

The debate on the bill was the most spirited contest over any legislation so far in that session. When Representative Green of Pottawatamie County made the charge that ninety-five percent of the people in favor of this bill were sincere, but were being misled by other individuals or organizations, Brown of Polk County silenced him by asking him to name the individuals or organizations that were misleading "some of the best friends I have." Toward the end of the debate Gallagher from Iowa County humorously remarked, "This is almost as bad as war itself, so far."

The House supporters of the optional bill presented views similar to those in the excellent nine-page statement made by Stoddard Lane for the Iowa CME in their seven-hour hearing held by the House Committee on State Educational Institutions, February 13, 1931.

Lane stressed the need to develop more courses in international relations; in the background, origins and results of the First World War; and in international trade and world finance. There needed to be more studies of the efforts for world cooperation and world organization instead of so much propaganda for more and larger military establishments. He pointed out that the Morrill Land Grant Act under which Iowa State College was established did not require that military training be compulsory, and that the state educational institutions would lose no Federal money for educational purposes, other than military, by making the change.

The educational value of military drill as physical education, discipline, or training in citizenship was insufficient to warrant its being made compulsory for all students, he argued. It ran counter to our obligations under the Kellogg Pact to train students effectively for settlement of disputes by peaceful means.

Stoddard Lane concluded his testimony by quoting a paper in College Corner, Ohio, which was commenting upon the action of the University of Cincinnati in abandoning compulsory military training: "To force men into military service is no function of a university dedicated to freedom of the conscience and freedom of the mind."

The optional drill advocates never deluded themselves that their drive to change the system would be either easy or short. The year 1931 was in the deepening depression and there never was much money to carry the issue to the people throughout the state as it should have been for adequate consideration and understanding. Almost everywhere it was discussed seriously we made converts to the cause. But while considerable efforts were continued in later years, the defeat was naturally a deep disappointment both to a great many people in Iowa and to the National Committee on Militarism in Education.

Peace Literature Study

In December 1929 and early 1930 I was granted a leave of absence from the Committee on Militarism in Education to make a preliminary study of the current literature dealing with peace and international relations. The material came from nongovernmental organizations and was designed for popular distribution. Our study did not include college textbooks or other scholarly publications. Elsie Lowenberg and I gathered together 780 separate items and 289 issues of forty-five periodicals from fifty-three organizations published or circulated in 1929.[19] We chose to study the peace literature because at that time, before the advent of T.V. and before radio was much concerned with educating people on international affairs, such literature was the most effective method for the widespread dissemination of peace ideas.

In the time available to us we were able to make an analysis of the 345 pamphlets and study courses from forty organizations. We collected but did not evaluate in detail a wide range of other material including posters, plays and pageants, programs for special occasions, bibliographies and fliers intended for general, widespread distribution. We attempted to make judgments about the study courses and pamphlets regarding attractiveness of printing, general content, groups for which the material might be useful, objectiveness of presentation, religious interest, and suggestions for specific action on the part of the reader.

---

[19]E. Raymond Wilson and Elsie Lowenberg, "Preliminary Study of Current Literature Dealing with Peace or International Relations," published by the American Community, 1930, DG 70, Series B, SCPC.

Few of the materials were illustrated; seventy-four percent were uncolored on the inside or the cover. One fifth were mimeographed. At least half seemed aimed at a "general public" rather than at any specific group. Some were designed primarily for religious groups and others had a strong religious emphasis, but most contained no religious emphasis. We judged that three-fourths of the pamphlet material was presented on a level too advanced for half the population to grasp. But we also decided that those who would be likely to give much attention to complex peace issues would probably have little difficulty with the material. We found no humor in the 9993 pages. Over seventy percent of the material had little or no explicit suggestions for specific action which the reader might take.

We summarized our findings:

> If we may say, roughly, that the task of the peace movement is threefold — namely to make peace, justice and goodwill intellectually convincing, emotionally compelling, and politically effective, then the reviewers would be inclined to say that so far as the literature was concerned, its intellectual level was fairly high, its emotional appeal terribly low.

And as for the political effect of the organizations and their literature, we continued, the United States still wasn't in the World Court or the League of Nations, nor were the marines out of Central America. No far-reaching disarmament agreement had been negotiated, and the world was already drifting toward World War II.[20]

At the time of our study the major source of news was the daily paper. Yet in a tabulation of newspaper coverage of the London Disarmament Conference from January 19 through 25 in the twelve New York City papers, we found that in those two weeks the two tabloids with the largest circulation, the *Graphic* and the *Mirror*, afforded the Conference the least coverage — sixty-four and seventy-seven lines respectively. In contrast, the *New York Times* gave the conference 2840 lines, 660 of these on the front page, and the *New York Herald Tribune* wrote 1884 lines of which 580 were front page coverage.[21]

This study was made, of course, before the U.S. involvement in the Second World War, the Korean War and the Vietnam War, and before our participation in an armaments race that has created a climate of violence and tension between countries which today has

---

[20]Ibid.
[21]Ibid.

vastly complicated the search for peace. But today peace literature is still important. Although skyrocketing publication costs have adversely affected distribution of serious studies, periodicals and books, these still play a much larger role in informing or convincing people than they did in 1929. Many daily papers carry greater coverage of international news than they did thirty-five years ago. In addition T.V. and radio now provide many hours of news, documentaries, panels and other informative programs. But whatever the source, the old dictum is still very true that "no man's thinking is better than his information."

The three years I spent working against compulsory military training crystalized my convictions against war, gave me a wide acquaintance among the leadership of the peace organizations and began to orient me to the multitude of issues to be pursued in the quest of world peace. It made me realize how deeply the war system was rooted in our society, in our economy and in our prejudices, and how enormous the task ahead of us was to achieve the elimination of war. It was a good introduction to my twelve years of work with the American Friends Service Committee.

CHAPTER 7

On the Road for the AFSC

In the early summer of 1931, Tucker P. Smith, executive secretary of the Committee on Militarism in Education called me into his New York office and said that because of declining receipts in a never well-financed organization, I should look for another job instead of expecting to continue as associate secretary. So I picked up the phone, called Ray Newton in Philadelphia, secretary of the Peace Section of the American Friends Service Committee (AFSC), and told him I was available. Sometime earlier he had indicated an interest in my joining the AFSC staff. He said he would take up my case with the Peace Section.

Their first question was "Is he a Quaker?" When Ray said "No," their response was, "Find a Friend." He asked their help, but the search didn't turn up a Friend with the experience which I had. So very reluctantly some weeks later they took me on as Ray Newton's associate for one year only. Ray Newton wrote in his letter inviting me to take the job that whether or not I would be asked to continue would depend not only on the enthusiasm which the Committee felt for the work I was doing, but on the availability of a Friend for the job in a year's time.

Happily for me I didn't entirely flunk the test. I am, perhaps, a measure of their tolerance. Today I am just rounding out my forty-fourth year working with the Society of Friends — the first twelve years with the AFSC, and the years since 1943 with the Friends Committee on National Legislation. It has been a happy experience for me, and since I haven't had to say or do anything I didn't believe in, I have been remarkably free from the inner spiritual struggles of conflict of interest or the kind of compromises so many people have to make. That doesn't mean that there hasn't been a lot of drudgery or hard work, or that I could always do just what I wanted to do, but it has meant I could throw myself wholeheartedly into what I was doing. Nor did it mean much success in the outward sense, because there has been little progress in the efforts for peace and disarmament during these four decades. These are goals for the human race still to be achieved.

My first assignment was a three-month speaking tour in Indiana and Ohio. The first month in western Indiana was arranged by Frank Streightoff. This initial itinerary took me into the territory of fifteen of the sixteen quarterly meetings of the Western Yearly Meeting. As a non-Friend who knew virtually nothing about the Society, it was an opportunity to get acquainted with them in their homes and localities, and to learn about their thinking, their hopes and their prejudices. These were mostly meetings with pastors. On one two-day stretch I spoke at eight high school assemblies in eight different towns, two each morning, and two each afternoon, plus an evening session with a local chamber of commerce. This meant a tight schedule.

I attended my first unprogrammed Friends meeting during that fall in Indiana. I had little idea of the practice of silence broken by one or more impromptu messages of a spiritual character. This was in 1931 during the year of preparation for the General Disarmament Conference which was to convene in Geneva in February 1932. So I spoke in meeting about the importance of this forthcoming conference in relation to the historic Quaker concern for peace. After the meeting closed a wizened old Quaker came up to me and said, "Raymond, we've never had a message like that in this meeting before, but maybe it's done us some good." I know now that it wasn't a particularly appropriate message for a Friends meeting, but he was generously giving me the benefit of the doubt. At least he thought the message might have done somebody some good.

At the Kokomo Rotary Club I spoke on a series of things that I hoped the United States would do in foreign policy including full support of the forthcoming Disarmament Conference, recognition of the Soviet Union, and advancing reciprocal trade. At the conclusion of the meeting a gentleman came up and said he had a crow to pick with me. I thought he would refer to recognition of Russia, which was a very controversial issue at that time. But he remarked that he disagreed vigorously about lowering tariffs. So I smiled and asked in what infant industry he was engaged. He replied that he was president of a steel company employing more than three thousand men. It is a frequent characteristic of the capitalist economy that its firms want competition — for the other fellow — but protection for themselves. I tried to point out how dependent our country was on exports, and that we couldn't keep up a high rate of exports without giving other countries a chance to pay for them by imports into the United States.

CARS WITH MORE HISTORY THAN FUTURE

In November I traveled over eastern Indiana and then spent three weeks before Christmas bounding around southwestern Ohio.

In Richmond, Indiana, on my trip out to begin my tour, I inherited an historic car which had been driven all summer by two girl peace caravanners. When I got to Indianapolis one nut on a back wheel was missing, another nut had only a turn or two to go before coming off, the right front door closed only with difficulty, and the engine sounded like a hand-cranked corn sheller. One time going down a seven-mile hill I got the speed up to thirty-five miles an hour. Some time later when Ray Newton came out to visit me, he remarked that he couldn't have a field secretary in the field standing still, so he bought another Chevrolet somewhat less aged and infirm.

Ray Newton was driving this newer car for a nine a.m. high school assembly at Wabash, Indiana, when just as he was passing a school bus the sign on the bus came down — "Stop." Braking, we skidded past the school bus and landed in the ditch along the side of the road, fortunately with no injuries. Seeing that we were from out of state, the bus driver was lenient and didn't press charges on what had been a technical violation of passing a school bus when stopping. We arrived just in time for the high school assembly. Afterwards, Murray Kenworthy, who was our host, said, "Raymond, you don't look very well." Then we told him about our near accident.

Frequently I changed the name of the car I was driving. The caravan girls had christened the car which I inherited *Carlotta Bunk*. After I had driven it seventy miles and one wheel was about ready to fall off I called it *Carload of Junk*. Since its speed limit seemed to be thirty-five miles an hour and it would climb hills only in low gear, I renamed it *Mississippi*. It would run downhill! When the speedometer clicked off twenty-five thousand miles, the name was changed to *Magellan*, once around the world. In anticipation of the drive back to Philadelphia over the Appalachians, it was suggested that we call the car *Zerubbabel* after a passage in the Bible which reads, "before Zerubbabel the mountains shall be made plains." Tires wore out and after I had bought the fourth new tire I affectionately named the car *Lassitude* because it was all tired out.

ON THE TRAIL TO MEETINGS AND CONFERENCES

My friends have often heard me say that if speeches would save the world, it would have been in good shape long ago. Even I am astonished to think how many speeches I have inflicted on a suffering public. Perhaps fortunately, I do not know how many hundreds of speeches I have made, nor on how many scores of subjects, nor in how many hundreds of conferences I have participated. That I didn't lead a life of complete leisure is indicated by the following summary of just a few of the many schedules which I undertook.

The 1933 Wilson Christmas letter reported that I had been with the AFSC almost two years. About half my time had been spent in traveling and field work to build up public opinion for peace and disarmament or to promote the Midwest Institute of International Relations. During that two-year period — and the records were far from complete — I had spoken to more than 299 meetings in 124 towns and communities largely in Ohio, Indiana, Illinois and Iowa. These included sixty-three high school or school assemblies and fourteen Rotary or luncheon clubs. If these speeches had been strung end to end they would have lasted more than thirty-one eight-hour days of continuous speaking!

Earlier that year Miriam and I had been on a forty-seven day cruise with Errol Elliott and Martha Hadley, a combined mission and peace tour of more than three thousand miles which took us into forty-nine communities in Iowa. On this trip while the Midwest was still in an economic depression, twenty-five of these addresses were on the effect of the First World War on agriculture, nineteen were on lessons from that war and twelve were illustrated talks on Japan. Other speeches dealt with the work of the AFSC, issues before the Geneva Disarmament Conference, impressions of the Soviet Union, the world tasks of the church, new demands on the foreign missionary enterprise, and a fifteen-point political program for peace.

During the summer of 1938 I went to International Relations Institutes in Oklahoma, Kansas, Iowa and Illinois, and then joined the American Seminar led by Sherwood Eddy in Eastern Europe. In October I rested up from a strenuous summer by traveling forty-five hundred miles by car in Indiana, Illinois and Iowa with eighty-two speaking engagements in forty-four communities. After my second trip to Eastern Europe I carried with me a suitcase of linens and fabrics, mostly bridge table-size from twelve countries, and costumes of four Formosan aborigine tribes. These were exhibited more than sixty times before Christmas. This collection, another hobby of mine, now includes more than twenty countries of origin with a striking range of colors and designs.

In 1939 I stayed away from home to the tune of twenty-five thousand miles by car going to meetings and conferences. One of the glorious experiences was bringing my mother and my aunt, Lois Honeyman, back to Philadelphia from the somber AFSC meeting in Indianapolis in late October, soon after the Second World War started. The drive over the mountains was an unequaled panorama of color. The oaks, maples and beeches shimmered in every shade of gold, brown, russet and red. After awhile adjectives become limp and useless, completely worn out because they have been used so much, or won't stretch far enough. Language runs a weak and extremely poor second to the glories of October's bright blue weather when autumn touches the Appalachians with its variegated paint brush.

After the passage by Congress of the conscription act in September 1940, I took off on a coast-to-coast tour reaching from Portland, Maine, to Portland, Oregon, to explain the implications of that legislation and to discuss the rights of conscientious objectors under the act. That itinerary covered 10,153 miles and involved participating in thirty-one Friends conferences in fifteen states with a total of 116 sessions. Participants in these conferences often came from great distances. One carload drove 125 miles for the conference at Central City, Nebraska. Another car drove 640 miles from Texas to Wichita, Kansas. Before I got home I had 'slept' in fifty-five beds or pullmans.

The four major topics with which I dealt were the problems of conscientious objectors under conscription, the Christian conscience in a world of violence, glimpses of wartime France and England, and suggestions for a constructive political and economic program for a durable peace. I found members of the Society of Friends far from unanimous in a positive, clearcut conviction against participation in war.

For eighteen days in December 1941, I traveled in Kansas with Tom Hunt from the AFSC regional office in Wichita. I spoke to forty-seven groups in twenty-three cities and towns. During that time we averaged 172 miles by car and three speeches a day without a break. We missed only one scheduled meeting — a luncheon at the Kansas State College in Manhattan — because we were delayed by icy roads.

On December 7 we were at Coldwater, in southwestern Kansas, when we heard over the radio news of the Japanese attack on Pearl Harbor. That Sunday night I spoke to a packed union service at the Presbyterian church summarizing the history of American-Japanese relations since the First World War. Some of the U.S. actions which had distressed the Japanese people, and had led to the dastardly attack, included the Japanese Exclusion Act in 1924, the anti-alien land laws, the adoption by Japan of compulsory military training in schools and colleges in 1925 modeled somewhat on the American ROTC system, the Smoot-Hawley Tariff in 1930, and the failure of the great powers to arrive at a disarmament agreement in the twenties and thirties.

The next morning at a convocation at McPherson College, a Church of the Brethren school, I spoke to an audience teary-eyed because of the American entrance into the war. And at noon, just at the time when President Roosevelt was asking Congress to declare war on Japan and Germany, I spoke to the Great Bend Rotary Club. That was one of the saddest days of my life to see our beloved country embroiled in a two-front World War of incalculable ferocity and destruction.

At the Peace Section meeting on May 20, 1942, I listed some of the conferences, many on postwar reconstruction or on problems arising out of the war, in which I had participated during the previous few months, or which I was scheduled to take part in in the near future. These included the World Order Study Conference on a Just and Durable Peace of the Federal Council of Churches at Delaware, Ohio; the All Friends Conference in Richmond, Indiana; a joint Historic Peace Churches conference also in Richmond; the Committee on Educational Reconstruction at New York University; and the annual Conference of the Young Peoples' State Federation of the New Jersey Baptist Convention at Bridgeton.

Other gatherings included the Conference on World Organization for a Lasting Peace at Poughkeepsie, New York, under the auspices of the Peace and Service Committee of the New York Yearly Meetings; the Interdenominational Young People's Conference on a Durable Peace at Wagner College, Staten Island; a weekend at the Buck Creek Civilian Public Service Camp in North Carolina; the annual conference of the Fellowship of Reconciliation at Lakeside, Ohio; a three-day conference on Civilian Public Service at Winona Lake, Indiana; and the annual meeting of the National Council for Prevention of War in Washington, D.C.

In addition I attended the annual two-day meeting of the

American Academy of Political and Social Science in Philadelphia; the meeting on the Transition Period of the Commission To Study the Organization of Peace in New York City; and a regional conference in Pittsburgh. I was soon to go to the Institutes of International Relations in Oklahoma, Kansas and Ohio; the Friends Yearly Meeting and a regional conference in Canada; the Indiana Yearly Meeting Pastors Conference at Dewart Lake; and the North Carolina Yearly Meeting where I had been invited to give two addresses on the New World Order and the AFSC. I visited the Student Peace Service Unit locations where peace caravanners were working in Indiana, Wisconsin and North Carolina. A few of the other meetings I addressed were in Wilmington, Ohio; Washington, D.C.; in Fallsington, Germantown, Coatesville, Juniata College and Pennsylvania State College, and at the rehabilitation center at Sleighton Farms, all in Pennsylvania; in Wilmington, Delaware; and in Plainfield, New Jersey.

FRIENDS AND COLLEAGUES

Ray Newton was a grand person to work with during my twelve years with the AFSC. He gave me a great deal of freedom to go ahead on my own initiative, and yet when I was about to go under for the third time on some difficulty in working out the organizing and financing of an Institute of International Relations, he or Guy Solt would come out and rescue me.

Ray had a lively sense of humor. One of his favorite stories was about too many people who would paraphrase the response of the boy Samuel to the call of the Lord, "Here am I Lord, send him!"

Clarence Pickett was the much revered executive secretary of the AFSC during my years with the Committee. Rufus M. Jones, one of the best known and best loved Friends, served as chairman of the Board of Directors. The staff of the Committee, including the secretaries of the Institutes, was a hardworking, dedicated group of people with whom it was a joy to work.

When I joined the staff, it was smaller and the budget was less than that of the AFSC area office in Pasadena today. During the Second World War the AFSC exploded to a staff of more than five hundred, to support its many overseas relief activities and the Civilian Public Service program for conscientious objectors in this country.

INSTITUTES OF INTERNATIONAL RELATIONS

During my first three years with the AFSC I spent the first six months of each year organizing, promoting, financing and conducting a ten-day Institute of International Relations at Northwestern University in Evanston, Illinois. Ray Newton's motto was "Educate the Educators," and these ten-day institutes were aimed at recruiting teachers, ministers, students and leaders of public opinion for dynamic peace leadership. The attendance was usually between one and two hundred people at each Institute.

The first one was held at Haverford College in 1930 followed by two there the next summer. At one of the second-year programs A.C. Goddard and Owen Geer brought together a key group of ministers from thirty-four states who not only took in the heavy schedule of the Institutes, but worked on plans for youth conferences in the Methodist Church. This group of Methodist ministers took leadership parts in more than a hundred young people's conferences later that summer. Due to a change in Methodist organization and policy this arrangement was dropped. Had such a program in that denomination been continued for ten years, who could have predicted the result in increased peace leadership?

The programs of the Institutes included discussions on the political, economic and spiritual aspects of peace. Intensive programs were held in the mornings and evenings, with the afternoons usually free for more informal discussions, reading and study.

When Ray Newton first said he hoped to have ten Institutes in as many different parts of the country, I thought he was crazy. But the Institute program grew to eleven scattered from Wellesley College in Massachusetts to Reed College in Portland, Oregon. In 1935 I was moved to Philadelphia to serve as coordinator of these programs from coast to coast, recruiting and scheduling faculty, and selecting literature for display or sale.

Faculty was recruited from the very best talent available. Among the scores of outstanding speakers were men like Sidney B. Fay of Harvard, author of *Origins of the World War*; Samuel Guy Inman, who spent his life on Latin-American affairs; Grover Clark, whose field was the Orient and colonial questions; Peter Drucker, whose books and articles have been so perceptive on the economic aspects of international relations: Kirby Page, author of many books and pamphlets on peace and war; and Leyton Richards and Maude Royden from England who probed the spiritual problems of peace and the personal commitment needed to keep up the struggle for world order and the elimination of war.

We tried to present a well-rounded perspective on international affairs. One year I paid a lecturer $1000 to come to the United States to present the case for collective security precisely opposite to the position of the American Friends Service Committee because I didn't want myself or others to hold a viewpoint that couldn't withstand the closest scrutiny and severest criticism.

I consider the Institutes of International Relations the most solid, productive and widespread peace education program ever carried on by the American Friends Service Committee. Lasting from ten to twelve days, and digging into the political, economic and spiritual problems of peace with an outstanding faculty of diverse views, they made a substantial contribution to understanding some of the complexities of achieving the elimination of war.

A note from Tucker P. Smith following his leadership in three of the Institutes in 1932 is typical of the many, many expressions of appreciation by Institute attenders over the years. Tucker Smith wrote:

> I want to express my great pleasure at the privilege of being with these various groups and my congratulations to all of you for the success which I feel they attained. They are achieving a degree of intellectual and educational strength which seems to me an invaluable contribution to the peace movement. I certainly hope that they may be continued, made larger, and increased. Everywhere I meet the people who attended these institutes, I find that they are carrying on a more substantial Peace program because of the solid training they have received. This is particularly true with regard to the work in economics which many of the ministers tell me is a great eye-opener for them.

The prolonged involvement in the war by the United States, however, meant the eventual phasing out of these projects. The AFSC still carries on a manifold series of peace education projects, but most of them lack the sustained intellectual focus by hundreds and hundreds of people which characterized the Institute programs. At the peak they were involving more than fourteen hundred people a year. And the problems of achieving peace have become much more complex and difficult than in the period between the two World Wars.

THE GATHERING STORM

The twelve years between 1931 and 1943 were a tumultuous period for the AFSC Peace Section, and created many difficulties and dilemmas for peace workers. At the beginning, the country was still staggering from the great depression. The 1930 London Naval Conference and the 1932 Geneva General Disarmament Conference failed to halt the race in armaments. In 1931 the Japanese seized Mukden and started on their conquest first of Manchuria and then of northern China. Hitler's rise to power in January 1933 was followed by the move into the Ruhr, then the Anschluss with Austria, the annexation of Czechoslovakia, and finally, on September 1, 1939, the attack on Poland and the holocaust of the Second World War. President Franklin D. Roosevelt had helped torpedo the World Economic Conference in London in 1933. The United States was not in the League of Nations nor in the World Court. The League had failed to halt Japanese expansion and had not been able to alleviate the frustrations of Germany which in part led to the rise of Hitler. The people of Japan and of Germany were not able or did not stop the rise of the military expansionists in Japan nor the rise of the Nazis in Germany, and they must share part of the blame for the tragedy that resulted.

The American peace movement, of which the AFSC was one organization among many, but an influential one, tried to arouse the American people to the unfortunate effects of many American policies, and to do what they could to change them. Among these were the treaties of 1918 which by disarming the Germans without disarming the Allies as promised rankled the Germans, and the imposition of reparations on Germany which helped undermine economic stability and progress, and which were not lifted until too late. The rise in tariffs was one factor in the Japanese decision to build up their navy in order to assure themselves of access to the oil of the South Seas. The failure of American leadership to push harder for disarmament agreements in the twenties and early thirties, and the unwillingness of the United States to participate fully in the peacemaking efforts of the League of Nations were critical failures.

The National Peace Conference brought peace leaders from thirty-one organizations (the number participating in early 1936) together monthly in New York City for many years to exchange information and ideas, and to discuss strategy either singly or in concert. I attended as a representative of the AFSC when possible. The Conference encouraged the launching of a fifteen-month campaign for world economic cooperation in 1937 with Clark Eichelberger as campaign executive.

It was envisaged that this campaign would deal with such

questions as a world economic conference, stabilization of currency, lowering of tariff and trade barriers, settlement of war debts, armament expenditures in relation to unemployment, problems of living standards and nutrition, work of the International Labor Organization, and examination of the economic section of the League of Nations and other machinery for economic cooperation.

The division of opinion over whether neutrality should be mandatory with an arms embargo to all belligerents, or whether the embargo should be lifted to countries judged to be the victims of aggression, began to divide the peace movement. The division deepened with American involvement in the war. The National Peace Conference terminated its active role on September 24, 1951. For some years the Peace Strategy Board, or the Consultative Peace Council as it was later called, brought together in Philadelphia pacifist and other groups for consultation and strategy planning, but this coalition was not as widely representative as the National Peace Conference had been.

During the decade between 1930 and 1940, the number of ten- to twelve-day Institutes of International Relations organized by the AFSC Peace Section grew from one to eleven. It was the Institute program to which I devoted much of my time. Harold Chance and his staff recruited, trained and directed hundreds of eager young peace caravanners who spent their summers traveling and working for a more peaceful world. Alarmed by the growing drift toward war, Ray Newton, executive secretary of the Peace Section, launched the Emergency Peace Campaign, which is reviewed briefly in the chapter, "We Tried To Stop Three Wars."

Even as the trend toward war deepened, efforts continued to keep the United States out of the impending conflict. A great deal of discussion before and after 1939 revolved around the threat of various measures of conscription, the potential difficulties of conscientious objectors, and the possibilities of some kind of alternative service. I kept advocating generous treatment of the absolutists — those who would not register or cooperate in any way with a Selective Service set-up. The British government gave some of these absolutists complete exemption from any required service. But this point was not included as I had urged in the statement to President Roosevelt by the representatives of the Historic Peace Churches who visited him on January 10, 1940. It was discussed, however, in the wide-ranging interview with Attorney General Frank Murphy by the deputation who saw him afterward.

THE TROUBLED WAR YEARS

After war broke out in Europe, the search for some kind of neutral mediation and a truce was initiated. The major effort involved the visit of two English Friends, Francis Pollard and Karlin Capper-Johnson to the United States, and the trip of Errol Elliott and myself back with them to Rome, Geneva, Paris and England related in chapter 10.

As the war went on and the United States became involved, there was increasing talk of the problem of relief in warring countries, of plans for postwar reconstruction, of the character of international institutions required for maintaining peace, and of the need for a clear statement of peace aims.

The pace of Peace Section activity did not slow down during the war. A seminar in 1940 dealt with the problems of the conscientious objector. A second seminar which I helped organize and conduct was held at Pendle Hill, near Philadelphia, January 14 to February 7, 1941, on the general subject of "Pacifism under Conscription, in Time of War, and in Time of Post-War Reconstruction." Naturally, projections for the future are subject to considerable error, but we tried as earnestly and honestly as we could to face the dilemmas ahead. The thirty-nine people who participated represented areas as widely separated as Vermont, Canada and California.

In order to share more widely the values of the conference, a committee of seven of us was asked to present in accessible form the implications of the group thinking on some of the fundamental issues confronting us. After two weeks' writing and editing effort, we produced an eighty-page pamphlet which was published under the title, *Pacifist Living Today and Tomorrow*, and which was given considerable circulation.

This publication was not considered as the official findings of the seminar, which adopted no formal resolutions, but did draw on the subcommittee reports and was to be used as a basis for study, discussion and action. The subject matter covered a wide range of topics including starvation in Europe, refugees, should a peace be negotiated or dictated, the possibility of war with Japan, efforts to keep the United States out of war, civil liberties in wartime, the responsibility of the churches for a new world order, a bill of human rights for mankind, minimum powers for an international authority, an outline summary of various proposals for world organization, and problems arising out of conscription.

Eight months after Pearl Harbor and the U.S. entrance into the

Second World War, a larger and more representative Friends Conference on Peace and Reconstruction was held in Wilmington, Ohio, from August 31 to September 4, 1942. I served as chairman of several of these sessions. More than eighty Friends from different parts of the United States participated. Ten thousand copies of the forty-eight page report of the conference, "Looking Toward the Post-War World," were printed by the Peace Section of the AFSC and the American Section of the Friends World Committee.

The report of the Wilmington Conference dealt with the spiritual basis of a durable peace, questions involved in the political and economic bases of peace, plans for relief and reconstruction, justice for minorities and dependent people, and Quaker peace testimony in wartime. Three paragraphs from the unofficial summary give a bit of the flavor of the conference:

> An enduring order will come only if the patterns and institutions of human life are founded upon eternal truth as revealed through the inward working of God in man. Successful reconstruction will depend on the degree to which it approximates the principles and spirit of Christ. Our planning and action must be guided by compelling love and forgiveness for all men, and be rooted in profound awareness of and repentance for our own deep sinfulness and in knowledge of our universal compassionate Father...

> The war with its unspeakable tragedy of suffering, hatred, fear and revenge should cease....Starvation as an instrument of policy is a particularly cruel weapon. It is politically unwise and morally indefensible....

> The peace settlement should be an agreed, not an imposed, settlement. It should be constructed to meet the basic needs of all men, provide for the beginnings of world organization, and be subject to revision and change. Instruments for the coercion of nations should be avoided, since world peace must be built upon justice, tolerance, mutual aid and the practice of brotherhood....A system of international security through adequate institutions of world organization, stressing justice and peaceful change and the abandonment of the use of force, should facilitate the reduction of armaments, both in letter and spirit, toward the goal of universal disarmament.

As American involvement in the war deepened, two other extended seminars were held to try to peer into the uncertain future of the war and the postwar period, and to prepare ourselves intellectually for the difficult problems ahead. One was the first

seven-week International Service Seminar with young people from
many countries, and the other was an intensive seminar on
conscription, coercion and disarmament. The latter wound up twelve
lively years of work with the American Friends Service Committee
before I went to Washington to undertake the strenuous life of a
religious lobbyist with the Friends Committee on National
Legislation.

KANESATAKE INTERNATIONAL SERVICE SEMINAR — 1943

In 1943 Miriam and I were asked, with the assistance of Jack and
Arlene Kavanaugh, to conduct the first of the AFSC's International
Service Seminars. The aim of these seminars, first proposed by
Wanneta Chance of the Peace Section, was to bring together a group
of students from various countries to discuss the problems of
achieving a durable peace.

The first seminar was held at Camp Kanesatake, near Tyrone,
Pennsylvania, from June 26 to August 14, 1943. This intensive
seven-week seminar, held right in the middle of the war, brought
together forty-six young people from seventeen countries: Austria,
Canada, China, Costa Rica, Czechoslovakia, Denmark, France,
Germany, Hungary, Holland, India, Latvia, Lithuania, Poland,
Scotland, Switzerland and the United States. They spoke a total of
twenty-four languages and represented Jewish, Catholic and
Protestant faiths.

It was difficult to achieve unity in a group so diverse, with strong
national prejudices and with deep memories of recent sufferings and
injustice. It took most of the time during the seven weeks for the
group to become closely knit together in real fellowship. There was a
rather heavy proportion of refugees from Central Europe who tended
to dominate the discussion. The American members, on the whole,
lacked a comparable experience either in training or travel, and so
participated less than they might have in the discussions.

The program, entitled "Can the Human Race Live Together in
Peace?", dealt chiefly with the background of the Second World
War, the breakdown of peace, and the political, economic, social and
religious problems to be faced after the war ended, and the major
tasks of the organization of peace. A rotating committee made up of
one person from each cabin, constantly planned and revised the
program in consultation with myself as dean.

The faculty had a wide background of experience to share. Hachiro
Yuasa was former president of Doshisha University in Japan.

Wilhelm Solzbacher, Hans Heymann and Hans Simon, exiles from Hitler's Germany, were distinguished lecturers on world affairs. Hans Simon had been a member of the German Peace Delegation to the Versailles Peace Conference and was dean of the Graduate Faculty of the New School for Social Research in New York City. Bertram Pickard was a British Friend and had directed the Friends Center in Geneva for fourteen years. He had followed the League of Nations closely all that time. Haridas Mazumdar was a follower of Gandhi and former editor of the *India Review*. Y.C. Yang had been president of Soochow University in China.

On the closing day the seminar adopted a three-page statement expressing their hopes and determination for the future. It said in part:

> We have tried to understand something of the crisis of our age, one of whose manifestations has been the Second World War in which our nations are now engaged. Mankind has been subject to totalitarianism, to political aggression, to economic exploitation, to racial prejudice and discrimination, to hatred and violence and the suppression of liberty of thought and speech and assembly, to rivalries over territory, and to economic warfare through tariffs and manipulation of currencies....
>
> We have sought to explore some of the common aspirations and needs of humanity and some of the steps that we believe must be taken within the next few years to heal the deep wounds of war and to begin the tremendous task of establishing a durable peace....
>
> War is fruitless and unnecessary for the solution of the problems of the world of today. It is possible and essential for nations to adjust their differences by peaceable methods, and so prevent war. The loss of life, time, materials and moral progress which is involved in war is a betrayal of the civilization which we are capable of achieving....We cannot have peace without a much greater realization of justice....
>
> Any eventual peace settlement, to be durable, should have the participation in, and consent of, all those who are bound by it. Any valid, lasting and effective post-war settlement must be free from the motives of revenge....The central task for the world now is to evolve an adequate world organization for continuous political and economic collaborations....
>
> With the great resources of the world, we believe that society should be so organized that every able-bodied man could be regularly

employed. Every man, woman and child has a right to provision of food, shelter and clothing essential to the preservation of good health; the nations must aid in the establishment and maintenance of a minimum economic subsistence level throughout the world....

We call upon the people of the world, and particularly the youth of our generation, to respond to the urgency of this hour and to prepare for the task of building a better world....Those who are sensitive to justice and anxious for peace must take the initiative now and remain in the vanguard of the march toward a world of justice, freedom, law and peace.

A letter I received some weeks later from one of the participants expresses some of the drive the seminar tried to inspire in those attending:

Whether or not a third debacle will arrive on the scene about the time that your son and mine are in the midst of fulfilling our hopes for them depends upon how much energy and common decency we put into the task of cleaning up after the war and demanding a real guarantee of a civilized world. We must shout out for adequate housing instead of destroyers, for five million trained farmers instead of five million trained killers, for experts on tuberculosis and social security instead of experts in tank combat and daylight bombing, for the drafting of the brain-power, strength and youth of the world for sane tasks rather than for savagery and purple crosses...

God grant that we may be sensitive enough to the wounds, horrified enough at the colossal waste, confused enough by thwarted ambitions, and tired enough from tenseness and strenuous wishing to become furious and mad with determination to compete in service and with an anxiety to see freedom and justice and brotherhood and peace, all four, in our world forever.

The seminar which started in an atmosphere of hostility and suspicion ended with affectionate goodbyes mingled with tears. Hans Simons wrote after attending the Kanesatake Seminar and a similar one at Guilford College:

The mere integration of a group as diversified as the student body of these seminars is something of a major achievement....It was remarkable to see how well they got along, how simple it was to discuss practically any problem without arousing antagonisms or creating tensions, and how perfectly at ease everybody was in the exchange of opinions.

This, I think, was due mainly to the atmosphere which the Friends' tradition and attitude impart to any group working with them. In addition, the faculties and leaders had very much to do with it....

I am sure that many of the members of these two seminars will pass on what they learned as well as what they felt during these weeks to friends and colleagues. But even if nobody outside of these two groups hears of what was worked out there, these hundred people must carry away a much deeper understanding of the characteristics, the concerns and the preoccupations of other nationalities as well as other individuals, and a much greater awareness of the complexity of international problems.

On the last Sunday of the Seminar, the students decorated our meeting place with tiger lilies, grasses and flowers from the fields. There they held an unusually moving and meaningful worship service. The mass was read by two Catholic students. Oriental students gave some readings from Eastern scriptures, and a Black theological student preached a thought-provoking sermon. The service ended in a quiet period of worship.

SEMINAR ON CONSCRIPTION, COERCION AND DISARMAMENT

The last project on which I worked for the AFSC was the organization and conduct of a seminar under the auspices of the Peace Strategy Board in October 1943. The seminar dealt with conscription, coercion and disarmament and was held at Pendle Hill, Wallingford, Pennsylvania. Our primary concern in arranging this meeting was the threat of permanent conscription and militarism in the United States and throughout the world in the postwar period. Consideration was given to previous attempts for worldwide reduction of armaments, the place of force and international police in world organizations, the pros and cons of sanctions, the need for justice and peaceful change, and the difficulties in maintaining democracy at home and abroad.

Mrs. Laura Puffer Morgan drew on her long years of residence in Geneva, Switzerland, to summarize the results of the Disarmament Conferences in 1922, 1927, 1930 and 1932, and to emphasize the relation of political settlements to the possible achievements of world disarmament. Various speakers stressed the need for the worldwide elimination of conscription and the desirability for an international convention against conscription.

About forty people met at this Quaker center from October 16 to

22. Those present were Friends, Mennonites, members of the Church of the Brethren, officers and members of the Fellowship of Reconciliation, the Women's International League for Peace and Freedom, the Episcopal Pacifist Fellowship, the Jewish Pacifist Fellowship, the War Resisters' League, the National Council for Prevention of War, the American Friends Service Committee, and men from Civilian Public Service Camps.[1]

Since this was a study conference, the members of the seminar came as individuals and spoke on their own authority. There was no attempt to pass resolutions or bind other individuals or organizations to any point of view advanced in the discussion.

Frederick J. Libby wrote afterwards that this was one of the finest conferences which he had ever attended. He commended "the debate adhering closely to the program and maintained throughout on a highly intellectual level in the best possible spirit." "There were frank differences of opinion," he continued, "but without controversy. All were seeking the truth. In fact, it was the kind of conference which all who want to see a lasting peace following this war should hope and pray will characterize international gatherings."[2]

Ray Richards, reporter for the Hearst press, came to see me the day before the seminar opened and said he had come to report the seminar for his chain of papers, particularly for the *Los Angeles Examiner*, clear across the country. I told him that the seminar had been called on an off-the-record basis, in order to maximize freedom of discussion, but that we didn't have anything to hide. He said he intended to write about it anyway. Faced with the dilemma of being written up by guess and hearsay or by distortion from the inside, I told him that while I could not change the rules unilaterally, I would, at our first meeting, recommend opening up the seminar to the press. This was agreed to by the seminar members. So for most of the time in the back row sat Ray Richards for the Hearst papers, correspondents for the Associated Press and the United Press, and sometimes other reporters.

What I did not know at the time was that various sensational and distorted stories had been circulated about the conference before it

---

[1] "Brief Study Report, Seminar on Conscription, Coercion and Disarmament, Pendle Hill, October 16-22, 1943," *E. Raymond Wilson Occasional Papers* Vol. III, DG 70, SCPC

[2] Libby's letter and the materials on the Ray Richards' story that follows can be found in the folder, "attacks by Ray Richards, Pendle Hill Conference, 1943," NCPW Box 497, DG 23, SCPC.

opened. On the one hand it was reported from Washington that the army, fearful of postwar disillusionment and pacifism, was carrying out a definite plan to disrupt pacifist organizations and to discredit conscientious objectors and pacifists with the public. On the other hand a letter from a certain worried author was being circulated to the effect that a "plot" was to be hatched at the conference to stop the war that winter.

Ray Richards started off his biased and highly inaccurate dispatches to the *Los Angeles Examiner* by declaring that:

> Pacifists of the United States are still maintaining contact with their fellows in Germany (with which the United States was at war) and hope for instant postwar collaboration with Japanese pacifists toward establishment of a Christian cabinet in Japan. That was revealed by degrees today as the leaders of the country's "peace-at-any-price" element gathered here for the first conclave of its kind.

A brief discussion of Frederick Libby's proposal, which was not a major item on the agenda, for "an honorable peace at the earliest possible moment by negotiation" (sometimes called "Peace Now" for short), was reported by Richards: "The United States is about to be flooded with stupendous millions of printed and spoken words in behalf of an immediate negotiated peace, total disarmament, and abolition of all economic monopolies and tariffs that might cause jealousy among other nations."

Frederick Libby wrote the *Examiner* regarding the Richards' dispatches that "I find in them remarks in quotation marks attributed to me which are pure inventions on the part of Mr. Richards and which apparently Mr. Hughes (a radio commentator) quoted recently before the City Club of Rochester."

The conference adjourned two days early because the last two scheduled speakers couldn't come. In Mr. Richards' story he asserted: "Split into camps of moderates and extremists, leaders of the nation's various pacifist movements found little peace among themselves as their seven-day conclave came to a premature end tonight."

The *Examiner* headline blazoned, "Friends Society Splits with 'Peace Now' Group. Quaker Hosts to Pacifist Parley Lop Two Days Off Program."

While the pacifists have no corner on knowledge or wisdom, I do not think that any of them are naive enough to expect instant peace or instant justice. They do hold up ideals and goals which seem far out to many people, but the realists have led us down the road of blood and slaughter for too many thousands of years. There is the temptation to be oversimplistic in analysis or in solutions. The most earnest and sustained study, discussion and action needs to be undertaken all one's life on the unsolved problems of achieving peace.

I do want to pay a high tribute to my country and to my fellow Americans that during the Second World War, the Korean War, and the Vietnam War I have felt free to express myself candidly in opposition to my government's policies without harassment or intimidation. In few countries of the world would this have been possible.

CHAPTER 8

The War Problems Committee, Forerunner of the Friends Committee on National Legislation

Between the outbreak of war in Europe in September 1939, and the launching of the Friends Committee on National Legislation on a permanent basis in November 1943, the Friends War Problems Committee (WPC) served to focus Quaker efforts against several pieces of Congressional legislation. The War Problems Committee was an ad hoc group of Quakers drawn largely from the two Philadelphia Yearly Meetings (with some wider representation), which met in Philadelphia some fifty times between July 26, 1940, and May 27, 1943, and carried on a struggle in Congress to oppose conscription measures and to uphold the rights of conscience in legislation.

In one sense the War Problems Committee was a trial run, although not intentionally so, for the Friends Committee on National Legislation (FCNL). It also gave me a chance to try my hand at lobbying and at following legislation in Washington.

After the introduction of the Burke-Wadsworth Conscription Bill in June 1940, I spent much of the next nine weeks in Washington working with Paul Comly French seeking fair treatment for conscientious objectors in that measure.[1] On leave from the

---

[1] This particular effort is related in more detail in my article, "Evolution of the C.O. Provisions in the 1940 Conscription Bill," *Journal of Quaker History* (Spring, 1975): Vol. 64, No. 1 pp. 3-15.

American Friends Service Committee, I served the War Problems Committee as part-time secretary, and made intermittent trips to Washington to follow developments in Congress, and to express opposition to a whole series of conscription bills, including total mobilization, draft of labor, draft of women, and a draft of eighteen- and nineteen-year-olds.

While these measures were actively promoted by their supporters, there was widespread opposition to them by various groups including labor organizations. Large numbers of Friends from around the United States visited Congress during this time to express their strong opposition to such measures. In the end none of them, except the Burke-Wadsworth conscription bill for military service, became law.

ANTECEDENTS OF THE WAR PROBLEMS COMMITTEE

Within a few days after the outbreak of World War II in Europe on September 1, 1939, the Peace Section of the AFSC appointed a committee empowered to research draft regulations and procedures during World War I, to prepare publications, to draw up suggestions for advising young men, and to make recommendations concerning further approaches to the President and the War Department.

Some weeks later a three-day conference was held at Guilford College, North Carolina, to assess problems American Quakers might face should the United States enter the war. Elbert Russell, chaplain at Duke University, and I served as resource leaders, and participants came from thirty-three local groups in North Carolina. One follow-up effort after this conference was to set up in every local meeting an active peace committee charged with the responsibility of counseling men and women of military age.

As part of the effort to get local meetings to take responsibility for questions that might arise out of conscription or war, the Representative Committees of both Philadelphia Yearly Meetings appointed Draft Committees to work with their own constituencies. (The Friends War Problems Committee concentrated almost exclusively on Washington.) By Christmas, the Race Street Committee decided that suggestions sent out so far for actions to help Quaker youth had been ineffective, and that they would have to concern themselves "with getting the message over the heads (or through them if possible) of many of the present officers of the local meetings." They concluded that while about eighty percent of all the monthly and preparative meetings had been reached with material, very few reported any activity and most felt little concern on the subject. So they planned personal visits to meetings, *not* letters, wherever feasible. The Race Street Committee undertook to list all Friends of draft age, and to encourage the overseers in local Friends' groups to counsel them in any way they could.

By the end of 1941 fifty-four meetings responded with the names of men between eighteen and thirty-five. Delegations went to see State Selective Service officials in Delaware, Maryland and Pennsylvania and the Governor of Rhode Island to discuss with them the rights of conscientious objectors.

In anticipation that conscription legislation might be passed later in the year, an important conference was held in Philadelphia on April 30, 1940, on "How Meetings Can Help Their Members Meet War Problems." This conclave brought together for consultation delegates from all but ten of the eighty-six monthly meetings and a number of Friends from New York and New Jersey. It laid stress on the religious foundations of Quaker pacifism, and emphasized the necessity of the love of God which would lead to reconciling love for human beings. If meetings for worship were held in the right spirit of seeking God, the leaders of the conference felt there would come strength of heart to bear the testimony of peace and the strength of mind to help solve the problems of making peace. This conference did not, however, reach agreement on the proposal to record conscientious objectors in advance of a draft.

As agitation for the enactment of a draft law mounted in Congress, Friends from twenty-two yearly meetings gathered in Richmond, Indiana, July 2-4, 1940, for a national conference on conscription. This conference stressed that conscientious objectors should be given much better support in their home communities than had been done in 1917; it urged continued opposition to conscription in any form, and sustained efforts to keep the United States out of war; and it advocated pressure for a negotiated peace. No country can be safe from the peril of war, it recognized, until the world is effectively organized for peace and justice. Friends were admonished to "bear an increasingly active part in developing the will to peace, the conditions of peace, and the institutions of peace."

ORGANIZATION OF THE FRIENDS WAR PROBLEMS COMMITTEE

Building upon the activities throughout the two Philadelphia Yearly Meetings, and the impetus of regional and national conferences, the Friends War Problems Committee drew together leaders from the two yearly meetings in the Philadelphia area and began its active life on July 26, 1940. It was the threat of the passage of the Burke-Wadsworth Bill for required military service that crystallized the formation of the WPC which was to devote itself on the national level to questions arising out of conscription and war, civil liberties and religious freedom. The WPC was a natural outgrowth of the activities of the local peace or draft committees.

The first meeting of the Friends War Problems Committee was initiated by the Board of Directors of the AFSC. In the beginning it was considered to be a subcommittee of the Peace Section, which provided secretarial services for calling meetings and circulating minutes. Soon it established a more independent status and always raised its own independent budget for any staff operations in Washington so that it could freely engage in legislative activities without fear of endangering the tax-exempt status of the AFSC.

The War Problems Committee had no permanent staff. Frequently I went to Washington on leave from the Peace Section, the longest stretch a four-month period from October 1942 through January 1943. Altogether a series of twenty-two memoranda were issued by the WPC on legislative developments in Congress. But it wasn't until the office of the Friends Committee on National Legislation was launched in Washington in November 1943, that there was a steady flow of information about bills in Congress which was widely distributed among Friends.

The genius of the WPC reflected the time and dedication of many Friends who spent long hours in committee meetings, or determining policy, or visiting Washington to lobby for the committee. On August 9, 1940, W.O. Trueblood wrote to Ralph Coppock of Damascus, Ohio, about his Washington experience:

> I have been here this week under the auspices of the Peace Committee of the Five Years Meeting, working with the Friends War Problems Committee and other Friends, stressing the views of those who have religious convictions against the war method. We are discovering that this is the only basis upon which we can get the attention of these realistic legislators. During these days I have been privileged to see a number of Senators and Representatives. In not a single case have I met with a rebuff. Friends stand on this issue for three hundred years is well recognized....

The WPC made a valuable contribution in enlisting the interest of a considerable number of Friends and in encouraging their efforts to express their concerns to members of Congress by letter or in person.

C.O. Provisions in the Conscription Bill

The first sustained effort by the WPC was to amend the conscience provisions in the Burke-Wadsworth Act, introduced in the Senate on June 20, 1940, by Senator Edward R. Burke of Nebraska, and the next day in the House of Representatives by James W. Wadsworth of New York. When this bill was finally signed into law by President Roosevelt on September 16, it fastened conscription on the United States for thirty-two years.

I had just returned from a month in wartime England where I had studied the workings of the British conscription laws which set up tribunals for deciding what service conscientious objectors should be required to give to their country. One provision of the British law provided that tribunals could grant complete exemption, which they were doing at that time to about eleven percent of the men.

Paul Comly French and I were asked by the Friends General Conference in session at Cape May, New Jersey, to rush down to Washington when the hearings opened on this proposed conscription bill. Between the bill's introduction and its signing we tried to amend several parts of the bill. The original language in the conscription bill was similar to the provisions at the end of World War I. It said that no person should be subject to training or service in a combatant capacity "who is found to be a member of any well-recognized sect whose creed or principles forbid its members to participate in war in any form." Another provision was that "no such person shall be relieved from training or service in such capacity as the President may describe to be noncombatant." These provisions were quite unacceptable because they made exemption a matter of religious affiliation rather than personal conviction and failed to allow exemption from noncombatant service.

Our efforts were directed toward six things. One was to base conscientious objector classification upon personal conviction rather than upon membership in a pacifist sect. We tried to broaden the basis of conscientious objection beyond "religious training and belief" to include the man who did not claim his objection strictly on religious grounds. We asked for complete exemption for the "absolutists" — those unwilling to register or to undertake any cooperation with military conscription. Other goals were to provide for a register for C.O.'s; to put them under civilian rather than military control; and lastly, to provide these men with opportunities to do "work of national importance under civilian direction" as an alternative to military service.

We were lucky to have a good friend in each Military Affairs Committee to keep us informed about what was going on behind the scenes — Representative John Sparkman of Alabama of the House Committee, now chairman of the Senate Foreign Relations Committee, and Senator Edwin C. Johnson of Colorado, who kept us posted regarding the Senate Committee.

Brigadier General Shedd, of the War Department general staff, suggested to Paul French and me that we confer with Colonel Victor J. O'Kelliher of the War College who was handling this part of the legislation for the War Department. We told O'Kelliher that the language of the bill as it then stood was completely unacceptable to us as spokesmen for those concerned about rights of conscience. Although the Quakers had had a corporate testimony for three hundred years against war, they didn't operate under a creed, and did not "forbid" their members to participate in war, although at their best they did discourage taking part in war. I still remember the surprise on the Catholic Colonel's face when I told him that after nine years of rather wide traveling among the Quakers, I estimated that not more than fifty percent were pacifists.

We urged that C.O. classification be based on personal convictions and not on membership in a certain church, and that consideration be given to members of any religious organization, and also to those who claimed no specific religious basis for objection to war.

Paul French and I and others concerned about the rights of conscience tried to anticipate the kinds of problems that would arise under conscription. We did foresee many of them, though we did not fully anticipate the number of men who would desert when they saw the futility and brutality of the Vietnam War. Three of us discussed at length with Colonel Frank A. Partridge the questions which the military would face with conscientious objectors who might land in the service or who might later change their minds while in the service and want exemption.

We maintained that the objector should not be viewed as a criminal, but as one who has a right under the law, that the objector should be subject to no cruel or inhuman treatment and that cases for consideration should be handled within twenty-one days. It should be possible, we argued, to furlough men from military service to perform work of national importance. To these and other suggestions the colonel was receptive.

But men and regulations change. Had the regulations for absolutists been included in the legislation and provided for in the law, and had the recommendations made to Colonel Partridge and General Hershey been accepted by the military and carried out, a large share of the persecutions and imprisonment of objectors and the flight of men in the army to Canada and Sweden because of the Vietnam War would have been prevented. These men could have served their country constructively in line with their attitudes toward war and military service.

It was unfortunate that very little discussion was held with members of Congress or General Hershey on issues of pay, dependency, service outside the United States or what might be included in "work of national importance" while the bill was under consideration. The burden of providing "work of national importance" in Civilian Public Service Camps was largely carried by the service agencies of the Friends, Mennonites and the Church of the Brethren at the expense of the C.O.'s or their churches. Later some government camps were set up. While the War Problems Committee followed these developments with interest, it was not deeply involved in these decisions.

Alternative wording for the Burke-Wadsworth bill was drafted with Colonel O'Kelliher and presented to the two Military Affairs Committees. Even then, while the bill was under consideration by Congress, the language went through various changes. As it actually worked out, the final text of the C.O. provision was rewritten in the Conference Committee after the legislation had passed both houses in somewhat different form.

The Conference Committee dropped the procedure for administration by the Department of Justice and placed it in the hands of the Selective Service System, thus turning down the pleas of the War Problems Committee for civilian control. The Department of Justice was, however, given authority to investigate appeals from the decisions of local draft boards. While the Selective Service was supposedly a civilian agency, conscientious objectors were actually under the jurisdiction of General Lewis B. Hershey and Colonel Lewis Kosch.

We did succeed in securing provisions for consideration of C.O. status on grounds of personal conviction rather than membership in a Historic Peace Church, and for work of national importance, but we failed to secure a national register of C.O.'s, to obtain exemption for the "absolutist," and to broaden the basis of C.O. status beyond "religious training and belief."

The language as finally enacted into law read as follows:

Nothing contained in this act shall be construed to require any person to be subject to combatant training and service in the land or naval forces of the United States who, by reason of religious training and belief, is conscientiously opposed to participation in war in any form. Any such person claiming such exemption from combatant training and service because of such conscientious objections whose claim is sustained by the local board shall, if he is inducted into the land or naval forces under this act, be assigned to noncombatant service as defined by the President, or shall, if he is found to be conscientiously opposed to participation in such noncombatant service, in lieu of such induction, be assigned to work of national importance under civilian direction. Any such person claiming such exemption from combatant training and service because of such conscientious objections shall, if such claim is not sustained by the local board, be entitled to an appeal to the appropriate appeal board provided for in section 10 (a) (2). Upon the filing of such appeal with the appeal board, the appeal board shall forthwith refer the matter to the Department of Justice for inquiry and hearing by the Department or the proper agency thereof. After appropriate inquiry by such agency, a hearing shall be held by the Department of Justice with respect to the character and good faith of the objections of the person concerned, and such person shall be notified of the time and place of such hearing. The Department shall, after such hearing, if the objections are found to be sustained, recommend to the appeal board (1) that if the objector is inducted into the land or naval forces under this act, he shall be assigned to noncombatant service as defined by the President, or (2) that if the objector is found to be conscientiously opposed to participation in such noncombatant service, he shall in lieu of such induction be assigned to work of national importance under civilian direction. If after such hearing the Department finds that his objections are not sustained, it shall recommend to the appeal board that such objections be not sustained. The appeal board shall give consideration to but shall not be bound to follow the recommendation of the Department of Justice together with the record of appeal from the local board in making its decision. Each person whose claim for exemption from combatant training and service because of conscientious objections is sustained shall be listed by the local board on a register of conscientious objectors.

MANPOWER LEGISLATION

As the United States' involvement in war deepened, conscription advocates increased their demands for overall manpower legislation. By August 1942, the War Manpower Commission had prepared a draft of a National Service bill providing that no one could be hired or fired without the authority of the U.S. Employment Service. Absenteeism or failure to report at the time of assignment would jeopardize citizenship rights or result in jail sentences. Those drafting the bill made no provision for a conscience clause because, it was argued, compulsory assignment for war production would not require the taking of human life.[2]

In October 1942, there were fourteen manpower legislation bills before the Senate alone.[3] Senator Hill of Alabama introduced a measure to provide for "universal service of all its citizens and. . . total mobilization of all the material resources, industrial organizations, and services of its citizens." The universal service bill offered by Senator Austin of Vermont applied to all males between eighteen and sixty-five. Neither of these two bills contained any conscience clause. They were forerunners of many different manpower bills to be introduced during the remainder of the war.

In the United States conscription of men for military service and the rationing of gas and some foods were already in effect. It was a major guessing game what might happen in Congress in the face of mounting pressure for national service legislation.

Beginning September 27, 1942, I was granted a four-month leave of absence from the American Friends Service Committee to go to Washington for the War Problems Committee in order to see what could be done in outright opposition to such proposed legislation and, if passage seemed imminent, to work for a conscience clause. By that time in England about two hundred Friends had gone to jail for violation of their national service requirements.

Most of the labor organizations and much of management were deeply opposed to manpower legislation, believing that free labor could outproduce compulsory labor anytime. The director of Selective Service himself, General Hershey, opposed such legislation, believing that Selective Service assignments and

[2]Minutes of the Friends War Problems Committee, August 18, 1942, DG 47, Box A, SCPC.

[3]WPC Memorandum no. 4, and no. 5, October 19, 1942, and October 21, 1942, DG 47, Box A, SCPC.

deferments would be sufficient to meet and distribute wartime manpower requirements. There was a sharp difference of opinion in the Roosevelt administration, and a lot hinged on what initiative the President himself might take.

Acting for the National Service Board for Religious Objectors and for the Friends War Problems Committee, Paul Comly French and I wrote to the War Manpower Commission on October 27, proposing alternative wording and provisions if manpower legislation were to be enacted. One suggested rephrasing was "that persons who, because of religious training and belief, have conscientious scruples against registration and/or compulsory service, may, upon evidence of sincerity, be exempted from registration and/or compulsory assignment."[4] Enclosed with the letter was a summary of the treatment of C.O.'s in Great Britain, Canada, Australia and New Zealand. We made a strong plea that if the U.S. passed manpower legislation, it should avoid the pitfalls of the British program, and employ an exemption clause for conscience.

Instead of pressing for legislation, however, the President on December 5 issued an Executive Order expanding the authority of the War Manpower Commission under Paul V. McNutt to assume full responsibility over the nation's manpower requirements. This points up the growing importance of administrative law and practice, and the reason any pertinent and comprehensive lobbying program must devote a great deal of concentration upon the executive agencies as well as upon Congress. Friends have never been able to follow administrative regulations in sufficient detail. The FCNL human relations secretaries have found that many of their most difficult problems arise in the executive agencies.

The *U.S. News* on December 11, 1942, revealed that in one year of war President Roosevelt had issued some 809 executive orders and the executive agencies had written a shelf of directives and rules that would fill a hundred volumes, while in two years Congress had enacted only 776 public laws, exclusive of private bills.

In February 1943, Senator Warren B. Austin and Representative James W. Wadsworth again proposed compulsory manpower legislation, entitled the "National War Service Act," and again there was no provision for dissenters. Support was led by the American Legion and the opposition by the American Federation of Labor, the Congress of Industrial Organizations, and the Labor Management Committee of the War Manpower Commission. Congressional

---

[4]In DG 47, Box A, Folder "Memoranda Nos. 1-22, 1942-43," SCPC.

Committees headed by Senator Harry S. Truman and Representative John Tolan argued that additional powers were not needed and that compulsion was unnecessary. Bernard Baruch was quoted in the *Washington Daily News,* March 1, 1943, as branding labor draft as "slavery. The attempt to draft labor. . .is impossible and dangerous."

Five Friends, Thomas A. Foulke, Edith Whitacre Cope, Harrop Freeman, Hannah Clothier Hull and D. Robert Yarnall, attended the Senate hearings, March 26, 1943, on the Austin-Wadsworth bill. They expressed Friends' opposition to the principle of conscription but asked that if the bill were passed, the following clause be included: "Provided, That persons who on the grounds of conscience are opposed to participation in war or conscription for war service shall be listed on a register of conscientious objectors and shall not be required to perform work or service to which they are conscientiously opposed." The delegation reported that they were courteously received and were given the impression that the omission of a conscience clause was an oversight.

I had the opportunity to testify in early December on the problems which would arise if conscription were extended to women and labor and to insert in the printed record the up-to-date British and American conscription figures. As so often happens in FCNL experience testifying before Congressional committees, there was only one Senator present at the Education and Labor Subcommittee meeting, but he questioned me for half an hour.

PROPOSED DRAFT OF EIGHTEEN- AND NINETEEN-YEAR-OLDS

Another piece of legislation the WPC was concerned about during the 1942 session of Congress was the proposed lowering of the draft age to include eighteen- and nineteen-year-olds. On October 14, 1942, after hastily called all-day Senate and House hearings, I wrote in a memorandum to the WPC:

> This was a brass hat day....Much of the discussion about drafting somewhere between 800,000 and 1,500,000 18-19-year-olds was as matter of fact as digging so many potatoes, or making so many biscuits. None of the boys were there, nor their mothers, nor their ministers, nor their teachers. (The legislators talked of drafting these boys) "For battle," "for offensive war," "for victory," but we weren't told where they would go, nor what they would do, nor what we should do with the victory...nor when the boys who survive will ever get home. . . .The biggest business in Washington is sending other men to their deaths.

Fortunately the opponents of drafting eighteen- and nineteen-year-olds were able to prevent enactment of this proposed legislation.

PROPOSED ELIMINATION OF CONSCIENCE PROVISIONS

When the new Congress convened in January 1943, a flurry was caused by a bill introduced by Senator Elmer Thomas of Oklahoma to end all provisions for exemption from either combatant or noncombatant service for conscientious objectors. This was in line with many resolutions passed by American Legion posts and was indicative of the growing prejudice against pacifists in wartime. Although the measure was later tabled by the Senate Military Affairs Committee, such bills had to be watched to see whether there was a real threat of enactment. Much depended on the zeal with which the authors of repressive legislation pushed for their passage.

DRIVE FOR UNIVERSAL MILITARY TRAINING BEGINS

The following month, on February 11, the Gurney-Wadsworth bill was introduced to provide for a system of permanent universal military training (UMT) for all male eighteen- to twenty-one-year-olds. This was the beginning of a long campaign by the military and preparedness advocates to indoctrinate every able-bodied young man. This drive for UMT was strongly opposed by the FCNL for eight years and culminated in the defeat of UMT by a recommittal vote in the House in March 1952.

PACIFIST STRATEGY BOARD ORGANIZED

On the intiative of the War Problems Committee a conference was held in Philadelphia in 1943 composed of representatives of pacifist groups. The Conference met to discuss problems growing out of the war, including conscription, peace aims, termination of the war, food for Europe, and concern for India where Gandhi was then in jail and talking about fasting unto death. Organizations represented included the American Friends Service Committee, Committee To Oppose Conscription of Women, Friends War Problems Committee, Fellowship of Reconciliation, Brethren Service Committee, National Council for the Prevention of War, the Mennonite Central Committee, Women's International League for Peace and Freedom and the War Resisters' League. Those present decided to invite other groups to join them and to hold regular meetings. This was the first gathering of the Peace Strategy Board which later became the

Consultative Peace Council and which met for many years to work on the exchange of information and the coordination of strategy on peace issues.

The WPC wanted me as a full time employee. Edward T. Steel wrote Thomas A. Foulke on February 2, 1943, raising the question "whether it would be desirable and practicable for the War Problems Committee to continue the employment of Raymond Wilson and to loan him to the Service Committee from time to time?" But because of heavy commitments in 1943 in promoting Institutes of International Relations and seminars as educational secretary of the Peace Section of the AFSC, I was unable to go to Washington even intermittently after the end of January though the WPC wanted me there. In late April Agnes K. Inglis agreed to take over the job I had with the WPC and to keep the War Problems Committee posted on the changing situation in Washington until she left the committee to enter government service.

Congress Favors Joining International Organization

One encouraging development during the war was that Congress gave serious attention to postwar planning and reconstruction. The Burton-Ball-Hatch-Hill Resolution (S. Res. 114), popularly known as B2H2, became a rallying point for individuals and groups concerned about postwar international organization. This resolution was very much along the lines of what the AFSC had been advocating all during the war — the establishment of an effective international organization in which the United States would play its appropriate role. The authors of the resolution and several of their colleagues traveled widely throughout the United States in their campaign to encourage the establishment of a world organization to replace the League of Nations and to promote U.S. membership in it.

In a dramatic move reversing the isolationism of the previous quarter century, the U.S. Congress in 1943 passed concurrent resolutions along the lines of the B2H2 proposal "favoring the creation of appropriate international machinery with power adequate to establish and maintain a just and lasting peace,"[5] and advocating U.S. participation in an "international organization based on the principle of the sovereign equality of all peace-loving States, and open to membership by all such States, large and small, for the maintenance of international peace and security."[6]

---

[5]*Congressional Record* 89, part 6: 7725.
[6]*Congressional Record* 89, part 7: 9202.

So, in the middle of the war, the U.S. for the first time expressed its willingness to join a postwar international organization. The U.N. in 1975 still faces the difficulty that nations have been unwilling to give up enough sovereignty to allow it to work as effectively as it should for the achievement and maintenance of peace, but it still remains man's best hope for peace.

The War Problems Committee operated on the conviction that religious ideals should result in political action and that the "liberties of the future have to be cherished and preserved now if they are to be enjoyed tomorrow."[7] While it was important to oppose conscription, the WPC believed that peace rested upon the principle of a governed world, and that conflicts must be settled by an effective world organization. The three-year attempt by the WPC to lobby in Washington laid a firm foundation for the establishment of the Friends Committee on National Legislation, which was to become a permanent program seeking to participate effectively in the political process for the advancement of peace and justice.

---

[7]"Proposed Statement of Purpose by the WPC," DG 47, Box A, Folder "Friends War Problems Committee Minutes, 1939-43," SCPC.

CHAPTER 9

Uphill on Capitol Hill

Quakers have been lobbying since 1659, or just about as long as the Society of Friends has been in existence. Leaders of early Friends like George Fox and William Penn buttonholed members of Parliament and appeared at committee meetings to champion religious liberty, justice and peace. Members of London Yearly Meeting even rented a room in a coffee house near the Houses of Parliament for a headquarters, much like the Friends Committee on National Legislation now has its offices on Capitol Hill in Washington.[1]

During my later years with the Peace Section of the American Friends Service Committee, Ray Newton and I used to discuss the need for more follow-up in Congress of the educational work going on in some ten Institutes of International Relations, scores of peace caravanners, and the other activities of the AFSC. But there were at least three obstacles to the AFSC opening an office in Washington specifically for influencing legislation.

As the Second World War was reaching its midpoint, the Foreign Service Section of the AFSC was involved in relief work in many countries which necessitated delicate negotiations with governments. In order to preserve its freedom of action, it followed a philosophy of political neutrality. That might be all right for a relief program, but in the Peace Section we felt that in the United States the citizens should stand up and be counted, and that it was our responsibility to seek to influence government policy in the direction we thought it should go. Second, the AFSC was primarily a project

---

[1] Frederick B. Tolles, *Quakerism and Politics* (The Ward Lecture, Guilford College, N.C., 1956), p. 10.

organization rather than a crusading propaganda agency and believed for the most part in letting its deeds speak for themselves. A third and significant factor was that with laws severely limiting legislative activities by a tax-exempt organization, there was fear that a vigorous program aimed at Congress would endanger the tax-exampt status of the AFSC.

There had been three years of intermittent effort in Washington on the question of conscription and the rights of conscientious objectors by the Friends War Problems Committee. On June 12 and 13, 1943, Friends from fifteen yearly meetings gathered in Richmond, Indiana, decided that the time had come to organize and launch the Friends Committee on National Legislation, and spelled out the basic philosophy which should guide it. They informally agreed to ask me to be its first executive secretary, and to help launch, on November 1, 1943, what was to become the first full-fledged, full-time religious lobby in the United States. For nearly thirty years it was the first and only religious agency registered under the Lobbying Act. The three decades of FCNL history are recounted in *Uphill for Peace*.[2] This chapter is merely an overview and recounts some of the highlights of the wide-ranging attempts to share in the anguish of Congressional decision making.

As befitting conscientious citizens, we tried to support the policies of our government when we thought they were right and worthy, to oppose the government when we believed it was wrong, to urge our government to do things which we felt could and ought to be done, and to refrain from asking the government to do that which citizens ought to do for themselves.

The FCNL was designed primarily to help thousands of Friends and non-Friends in its constituency across the country be more articulate and effective in their relations with the legislative and executive branches. In some areas like California and Indiana its autonomous affiliates put heavy emphasis upon influencing state legislatures. The FCNL encourages citizens to come to Washington or to interview their members of Congress in their districts, and to send letters and telegrams about their concerns. In cooperation with William Penn House it holds seminars and conferences, visiting not only members of Congress, but officers of the Departments of State and Defense, the World Bank and other executive or international agencies.

---

[2]E. Raymond Wilson, *Uphill for Peace* (Richmond, Ind.: Friends United Press, 1975).

The FCNL publishes the monthly *Washington Newsletter*. It carries on hundreds of interviews each year by staff or constituents with Congressmen or their legislative or administrative assistants. It has encouraged more than 150 different witnesses to testify for the FCNL before Congressional committees. FCNL staff travel widely within the United States discussing programs and policies of the Committee, and several FCNL members gained international experience as well. On leave from the FCNL Edward Snyder served the AFSC in Southeast Asia for two years, traveling fifteen times to Cambodia. I was Quaker International Affairs Representative in Japan for a year. Robert Cory visited the People's Republic of China in 1975.

Action Bulletins are rushed into the mail when immediate action is desirable on an important piece of legislation. From time to time serious in-depth studies are prepared on crucial issues in Congress. Contacts have been recruited in many Congressional districts who are sent special mailings and are expected to encourage their friends to spring into action for or against proposed legislation. In various ways the FCNL seeks to be an effective leaven in a country where apathy and inertia are all too common or where people feel helpless in knowing where, when and how to take ahold of burning issues.

The Friends Committee, I believe, has won respect but not necessarily agreement, in and out of Congress because it has stressed the moral questions involved in legislation, because it has been persistent and hasn't given up when the going was hard, or the victory seemed a long way off. It has been receiving increasing support from Friends and non-Friends, although not nearly enough to carry on as vigorous a program as the seriousness of the times demands.

It has been a great privilege to have served from 1943 to 1961 as executive secretary of the FCNL, and from 1962 to 1975 as full-time executive secretary emeritus. Much of the limited success which the FCNL has had is due to the dedicated, loyal and hard-working staff and to the cooperation of many nongovernmental organizations which work together on given issues like civil rights, civil liberties, world hunger or support for the United Nations. While I have used the first person in this chapter, most of the credit for labors done and the achievements recounted go to my colleagues in the FCNL and to the joint efforts of many like-minded organizations working in concert.

Two Million Dollars in Twenty-four Hours

I picked up the phone about four o'clock on the afternoon of June 1, 1949. A friend of mine in the State Department was calling to say that the Senate Appropriations Committee had cut two million dollars from the requested $16 million appropriation for refugees in the Middle East, that the money was greatly needed, and that the measure would be on the Senate floor the next afternoon. What could we do to help?

I dashed over to the Capitol by taxi, but couldn't locate any members of the Foreign Relations Committee or the Appropriations Committee. So I wound up the afternoon with no visible progress.

That evening at a civil liberties dinner I was sitting next to Senator Hubert H. Humphrey. I told him about the request and asked if he would be willing to move the restoration if we couldn't find someone on the Foreign Relations Committee or the Appropriations Committee who was already familiar with the legislation. He agreed and asked me to report at ten o'clock in the morning what the situation was.

James M. Read, secretary of the AFSC Foreign Service Section, was called to dash down from Philadelphia and join the effort because he was familiar with the needs of the Middle East and since he had been my first associate in the FCNL as legislative secretary, he knew his way around Congress. At the time the AFSC was caring for about one-third of the refugees in the Middle East.

The next morning we telephoned to the State Department and went to the Senate Foreign Relations Committee in search of active support. The State Department said they could not produce a statement by Ralph Bunche whose prestige was at its height from working as U.N. negotiator in the Middle East, because of lack of time. Francis Wilcox, chief of staff of the Senate Foreign Relations Committee, told me they were in trouble for $800 million in the foreign aid budget so they couldn't mess around with just two million dollars. Both spokesmen said, "Good luck to you, Raymond!"

Ten o'clock saw no substantial progress. When I arrived at Senator Humphrey's office, he was leaving for a committee hearing with his coattails flying. I trotted down the hall with him and told him we needed his initiative. "All right," he said, "meet me in the Senate lobby at 11:45 and brief me."

The legislative assistants to Senators Flanders and Aiken both promised the support of their Senators. Senator Sparkman said he would work on the Democrats and that we should concentrate on the Republicans.

At a quarter to twelve Jim Read and I sat down with Senator Humphrey, who is very quick on the uptake, rattling off the history of the legislation, the need for it, the action of the House of Representatives in accepting the amount requested, and of the Senate Appropriations Committee in cutting the request. We reviewed the arguments pro and con and put in his hands the relevant documents. Humphrey thanked us, said he believed he had the necessary information and went into the Senate as it convened at noon, to await the call-up of the appropriations bill.

I buttonholed Senators as I could, including Senators Taft and Hoey who said what a serious thing it was to override an appropriations cut. Jim Read stayed in the gallery most of the time. After the measure had been called up, Humphrey moved for restoration of the two million dollars and the debate was on. Jim came dashing down at one point and said that Senator Humphrey needed certain facts. Since you can't send in material by the pages, I grabbed Senator Langer from North Dakota by the coattails as he was entering the Senate chamber and asked him to put the information in the hands of the Senator from neighboring Minnesota. By the time I could get up to the gallery the critical material had been put into the debate.

Flanders and Aiken strongly supported the restoration move. There was a cluster of Senators seeking to reach consensus when it was proposed to recess the discussion and come back to it later as is sometimes done in a Quaker business meeting.

Humphrey's aide, Max Kampelmann, came out and asked if Jim and I would accept an amendment which would require matching funds from other countries. I told Kampelmann that we didn't like the idea of playing arithmetic with human misery, but that if that were the price of restoration, we would reluctantly accept it. So the amendment to the amendment was drafted. After a period of time the Senate returned to consideration of the appropriation, the cut was restored and the full $16 million for Mideast refugees was accepted almost exacty twenty-four hours after I received the distress call from the State Department.

There have been other dramatic moments in FCNL work like commending Adlai Stevenson for his early opposition to bomb testing as we rode down four floors together in a hotel elevator or, after waiting five hours to speak to him, catching Senator Russell in a revolving door as he left the Capitol in order to ask his support on a certain piece of legislation. But FCNL work is not always so dramatic. Most of the time it has been long, hard work.

BLITZ TO RELIEVE HUNGER: 1956

I had a brainstorm in March 1956 to try to increase the person-to-person distribution of surplus commodities abroad through the eighteen voluntary agencies licensed to distribute food in some seventy countries. This would be done by authorizing more payment of ocean freight and processing costs and by raising the amount of commodities which could be distributed overseas under Title II of the Agricultural Act from $300 million to $500 million.

The Agricultural bill had already passed the House and was being debated on the Senate floor when the idea struck me. I drafted a proposed amendment, got Senators Humphrey and Lehman to introduce and to sponsor it, wrote out an explanation and justification for it over my signature which a letter company processed and put on every Senator's desk on Monday morning. Five of us worked on this measure intensively for five or six days. We talked to thirty-three Senators and sixteen legislative assistants in person. Some of us went to the White House and asked Governor Pyle on President Eisenhower's staff to have the White House telephone the chairman of the Senate Agricultural Committee, Senator Aiken, that the White House supported the measure.

I told the general counsel of the Department of Agriculture what we were doing so he wouldn't block the effort. The *Washington Post* responded to our request for a favorable editorial on the crucial day. We interviewed the ranking members of the Senate and House Agricultural Committees, and since this amendment was not in the House-passed version, we urged them to accept the amendment when it came to conference between the Houses. The measure finally passed the Senate without opposition and our amendment was accepted in conference. But when the farm bill in its final form as agreed upon by the conference committee was passed by both Houses, it was vetoed by President Eisenhower! The veto was not aimed at our amendment, but toward other provisions of the bill. Since we had done a thorough job of talking with all the major people involved, the revised bill when it was later presented included this amendment word for word and it soon became law.

During the following twelve months I had the unique privilege of visiting Japan, Okinawa, Taiwan, the Philippines, Hong Kong and South Korea, and witnessing some of the distribution of American surplus food in each country. This gave me a firsthand picture of how food aid was received and distributed, and how thankful people were to receive it. This aid was partly a result of legislation which the FCNL had originated and which, with the help of our allies from the Cooperative League and the Women's International League for Peace and Freedom, we had engineered through Congress in less than a week.

THREE DECADES OF FOOD AID

During the last three decades the FCNL has pushed for many measures designed to alleviate world hunger. The first *Newsletter* urged that efforts be made to get food through the wartime blockade to beleaguered Europe as former President Hoover had proposed. We supported opening up and expanding food parcel shipments to Germany and Japan after the war was over as well as various measures for emergency relief. Congress was strongly urged to divert grain from the manufacture of whiskey to feeding human beings. We worked for generous appropriations to UNRRA, the United Nations Relief and Reconstruction Administration, which distributed relief after the Second World War, and for support of the Marshall Plan for the reconstruction of Europe.

The Agricultural Act of 1954 became the basic Food for Peace Legislation regulating distribution of food abroad and at home. Over the ensuing years we testified or lobbied for continued appropriations and for needed amendments. We kept closely in touch with Food for Peace Director, later Senator, George McGovern, or his staff. In fact Edward Snyder, my successor as FCNL executive secretary, and I went to see George McGovern right after his appointment by President John Kennedy. This was before he had been confirmed. He didn't yet have an office, a desk or a secretary, so we sat on three chairs and talked about his new job and the need to get food to Communist China which had suffered the worst series of natural disasters in a century. He was a very sympathetic listener.

Although the FCNL worked intensively for more than a year, including discussion with President Kennedy by a six-member Quaker delegation on May 1, 1961, unfortunately no formula was achieved to break the diplomatic and psychological deadlock in order to get American food to the needy people in Mainland China.

Twice a major drive was made to get grain to India which had suffered from drought and floods. I was the only witness from any religious agency to advocate grain to Russia on the same terms as to other countries. Over a period of many years we tried to get our government to quit using food as a weapon and to take food out of the Cold War. While we differed from the Communists in their philosophy, they were human beings, too, and food should be a basic right, not a political tool against any nation.

Senator Peter Dominick glowered down at me after my testimony on putting the Soviet Union on the same terms as other countries regarding purchasing grain. He said the Soviet Union never kept any of its treaties. I conceded that the Soviet record in keeping political treaties, as with the Baltic countries, for example, was not good, but that the State Department had furnished a list to the Senate Foreign Relations Committee of more than thirty treaties which the Soviet Union had generally kept. I reminded the Senator that the U.S. record in treaty keeping was nothing to brag about. American Indians were saying to me that the United States had made over three hundred treaties with them and none of them had been kept.

In 1950 and 1956 more than fifty farmers or farmers' wives came from all over the United States for eight-to-ten-day agricultural seminars sponsored by the FCNL. These intensive seminars met with an enthusiastic response from the participants as they discussed the anomaly of American surpluses in a hungry world and wrestled with the various policy questions facing American agriculture.

The forty-eight-page report from the first seminar entitled *American Surpluses in a Hungry World* was widely circulated. The initial request from the U.N. Food and Agriculture Organization was for two hundred copies. Several ideas discussed in the seminar were objectives of active lobbying later by the FCNL staff.

The FCNL joined the coalition of the Point Four Information Service at its inception. This coalition labored for years for widespread and appropriate technical assistance toward improving agriculture in developing countries through a whole complex of measures designed to increase the production, storage and distribution of food and other agricultural products.

The Food for Peace Act of 1954, popularly known as Public Law 480, provided for concessional sales to other countries in their own currencies or in dollars on easy terms. It also provided for donations to other governments for disaster relief, and for grants to voluntary agencies for relief in more than one hundred countries. Between 1954 and 1973 about $22 billion worth of commodities were exported under P.L. 480 as concessional sales or as donations. This was generous but by no means sacrificial, for much of it was a means of getting rid of agricultural surpluses after World War II. Food aid has been shrinking terribly in the face of world needs. The number of people aided dropped from 74 million in 1973 to 55 million in 1974.

Unhappily, money for the Food for Peace Program was diverted to the war in South Vietnam and Cambodia until that diversion was halted by Congress in 1974. At the height of the Sahelian drought in Africa (1968-1973) the five most seriously affected nations — Chad, Mali, Mauritania, Niger and Upper Volta — received $38.6 million worth of commodities under the Food for Peace Program, while South Vietnam received $792.8 million or 20 times as much, the receipts of which were used for the war.

In 1975 the goal the FCNL worked for in concert with the Senate committee headed by Senator Mark O. Hatfield was to allocate one hundred percent of Food for Peace commodities to the most needy nations rather than allow them to be used for political purposes. The legislation as finally passed designated seventy-five percent for nations with a per capita income of less than three hundred dollars.

FIGHTING MILITARISM FOR THIRTY YEARS

In addition to eliminating world hunger, another long-time concern of mine has been the abolition of war and conscription and the achievement of general world disarmament. The campaign against universal military training (UMT) was perhaps the most intensive and sustained effort in FCNL history. It began with opposition to the bill introduced by Chairman Andrew J. May of the House Military Affairs Committee in 1944, and culminated in the defeat of UMT legislation March 4, 1952.

During that period I recruited and briefed witnesses for the many hearings, helped raise $57,000 (equivalent to less than what the Defense Department spends every two-and-one-half minutes) in extra funds for two special augmented efforts with additional staff, and devoted a major part of my time to the struggle. At one time we rented extra space across the street for headquarters for the anti-UMT campaign which was dubbed "Turmoil." This anti-UMT campaign meant fighting against the tremendous weight and power of the Defense Department, Presidents Truman and Eisenhower, the American Legion and other patriotic and military organizations, the U.S. Chamber of Commerce, and much of the American press.

Before the campaign was over, opponents to UMT included most of the churches, except Carl McIntire's conservative American Council of Churches; labor groups except the Teamster's Union; and most of the farm and educational organizations. We worked closely with John Swomley and Marjie Carpenter of the National Council Against Conscription who put out 262 issues of *Conscription News* and prepared much of the literature used in the anti-UMT drive, and with Annalee Stewart and Mildred Olmsted of the Women's Committee Against Conscription.

Clarence Pickett, Harold Evans and I had about an hour-and-a-half in the White House before Truman's Commission on Universal Training. Instead of arguing against UMT directly, I raised sixteen questions which I thought the Commission should answer before making up their probably already-made-up-minds. All but one of the Commission were already on record favoring UMT. The rather informal give-and-take stretched over a considerably longer period than originally scheduled. Finally the door opened and in walked quite a number of generals in uniform with their charts and maps. Clarence Pickett said to the Commission in a stage whisper, "Does it take a dozen generals to offset the testimony of three unarmed Quakers?" These hearings were never made public.

We did what we could to back up House Speaker Joseph W. Martin, Jr., and Senator Clyde Hoey of North Carolina, who introduced measures favoring the international abolition of conscription. Partly because of the opposition of President Harry S. Truman and Secretary of State James F. Byrnes, neither measure got out of committee.

The defeat of universal military training was something of a hollow victory because conscription for military service under the aegis of the Selective Service System continued until the power of induction was terminated in 1973, so that meant twenty-one more years opposing the draft.

Conscription, the Taproot of Militarism

Prime Minister Jans Smuts of South Africa said on December 16, 1918, at the close of the First World War:

> I would go so far as to say that while the Great Powers are allowed to raise conscript armies without hindrance or limit, it would be vain to expect the lasting preservation of world peace. If the instrument is ready for use the occasion will arise and the men will arise to use it. I look upon conscription as the taproot of militarism; unless that is cut, all our labors will eventually be in vain. [3]

---

[3]David Hunter Miller, *The Drafting of the Covenant* (New York: G.P. Putnam's Sons, 1928), II, 48.

The draft was extended nine times between 1946 and 1971. At every opportune time the Friends Committee pleaded for ending the draft, pressed for investing the necessary energy and brains in preventing wars, and in strengthening the United Nations, and voiced the crucial importance of general disarmament. Between 1955, when the threat of UMT was over, and 1971, ten witnesses for the FCNL appeared before the House or Senate Armed Services Committees to oppose continuation of the draft.

Conscientious Objectors under Conscription

Aside from abolition of the draft, there is no satisfactory solution — only various more or less unsatisfactory compromises — for the problems of the conscientious objectors under conscription. A sweeping change for the better was provided for in the revision of the Selective Service Law passed in 1951. This change provided for individual assignment by local boards to work of national importance in the national interest with prevailing pay for the work performed, rather than assigning conscientious objectors to Civilian Public Service Camps with no pay.

The FCNL was one of several organizations urging recognition of the right of selective objection. These were men who objected to the Vietnam War but weren't ready yet to say that they opposed all war under every circumstance. After all, one war is about all young men are likely to face the draft in anyway.

Senator Philip Hart proposed an amendment to the Selective Service Act which would have provided for the recognition of the right of conscience for those opposed to "all wars or a particular war." The Senator said in the floor debate, "One proud element of our free society is the willingness to recognize individual conscience as worthy of respect by the government and, where possible, to permit fulfillment of society duty in ways which do not offend it." Unhappily there were only twelve Senators who voted for recognizing selective objectors on June 8, 1971, and fifty who voted against it.

Two of our many frustrations and disappointments were the attempts to repeal the Starnes rider and to get the so-called "frozen fund" appropriated for some useful purpose in line with the ideals of the conscientious objectors who earned the money.

In 1943 Representative Joseph Starnes of Alabama put a rider on a War Department bill to prohibit any government money being used for conscientious objectors for overseas service. General

Hershey, director of the Selective Service System, approved the idea of training C.O.'s to transport medical supplies from Rangoon over the Burma Road to the interior of China at the request of the Chinese government. They were trained in first aid, Chinese language, and how to handle charcoal-burning trucks under trying mountain conditions. The first contingent sailed, and got as far as Durban, South Africa, before they were recalled by the State Department after the Starnes rider had passed. It was a pure technicality because the only government money involved was the few cents of Hershey's salary while he signed the necessary papers. We got a repeal through the Senate three times, but each time Starnes and Representative D. Lane Powers of Princeton, New Jersey, were able to throw it out when the bills went to conference between the Houses. Finally Starnes was defeated for reelection in Alabama and his rider was dropped. We didn't have any part in that welcome retirement.

The frozen fund, which eventually totaled more than $1,300,000, was money taken from the wages of conscientious objectors on individual assignments such as farm work or dairy testing, and put in escrow by the Comptroller General, Lindsay Warren. For fifteen years we tried to get that fund appropriated to the CARE book fund or for the United Nations Children's Fund or for the use of the Historic Peace Churches for relief and rehabilitation of war torn areas. During the fifteen years between 1943 and 1958, nine measures had been introduced in the House and two in the Senate. The Cole Bill with the United Nations Fund as the beneficiary, had passed the House in 1947, and the Sparkman-Saltonstall measure to appropriate the fund to the CARE Book Program had cleared the Senate in 1959, and yet neither had been accepted by the other House. The money stayed in what the men viewed as "Uncle Sam's War Chest," and was absorbed into general Treasury receipts.

DISARMAMENT OR REARMAMENT?

If peace is to be assured, disarmament must come. The achievement of general and complete disarmament is perhaps the most difficult political step which the human race has undertaken — perhaps I should say has not undertaken. If I were an easy victim of frustration, which I am not, I would be totally discouraged by the lack of progress. It reminds me of the general who wired back to headquarters, "We are advancing backward, and the enemy insists on retreating upon us." The United States has spent much more than one trillion seven hundred billion dollars on military defense since 1945, but it has brought us neither peace nor economic nor political security.

The FCNL took the initiative toward convening the first of seven national conferences on disarmament, which was held during the week of President Eisenhower's inauguration, and played an active part in arranging and promoting all of them. The first was called by the officers or secretaries of ten national organizations. The last one was sponsored by forty-three nongovernmental agencies. I was asked to be chairman or coordinator of five national conferences, which discussed the need for reducing arms, the obstacles to be overcome and what the United States could do either by international agreement or by taking the lead itself. These conferences also recognized that political settlements must either precede or accompany arms agreements.

Sir Edward Grey, British Foreign Secretary, who committed Great Britain to enter the First World War, in reflecting on his experience, wrote in his book, *Twenty-Five Years*, "More than one true thing may be said about the causes of the war, but the statement that comprises most truth is that militarism and armaments inseparable from it made war inevitable."[4]

Within two weeks after the dropping of the bombs on Hiroshima and Nagasaki, thirty-four religious and educational leaders appealed to President Truman "to take immediate steps to discontinue its production and to press for commitments by all nations outlawing the atomic bomb and also war."[5] Rufus Jones, Clarence Pickett and I were the signers from the Society of Friends.

We worked closely with Senator Brien McMahon in seeking to establish civilian direction through the Atomic Energy Commission and government ownership of all fissionable material and its production. Efforts to get agreement with the Russians for international control of atomic energy and the outlawing of the bomb failed for a number of reasons including the rigidity of the American negotiators. The United States has produced enough atomic bombs to destroy all the major cities in Russia forty times over and vice versa, and still the race goes on virtually unchecked. I was in the audience in the State Department when President Nixon and Ambassador Dobrynin affixed their signatures to the nonprolifera-

---

[4]Sir Edward Grey, *Twenty-Five Years*, Vol. II, (New York: Frederick A. Stokes Co., 1925), p. 63.

[5]DG 47, Series D, Box 35, Folder, International and Civilian Control of Atomic Energy, SCPC.

tion treaty which sought to retain the monopoly of atomic weapons by the five countries who now make them and to prevent their spread to other countries. But unless the Soviet Union and the United States set an example by stopping the manufacture of atomic weapons, other countries will probably soon join the suicidal race in terror.

I was the spokesman for a delegation in September 1952, which appealed to candidate Eisenhower to make general disarmament a major item in his campaign for the presidency and if elected to make it a major goal in his foreign policy. Later we made a similar appeal to presidential candidate Adlai Stevenson for vigorous leadership toward general disarmament. Eisenhower had the best chance of any President since the Second World War to lead the world in that direction, but he didn't take the U.S. or the world very far along that road. His most eloquent appeal was his last speech on January 17, 1961, just before turning over the Presidency to John F. Kennedy, when he declared: "In the councils of government, we must guard against the acquisition of unwarranted influence, whether sought or unsought, by the military-industrial complex. . . .Disarmament, with mutual honor and confidence, is a continuing imperative. . . .I confess that I lay down my official responsibilities in this field with a definite sense of disappointment."[6]

The first disarmament conference recommended that efforts be undertaken to secure a strong Congressional resolution pledging the United States to press for general disarmament. The resolution which I drew up went through eight revisions before being introduced by thirty-four Senators in 1953. Two of us were asked to take the initiative in drafting legislation, securing sponsors and pushing for enactment of such a measure. Annalee Stewart of the Women's International League for Peace and Freedom talked in person to sixty-six Senators and I interviewed a good many, too. The ensuing resolution was a good one, stating that the purpose of the United States should be to obtain, within the United Nations, agreements by all nations for reduction down to forces needed for the maintenance of domestic order and international control. It advocated effective control and elimination of atomic and other weapons of man's destruction. Resources and manpower would be diverted to constructive needs at home and abroad, toward overcoming hunger, disease, illiteracy and despair. It provided for governmental help in converting military production to civilian

---

[6]*U.S. News and World Report*, 50, January 30, 1961.

purposes without a depression. The aim was to encourage hearings and Congressional and public debate. But this was short-circuited when the resolution was sent to Secretary of State John Foster Dulles who gutted the measure. The weakened version passed with only brief discussion and without expressed opposition or a roll call vote, so the educational value was largely lost.

An eight-year campaign to end nuclear tests which were poisoning the air with strontium 90 wound up in 1963 with the adoption of a limited test ban treaty. The treaty stopped testing in the atmosphere and outer space but not underground. It did not inhibit the use of nuclear weapons, nor slow the arms race in its most crucial area, the perfection of missile delivery systems. The treaty did not create even a rudimentary international inspection system. During this campaign I helped draft an appeal which I mailed, with twenty-one other co-signers, to President Dwight D. Eisenhower, British Prime Minister Harold Macmillan and Soviet Premier Nikita Khrushchev, urging them to "exert vigorous, constructive and constant leadership to find a way to end the arms race."[7]

In regard to civil defense it is difficult now to portray the hysteria in the country between 1957 and 1964 caused largely by a propaganda campaign waged by a section of the Defense Department and by various private organizations to encourage the building of fallout shelters for alleged protection in a nuclear war. The FCNL contended that "the only defense against nuclear attack is to abolish war itself." Opposition to the tidal wave of pressure for shelter appropriations was a high priority for years for Frances Neely of the FCNL staff who has labored hard against high military spending. The study by Edward Snyder, "Civil Defense: Shelters or Tombs?", was widely distributed as was a pamphlet by Trevor Thomas of the San Francisco office.

By 1963 the shelter program was turned down temporarily but civil defense advocates were back for a massive program in schools and public buildings. A friend of mine defined civil defense as a frank admission on the part of the military that they cannot defend us by military means, and that if the citizen is to survive he must dig his own rat holes and dig them now.

From 1957 to 1963 I was active in launching and conducting the Disarmament Information Service which brought together at luncheon the representatives of about forty national organizations.

---

[7]DG 47, Series D, Box 37, Folder, Appeal to President Eisenhower and Premier Khrushchev To End Nuclear Tests, SCPC.

It was a clearing house where information, ideas and action suggestions could be exchanged without approving joint statements or binding any organization to a given position. We listened to an impressive list of speakers, including two Presidential Advisors on Disarmament; Philip Noel-Baker, M.P., who had been awarded the Nobel Peace Prize; the Counselor of the Soviet Embassy who explained the Russian point of view; nuclear physicist Hans Bethe; and anybody who could throw light on some aspect of the problem of disarmament. These examples of actions taken by the FCNL are only suggestions of the range of activities in behalf of the unattained goal of a disarmed world that relies on the process of law and justice for achieving and maintaining peace.

Two New Organizations

In February 1960, a journalist in the Senate press gallery tipped me off that Senator John F. Kennedy was preparing a major address in which he would propose a disarmament agency. Edward Snyder and I went over and had an hour's talk with his speech writer, Meyer Feldman. The Senator and his staff were thinking creatively about mobilizing the best brains they could recruit for a real attack on the many tough problems in the disarmament field. The FCNL distributed 16,000 copies of the Senator's speech which was delivered in Durham, New Hampshire, and we worked intensively for the establishment of what emerged as the Arms Control and Disarmament Agency in September 1961.

Diminutive Marion Krebser put on a remarkable demonstration of what an FCNL volunteer could do by interviewing seventy-two Representatives, six Senators and ten members of President Kennedy's staff, urging members of Congress to introduce bills to create a disarmament agency. The ACDA hasn't lived up to our high expectations, for it has never been adequately funded by Congress nor freely supported by successive Presidents. Though the agency does have a record of nine disarmament treaties ratified in which it played a part, its biggest job is still ahead in trying to halt and roll back the race in weapons of mass destruction.

Congressman Henry Reuss has credited the FCNL with having tipped the scales in Congress for reporting out a bill to study the idea of a Peace Corps. Soon after the election of President Kennedy, the Congressman asked me to chair an all-day session in the House Office Building on December 20, which brought together people representing six government agencies, thirty-eight nongovernmental organizations, eight colleges or universities and seven Congressional offices. The purpose was to draw on the extensive experience of these persons in recruitment, selection, training and supervision of young people in overseas projects. Present was Maurice Albertson with two of his staff who were drawing up proposals for the Peace Corps under a Congressional grant to the Colorado State University Research Foundation at Fort Collins. President Kennedy launched the Peace Corps as a temporary pilot project and recommended that it be established on a permanent basis which was done in September 1961. Through the Peace Corps, thousands of young people have been enabled to work person-to-person on a multitude of useful projects in more than seventy countries.

OUR LIBERTIES WE CHERISH

Late in 1947 a few of us religious lobbyists were talking together about the almost unbroken pattern of racial segregation in Washington D.C., and the many threats to civil liberties including the rights of freedom of speech, petition and assembly. Out of our discussion grew a day-long National Citizens' Conference on Civil Liberties which was held at the Washington Hotel a block from the White House. It was one of the first fully integrated conferences held in the Capital. Out of that developed the National Civil Liberties Clearing House which gathered together monthly representatives of many organizations and which held twenty-two annual national conferences before it folded for lack of funds.

I was asked to serve as chairman during the first three formative years, and members of the FCNL staff were on the steering committee or the planning committee or were active participants during the life of the Clearing House. The Clearing House addressed itself to four main areas: (1) civil liberties involving protection from tyrannical or arbitrary acts of government, including the government loyalty-security program, wiretapping, surveillance, capital punishment and attacks on civil liberties from the House Un-American Activities Committee and the Senate Internal Security Committee; (2) civil rights for Blacks and other minorities; (3) academic freedom from arbitrary actions by school boards, citizens' groups and super-patriotic societies; (4) international rights such as U.N. Conventions.

Some of us worked up to the minute of the execution of Caryl Chessman in California trying to get a Supreme Court Justice to stay the execution. The FCNL maintained a consistent position against any and all wiretapping. It upheld the right of dissent and the right to refuse to testify against oneself under the Fifth Amendment. As this chapter is being written, the revelations about CIA and FBI actions, including wiretapping, burglary, opening mails, infiltrating dissident groups, emphasizes again that eternal vigilance against unwarranted intrusion upon privacy by government is still the price of liberty.

JUSTICE FOR MINORITIES

Edward Snyder and Irene Heine interviewed every member of the two subcommittees dealing with Alaskan Natives as part of the FCNL campaign for what turned out to be a fairly generous settlement of their claims. These natives were awarded 40 million acres though that was less than twenty percent of what the Aleuts, Indians and Eskimos felt was rightfully theirs. In addition they were awarded more than $900 million which would in part be derived from revenue from minerals and oil. The legislation left many questions unanswered, but it was much better than the earlier proposals, and much more generous than most Indian treaties in the other states.

The FCNL has maintained a continued interest in the rights of American Indians for health, sanitation, education and other measures to insure their well-being. For years a special *Indian Newsletter* on legislation was prepared and circulated. In 1974 Nebraska Yearly Meeting took the initiative toward underwriting two people to concentrate in 1975 on Indian affairs. Bryan Michener and Diana Payne have undertaken that responsibility.

From its inception the FCNL has been concerned with the rights of Blacks. The second *FCNL Newsletter* dealt at length with the poll tax which was a major block to voting for Blacks in many states. In the early years of the FCNL we struggled for fair employment practice legislation and made efforts to set up a Fair Employment Practices Commission. We also pushed for anti-lynching legislation. Then came the 1954 Supreme Court decisions outlawing segregation in the schools. In 1954 seventeen Southern and border states still had segregation laws on their statute books, and three others allowed local option. While the Supreme Court decision didn't end segregation, it did put law on the side of integration and made it possible for civil rights advocates to work *within* the law for its implementation. As participants in the Leadership Conference on Civil Rights, the FCNL played an active role in the passage of the two landmark statutes, the Civil Rights Act of 1964 and the Voting Rights Act of 1965. There is still a long way to go to assure Blacks and other minorities equal rights in education, housing, employment and other aspects of American life, but progress is being made.

I worked closely with Mike Masaoka and the Japanese-American Citizens League to try to secure compensation to the Japanese-Americans who were arbitrarily evacuated to relocation centers in an atmosphere of hostility at the outbreak of the Second World War. This was a great and evil blotch on our national history. At its annual meeting in January 1947, the FCNL called for the setting up of an Evacuation Claims Commission to make restitution to those who were evacuated from their homes by our government. It took more than seventeen years to complete payments after the Attorney General had been authorized to receive and adjudicate those claims. Settlements on the average ranged from five to ten cents on the dollar. One of my great regrets was that we weren't able to persuade Congress to make a really fair settlement. Nothing, of course, could erase the injustice of the evacuation itself. The *Washington Post* said on October 6, 1965, "The injustice done to the Japanese-Americans will remain forever a stain on American history."

TOWARD AN ORGANIZED WORLD

Seven of us appointed to attend the 1945 San Francisco Conference as observers from various Friends organizations sent a memorandum to all the fifty delegations urging a dozen points for consideration in improving the final text of the United Nations Charter including a recommendation for power to review treaties and for universality of membership.

There is no full-time lobby for the U.N. in Washington, but I think it is fair to say that the Friends Committee on National Legislation is about the most active legislative supporter of the United Nations. We lobbied for U.S. joining the U.N. and the World Court without the Connally reservation which declared that the United States would be the judge in its own case, for U.N. Bonds when the organization was in financial straits, for more adequate U.N. appropriations, for U.N. seating of the People's Republic of China, for channeling more economic aid through U.N. agencies, for referring the Vietnam War to the U.N. for settlement and for making the United Nations the cornerstone of U.S. foreign policy.

One of the most important crusades in recent years has been the remarkably able leadership of Samuel and Miriam Levering aimed at worldwide agreement for a law of the seas which would include oil, mineral, fishing and navigation rights. They began as Friends-in-Washington for the FCNL, then developed resources for continuing under the banner of U.S. Committee for the Oceans (Save Our Seas) with former Supreme Court Justice Arthur Goldberg as one of the co-chairmen. Sam has worked hard against exploitive legislation aimed at monopolistic control of large areas of the seabed by American oil and mineral companies, while Miriam organized educational programs to acquaint the American people with the great importance of the issue involved. They spent considerable time at the two U.N. Conferences at Caracas and at Geneva conferring with delegates and working with other representatives of nongovernmental organizations. Unless the trend is reversed the vast resources of man's last great heritage are going to go mainly to strong nations and multinational corporations rather than much of it being set aside for the benefit of the developing nations.

EPILOGUE

For many years I used to take my quarterly lobby reports over to the Senate Office Building to be notarized by a man who had spent nearly fifty years on Capitol Hill. Hanging behind the notary public's desk was a plaque on which was inscribed, "The price we pay for not being interested in politics," says Plato, "is to be governed by people worse than ourselves."

Democracy, if it is to meet the many complex and demanding challenges of today, must have stronger leadership and much more active participation by citizens all the way up from the local precinct to the actions of Congress, the President, and executive agencies of government. Religious institutions need to stress the moral and humanitarian considerations in viewing proposed legislation and executive policies, and to look upon the whole of mankind as one family under God, each with a fair claim on the world's resources. They need to provide the persistent drive for peaceful change in international relations and in domestic policies, the courage to champion new ideas, and the dedication to persevere over delay, defeat and inertia in working for needed legislation. I hope it can be said that the FCNL played a worthy role in this endeavor to translate religious faith into political action.

CHAPTER 10

We Tried To Stop Three Wars

Somebody has said you can't win a war any more than you can win a fire. What the world tends to get out of one war is another one. How to break that cycle is still the overriding question before the human race.

Most of my life has been devoted to working for the establishment of the conditions and institutions which would make world peace possible. But three times I was part of an earnest, long shot, but ultimately unsuccessful endeavor by a group of Friends to end a war that had already started.

The first was in Geneva in the fall of 1932 when the Manchurian conflict between China and Japan was before the League of Nations. The second was in Europe in April and May 1940, just before the blitzkrieg that dragged much of Europe into total war and later drew the United States and Japan into the holocaust. The third was in the first few weeks of the Korean War in June and July 1950. FCNL efforts to stop the Vietnam War are not pursued in this chapter.

FRIENDS AND THE MANCHURIAN CONFLICT: 1932

The small group of Friends in Geneva were much concerned over the near paralysis of the League of Nations in trying to effect some acceptable solution in Manchuria. Miriam and I were on our honeymoon. I had been granted a Biddle scholarship to Geneva. We were doing our best to understand the workings of the League of Nations, which the United States had not joined, and the difficulties of the General Disarmament Conference, which convened in February 1932 but which recessed in July, largely over the problem of the granting by the other Great Powers of equality of status to

Germany, which had been subject to the unequal treaties of 1919.

The Japanese Army had seized Mukden on September 18, 1931, and was in control of Manchukuo. The League Council had dispatched a Commission of Enquiry, popularly known as the Lytton Commission, to study the situation firsthand and to make recommendations to the League for a settlement which would then be before the Council and the Assembly. The Lytton Commission report was issued on October 2, 1932.

Before we arrived in Geneva a two-page statement was issued on August 20, 1932, by a group of Friends in Geneva under concern of the Members Meeting. This statement summarized the views of Japan, China and of other nations in the League, and commented that the present situation of an undeclared but virtual state of war was regarded in Geneva as perhaps the gravest condition of the postwar period. The statement said in part:

> Our object is two-fold: first, to urge upon Friends with all earnestness the gravity of the moment; second, to urge that every effort should be made, before it is too late, to help in finding a way out of an apparent impasse. The gravity of the deadlock arises from the passionate conviction of the justice of its cause felt by each of the interests concerned.

> We want to rally Friends and others to further supreme efforts toward reconciliation and basic adjustments which is not only the particular province of a religious society like our own, but which clearly offers the only practical escape from political disaster.

> Before irrevocable decisions are taken we must try to create the spirit of the real Round Table whose purpose is to find an inclusive solution big enough to embrace the essential needs of all and to persuade contending parties to withdraw claims that cannot be conceded to one without endangering the common life of the whole. [1]

This was followed by another statement on October 14, 1932, that Japan and China work out a settlement along the main lines of the Lytton Commission report. Since the Japanese were the main holdout it was suggested by the Friends that there should be some proof of sincerity and repentance on the part of the governments of the West for their past actions that set a bad example to Japan. Among the suggestions was an honest recognition by governments

---

[1] "Friends and the Far Eastern Crisis," in folder: Friends and the Manchurian Situation, 1932, DG 70, Series C, Box 1, Swarthmore College Peace Collection.

of the West or by the League of the principle of racial equality, which had been proposed by Japan but rejected when the Covenant was framed. Another recommendation was a sympathetic consideration of the question of Japanese immigration by the United States and Australia. The Friends group asked whether as part of a general and radical scheme of disarmament, the demilitarization of the Pacific Ocean might be achieved, and whether some far-reaching economic agreement might be concluded which would remove or at least reduce Japanese fears concerning Japan's access to raw materials and her major markets. International assistance was proposed for China in such fields as transportation, education and health.

The Friends' October statement concluded with the recommendation that in the event of the League's Extraordinary Assembly failing to secure agreement, a provision should be made for calling a conference of the Signatories of the Pact of Paris at which a further attempt would be made to find a durable solution of the conflict.[2]

On December 2, 1932, the tiny band of Friends in Geneva issued their third appeal. They declared that:

> Under Covenant and (the Briand-Kellogg) Pact no single nation can now claim the right to impose a solution by force without reference to the collective moral judgment of the peoples of the world. . .We appeal to the Chinese and Japanese governments to uphold this principle in relation to the present conflict over Manchuria. . . .
>
> But if we dare to make this particular appeal in the present circumstance, we are likewise convinced that permanent peace will be possible only when all nations are prepared to recognize and provide for one another's vital economic and social needs.
>
> For our part we are urging our respective governments to consider what disinterested and friendly cooperation could be offered to the Japanese and Chinese people which would foster in them a greater confidence in each other and in the West, and so ensure the growth of that spirit which "taketh away the occasion of all war." [3]

INTERVIEW WITH MR. Y. MATSUOKA

Immediately upon receipt of the third appeal, Mr. Y. Matsuoka, Chief of the Japanese Delegation at the Extraordinary Session of the

---

[2]Ibid., "Next Steps in the Far East Crisis."
[3]Ibid., "The Manchurian Conflict."

Assembly of the League of Nations, wrote saying that he would be pleased to forward the appeal to his government as desired and also to receive a deputation. All the signatories to the appeal, with the exception of Richard Cary who had returned to Berlin, took part in the deputation. These included Emma Thomas and Bertram Pickard, who were resident in Geneva; Edith Bigland and Hilda Clark of the Society of Friends in England, and myself from the Society of Friends in America. Bertram Pickard had been representing the British Friends Service Council and the American Friends Service Committee in Geneva for several years, and played an important role among the representatives of nongovernmental organizations concerned with supporting the efforts of the League of Nations for justice and peace. The interview on December 4 lasted for an hour and a half.

As soon as we had explained briefly the purpose of our interview, emphasizing the fact that we were a religious and not a political organization, Mr. Matsuoka launched into a long statement setting out the Japanese case. Japan stood first and foremost for its own integrity and for peace and order in Eastern Asia. An examination of the history of Japan during the last sixty years would reveal its peaceful policy; moreover, Japan had always opposed the dismemberment of China and still maintained that her policy in Eastern Asia was directed for the good of China as well as that of Japan. The West found it peculiarly difficult to understand the realities of the Far Eastern situation. The Japanese were at a disadvantage in getting their point of view understood because the Japanese tradition had always been the way of silence and action while the Chinese were masters of propaganda. In private conversations with the Chinese representatives, Dr. Yen and Dr. Koo, he had found the differences of opinion in his judgment to be relatively slight.

At this point the delegation intervened and explained that there was no lack of sympathy in the United States and England for the serious grievances that Japan felt. However, we pointed out that opinion in the West was increasingly unable to understand why Japan — a permanent member of the Council and heretofore a loyal supporter of the League — now seemed unwilling to utilize to the full the machinery for the pacific settlement of disputes offered by the League. In particular Japan's seeming total rejection of the thoughtful conclusions of the Lytton Report was difficult to understand.

Mr. Matsuoka proceeded to justify the policy of Japan by reciting a long series of examples where, in his view, other countries had failed to adopt a League procedure, including the U.S. seizure of Panama and its actions in the Caribbean. He stressed the defensive character of Japanese action in Manchuria, explaining how long-suffering the Japanese had been in the face of repeated provocations along the South Manchurian Railway for which the Chinese refused responsibility.

We countered that liberal opinion in the West had always been opposed to arbitrary acts. It was important to recognize that the situation had changed with the adoption of the League Covenant and the Briand-Kellogg Pact. Mr. Matsuoka insisted that Japan had in fact neither violated the Covenant nor the Briand-Kellogg Pact. Japanese sacrifices justified a special position in Manchuria. A very large factor was Japan's fear of Russia. He had made it clear to the Soviet authorities during his recent visit to Moscow that while Japan desired a policy of friendship and cooperation with Russia, yet remembering the history of the last fifty years, Japan was obliged to consider its strategic position on the mainland.

In Matsuoka's view the settlement would have to be worked out between Japan, China and Manchukuo. He hoped that Japan could remain a member of the League, but if the League failed entirely to understand the Japanese point of view Japan might feel compelled to withdraw from it. He was surprised how greatly Japan was misunderstood in Geneva. He believed that in two or three years it would be recognized that Japan's policy was one of peace and essentially helpful to China. While some good things in Japan had been learned from the West, there were many evil things that had been taken over by Japan from Western civilization.

He claimed that the spirit of the Japanese people was essentially pacific as witnessed by the long centuries of nonaggressive life lived on their small and inadequate islands. He personally wished that the Japanese people were ready to disarm and risk the possibility of invasion though he admitted that public opinion in Japan was not ready for any such step. He spoke of his own faith as a Buddhist, stating that when he left Japan on this important mission he felt that he was standing before God and must pursue what he felt to be the truth at all costs. He explained that in his final radio talk to the whole nation before leaving Tokyo, he had emphasized the need to come to Geneva not to fight but to persuade. He was trying to fulfill his mission in that spirit and would take any amount of trouble to explain his country's position and actions.

The deputation came away with the feeling that while Mr.

Matsuoka was a very able and determined patriot, he did have a softer side than might have been imagined as we had seen and listened to him at the Council table. He was not prepared to admit the weakness of the Japanese case nor recognize that Japan had not faithfully observed her obligations under the Covenant and had now done things which he condemned other countries for doing in pre-Covenant days. His arguments indicated that as far as Manchuria was concerned, Japan proposed to follow the policy she deemed essential in her own interest. He showed little comprehension of the general condemnation of the military actions of the Japanese in Manchuria, nor of the stalling and obstructive tactics consistently pursued in Geneva by the Japanese representative.

Interview with Dr. V.K. Wellington Koo

When Dr. Koo, Chief of the Chinese delegation to the Extraordinary Session of the Assembly of the League of Nations, received Bertram Picard and me on December 16, 1932, he had in his hand the appeal which he had heavily underlined in red, and copies of the two previous statements issued by Friends in Geneva.

Dr. Koo thanked us very cordially for the spirit and intent of the appeal and for our concern on the Manchurian question, and asserted that it was quite in line with the Chinese case. He himself took part in the Peace Conference after World War I and helped draft the Covenant of the League. We were now living under a new order of things in the world, and it was not only Manchuria, but the whole new world order that was vitally at stake in the present issue.

China had acted, according to Dr. Koo, in strict accordance with the Covenant by placing her whole case in the hands of the League from the beginning. When one looked realistically at Japanese history, their "Manchurian adventure" was nothing new. It was only part of a military policy of expansion which was, for a time after the First World War, held in check by the liberal element in Japan. It was the same policy which led to the annexation of Korea in 1910, to the secret agreement with Russia partitioning spheres of influence in Mongolia in 1912, to the Twenty-One Demands in China in 1915 and to other events which he could have mentioned.

If not checked now, the Japanese would take Inner Mongolia as the next step, then Outer Mongolia, then North China. Control of Manchuria would not diminish their expansionist policy, but greatly increase it for they would only use the resources for more extensive campaigns. Unless the world united to check Japan now they were only laying up much more serious trouble for the very near future.

Just as Mr. Matsuoka told us that the Japanese understood the Chinese much better than the West, so Dr. Koo asserted that the Chinese understood the Japanese better than did people in the West. Japanese diplomacy, he said, was very much of a double character. They said one thing to the people in the West and pursued quite a different policy in Asia with the Chinese.

Yet Japan would be the last country in the world really to defy a united front of world opinion. History had shown that in 1895, 1905 and 1922, Japan put up a bold front but gave way at the last moment when faced with determined world opposition. Her present intransigence was a result of the divided opinion in the West and would suddenly change in the face of something more substantial than mere paper resolutions. While admitting that measured by the most progressive and stable nations in the West, China still had a good way to go, Dr. Koo definitely denied the common assumption that the internal situation in China was chaotic.

As one example of what China had been able to do to meet one of her serious internal problems, Dr. Koo related that within eight months, after one of the worst floods in two hundred years in the Yangtze valley on top of all their other difficulties, the Chinese people had built sixty-five hundred miles of dikes ten feet high at an expenditure of twenty-five million dollars from the national treasury in addition to all that was spent by provincial and local government. At one time there were twenty million people at work on these projects and for most of the time from seven to ten million people. In spite of that herculean effort they had actually balanced their budget without any foreign loans, which most of the other nations had not been able to do.

When we asked Dr. Koo if the resumption of full diplomatic relations with Russia, which had only been restored in Geneva during the previous week by Mr. Litvinoff and Dr. Yen, meant that the Soviet Union would not recognize Manchukuo, he implied that China expected Russia would not. "Would the recognition of Russia by the United States aid materially in furthering a settlement of the Manchurian dispute?" we asked. "Yes, very materially." (The U.S. recognized the Soviet Union in 1933.)

Dr. Koo gave us his candid comments on the two Friends statements which had been circulated. He felt that the Manchurian issue should be kept foremost and simplified, and he questioned the wisdom of raising the issue of repeal of the Japanese exclusion act or recognition of the principle of racial equality. He took exception to the suggestion in the October 14 statement that after recommending internal technical assistance for Chinese reconstruction "China might properly be asked, in such circumstances, to discontinue any official support of the boycott movement."

He claimed that the Chinese boycott of Japanese goods was a weapon of self-defense. The last one was started only after the massacre of 140 Chinese in Korea over a period of about ten days under the cognizance, if not the connivance, of the Japanese, and the Chinese could get neither justice nor convictions of anybody. Bertram Pickard reiterated our position, that even if the boycott were used in self-defense, it too must be brought under international judgment and review. Regarding the boycott we argued that no nation could any longer claim the right to be sole judge in its own cause, at least morally, if not legally.

When I asked Dr. Koo what could be done officially or unofficially in the United States, he replied:

1) Uphold the Kellogg Pact and insist on the pacific settlement of all disputes.

2) Hold to the nonrecognition policy as advocated by Secretary Stimson. This would logically imply the recall of consuls and mean a temporary sacrifice of trade.

3) Exert pressure, economic or diplomatic or both. The threat of a united withdrawal of all ambassadors from Tokyo would bring Japan to terms without even having to carry it out, if the nations really meant business. Impose an embargo on loans and munitions and an economic boycott if necessary.

We thanked Dr. Koo for his cordial reception to us and the generous and free way he had talked to us. I expressed sympathy and encouragement for China's efforts to keep the dispute before the League of Nations which would have tremendous significance for the future, and appealed to him to be patient with the apparent failure of the peace machinery so far. Dr. Koo replied, "Yes, but we have done this at a great sacrifice."

We felt that if the dispute had been left to Matsuoka and Koo they might have been able to work out a settlement. But publicly each had to be the mouthpiece of his government back home, and the Japanese in particular weren't softening their position much.

While the conflict went to the League and a very able Commission of Enquiry studied the question on the spot and gave a thoughtful and generally conciliatory report, while the matter was debated for weeks and weeks, the League in the end failed to settle the

Manchurian dispute and to forestall war between China and Japan. The Japanese withdrew from the League and moved deeper into China. Nine years later they struck the United States at Pearl Harbor.

This failure was a major tragedy in the struggle to solve disputes through international mediation. Unfortunately international institutions have still not been able to prevent all wars even when they are consulted. Perhaps as Americans we might humbly reflect that the United States never allowed the Vietnam War to go officially to the United Nations for settlement. As Britain's most famous modern military writer, Captain Liddell Hart, put it, "What we learn from history is that we don't learn from history."

EMERGENCY PEACE CAMPAIGN

Ray Newton, with whom I worked as a colleague for twelve years on the staff of the American Friends Service Committee Peace Section, organized and directed the Emergency Peace Campaign (EPC) in 1936 and 1937. E. Charles Chatfield in his dissertation, "Pacifism and American Life, 1914 to 1941," called this crusade the "most important and most impressive effort in the history of the American Peace Movement"[4] up to that time. I concentrated on coordinating Institutes of International Relations and other Peace Section activities in order to free Ray Newton to devote almost his entire time to the Emergency Peace Campaign which sought to stiffen the opposition in the United States to becoming involved in a possible Second World War.

The Emergency Peace Campaign organized thousands of meetings scattered over forty-seven of the forty-eight states. Through twenty area offices staffed with seventy-five workers for six months, committees or active working contacts were organized in more than two thousand towns and cities across the country. On the evening of April 6, 1937 (the anniversary of America's entrance into the First World War), over seven thousand meetings were sponsored by farm groups alone in addition to gatherings on five hundred campuses and in a large number of cities and towns.

More than six hundred prominent men and women volunteered their services as speakers, giving from one day to six weeks without remuneration. Among these leaders were Admiral Richard Byrd, the first man to reach the South Pole; Charles A. Lindbergh who made

---

[4]E. Charles Chatfield, "Pacifism and American Life, 1914 to 1941," 3 vols. (Nashville, Tenn., 1965), 2:321.

the historic solo flight to Paris in 1927; Eleanor Roosevelt, and scores of other notable people.

The main legislative objective was to secure and maintain mandatory neutrality legislation in Congress aimed at preventing involvement of the United States in the arming or the fighting of other nations' wars. Because of the pressure for arming Western Europe, this dike of neutrality legislation did not hold. The only certain way of staying out of war is to prevent wars from occurring. Neutrality legislation was modified after the outbreak of war in Europe, but Congress still forbade, in the earlier part of World War II, the arming of American merchant ships and the carrying of arms, ammunition or the implements of war in American ships.

There was no effective political program to stem the rising tide of Fascism and Nazism in Europe. Nazism developed in part because of the inequalities of the Versailles Treaty, the failure of the Western Allies to carry out their promise to disarm and to work out a movement for world disarmament, the crippling of the League of Nations by American, Soviet and German nonparticipation, and the growing frustration in Europe in the twenties and thirties as part of the aftermath of World War I.

WORLD WAR II ERUPTS IN EUROPE

The armies of Hitler attacked Poland on September 1, 1939, and World War II had begun.

On that fateful morning Miram and I were dressed to go from Philadelphia to the World's Fair in New York City. We were stunned when we heard on the radio what we had feared for years — that war had broken out in Europe. Some of my feelings were expressed in the letter which I wrote to my family in Iowa.

September 3, 1939
Philadelphia

Dear Mother, Ralph, Martha and all:

The day of disaster has arrived. Today Britain and France have declared war on Germany who is already at war with Poland.

The day many people said couldn't come is here. The day the Emergency Peace Campaign tried to steel the American people against, the day we hoped and prayed could never come — the outbreak of the Second World War — broke the stillness and peace of the Sabbath of the world.

Men will say — have said — it is in a good cause — for freedom, for right, for peace, for justice, for international order, for the right of all men and all nations to live, for the pledged word.

It shows again the futility of the dictum that huge armies and navies and the threat of using them will maintain peace.

It means that men and women of goodwill who for twenty years have sought to weave the fragile fabric of peace have seen the tapestry trampled upon by the unprovoked invasion of Poland by the marching men of the German army.

Once again the floodgates of propaganda will be opened. The Germans are told that the mendacity of the British made the Poles unreasonable. The British are told that every peaceful avenue was explored but the fickleness and self-will of one man drunk with love of power for himself and his people plunged the world into a whirlpool of blood. Up to now we have many of the facts. But with censorship in Great Britain, France and Germany from now on, we are at the mercy of government censors who will pass what they want us to know.

It is too early to predict how long the war will last, who will finally be involved, what it will cost in lives and money and in ideals. But the ultimate victor will be Death and at his side will be Economic Depression and Ruin for all peoples. From any evidence available now it will not be a short war this time.

Hitler dashes to the front like young Lochinvar to "personally lead his troops" like the fire horses dashing down the street at the sight and smell of fire. One wonders if he is not already a prisoner and casualty — a prisoner of his own propaganda of hatred, force and bloodshed — a casualty who has slain his own future with his own hand. The First World War put the Czar and the Hapsburgs in their graves and the Kaiser in retirement. Hitler rode in triumph into the Rhineland, into Vienna, and into Prague, into Memel. I doubt very much if he will ride in triumph back to Berlin when this war is over.

I don't know what the President will say in a few minutes but it looks now as if American industry would be turned into a forge for Mars. Repeal the Neutrality Act and become the arsenal for France and England, the newspapers cry. If so, we transfer American ingenuity and industry into drops of blood by the alchemy of trade and sympathy and become partners in the mutual destruction of the Western civilization.

Passions will rise and feeling well upward into springs of hate. It will be hard to hate war without hating individuals, to hate the wrong without hating the wrongdoer. Millions of Americans will want to join in the slaughter vicariously and spill blood with dirty looks and vengeful phrases.

What this will mean in any of our lives we do not know. Can we maintain a sympathy for the Germans of goodwill who are as much victims of National Socialism and war as the Poles themselves? Can we stand beside the pacifists of Great Britain who will be tried by the seeming justice and inevitability of a Second World War? Can a peace come out of a Second World War which will bring freedom and make the world safe for democracy any more promising and durable than twenty years ago?

For the Service Committee it will mean new and difficult demands of leadership, ideals and personnel. For the world this is unmitigated tragedy. How deeply can we share it without adding to it or becoming a party to its method?

Friday afternoon and yesterday Miriam and I were at the (World's) Fair (in New York City) dedicated to the World of Tomorrow. Here was portrayed man's assault upon the unknown, his struggles to overcome time and space, his efforts for education, for security, for housing, for expression in the arts and music, his capacity for creating beauty in design, in form, in structure, in color, his past to be a steppingstone to a better world.

How incongruous war seemed! Crowds huddled around bulletins and ticker machines waiting silently, stunned, for scraps of news from the world on the edge of a precipice. Beauty for ashes, historic buildings as targets for bombs, transportation and communication leased by Mars for speeding destruction on the progress of yesterday, man's capacity for construction prostituted into relentless fury of destruction and put in the hands of more than eight million men. Bread cards when America is glutted with wheat and meat, ersatz clothes with ten million bales of cotton unsold, life insurance companies trying to lengthen life while bullets search for death.

Man is more than savage. Sometime the divinity within himself must rise to join the Divinity of the Universe and live in harmony with God and his fellow men. The torch of peace and goodwill must not be extinguished even when Mars rules the earth.

We may not see all the way. But we can say we will not hate, we will not fight, we will not help the war knowingly, but at the same time we will open our hearts to share the tragedy of our brothers and our time as we can, even now, try to build for peace and justice which sometime must come if man is to live upon this earth.

Raymond

TRIP TO WARTIME EUROPE: 1940

Months later during the lull in the fighting in Europe in 1940, sometimes called the "phony war," British Friends sent Francis Pollard and Karlin Capper-Johnson to confer with Friends in the United States to see if there was anything which could be done toward mediation or seeking an end to the war. In cooperation with leaders of the American Friends Service Committee various interviews were held including one with Eleanor Roosevelt in her New York apartment exploring conceivable steps which the United States might take. But no major initiatives grew out of these consultations.

Errol Elliott, later editor of the *American Friend*, and I were asked by the American Friends Service Committee to return to Europe in April with these two British visitors to express the loving concern of Friends in the U.S. and to pursue the quest further on the chance that some fruitful move might be encouraged. On the way over to Naples on the *S.S. Rex* we sat at the same dining table with Sir Stafford Cripps and his secretary, Geoffrey Wilson. Geoffrey had been granted complete exemption from military service as a conscientious objector by a British tribunal and was serving in the British Foreign Office.

They were completing a 33,000-mile journey to Russia, India, China, Japan and the United States. A short time later Sir Stafford Cripps was appointed British Ambassador to Russia and took Geoffrey Wilson with him. Some of us had a delightful visit with Sir Stafford after his appointment. This assignment for Geoffrey Wilson was an example of a more enlightened attitude displayed in Great Britain than in the United States toward some of their conscientious objectors in letting them serve their country in ways they could without violating their conscience. The United States Congress has never been willing to grant complete exemption to C.O.'s who were opposed to all cooperation with conscription or registration.

In Rome, Errol and I saw William E. Phillips, the American Ambassador. I told him something about the attitude of the churches and peace organizations in the United States and the hope of such groups that the United States and Italy might act together in trying to prevent a further spread of the war. They hoped that in associating Italy with other neutrals, it would engage in a search for some formula for an armistice. Without saying so directly, Phillips implied that the Italian government was not interested in mediation, and that when the decision would be made regarding Italy's entrance into the war, it would be made by one man, Mussolini.

As we were leaving, we asked the Ambassador what Quakers could do at this time. He said in effect: "Keep open the doors of communication as best you can when so many doors are being closed. Some day the world must change for the better. Now the world is in the grip of fear and force and war. You must keep alive the hope in, and the belief in, a better way and a better world."

Our interview with the American Ambassador to the Vatican, Myron Taylor, was very short and confined entirely to the question of refugees. We received no encouragement in Rome that there was any prospect that the Pope might use his good offices to challenge the continuation and spread of the war. In London, we saw American Ambassador Joseph P. Kennedy, father of John F., Robert, and Edward Kennedy, who expressed his hope that the United States could stay out of the war.

Karlin Capper-Johnson and I saw Mr. R.A. Butler, parliamentary undersecretary at the British Foreign Office, and Sir Herbert Emerson of the Intergovernmental Committee regarding what the United States might do, either in halting the war or helping with refugees. At that time there were between sixty and seventy thousand refugees in England from Germany, Austria and Czechoslovakia.

In my interview with Herschel Johnson, Counsellor at the American Embassy in London, I mentioned the concern of many people in the American peace organizations and churches that a negotiated peace would be more desirable than an all-out continuation of the war, leading to a possible decisive military victory. He launched forth in a tirade against Hitler as a "leopard" and a "tiger," so I saw that we would get no consideration from him for efforts to limit or halt the war.

On May 8, 1940, Karlin Capper-Johnson and I talked with Arthur Jenkins, a member of Parliament, and secretary to Clement Atlee, head of the British Labor Party, in the bomb-proof shelter of the House of Commons. He urged that the United States call an immediate conference of the belligerents to deal with economic frontiers, cultural frontiers, and disarmament, even without waiting for an armistice, believing that such a move, if sincerely and strongly made by the United States, would in the end compel the people of Germany and England to undertake some kind of negotiations.

I tried for hours to get through by phone to Clarence Pickett in Philadelphia in the hope that he could implore President Franklin D. Roosevelt to intervene morally in the war at this point to see if the impending holocaust could be prevented. But the censor wouldn't let me through.

It was already one minute to twelve in the military timetable. Karlin and I had lunch with a German emigre on May 4, who predicted that the blitzkrieg would begin on May 10 which it did. When I met this former German citizen in the United States some years later and asked him how he knew that the war would resume on May 10, he explained that he and his friends had been in touch with the underground in Germany by radio.

On May 9 it seemed to us that there was an impenetrable cloud of approaching doom over official London. On the morning of the tenth we had been visiting the grave of William Penn at Jordans and came in at eight o'clock to hear the BBC radio broadcast to which most of Britain listened. After a long pause, a voice said in anguished tones, "Pardon the delay, but Holland, Belgium and Luxembourg were invaded this morning at five a.m." We turned to each other in silence. It was now total war and our mission had failed.

KOREA: JUNE-JULY 1950

A much fuller account of the efforts to halt the Korean War is related in my book *Uphill For Peace.* The postwar settlement had divided Korea at the 38th parallel into two hostile camps, each of which threatened to reunite the country by invading the other. The U.S. military authorities deliberately withheld certain military equipment from the South Korean government under Syngman Rhea for fear the South would attack North Korea which was under the dictatorship of Kim Il Sung. The North Korean radio kept up a running tirade against the South.

On Sunday, June 25, 1950, units of the North Korean Army crossed the 38th parallel and fought their way toward Seoul, the South Korean capital. I rushed back to Washington and as executive secretary of the Friends Committee on National Legislation (FCNL), on Monday morning telephoned the American Friends Service Committee in Philadelphia, the National Council of Churches and the United Nations Association in New York City, asking if each of them, singly or in concert, would ask President Truman not to commit American troops to Korea, but instead call for a cease-fire and try to stop the war immediately. None of these organizations was willing to act. I didn't know until weeks later when the U.N. documents were published that this suggestion was very much in line with the recommendations of the United Nations Commission on the spot in South Korea.

Two or three days later the American Ambassador to Nicaragua spoke to the Point IV Information Committee luncheon. This was a group of representatives of nongovernmental organizations concerned with technical assistance and foreign economic aid. After the luncheon I rode back to the State Department in the taxi with the ambassador. I asked him what the chance would be of stopping President Truman from ordering American troops in Korea into action. He replied, "Sonny, you are too late. The President ordered the Air Force into action this morning at eleven o'clock."

But the Friends Committee on National Legislation took the position that even if a war had started, even if not only the American Air Force and Navy, but American ground troops were involved, still the war had to end sometime and efforts to stop it should be continued. During the next few weeks, I conferred with a string of Senators including Wayne Morse of Oregon, Robert C. Hendrickson of New Jersey, Frank Graham of North Carolina, Burke L. Hickenlooper of Iowa, and Hubert Humphrey of Minnesota in an effort to halt the war.

The Korean War represented one step upward in the long climb to a peaceful, ordered world in that the war was carried on under the United Nations banner against North Korea which was judged to have been the aggressor. This was a somewhat simplistic view in the light of the previous five-year history of threats and counterthreats. The *goal* was noble, but the *method* was the age-long method of brutal war. I argued that the longer the war continued, the more the United Nations became a belligerent, instead of a judge and peacemaker, its proper role. The longer the fighting went on, the more the country would be destroyed that we were trying to defend. The money used for destruction ought to be used for reconstruction. Every honorable effort should be made to seek a settlement, including mediation, third party judgment and pressure from nations not involved in the fighting.

Catching Senator Humphrey near the end of a long day, I put the case as strongly as I could for seeking an end to the war. "You can't negotiate when you are losing," countered the senator from Minnesota. This was at a time when it looked as if U.S. troops might even be pushed out of South Korea. I attended a State Department briefing about this time when they were preparing nongovernmental representatives for such a possible eventuality. "You can't negotiate with the Communists," Humphrey asserted, "You can't negotiate."

It was a vigorous discussion that ended in a draw. Neither of us convinced the other. Then the senator picked up an editorial from a Minnesota paper bitterly attacking him for one of his virtues, his strong support of civil rights. He turned to me a bit wearily and said, "Raymond, I've been asking myself all day whether it is worthwhile to stay in politics. I get attacked like this not only from one paper in my state, but from many of them, and not just occasionally but quite often. Is it worth it to take all this abuse?" I told him I hoped he would stay in the Senate to continue the struggle for civil rights, for world disarmament, for stronger measures toward feeding a hungry world, and that I thought his leadership was needed.

E. Stanley Jones, one of the world's great Christians and a long-time resident in the Orient, and I conferred that summer with Dean Rusk, then Assistant Secretary of State for Far Eastern Affairs. We argued vigorously for U.S. acceptance in principle of the suggestion by Nehru of India that a U.N. Commission consisting of the twelve members of the U.N. Security Council be established to receive or make recommendations for a Korean settlement.

It was imperative to establish the principle of third party judgment if two antagonists couldn't settle the conflict between themselves, we told Rusk. Let the United States recommend the number and the members of such a commission. We weren't arguing for the Indian proposal in detail, but for the necessity of setting up machinery for mediation or for searching for a settlement. Some day the world would have to come to such a process actually envisaged in the U.N. Charter and why not try it seriously now? But Rusk wouldn't accept our suggestion, perhaps because of the military situation at the time we talked with him.

Later I was lobbied in reverse when Senator Ralph Flanders of Vermont called me in and expressed his disappointment that the Friends Committee on National Legislation hadn't gotten more strongly behind a bill he had introduced aimed at terminating the war. His bill had some limitations, but I felt his rebuke had been justified, and that while suggesting some modification of the bill, we should have strongly supported his initiative in seeking an end to the war.

Unfortunately, there is still no stable peace between North and South Korea. While talks began some four years ago, little progress has been made between these two dictatorships toward reuniting families or reciprocity between the two sections of what had been one country and one people. President Park of South Korea at one time threatened the death penalty for some students who in dissenting from his repressive regime had been accused of sympathy for the

communist-oriented government of North Korea. At the Governing
Board of the National Council of Churches which met in Los Angeles
in February 1974, a resolution was adopted expressing concern over
the arrest of certain South Korean churchmen. In January 1975,
reports indicated that about 160 persons were still in jail for
expressing opposition to the Park regime. Many of these have been
released, but in April 1975, eight persons were executed after secret
trial. They had been accused of being revolutionaries against the
Park government.

I expressed my apprehension about the limitations of freedom in
South Korea to the American Ambassador and the political officer in
the American Embassy as strongly as I felt I could during an
extremely brief visit to Korea in 1972. The United States has
invested over nine billion dollars in economic and military aid since
the end of the Korean War in 1953, plus an undisclosed amount of
troop support. More than twenty years after the end of open
hostilities, the U.S. has about thirty-eight thousand troops in South
Korea ostensibly to deter further aggression from the North. While
there are many fine officers and men in the Army, the general effect
of foreign troops on the country is unfortunate. I think these troops
should be brought home.

THE VIETNAM WAR

In 1954 at the time of the Geneva Conference designed to work out
a settlement in Indochina after the French debacle at Dien Bien Phu,
the editors of the *FCNL Washington Newsletter* warned against
possible U.S. military involvement in Southeast Asia. For twelve
years, from 1964 to 1975, the FCNL worked actively against the
Vietnam War.

Most of the story of FCNL opposition to the Vietnam War is told
in two chapters in *Uphill For Peace*. Since other staff members
played a leading role in that struggle while my concentration was
largely on other issues, I have not tried to review here in detail the
sorry tale of U.S. involvement in Vietnam and FCNL efforts to end
it.

Some thoughtful observers believe that unless U.S. policy is
changed away from so much support of dictatorial and repressive
regimes, that there is serious danger of U.S. involvement in other
Vietnams. I hope and pray that I don't have to try to stop another
war. Let's work harder to prevent any more wars in the Middle East
or in Latin America or anywhere.

CHAPTER 11

Say It with Flowers — Don't Grope for Words

All my life I have loved flowers. Even when I was a toddler and before I can remember, my parents said I used to go around clutching a flower in my hand.

My favorite flower, among all the others, is the peony. On the farm I planted four rows of peonies running down the garden in full view from the bay window of the living room. One Memorial Day only a few were in bloom when we left for the memorial service in Morning Sun and the laying of home grown flowers on the graves of departed relatives. It was a bright and sunny day, and when I came home I went out and picked twenty dozen red, pink and white blooms — my idea of a bouquet. When my Uncle Will died, his son Cecil and I took some chicken wire and made a beautiful blanket of peonies to cover his casket. We shipped many boxes of peonies to relatives and friends. One bouquet went to my aunt as far west as Rock Springs, Wyoming, near Yellowstone Park. I mailed a box to Dora Willson on the boat just as she was sailing for England to visit her relatives. During the trip one of the buds burst into bloom and she stepped off the boat in England wearing a peony from Cloverdale Farm in Iowa.

My father was a great planter, especially of trees, and a love of planting was in my blood. When Miriam and I built our first home on the Bryn Gweled Homestead in Bucks County outside of Philadelphia, it was a great joy to plant more than a hundred varieties of flowering trees, shrubs and perennials on our lot. Many were easy to propagate by cuttings or divisions, and I was fond of sharing them with my neighbors, telling them I was very selfish since I could enjoy them while they would have to work to care for them. I have often said it is nice to give flowers as expressions of appreciation to people while they can still smell them, and not save them until after they are dead.

For a birthday present once my son Kent gave me a book describing many of the gardens and parks in the United States open to visitors, and I have been privileged to see many of them. The most spectacular one I have seen, and that one many times, is the National Arboretum in Washington during the spring when azaleas and dogwoods emblazon fifteen or twenty acres of hillside. At any time of the year the bank of evergreens and border and bedding plants is a sight to behold.

VISITS TO FAMOUS GARDENS

On February 20, 1964, I was thrilled when Franklin and Ruth Pineo and I visited two outstanding old gardens near Charleston, South Carolina. The Middleton Gardens which were awarded the Bulkley medal, the highest honor of the Garden Club of America, in 1941, "in commemoration of two hundred years of enduring beauty," have been called the most important garden in America. They were started in 1741 on the bank of the Ashley River by Henry Middleton, President of the First Continental Congress and father of Arthur Middleton, a signer of the Declaration of Independence. He is reported to have put one hundred men, slaves I would guess, to work for ten years building magnificent terraces, the Butterfly Lakes, and laying out the floral paths of this horticultural wonderland. In 1783, at the close of the Revolutionary War, the first four prized camellias were planted there by the celebrated French botanist, Andre Michaux. This may have been the first camellia planting in the United States. After 180 years, three of them are still thriving. How is that for age and beauty? Many, many camellias have been planted in this garden since.

We walked through great tunnels of camellias, often with the ground covered with fallen blossoms. While I am not as enthusiastic about camellias as I am about flowers with fragrance, this garden was certainly an eyeful of color and form — white, pink, red, variegated, single, semi-double and quite double. It was a little too early to see the 35,000 azaleas in bloom, but I hope to return sometime to see them in all their glory.

The second garden we visited, the Magnolia Gardens, has been owned by the Drayton family for more than 275 years. When I get tired of pulling weeds I can think of the twenty-five acres of the

Magnolia Gardens with three lakes, and a lawn of sixteen acres (I am glad that I don't have to mow it) set in live oaks two centuries old along the Ashley River. Here there were so many intriguing views of cypress, oaks and magnolias dripping with Spanish moss which gives the scene the haunting strangeness of an attic which has been gathering cobwebs and dust for three hundred years. The big feature of this garden was the tremendous variety of camellias, labeled as to variety, three to ten feet high and planted so close together I wondered if in a few years they would create an impenetrable jungle.

I cherish memories of so many other gardens visited, including three in Florida, the Bok Singing Tower in the Mountain Lake Sanctuary, the Cypress Gardens at Winter Haven with the spectacular water-skiing exhibitions, and the Tropical Gardens near Miami, with more than five hundred varieties of palm trees from all over the world, and the gorgeous range of colors in the bougainvillaea vines.

One feels almost overwhelmed in some seven hundred varieties of camellias in the Descanso Gardens in Los Angeles or the fifteen hundred varieties in the Huntington Gardens in San Marino near Pasadena, which I have also enjoyed several times. In my youth I did not see azaleas, rhododendron or camellias since the climate in Iowa is so cold, but when I finally saw them in the East and South, I really fell in love with them.

Gardens like these require an enormous amount of care to keep the places tidy, to see that trees are properly pruned, grass trimmed, weeds pulled, walks and trails in good repair, leaves and trash picked up. A great deal of credit goes to the maintenance people who do this unheralded work.

In my colored slide collection I prize the photographic record of two visits to the city park in Oakland, California, with some three hundred and fifty varieties of chrysanthemums in bloom, including the backdrop of cascading flowers that makes up a brilliant mosaic. My assortment of colored slides which I call "America the Beautiful" is mostly a panorama of trees in brilliant fall colors — maples, oaks, gum, sassafras, sumac and other trees saying goodbye to summer with a thousand shades of beauty. One of my favorites is a row of tall, columnar Lombardy poplars marching across the horizon like pillars of gold.

CHRYSANTHEMUM TIME IN JAPAN

I was not in Japan very long in the fall of 1927 before I was very much impressed by the love of beauty which seemed so common. Wherever a home had a backyard big enough for a cat to turn around in, there would usually be a few plants or flowers, or a stone lantern, or a gold fish, or a chrysanthemum, or something with an artistic touch. I visited three art exhibitions and five chrysanthemum shows and marveled at the way people crowded them for weeks and weeks.

At the chrysanthemum shows I saw no individual flowers that were any more beautiful than those raised by "Dad" Reardon, horticulturalist at Ames, but there were two features that were quite noteworthy and different from our shows which I have seen. First was the amazing variety of shapes and colors — globular, flat, peony-flowered, with flat petals, curved petals, spidery ones, some which towered up like the fronds of ferns, others that hung down and curled up like the tail of a monkey, some that stuck out like a porcupine's quills, others which tasseled out like corn silks. Some hugged themselves tight like a popcorn ball; others looked anemic like damp spaghetti. Some spruced themselves like a dandelion half through finishing school; others sprawled out like an octopus. Here was a fountain of snow and there a trickling bit of molasses, and yonder a bubbling bit of sunshine.

The second feature was the mass formations and the huge single plants trained in various shapes. Many were five and six feet across. I remember the following as typical, formed by training single plants — fish in a basket, a bicycle going over a bridge, four open fans made from one plant, a three-wheeled cart, a butterfly, a sailboat, a fountain, a street car, a houseboat or an automobile. The Japanese made a great deal of the pompoms and singles, especially training them as they grow downward in a huge spray. I saw one in Mr. Endo's house that had over six hundred blossoms on it, and that was not at all unusual. So you can see why I nearly went out of my mind reveling in the beauty I saw in Japan, especially when you add the great variety of blossoms in the flower markets, azaleas, wisteria, cherry and plum blossoms, iris, peonies and flower arrangements of infinite range and beauty.

Flowers are not only fun to grow and beautiful to look at, but they also can call us to reverance and worship. The sight of several bunches of early snowdrops on the lawn of the Florida Avenue Meeting House in Washington evoked the following meditation which I shared with the other worshipers there.

SALUTE TO THE SNOWDROPS

All flowers are special to me, but the snowdrops are very special because they speak of hope. The blue and white and gold crocus bloom later, and declare that winter is over. The snowdrops don't wait until winter is over, but say that in spite of winter, spring will come.

This is a day of great pessimism and cynicism among high school and college students who look upon the future with disillusionment. We all share that to some extent, the disillusionment that progress toward the spiritual ideals of a better world of peace and justice hasn't been faster. But we should not give up our dreams.

To gain a bit of perspective, drop back in history only thirty short years. Then there was no United Nations. Now the flags of 138 countries fly in the wind in front of the United Nations building in New York. Thirty years ago man was earthbound except for the airplane. First there was the sputnik, then mice, a dog, a monkey, and later men zoomed around the moon and returned to earth, because men dreamed that man could reach the moon. Thirty years ago discrimination and segregation were the law in many states. Then came the Supreme Court decision in 1954 outlawing such practices.

Thirty years ago the Friends Committee on National Legislation had only just been launched. There was no National Council of Churches and no World Council of Churches, but now denominations in countries all over the world are building spiritual and personal bridges East and West and North and South.

There are many dreams yet to be realized: a world without war, a United Nations with sufficient political authority to make peace and maintain it, and the time to come when children who are born are wanted, are loved and no longer cry from hunger, when preventable disease is erased, when men are judged on their merit and not on their color. There are new cities to be built, new institutions to be created, a divided world of hostility to be knit together in friendly cooperation. Perhaps we can overcome these problems too. "Some men see things as they are, and say why. I dream things that never were, and say 'Why not?' " said John Kennedy. When the calendar says it is February and winter the snowdrops promise spring. I salute the snowdrops that say to us "Keep hope in your heart!"

If Flowers Behaved Like Human Beings

On ten different occasions I have imagined how the flowers would mimic some of the human frailties at the time. My first flower fable was given during the Twentieth Anniversary of the American

Friends Service Committee in Philadelphia in 1937. The others were meditations given in substance during Quaker meetings for worship, usually in the Florida Avenue Friends Meeting in Washington and often sparked by the sight of the first yellow crocus. I have included here the latest of these fables, a sample of what the flowers have told me about how the human race was doing.

EASTER AMONG THE FLOWERS

As the sun rose over the Anacostia River, the flowers in the National Arboretum in Washington had a beautiful early Easter morning service. Even the Resurrection didn't seem unusual to them for many of the flowers had awakened from a long winter's sleep.

When the service was over and the music of the Bluebells, the Coral Bells and the Canterbury Bells was just dying away, the flowers had their breakfast of hard boiled Eggplant, toasted Breadfruit and Milkweed to strengthen them for their annual festival — a spoof on the foibles of the human race, billed on the bulletin board as "If Flowers Behaved Like Human Beings in 1973." I was there in my mind's eye — the tenth time I've been invited to these seldom-seen performances.

The first scene I saw was one of great activity by an organization whose full title was the "Ladyslipper's Liberation League for Full Equivalence with the Johnny Jump-ups." They complained that the Ladyslippers had been discriminated against, had been trodden over and abused since the dawn of history and the time was long past when there should be a constitutional amendment to insure their rights. They had secured thirty out of the necessary thirty-eight flower beds to endorse their campaign.

But the Ladyslipper Liberation League ran into heavy opposition from the Ancient Order of Queen Anne's Lace who teamed up with the Jacarandas to try to defeat the equivalency proposal. They argued that the Ladyslippers were superior to, or at least different from, the overbearing Johnny Jump-ups and that ought to be recognized. For one thing, the Ladyslippers under this new proposal might be conscripted into the Sword Fern Army. In the second place, the Ladyslippers usually had to take care of the Baby's-breath. No equivalency law would make the Johnny Jump-ups do their share of the homework including bathing and changing the Baby's-breath.

There was a good deal of noise and some picketing and some heckling in the center of the Arboretum where the big Nicotiana — some cynics called him the Big Emperor Tulip — was making one speech after another. Some of the returning flower veterans from the war in Verbenaland said it was time to wipe the slate clean and give amnesty to those who were unwilling to Viburnum the Verbenas just because they were told to. You could hear the thunderous reply for a long way. "Never, never while the unending Verbena War never ends. Let the Yellow Dog Tooth Violets stay up there with the Canadian geese. They don't deserve any compassion. Save compassion, Henryi Lily tells me, for the leaders of the Watercress Affair. Law and order is the order of the day, but don't ask me any questions about international law. We will use our prisons to jail the dissenters from the Selective Slave Law, and those who wouldn't commit murder by napalm."

And then turning to the Verbena War, Nicotiana exclaimed, "I don't want to be the first President since LBJ to lose a war. I want a Geranium of peace. Even though the war is over, I'll blow up every road in Cosmosland and Lotusland and every fish in the Mekong River to get peace if I have to, so long as those North Verbenas keep on fighting. I call those bombs, 'Peace Roses' because they glow in the sunlight, and you rest in peace if they hit you. If we can't get peace with honor, we will get peace with horror."

A lot more was going on in Verbena land but I wanted to get to the sensation of the day before the festival closed. So I hurried on to the bog near the Anacostia River to see the Watercress Affair. The Rudebeckias wondered if the Dahlias were still the party of treason, or what they might be up to to get control of the Big House in the middle of the Arboretum. So somebody in the Committee To Re-elect the Big Man in Power, arranged a deal with the Water Bugs to find out what was going on in the Dahlia Daze. Ordinarily Water Bugs skim over the surface as if they were skating on ice, but they got the Water Bugs to do some underwater bugging at night and they were caught flat-footed by night crawlers who seldom catch anything. For a long time Big Jonquil said he didn't see anything, hear anything or smell anything about any payola, but Martha Jonquil said if she could just get to a telephone she would tell all or at least tell something. But finally Big Jonquil said he had told the boys not to be naughty but you know how boys are. We don't know yet who is going to get the gate in the Watercress mess or where the Goldenrod came from, but some of the sweet-smelling flowers in the Arboretum said that when the wind blew from the Anacostia River over the Watercress mess, that it smelled like Skunk Cabbage or walking down Gingko Avenue in Georgetown in the fall.

When high noon came the flowers reverted to their own sweet

selves. They usually close the farce with a benediction, so they called
on the Jack-in-the-Pulpit to say a prayer. He prayed:

"Oh Lord of the Flowers, we pray for the human race that they
may learn to live together in peace and harmony like the flowers in
the Arboretum and make this old world the beautiful place it ought
to be. And may the flowers smile with joy as their fragrance goes up
in praise and thanksgiving to the Lord of us all on this Easter Day as
we think on the life of Jesus Christ, the Prince of Peace."

WINDOWS TO MY SOUL — IN AN ENGLISH GARDEN

Some men wear their souls
Like a diamond ring
Flashing in the light
Showing everything.

Other souls are hidden —
Gold still in the ore —
Only found by digging
For such precious store.

Not soon discovered —
Not soon forgotten.

Some men find their souls
Among the crowds prosaic,
Snatching little bits from each
To make their own mosaic.

Would you match the colors play
Like rainbows on my face?
Put your hand in mine and stray
Into an English garden place.

Flowers born of gardeners' pride,
Treasures there for the beholding —
Faded flowers where dreams have died,
Buds with promises unfolding.

Airy grace of columbines,
Sturdy strength of English pines,
Tenderness of clinging vines,
Labyrinth of strange designs —
In an English garden.

Coyness of the pansy bed,
Youthfulness on fountains fed,
Passion of the roses red,
In an English garden.

There's a doorway to my soul
Never opened to the crowd,
Multitudes may past it roll
With their vaporizings loud.

There's a window hid from view
Till sometime I walk with you
In an English garden.

CHAPTER 12

Hitchhikers Are People, Too

For more than forty years I have made a practice of picking up hitchhikers when I have room in my car. What a wide variety of stories I have listened to — such a kaleidoscope of human experiences. I am sorry that I haven't kept a diary of what hitchhikers have told me. I always feel that I get more out of my conversation with them than they get out of riding with me, so I am the beneficiary. My experience has been that on the whole trusting people brings a positive response, and that having transportation to share has been a rewarding and enriching experience.

In the spring of 1974, driving up from Washington to Haverford, I picked up a young man on the north side of the Baltimore Beltway. He had been in Florida trying to get ready to settle his young family down there. A telephone call from his father-in-law relayed the shattering news that his wife and three-week-old twins had been killed in a truck accident on the highway in New Jersey. His father-in-law, who was commandant of a large military installation, offered to send down a plane for him, but he said no, he would hitchhike. I was the ninth person that had picked him up in about twenty-nine hours, so if his story was true, he had make remarkably good time. Naturally, he was tired after the shocking blow and the exhausting ride without much, if any, sleep.

"God must have some purpose in this," he remarked. I didn't try to argue with him about that thesis. Yes, there is a destiny that shapes our ends, yet it seemed to me that rather than blame that kind of accident on God, I would rather explain it that God does not repeal the physical laws or the moral laws of the universe. If a truck runs over you, you may be dead. God's purpose comes in for humans to try to overcome whatever circumstances they meet with. We should try to overcome tragedy and to overcome evil with good.

Now this boy was up against the task of trying to go on without his wife whom he had known and loved since elementary school. They had certainly been an affectionate couple, and I could see the tragedy written in his face though he held up remarkably well. I did the best I could to comfort him, but one feels somewhat helpless trying to share the depths of such suffering.

He had been a prisoner of war in North Vietnam. Since we hear so many different stories about the treatment of prisoners, I asked him how he had been treated. He replied that he had been beaten pretty brutally. He had one tooth missing and I assumed that the beatings may have done that. This young man had finally been discharged and was looking for his back pay which was due him for the time he spent as a prisoner of war. As I recall, the sum he gave was $46,000. He was a very religious person, and he said to me, "I want to go somewhere and start a church, then build a church." "How much education have you had?" I asked. "The equivalent of high school."

I suggested that rather than spend this money which he was expecting in a few days, that he put it in the bank. I told him that he rated G.I. education benefits which would go a long way toward giving him a college education. If he could finish college and seminary he would be much better qualified for the kind of religious leadership to which he aspired. Then he might explore the possibilities of using that money in establishing a church or for some religious purpose.

He was an extremely conscientious and idealistic person and had used his influence to the best of his ability in the army among his fellow soldiers. He seemed very dedicated and sincere.

Since I was leaving the turnpike at Wilmington, I stopped at the first restaurant we came to and asked quite a number of people if they were going up the New Jersey Turnpike to his destination. One very beautifully dressed man in dark clothes looked at me with an astonished expression as if it were an insult to ask such a question even though I told him briefly about the young man's tragedy. He turned me down flatly.

I didn't succeed in nearly half an hour in finding a ride (of course, many people were going in the opposite direction), so we drove on to the next restaurant. I began to think the milk of human kindness had pretty well curdled among the travelers I was meeting. This reluctance to aid a fellow human being in deep distress shocked me almost as much as the man's story.

Finally I found a man who hesitated, because he said his wife was very nervous. I told him the story as directly and vividly as I could, and he finally agreed so I got them together. When I introduced them, the driver frisked the fellow to be sure he wasn't carrying concealed weapons. The ride would take him within a very few miles of his destination where he could telephone, so I assumed this would be his next to last ride before reaching home.

Here was a young man who had gone through one of the greatest and seemingly most senseless tragedies which a man could go through, who would have to face that situation of a dead wife and twins in a couple of hours, and yet he was dedicating his life to what he felt was a religious call. I was deeply moved by a sense of triumph in this man as I parted from him.

It made me feel thankful for the unmerited benefits and mercies which I have received all along the line. It makes one ask why some of us should be as fortunate as we have been when so many other people are faced with illness, or accidents, or tragedy week after week and month after month.

Another hitchhiker turned out to be a staff sergeant who had been in the Army for twenty years. During his service he had been stationed not only in the United States, but had spent three-and-half years in Germany, and had been both in Vietnam and Korea for a time. So I asked him quite a number of questions about army life.

"What's the modern army like?" I asked.

"Well, it's not like the Army used to be. You don't have the discipline you used to have."

I guess now the staff sergeants can't tell the fellows off quite like they used to in the good old days when the staff sergeants' language was one of the most colorful things in the Army. But he seemed to like the Army and was expecting to stay with it until he finished out his career in six more years and could retire with a modest income. I asked about his tour of duty in Korea, whether he got up to the thirty-eighth parallel.

"Yes, I got up where I could see the foliage on the other side."

I did not get from him any detailed story about how the parallel looked. I told him about some of my experiences in Korea in 1972, that my interpreter had since been imprisoned for being a liberal and speaking his mind. The way the repressive Park regime handled dissenting students was to find the leaders of demonstrations, induct them into the army and work them over. Now some of them have been threatened with the death penalty. I had been told that every one of the forty-two newspapers had a CIA man on the editorial staff, so that many of us were very much concerned about American support, implicit if not explicit, for such repressive governments. (As this is being written, the paper today recounts that the U.S. government has been making some representations to the South Korean government against such repression).

This sergeant was a man who had made a real effort to get acquainted with the people in the countries where he had been stationed, but he said that that was unusual among the G.I.'s. Some of them would try to make friends, but a lot of them didn't mix very much with the local population. When he was in Vietnam one of his activities was to train a Vietnamese couple how to run a supply depot of automotive parts. He had been able to train them in a short time so they could handle that kind of a job.

The sergeant had enjoyed his three-and-a-half years in Germany on the edge of the Ruhr. He found the German people very nice and he made some effort to make friends with them. While he wasn't technically religious, he seemed a man of genuine principles. For example, he didn't even smoke, which is unusual in the Army. When I asked him how he escaped that while being in the army for twenty years, he said he just didn't believe in it, and besides he tried to save his money.

One of his recent experiences in the Army was with a white boy from Philadelphia whose family was on welfare. There were five or six children at home. When his younger brother got hooked on drugs, the G.I. went AWOL trying to help his brother and his family. In an attempt to help the situation, the sergeant recommended to the commanding officer that the G.I. be released, if not discharged, so that he could go home to try to help his brother and his family. What did the commanding officer do but throw him in jail for a week?

"Sounds like an absolutely cruel, inhuman and inapplicable treatment under the circumstances," I remarked. "The Army doesn't have much in the way of compassion, does it?"

"No, it doesn't."

While he was in Vietnam for three years, his wife became alienated and the marriage broke up. He married again to a woman who already had four children. He was also trying to keep in touch with his own children. He would hitchhike home on weekends, nearly a hundred miles, and would have his boy come visit him on some weekends for picnics.

Here was a man who put a high value on family life, and upon his relations with his children. He was trying to save enough money to buy some land and raise a garden, partly because the cost of food was so high. He was happy where he lived but his father had a garden and he wanted one too.

I asked him if he thought the military chaplains had sold their souls, or if they ever criticized the war. He replied that they did not criticize the war, but he felt that many of them had been helpful in counseling with the soldiers. When you think of all the temptations in military life, nobody can tell me the Army's run like a Sunday school. I commented that some of us were working hard to bring home the 600,000 U.S. troops stationed abroad, and that I was trying to work him out of a job, because we were hoping to get down the road toward general disarmament and the conversion of our huge military establishment all over the world. I might have said our progress was excruciatingly slow.

When I dropped him off at the parting of our ways, I told him it had been a real blessing to visit with him because of his character and the fine way he told me about his experiences.

One day I headed out from Richmond, Indiana, for Chicago. Soon I passed a fellow walking along the road, so I waved by a truck that was tailgating me, pulled over to the side of the road, and waited for the man to catch up with me. He got into the car and sank back wearily in the seat. His greeting to me was, "I've been feeling all day that all the Christians are dead."

I tried to cheer him up. The story he told me was that he was hitchhiking home to Denver where his father was very ill. So I took him all the way into Chicago. He said he was going to ride the rails from there. I often wondered what happened to him because the weather turned bitterly cold that night and I was afraid he would freeze to death riding under a freight car.

Many of the men were veterans. One ex-soldier told me he had been in the American expedition in Archangel, along about '21 or '22, I guess, when the American Army invaded Northern Russia. I asked him what he was doing there.

"I was in the intelligence division."

"Why?" I asked. "What were you doing there?"

"I didn't know then and I don't know now," was his reply.

Another time I was south of Chicago headed west when I saw a man and his wife and child looking for a ride, so I invited them to ride with me as long as I was going in their direction. The man was in good spirits because he had just achieved his lifelong ambition to ride in a rodeo in Madison Square Garden. Now he was hitchhiking back to the range and mountain country having ridden a bucking bronco or a wild steer in the middle of New York City. At least he knew where the action was.

When I began traveling for the American Friends Service Committee in the Midwest in 1931, it was my first close experience with members of the Society of Friends. It was years later that Miriam and I joined the Society, but I asked myself what would a Quaker do in my circumstances. It was in the depths of the depression, thousands were out of work, hundreds of desolate men were on the road. My question to myself was — what do I have to share? The answer was transportation.

My philosophy was that if a person were riding with me he was my guest. If I stopped for lunch or dinner and he didn't have the money for a meal, I bought a meal for him where I ate. The same way for overnight. I never carried more than about twenty-five dollars in cash, so if somebody wanted to hold me up, he wouldn't get very much and I wouldn't lose very much. The cars I drove were usually relics and were insured so I didn't worry about the car. So I figured there wasn't much to worry about or be afraid of. I never was seriously afraid although I had a variety of experiences that made me wonder a bit.

I remember once I had four fellows riding with me. One was beside me, the other three were in the back seat. They were a pretty rough-looking bunch. I thought they might be tough guys, but they were my guests and I never let on. So I have never felt that I have really been taken advantage of or that my life has been in danger. With the amount of hijacking and gun play and rising crime I would be a little more careful today, but on the whole I think it is better and safer to trust people than to fear them.

Since I didn't particularly like to drive a car, I often let the fellows I picked up drive. A lot of them were truck drivers and knew more about cars and how to drive than I did. One morning I started out early from the Loop in Chicago. I picked up a man near the Art Museum, and it wasn't too long before he was driving. My ears picked up as we drove out toward the South Side and he pointed over to the right and said, "That's where Al Capone lives."

When we got to Gary, Indiana, he turned off the road and drove catty-cornered across a vacant lot, looking up at a house. I wondered what kind of a den of thieves might be in there. He didn't say a word; I didn't say a word. Then he turned back on the road and drove on down toward Fort Wayne. After a while we caught up with a fellow hiking along the road carrying his shaving kit and personal effects in an open mesh onion bag. So I said, "Let's pick him up." He stopped the car, got out and frisked this hitchhiker before he let him in the car to ride with us. We went on to Fort Wayne. I was a little bit relieved when my companions got out and I went on toward Pittsburgh.

When I was driving an AFSC station wagon with a German student guide in the Ruhr in 1952 on the way to the Friends World Conference in Oxford, we caught up to a fellow hobbling along, whom I took to be a wounded German veteran. He was carrying an open mesh bag with just a few things in it. So I turned to this student and said, "Let's pick him up."

He got in the car. My German is fairly nonexistent, but I said to him in my best German, "I'm a Quaker." His face lit up. He grabbed the lapel of his coat to indicate that he had been clothed by the Quakers. Then he raised his hand to his mouth to say that he had been fed by the Quakers. I've been humbled not only in Germany but in several other countries by the gratitude of unknown people expressed to me for what Quakers or Church World Service, or the American aid and Food for Peace Programs had done for them when they were homeless or hungry. By what right do we fortunate Americans merit the blessings we enjoy when half the world is hungry? Charity may ameliorate the situation, but only justice to share the world's resources is a great enough goal toward which to strive.

During one political campaign a professor was running for Congress in Indiana. His attitude was similar to mine, that someone riding with him was his guest. He picked up a fellow one day who rode with him awhile. A day or two later he got a post card which said, "If you look under the back seat of your car, you will find a gun. When you picked me up, I was desperate. I had made up my mind that the next person who picked me up, I was going to shoot and steal his car. But you treated me like a Christian gentleman and I decided to give up the racket."

Come, be my guest.

CHAPTER 13

Homesteading —
One Step This Side of Utopia

In 1939, Ray and Babette Newton, Tom and Florence Potts, and Miriam and I were living in adjacent apartments in the Carl Mackley Houses. This was a remarkable PWA housing project of excellent design, but we longed for something more rural and more productive. We began to talk and dream about moving to the country, living cooperatively and raising our own food. We even went to visit a big house overlooking a beautiful valley — the site now of the Holy Redeemer Hospital, about three miles from where the Bryn Gweled homesteads were to be — to see whether the house's floor plan was adaptable for cooperative living, whether we could share kitchen and laundry facilities there, and escape the dust and grime and sidewalks of Northeast Philadelphia.

As we were probing around we heard of another small group with similar interests who were yearning for a combination of cooperative effort coupled with a large measure of freedom. They were meeting at Bedford Center, a social settlement in South Philadelphia. The two search parties coalesced into a group of a dozen families and began serious discussions which brought the group together almost weekly for about a year to hammer out the main ideas later embodied in this venture.

EARLY HISTORY OF BRYN GWELED

To a considerable degree setting up the organization and deciding basic policies was an uncharted process because there was no precise model to follow for what we wanted to do. It was a pioneering adventure, not so bold or difficult perhaps as the trek of hundreds or thousands of miles which some of our ancestors had undertaken to find new homes between the Appalachians and San Francisco, but a search nevertheless for a new way of life.

Some members of the group went twice to visit the School of Living and the Bayard Lane Homestead Association at Suffern, New York, which had been started by Ralph Borsodi. Borsodi himself came down and conferred with us, and we benefited greatly from the advice and stimulus which he and his staff gave us in the formative stage of our development.

Our group's first plan was to organize under the banner of the Independence Foundation, the financial arm of Borsodi's cooperative enterprises. But this was later abandoned in favor of a totally independent organization. Borsodi's projects emphasized self-help and doing what could be done to produce food and clothing or to meet other needs of the family, but none of his projects had the number of starting families ours did, and they lacked the emphasis on initiative and responsible participation of the individual homesteader which has characterized Bryn Gweled throughout its history.

After weeks of exploration and discussion, an organizational meeting to crystallize preliminary plans was called at Bedford Center on December 11, 1939. Temporary officers were elected including Herbert Bergstrom, chairman; meetings that followed began to come to grips with important policies — membership, name, open meetings and particularly the site, but some of the answers took months more of exploration.

The site was, of course, a very important decision and during the months of October and November various locations were explored. Since we expected many children on the Homesteads, a nearby college would be an advantage to some of them for study and to all of us for the lectures and musical programs which are often open to the public. In the vicinity of Swarthmore or Haverford Colleges or Pendle Hill, however, an area I facetiously called the Athens of Quaker education, land was too expensive and no large tracts were available.

I suggested we buy an operating dairy farm within walking distance of the Trevose station on the Reading Railroad. It seemed to me that this site would have two important advantages. The good earth on this farm promised fine yields of vegetables or good soil for lawns, and the location near a railroad with good transportation into Philadelphia meant that many families would not need a second car for transportation. But perhaps wiser heads prevailed.

The site finally chosen was the Read estate, an abandoned dairy farm of approximately 240 acres located in the beautiful rolling land of lower Bucks County in a triangle between Feasterville, Churchville and Southampton, about twenty-three miles northeast of City Hall, Philadelphia. The estate was in the hands of about a dozen heirs who wanted to dispose of it. Some of the land was badly eroded; some was gravel or heavy clay, terrain I frequently referred to as land no Iowa farmer would be caught dead with. But if properly fertilized and cultivated it could grow good gardens. Weeds, I found, grew very well. As a location for homesites and a community this land had marvelous advantages.

First, we were able to purchase it at the very attractive price of about seventy-seven dollars an acre. Unimproved land in sprawling suburbia now sells for eight to ten thousand dollars an acre. So even with the cost of internal roads which the Homesteads put in, the capitalization was very modest for what we received.

Second, the land itself was lovely. On June 23, 1663, William Penn purchased from the Lenni Lenape Indian chiefs Essepenaike, Okettarickon and Wessapoak, all the lands "lying between the Pemmapeck (Pennypack) and Neshenineh (Neshaminy) creeks, and all along upon Neshenineh creeks, and backwards of same, and to run two days' journey with a horse up into the country." Included in this territory was the land which was to become the Bryn Gweled Homesteads.[1] The land we bought had three woodlots covering several acres altogether. These we soon called the High Woods, the Picnic Woods, and the Beech Woods. The oaks, tulip poplars, beech, ash, sour gum, maple and other native trees were interlaced with scores of white dogwoods which bathed the landscape in white in early May. Huge sycamores lined Gravel Hill Road bordering the Homesteads, and there was a lane of sycamores leading to one of the houses on the tract.

All the woodlots, land along the two streams and the gullies, and a large plot for community activities, an area totaling more than fifty acres not counting the roads with their fifty-foot right of way, were set aside and dedicated for common land. So everybody owned the big trees, the dogwoods, the wild flowers and the streams. This arrangement provided a natural habitat for many kinds of birds and wildlife including rabbits, deer, pheasants, raccoons, opossums, skunks, ground hogs and, when a skating pond was constructed, a

---

[1]Wayne A. Dockhorn, "A Brief History of Bryn Gweled Area since Latter Part of the 17th Century," in *Bryn Gweled 1975 Heritage Trail,* prepared for the Annual Meeting of Bryn Gweled Homesteads, May 17, 1975.

home for a pair of mallard ducks.

How should title to the land be held and how should the area for homesites be divided? These two decisions took months to work out. The group finally decided to set up a nonprofit cooperative chartered May 20, 1940 by the State of Pennsylvania to hold the title to all the land in the name of the Bryn Gweled Homesteads. Member families would then lease their homesites on a ninety-nine year lease, and, if they liked it, the lease could be renewed! Ownership of the land by the Homesteads was designed to discourage rapid turnover in what we hoped would be a reasonably stable community and to avoid the inflation and skyrocketing price of land which has characterized so many housing projects.

However, leasing rather than outright ownership of the homesite by member families raised a good many difficulties in borrowing money for home construction. The practice has been for the Homesteads to co-sign the mortgage. In case of foreclosure and failure of the Homesteads to redeem the indebtedness, there was a release clause for ownership of the land to go to the mortgagor. So far there have been no foreclosures.

In order to give families privacy it was decided to parcel out homesites averaging about two acres each, an area, as we found on our 1956-57 trip to Japan, nearly the size of the average Japanese farm. Personally I think two acres is too much ground for most city families to cope with. One or more families asked for smaller lots but were overruled. With such large lots it is easy for half the property to remain unusable thickets of briars or to revert to trees, as many families prefer. The acreage allotment was decided, however, before today's increased sensitivity about urban sprawl, population pressure and the need to produce more food, and the deepened concern for the wise use of land.

When the survey had been completed, the common land set aside, and the remainder broken up into about eighty lots of approximately two acres, the lots were graded according to view, location, size, arable land and access, computed on a point basis, with the most desirable rating 10.5 and the least desirable 7.5. For example, the Wilson lot, No. 48 on the chart, was graded a 10.5 lot because in size it was slightly over two acres, it had a fine view of the High Woods and the Picnic Woods, and every foot of it was arable.

The dramatic time came for the first thirteen charter member families to choose their sites. The order of choice was by lot. Because of the variety of desirable choices and the different things people wanted, eleven got their first choice of homesites, and the other two got their second choice, and everybody was happy.

Gordon Fredendall headed the months of negotiations with the Philadelphia Electric Company and Bell Telephone which resulted in putting all the utility wires and a telephone cable underground. We paid only a modest deposit, plus the costs of ditching, backfilling, and the transit pipes through which the telephone wires were threaded. So our entire homestead is without poles and overhead wires except at the perimeter where the Homesteads abut public roads.

What a time we had choosing a name! Altogether at least fifty-three names were proposed, including Briar Ridge, Bucklands, Stumpbridge Homesteads, The Cross Roads and The Quest. Although people found it hard to spell and difficult to pronounce, the members at long last settled on the name Bryn Gweled, which is Welsh for "Hill of Vision," and which echoes the names of early Welsh settlements in the area. While not every vision we had was fully realized, I think the name reflects our efforts to keep our sights high.

An early action in the formative period of the community was the adoption in the statement of purpose of the declaration: "The rights of the members to absolute freedom of religion, politics, association and expression shall not be abridged or impaired by the group, except insofar as such freedom conflicts with the equal rights of the other members of the group."

After long consideration members adopted an early bylaw that "no liquor should be served on public grounds or at public functions of the Homesteads, leaving each family free to do as they wished in their own home, keeping the welfare of the community in mind."

At the outset it was agreed that the community should be interfaith and interracial. The first Black postmaster in Pennsylvania and one of the first in the United States was Paul Gibson, an early member of Bryn Gweled. In 1965 he became postmaster in Southampton, the mailing address for the Homesteads now.

Bryn Gweled was an early pioneer in suburban integration. There were problems within the Homesteads as well as on the outside, but on the whole the policy has worked well. One Black family was very unhappy because they felt that though several Bryn Gweled residents had actively supported the pioneering Blacks in Levittown, a nearby all-white community, the Homesteads as a whole had not been active enough in championing integration. But one of the great virtues of Bryn Gweled has been its racial, cultural and religious

diversity. Today at Bryn Gweled there are thirteen Black families, a
Japanese family, and Chinese-Americans. The religious heritage
includes Protestants, Catholics and Jews.

One of the most important factors in the success of Bryn Gweled
has been the time and effort taken to gather facts and talk through
all important decisions as a group. While unanimity is not always
easy or possible, there has been continual striving to reach
consensus. If there is a close vote, a decision is deferred, when action
is not imperative, in order to take more time to seek agreement.
Procedurally it was agreed at the outset that each member, not each
member family, should have one vote, and that all matters requiring
a decision should be brought to the membership, except when a
matter had been specifically delegated. This has kept the basic
decision making quite a democratic process. Although the
seven-member Board of Directors, elected from the Homesteads, has
the responsibility of wrestling with difficult questions of
Homesteads policy, it reports to the monthly meetings and its
actions are subject to ratification or rejection by the membership.
From the beginning women have had an equal share in the business
affairs of the community and several women have served as
chairperson for a year conducting the monthly meeting of the
Homesteads and the other duties naturally falling to the chief officer
of the organization.

The Development of Bryn Gweled

By 1941 the site for the Homesteads had been chosen, the land
bought and paid for, the surveys completed for the different lots,
roads laid out, and utilities buried in the first area to be developed.
By summer the war in Europe had been going for two years, the
prospect for U.S. involvement was rapidly increasing, and building
materials were getting scarce. The first few families who wanted to
build were letting contracts and scrounging around for supplies.

In the fall of 1941, Ray and Babette Newton became the first
family to move into their house. But almost immediately Ray went
on a trip leaving Babette and their small daughter, Jay Jay, alone in
the house with no lights. One night Babette heard a noise and opened
the door to find a strange man on the doorstep. He thrust a carton of
milk into her hand, and frightened, she slammed the door in his face.
Some days later he came by again and explained that since they had
just moved in he had thought they might be unfamiliar with the
grocery stores in the vicinity, and he was trying to welcome them in

a neighborly way. He warned her that alone as she was she should have a gun. If she'd had a gun, Babette replied, he might not still be around to advise her, since hearing the noise outside that night she'd have shot right through the door and killed him! Perhaps Bryn Gweled's policy forbidding the use of firearms on the property saved at least one life at the outset.

At the housewarming for the Newtons in October, members of the Homesteads sanded and polished woodwork, washed windows, puttied nail holes, filled ditches, graded the lawn and laid flagstones — an enthusiastic and utilitarian welcome for our first family on the land.

Miriam and I were moved in on January 2, 1942, less than a month after Pearl Harbor and U.S. entry into the war. We camped in the house until our sink, which had been missent to Homestead, Pennsylvania, was enrouted to us.

Miriam and I sandpapered and shellacked all the inside woodwork and did some of the outside painting. Kent, who was not yet five, enjoyed every detail, the framing of the house and the roof, putting in partitions, windows and floors, drilling the well, paving the driveway, mixing concrete for the foundation and floor, and all the details which one misses living in an apartment, or moving into a ready-made, let-the-other-fellow-worry kind of a house. He and his playmate Tony Potts also loved playing in the tall bunched grass that grew scattered over much of the land at the Homesteads. They called it "bumple ditty," a name that has stuck to this day.

Unaware that we wouldn't be permanent and continuous residents of the Homesteads, we planted apple and peach trees, sixteen varieties of grapes, boysenberries, red and black raspberries, asparagus, strawberries and a large garden. It seemed we were visited by every variety of insect, bug or beetle that walked, crawled, hopped or flew above, on, or under the earth. With a pitchfork Miriam used to fight off the skunks or ground hogs that came in the bright moonlight to sample the delicious sweet corn when it was just ready to eat.

One cold winter day while we were still getting settled in our house, a young man dressed informally in heavy winter clothes walked into my office in the American Friends Service Committee in Philadelphia. It was Edward Myerding from Rochester, Minnesota. His father was on the staff of the Mayo Clinic and was one of the most famous bone surgeons in the United States. Because Ed was a conscientious objector and didn't want to enlist in the armed services, his father disowned him and told him to leave home. He had hitchhiked all the way to Philadelphia. I took him home with me and he stayed with us several weeks helping us put in shelves and finish up the woodwork in the house and garage. He and his father were later reconciled in our home.

Nearly all the Bryn Gweled houses are modern style architecture. In the early forties these functional and organic homes were largely unknown in the Philadelphia area and we received many derisive comments from the residents in Bucks County. Ray Newton's house had a slanting roof over an upstairs bedroom and a broad deck over the living room where the family could eat or lounge. It was dubbed the "chicken house." Our house had a 20 x 24 foot overhang (nicknamed the "Wilson hangover") between the house and the garage, and our house became known as the "filling station." It was some years after our member architects had begun designing such functional houses before the style swept the Philadelphia area.

Our house was designed by Paul Beidler, a pupil of the great modern architect, Frank Lloyd Wright, and it was featured among other Bryn Gweled homes in illustrated articles in *Progressive Architecture, Pencil Points,*[2] *Living,*[3] and by itself in *Household*[4] magazine. Miriam and the architect planned a small home with no space wasted, a home in which the rooms could expand or be converted from one use to another.

A special feature of this versatile use of rooms was a movable partition between the living room and the study. This consisted of three thick panels with thorough insulation to provide a completely private study or bedroom. When the panels were out and stored in the attic, one could see a more than 180 degree panorama of Bryn Gweled. Two bay windows gave a wide view of the High Woods and the Picnic Woods. There are no fences on Bryn Gweled except around gardens so there are many, many unobstructed views to enjoy.

The large lawn in front of the house was used as a baseball and football field until the community playing fields were prepared. Only one window was a casualty from a stray baseball. The overhang between the house and garage was the coolest place in Bryn Gweled. Since there was so much cross ventilation we never felt the need for air conditioning. Another feature which Miriam proposed was to make all the woodwork flush with the plastering, leaving fewer

[2]March 1946, p. 72.
[3]Autumn 1947, p. 63.
[4]December. 1949, pp. 8p9.

places for dust to collect. Walk-in closets and a large attic provided lots of storage space. The many bookshelves were soon filled with books and albums. Altogether, Paul and Miriam designed a compact, efficient, and very livable house.

There was only one drawback. For seventeen years our family lived in the house only during the summer. Two years after our house was built, I helped launch the Friends Committee on National Legislation in Washington. For the next two years I commuted, getting home some weekends and for a vacation in the summer. Then in 1945 we started a cycle of living in Washington during the school year. The day after school was out Miriam and our sons, Kent and Lee, would return to Bryn Gweled for the summer. Then the day after Labor Day we would haul a truckload of clothes, bicycles, baby cribs, canned fruit and miscellaneous items back to Washington. That schedule involved renting the Bryn Gweled house — often to a member who was building a home or to an applicant — for nine months and the house in Washington for three months during the summer. Neither house was vacant during the seventeen years we kept up that rotation. Miriam and the boys were left with most of the gardening to do, however, since except for my vacation, I was in Washington or on the trek to yearly meetings and conferences.

Since Miriam's death in December 1965, I haven't lived in the house at all, but have based my activities in Washington, D.C., and lived in our house there. During the period of research and writing on *Uphill For Peace* and these memoirs, I have roomed first in Ardmore and then in Haverford, commuting to the Swarthmore College Peace Collection where the FCNL and my own archives are stored. Now my visits to Bryn Gweled are infrequent, but I usually return with a carload of flowers from the 110 different trees and shrubs or perennials which I planted on our lot. Maybe one of the reasons I am so excited and nostalgic about Bryn Gweled is because my responsibilities in Washington have not allowed me to live there continuously.

Until recently when a lifeguard was hired to oversee the swimming pool, there has been no regular paid staff at Bryn Gweled. The community has depended on its members for staffing and upkeep. Work parties at least once a month have done a myriad of activities — planting trees, surveying, painting, mowing, filling in ditches, swimming pool maintenance, and general repairs.

The biggest single project was building the community swimming pool. Members installed the pump and filter system, constructed the shower rooms and the walls and aprons for the pool itself. The day before one Fourth of July fifty-five cubic yards of concrete were delivered, but only one extra man was hired to help with the troweling. The swimming pool is now open from Memorial Day to Labor Day and has been a wonderful socializer and a focal point for summer activities. Two surfaced tennis courts added later are also widely used much of the year.

The Homesteads converted the old carriage shed adjacent to the pool into a community center where monthly meetings of the Homesteads members are held. There are sixteen committees that look after the various concerns of the community — such as children's activities, property and utilities, swimming pool, public relations, pest and safety, membership, soccer, grounds and planting, and so on.

At one time there were nearly one hundred children on the Homesteads. The skilled leadership of parents, often mothers, encouraged a variety of summer programs for them including swimming, archery, painting, nature walks, basket weaving and making bird houses. There was something for almost every taste and size.

Hans Peters engineered the layout for two soccer fields and has been the driving force in the Intercounty Soccer League which is now made up of more than two hundred teams. He is general secretary and games commissioner and among other duties he has the power to call off games on account of inclement weather.

There are now nine Bryn Gweled teams that compete — six boys' teams and three girls' teams. They start with the Pee Wees at seven and run up to nineteen-year-olds. Not only do they play a wide variety of teams in the area northeast of Philadelphia, they have played visiting teams from Brazil and several from Canada. Carolyn Eckel, Hans' daughter, was the first woman in the area to qualify as a soccer referee.

The object in the games has been good sportsmanship. Coaches tried to get all the boys into the game at some time rather than emphasizing winning. But there is a cabinet full of trophies won by the Bryn Gweled teams. Hans has become a national authority on soccer, and many Bryn Gweled members have coached, refereed or transported teams to games in southeastern Pennsylvania.

Naturally in a community of nearly eighty families there are some tensions and sharp differences of opinion. At Bryn Gweled members have held various views on the use of land, particularly the use of the woods and areas set aside as common land. All are interested in ecology, in respect for wildlife, and in the preservation of our beautiful woods and streams. I have belonged to what might be called the utilizationist school of thought that advocated use of unallocated land for raising corn or other food during the war, the maximum use of productive gardens and some check on garden predators like ground hogs which play havoc with crops. I wanted to carry on a relentless warfare against the further encroachments of thorny catbrier, Canada thistles, climbing honeysuckle and poison ivy.

Other members wanted to preserve anything natural and to encourage the birds and wild animals to roam the Homesteads at will. They urged that we lay no hand on catbrier or poison ivy except on our own lots and at the edge of the roadways which are mowed from time to time.

In general this conservationist view has prevailed at Bryn Gweled. While some branches may be removed, sawing up of trees in the woodlots for firewood is forbidden in order to preserve the ecological cycle. Nature is usually allowed free rein on common land. In fact a considerable portion of the common land has recently been set aside in an agreement with the county for its permanent preservation as a wilderness area. Individual gardeners can put up fences, often electrified, to protect their gardens, but there is no hunting or shooting of rabbits, deer, pheasants, raccoons, possums or the many birds which liven the air with their songs.

Another difference of opinion among the Homesteaders has been on membership policy. The procedure has been for applicants to visit one or more monthly Homesteads meetings and to visit as many member families as possible. Later the applicant's references and written views on cooperative living are read in a closed meeting. The applicant must receive an eighty percent favorable vote cast by secret ballot in order to be accepted. The idea was to develop a community with enough ideals and viewpoints in common to make a happy working fellowship. It was hoped that new members would be flexible enough to undergo the give and take of life in a cooperative community, and if physically able would be willing to do their share on work parties or in committees. Since many members hold strong sentiments, applicants are often asked whether they would be happy in a community where there are many pacifists.

Some members object to this procedure of visitation and voting and think that applicants should be accepted without voting — in other words they favor an open membership community. During the past few months there have been many small discussions about membership procedure, but so far there has been no resolution of this division of opinion. Partly because three applicant families recently failed to receive the necessary votes for membership, efforts are being made to improve the procedure of visitation and conferences with the membership committee to increase the chances of acceptance or to counsel applicants that their application might be turned down.

Since the purpose of Bryn Gweled from the beginning was to build a cooperative community and not just an aggregation of people living in adjacent houses, I still favor some such procedure as has been used in the past for acquainting prospective members with the history and ideals of the community and for judging their adaptability to such an association.

Despite such differences of opinion, one of the joys of Bryn Gweled is the variety of occupations and the great diversity of talents in the membership. Just to name some of the different occupations is like going through the yellow pages of the telephone book. The variety of training, skills and crafts has greatly enriched the community.

There are or have been construction and factory workers, secretaries, accountants, engineers and scientists, teachers, administrators, counsellors in private and public schools, colleges and universities. At least seven members have been on the staff of the American Friends Service Committee at some time or other. Three have been Y.W.C.A. secretaries. Three of our several scientists worked in the RCA Research Laboratory at Princeton Junction, New Jersey, and one of them played an important role in the development of color television. One served as president of the Society for Social Responsibility in the Sciences.

Another member spent his life making stained glass windows. Our membership has included artists, painters and musicians, lawyers, writers, editors and journalists. One of our two doctor members moved away to serve as a pathologist in three upstate New York hospitals. A businessman was head of a company that made floor cleaning materials; another was partner in an iron and steel distributing firm.

The outreach in the nearby or the larger United States community has been varied. One neighbor ran successfully for one of the town commissioners' posts and has been in the thick of the struggle over zoning regulations and other problems of local government. Another has been an active participant in the Southampton Volunteer Fire Company which helped control the grass fires that threatened Bryn

Gweled in its early years. Still another resiaent coordinates the work of several hundred volunteers at the Holy Redeemer Hospital nearby.

Members have been active in organizations focusing on peace or race relations, on recreation activities like swimming, square dancing and soccer, on the School Board, the Sewer Authority, Library Board, Home and School Association, Churchville Nature Center, on possible zoning changes, on conservation and protection of the environment, on consumer affairs, on prison visitation, on legislation, and other current good causes. The Homesteads does not officially sponsor organizations and movements but encourages members to participate in such activities on their own initiative and responsibility.

The children of Bryn Gweled residents have scattered from Boston to California and Oregon and are employed in a dazzling array of occupations and enterprises. They plan a reunion in August 1976. At the present time there are five second-generation Bryn Gweled residents.

So far as we know, Bryn Gweled is the oldest and largest nonchurch-related cooperative and intentional community in the United States. It was founded to give our children an opportunity to know that people of various ethnic, religious, economic, professional, vocational, political and national categories could live together and that this would be the most valuable experience for living in the world.

What is the value of Bryn Gweled? It is those undefinable and indescribable ties of friendship developed over the years from common endeavor, from shared experiences, from understandings hewn out of vigorous discussion and debate. Obviously seventy-seven families can't get to know each other intimately. Smaller groups tend to develop their own close friendships. One's relation to others is partly determined by one's own readiness to reach out to communicate and reciprocate. The original members forged close ties in those weekly meetings that crystallized Bryn Gweled from a romantic vision and a vague desire for a creative new fellowship of living to its realization. A lot of hard work went into backfilling utility ditches and other work projects in the early days. The covered dish suppers in the summertime with tables laden with all sorts of tempting delicacies, the evenings of folk dancing and other group activities were important welding factors. I can only hope that later Bryn Gweled members could and did experience the depth of fellowship that those of us in on the creation felt.

In May 1975, the Bryn Gweled Homesteads celebrated its thirty-fifth anniversary as a successful cooperative, with the joys and satisfactions and problems inherent in building a community of people with many common but also rather divergent interests. What has made Bryn Gweled succeed as well as it has when so many cooperative ventures have failed? Different people would give different answers, and no one answer would suffice. One answer is that Bryn Gweled was founded with high ideals and with a membership determined to put them into practice. The founders hoped to:

> Establish, maintain, and develop a homestead community for the mutual benefit of all its members, who are seeking stable, productive homes on adequate ground, free from land speculation, with the positive advantages of land controlled by the community, permanent provision for recreation and a wholesome outdoor life, opportunity for individual freedom and creative initiative, as well as for sharing in the responsibility for and development of community facilities and activities. [5]

Another factor in its success has been the quality of the people it attracted, people with a high sense of responsibility to themselves and to others. Still another factor has been the emphasis on wide sharing of leadership, with nobody being "king" or "queen." The fact that decisions have been cooperative rather than imposed has given members a sense of participation in the affairs of the Homesteads. There has been a nice blend of cooperation and individual freedom and an encouraging sense of tolerance among all segments of the community.

Frustrations can be worked off cutting weeds or grass, raising a garden, swimming in the pool or in many other ways. I don't want to give the impression that Homestead members are saints or that there have been no problems. But the process of sharing work and recreation, fun and sadness, ideas and decision making in the Homesteads has knit together what I think is a unique experiment. One description of Bryn Gweled captures the essence of our cooperative venture in this way:

> The significance of Bryn Gweled is in our dream and the ability to make our dream a reality. It is not only the land and all our homesteads, the members and their families. It encompasses and

---

[5]Articles of Incorporation and By-laws, Bryn Gweled Homesteads, DG 70, Series A-1, Box 8, Folder: Bryn Gweled Homesteads, SCPC.

is dependent upon values we cannot prove statistically, nor touch nor see. It is a vision of a way of life based on the belief in the importance and the fundamental dignity of the individual, and the necessity for individuals to work together responsibly to build a community. [6]

[6]"Bryn Gweled Homesteads, the Story since 1939," DG 70, Series A-1, Box 8, Folder Bryn Gweled Homesteads, SCPC.

CHAPTER 14

The Struggle for Peace and Cooperation in the Churches

Once, during a banquet I attended at the Cosmos Club in Washington, I found myself seated beside an old friend of mine, retired Congressman Brooks Hays from Little Rock. When I asked him what he had been doing with himself since his retirement from Congress, he replied with a smile that he was an "ecumaniac" — working in an ecumenical institute for greater cooperation among religious groups. Perhaps I could call myself an "ecumaniac" too because much of my life has been spent in efforts with various religious groups to foster more exchange of information and to stimulate greater common action on the great unsolved problems of humanity about which the churches should be doing much, much more, both individually and in concert. A great deal of my concern over the years has been not only in working for greater cooperation between religious groups, but in encouraging greater participation by the church in seeking to influence government and society to build a more just, humane and peaceful world.

I was engaged in ecumenical activities during my three years as a student in New York City when I was in close touch with the leadership in the student YMCA and the student YWCA, and took an active part in the Student Volunteer Movement for Foreign Missions. All of these organizations cut across denominational lines. There was increasing ferment in all of them about issues of war and peace, and racial and social justice.

For a time I served on the executive committee of the Student Volunteer Movement (SVM) and became acquainted with the very fine traveling secretaries, Robert P. Wilder, founder of the SVM, and his associates, Milton Stauffer and Stan Pier. The SVM emphasized a world view of man's spiritual needs. The crosscurrents of discussion in missionary circles were a helpful background for my year's residence in Japan which followed my study in New York City.

THE REFORMED PRESBYTERIAN CHURCH —
BEYOND EXODUS AND LEVITICUS

An effort of mine to encourage a stronger peace stand on the part of the churches was directed toward my own denomination, the Reformed Presbyterian Church. In August 1934, I spent three days at Winona Lake, Indiana, where the Annual Synod, or legislative body of the Reformed Presbyterians, was meeting in conjunction with the Women's Synodical and the Young People's Convention. This was while I was still a member of that church which I had joined as a boy. About twelve hundred of the 6700 membership had gathered for this meeting.

The Reformed Presbyterians, or Covenanters, were Protestant dissenters who had broken away from the established church in Scotland and Ireland before the Society of Friends had been founded. They suffered a great deal of persecution in their native countries and sacrificed a number of martyrs to the faith before many of them emigrated to the United States.

In America the Reformed Presbyterians took a position of political dissent, refusing to vote because they believed the Constitution did not recognize the supreme authority of God and the Bible. Only recently have the Covenanters allowed their members elective franchise. Some of us, including my brother Ralph and I, wanted to expand the church's dissent to include a strong antiwar stand, and we tried to push as hard as we could at this 1934 Synod for a renunciation of war by the denomination.

Dr. Walter McCarroll, a New York City minister who was a strong pacifist and a good friend of mine and who served as chairman of the Committee on International and Social Justice of the Reformed Presbyterians, opened the issue by reading to the Synod a long antiwar paper. He then presented a resolution which, though it had been considerably modified and weakened by the committee, did, when adopted, put the denomination on record in support of members who might choose to be conscientious objectors.

Three of us then drafted another stronger antiwar resolution which said in part that war was unchristian because it was contrary to the life and teachings of Jesus Christ. "If these premises are correct," it continued, "it follows that no Christian should engage in any war for any purpose whatsoever, nor give it his sanction or approval." The resolutions committee agreed with the analysis, but gagged on the conclusion.

Several members of the church, among them George Coleman, a professor at Geneva College and perhaps the best informed man in the church, and my cousin Bruce Willson, now president of Pittsburgh Seminary which trains ministers for the denomination, opposed such a stand on war. Their argument was that it was clear that God had commanded wars in Biblical times. While none of the wars in the past three hundred years appeared to have been ordered by God, and while it seemed unlikely that God would, in the future, step out and command the Covenanters to slay their Christian brethren, still, war might be God's judgment again, and it was not the place of the church to take a stand against what He might ordain.

The final debate on the issue, which took place after I had left for another engagement, was limited to twenty minutes — hardly time enough to consider in depth the enormity of modern war, nor to review a three-hundred-year-old theological position which the church was unready to change.

I used to chide the church fathers that it was very hard for them to get past Exodus and Leviticus and face seriously the life and teachings of Jesus Christ as they might apply to today's world. I have often said, tongue in cheek, that if we could just get the Christians to give up war, I believed the pagans would be doggone glad to.

THE NATIONAL COUNCIL OF CHURCHES

For nearly forty years I worked in a variety of programs of the Federal Council of Churches and its successor, the National Council of Churches (NCC), and for much of that time I was a member of one or more committees of the cooperative agency of the Protestant churches in the United States.

When I landed in Portland, Oregon, on the evening of February 22, 1965, to attend the four-day General Board of Meeting of the National Council of Churches, several friends of mine, including one of the vice-presidents, said to me: "Raymond, you must bring in a resolution on Vietnam. Nothing has been prepared by the staff nor by the Executive Committee which met today."

So at breakfast I wrote out a draft resolution on the back of an envelope, got the necessary co-sponsors, and introduced the measure by title when new business was called for. Then Vernon Ferwerda, National Council staff member for International Relations in Washington, D.C., and I worked on possible language for more than half a day with frequent phone calls to New York and Washington. When we were reasonably satisfied with the draft, it went to the Committee on Reference and Counsel which acted as a review and steering committee for proposed actions.

The draft language as it came out of this process was mimeographed and distributed and then slated for consideration immediately after lunch the third day. As the Board recessed for lunch that day I was told that a delegate from Princeton who disagreed with one of my points was all ready to shoot the resolution down when it was brought up for action. I got hold of him and we talked it over at luncheon, rewriting it until both he and I felt we could accept it. Then I rushed to the office secretary who typed and mimeographed it in fifteen minutes so I could take the revised resolution to the Board as it convened. Though it took a bit of awkward maneuvering with the chairman after the meeting started to replace the draft already circulated with our revised version, the resolution was adopted in substantially the form in which it was presented. It read in part:

> Conscious that there are many difficulties and dilemmas facing our country in negotiations for political settlement, but mindful also of the seriousness of prolonged military conflict, the danger of escalation of hostilities, and the possibility of a third World War:

> The General Board of the National Council of Churches urges the United States Government:

> To engage in persistent efforts to negotiate a cease-fire and a settlement of the war which will attempt to achieve the independence, freedom and self-determination of the people of South Vietnam;

> To utilize United Nations assistance in achieving a solution and in seeking to reduce the area of conflict by effective border control and internal policing; and

> To give bold and creative leadership to a broad international development program for the Mekong Region and to continue fullscale U.S. economic and technical assistance where necessary.

> The General Board pledges support and cooperation in the urgent tasks of reconciliation and reconstruction in Vietnam. [1]

---

[1] "Resolutions by the National Council of Churches," SCPC.

The next morning there were two parallel columns on the front page of a Portland newspaper. In one President Johnson declared that the United States would not negotiate. The other column carried the NCC statement that the U.S. must negotiate a cease-fire and settlement if we were to end the war in Vietnam.

I have served since 1963 as a member of the General Board, now the Governing Board, of the National Council of Churches representing the Philadelphia Yearly Meeting of Friends. I have been a member at one time or another of the Program Board of the Division of Christian Life and Mission, the Department of International Affairs, the Government Relations Committee, the Unit Section on Human Need, and the Nominating Committee. This account deals largely with my participation in the Governing Board and with the National Conferences on World Order, and does not attempt to portray the variety and importance of the wide range of NCC activities nor my relationship with them. My service on the Governing Board terminated in October 1975.

Though the NCC holds one Board meeting a year in New York City where its home office is located, the other Board sessions are scheduled in different parts of the country in order to encourage wide participation of churchmen outside of the East Coast. Board meetings have been held in Washington, D.C.; Baltimore; Pittsburgh; Indianapolis; Chicago; Des Moines; Portland, Oregon; San Diego; Tulsa, Oklahoma; Houston, Texas; New Orleans; and Atlanta. I have been able to attend all these and the triennial General Assemblies which met in Philadelphia, Miami Beach and Detroit.

My interest in Board meetings has been to encourage actions on pronouncements and resolutions which would give the Council authorization for projects which it should undertake, or which would define positions on crucial issues to member churches or to the government. Pronouncements are basic formulations of policy. Resolutions update or apply the implications of pronouncements previously adopted. It is not that resolutions are so important in themselves, but that they provide a basis for action. Among the issues I either took some initiative in drafting or defended on the floor were statements on world hunger, the abolition of poverty, disarmament, conscription, the rights of conscience, the selective objector, the Vietnam War, the United Nations, the Mideast and guaranteed income.

On occasion there is not time enough for adequate preparation or for sustained consideration of specific measures in Board meetings, but after participating in this process for ten years, I feel that the pronouncements and resolutions represent, on the whole, courage, timeliness and foresight. They have not always gone as far as I wanted. The Council has never, for example, taken an outright and unequivocal stand on the renunciation of war. Some resolutions, however, have reflected bold but controversial positions, and have taken stands unpopular with many parishioners, as did the NCC support of minority groups and its statement upholding the rights of the United Farm Workers to organize and bargain collectively and its subsequent call upon members of the churches to boycott nonunion grapes and lettuce. Often the NCC is ahead of its time. Long before Nixon and Kissinger ever visited China conferences initiated by the National Council recommended the resumption of diplomatic, economic and cultural ties with the People's Republic of China. Some of the severest criticism has been leveled at the National Council because of such stands on controversial issues. But if the churches are to be relevant today, they have to speak out forthrightly on issues with which not all of their members are in accord.

The National Council, among its many other major activities, has made sustained efforts for the victims of war and hunger through its agency, Church World Service. At the present time there is a determined push to get the U.S. to ship more grain to the neediest nations and for the NCC through the World Hunger Task Force, to coordinate Protestant and Orthodox hunger programs with their Roman Catholic and Jewish counterparts.

While peace has been one of its priorities for several years, the Council has done less in the field of international affairs and world disarmament than I had hoped it would. I wanted the NCC to recruit the best persons they could find to work on the political and economic problems of world disarmament. One person might follow the bilateral negotiations between the United States and the Soviet Union in Helsinki and Vienna, the Eighteen Nation Disarmament Conference in Geneva, the work of the United Nations Secretariat in New York and the Arms Control and Disarmament Agency in Washington in order to exercise, as far as possible, the influence of the churches on international negotiations. Another staff member could initiate a campaign for conversion from military spending to civilian programs and seek ways to encourage reduction of armament expenditures. Many economists say this could be done without creating a depression if the appropriate political decisions are made. Unfortunately, instead of providing such broad scale leadership, the

NCC, partly for financial reasons, has been forced to close its liaison office with international agencies in the Church Center for the United Nations. For most of the calendar year 1974 the Council has not even had one full-time staff member at work on international affairs. Now Alice Wimer and Rev. Eileen W. Lindner are staff persons on international affairs and peace.

CONFERENCES ON WORLD ORDER

As a representative of Friends agencies I was an active participant in all six of the Conferences of the Churches on Peace and World Order, and was usually on one or more of the section-drafting committees drawing up findings of the Conferences. The first two conferences were held under the auspices of the Federal Council of Churches, and the last four were organized by its successor, the National Council of Churches. The first was held in Delaware, Ohio, in 1942, and others followed in Cleveland in 1945, 1949, 1953, 1958, and in St. Louis in 1963.

These conferences did not speak officially for the National Council nor for the member denominations. Each conference adopted a brief message to the churches. The substantive findings were discussed and debated but not acted on as official pronouncements. They were to be considered as serious formulations for study and possible action by the churches. These findings did have considerable influence on the thinking of many church members, and usually the pertinent recommendations were taken up by delegation or letter with key officials in Washington, including the President. Each conference served as a steppingstone in the evolution of church opinion in these two tumultuous decades.

I wish that church conferences today could play the role they used to in reaching consensus and influencing action. It leaves with us the unanswered question how to persuade people to accept and act upon the essential changes in society which must be made if we are to achieve and maintain a world of justice and peace.

The first conference at Delaware, Ohio, in March 1942, gave primary consideration to the political, economic and social reconstruction of the world which was being devastated by the Second World War. The findings spoke out strongly even then on the need for drastic change in our racial policy — twelve years before the Supreme Court decision of 1954 outlawed segregation. The report stressed the need for international machinery for world order, and considered at length the kind of problems to be met in a peace settlement and in the immediate postwar period such as hunger, refugees, prisoners of war and reconstruction.

Sensitive to the kind of problems to be faced after the war, the conference advocated that:

> The efforts of the peoples of the world be devoted, in proportion to their ability, to the reestablishment of order, the provisions of food, shelter and medical service, and the restoration of stable government and economic activity, especially in the devastated territories. These emergency measures must include policing by joint action of minorities and disarmed populations, and positive measures of economic and cultural cooperation. They should be carried out under international authorities, representative of all peoples concerned. There should be no punitive reparations, no humiliating decrees of war guilt, and no arbitrary dismemberment of nations. All of these emergency measures should tend toward a growing structure of international order. [2]

"We believe," the Conference continued, "that:

> As Christian citizens, we must seek to translate our beliefs into practical realities and to create a public opinion which will insure that the United States shall play its full and essential part in the creation of a moral way of international living. [3]

The Second Conference on a Just and Durable Peace, held in Cleveland in January 1945, concerned itself with suggesting improvements in the Dumbarton Oaks Proposals, the first major draft for the United Nations Charter, which had been drawn up the preceding October. The Conference made a number of recommendations: that there should be progressive subordination of force to law, that a Special Commission on Human Rights and Fundamental Freedoms should be established, that eventual universal membership in the United Nations should be encouraged, and that the Charter should be easier to amend. While the findings urged more specific provisions for limiting and reducing armaments, this recommendation was not as strong as it should have been in my judgment.

In other matters, the Conference urged economic cooperation between nations despite their political differences, and it made specific recommendations for an effective peace settlement:

---

[2]"A Message from the National Study Conference on the Churches and a Just and Durable Peace," March, 1942, pp. 18-19. DG 48, Series 1, Box 5, Folder: "The Commission To Study a Just and Durable Peace." SCPC.

[3]Ibid., p. 13.

The settlement should make possible the reconciliation of victors and vanquished. . . .The partition of Germany into separate states should not be imposed upon the German people. The treatment of Germany should be calculated to strengthen the forces within that country committed to liberal civil policies and to international cooperation. . . .

We cannot in good conscience be a party to the dismantling of Japanese colonial possessions without at the same time insisting that the imperialism of the white man shall be brought to the speediest possible end. We cannot have a sound or stable world community so long as there is enforced submissions of one people to the will of another whether in Korea, in India, in the Congo, in Puerto Rico or anywhere else. [4]

Instead of incorporating these suggestions into the peace treaties, however, the postwar settlement left a divided Korea and Germany and an escalating nuclear arms race. The Third Conference on World Order convened in this troubled atmosphere in 1949, just after the North Atlantic Pact had been negotiated, but before the final text was released. The Conference's theme was "The Moral Use of Power," but this conference seemed to me unsatisfactory because it accepted too much the spirit of the Cold War and failed to grapple seriously enough with the burgeoning arms race. Granted the extreme difficulties of making progress on either of these two issues, the prophetic role of the churches seemed to be dampened.

John Foster Dulles, who had played a leading and quite a constructive role in two previous conferences, and who was later to serve as Secretary of State in the Eisenhower Administration, and Charles Bohlen, later to be Ambassador to the Soviet Union, explained the new pact in general terms and seemed to me quite anxious to have the Conference adopt it in principle.

It seemed incongruous to many of us in the Conference that the churchmen might give their blessing to the arming of one group of Christians against another even for the purpose of deterring war. Many of us felt that the better way to build international security in an unsettled world would be to place primary emphasis on worldwide disarmament rather than to rely on regional military alliances such as the North Atlantic pact. Our argument was that an all-out effort should be mounted for general disarmament and for strengthening

---

[4]"A Message to the Churches from the National Study Conference on the Churches and a Just and Durable Peace," Cleveland, January 16-19, 1945, pp. 12-13. DG 48, Series 1, Box 5, Folder: "The Commission To Study the Bases for a Just and Durable Peace," SCPC.

international security through using and improving the United Nations.

The FCNL had already taken a strong position against the Truman Doctrine of unilateral military aid to Greece and Turkey, believing that policy would lead, as it did, to a series of unfortunate military actions, including the landing of troops in Lebanon in 1958, in the Dominican Republic in 1965, and the anomaly of armed conflict between the Turks and Greeks in Cyprus in 1974 using largely American military arms. The Vietnam War too was in the Truman Doctrine tradition.

In the end the Conference urged the U.S. Senate not to ratify the Pact until citizens had a chance to fully understand its meaning.

In this and later conferences Dulles was more the Cold Warrior than he had been in the two early conferences, and he was a strong advocate of some policies which seemed to me disastrous. I felt that while the churches should recognize the immense difficulties of improving relations with the communist world, they should go more than half way in seeking understanding, mutual exchange and reconciliation. I often found myself in deep disagreement with Dulles, but he was always friendly and courteous to me personally.

At another of these conferences John Foster Dulles had said to some of us dissidents that when the drafting committee had completed its proposed text that they would call in representatives of our minority point of view to comment on them before they were considered final. It was a generous move on his part that I appreciated. Norman Whitney and I were appointed spokesmen. About 2 a.m. the telephone summoned us to a sleepy-eyed drafting committee sitting around a table drinking strong coffee. Not all of our points were accepted, but at least we had our hearing before the text of the findings was released to the conference the next day for discussion and acceptance.

A number of us attending this Third Conference on World Order were dissatisfied with the results of the meeting. We were unhappy (1) that the preliminary text of the findings went as far as it did in accepting the idea of regional pacts while admitting that they would add to insecurity if their words concealed what was essentially a military alliance, (2) that in considering the moral uses of power not enough emphasis was placed on reducing military power and pressing for far-reaching disarmament, and (3) that while in no sense the injustices and totalitarianism of the communist world should be ignored, it was time to try harder for detente.

Some of us talked about introducing a minority report, but finally settled for a very unsatisfactory footnote registering dissent on certain points. In retrospect I think we should have insisted on a clearcut statement of our views in the conference findings. I have always striven for consensus where possible, but believe consensus is wrong when it is papered over by compromising deeply held principles. Absolute right and wrong is seldom clear in complex political issues, but that does not excuse us from the responsibility of making judgments to the best of our ability.

In his article, "Footnote to Cleveland," published in *The Christian Century* for December 9, 1953, A.J. Muste wrote, regarding the fourth conference in this series, that:

> The general trend (in these conferences) has been toward less "controversy," more "unanimity." Cleveland 1953 went farthest in this direction. . . .The impact of all these conferences has been to put the American churches back of the Administration of the moment and of the internationalist elements in the major parties, to give sanction in effect to World War II and the Korean War, to avoid revolutionary analysis and proposals, to play down the prophetic and to hew out a "responsible," practical middle-of-the-road line. . . .We live in an era of permanent though as yet limited war. [5]

Muste believed the object of the promoters "was to come out with a program which would strengthen the hands of Mr. Eisenhower and Mr. Dulles, not one which would cause them any concern."[6]

On the train from Cleveland after the conference I jotted down a few of my reactions to this conference, the most disappointing of the series. While the Delaware Conference had opposed military alliances and the previous conference had withheld its support of the proposed North Atlantic Treaty, this conference had supported NATO and the current collective defense system. The major issues were whether the church should bless the Korean War and be an instrument in the Cold War, and whether a church conference should hand over its supposed ecumenical view and responsibility in order to give religious sanction to regional military alliances.

I wrote in part:

> To a layman unversed in the deviousness of contemporary theology and somewhat calloused to ecclesiastical rationale, it seemed that in many common "matters of the law" the decisions were earnest steps forward ranging from the timid to the

[5]p. 1421.

[6]Ibid., p. 1420.

courageous. But when the chips were down, the bite was on, and the hands were counted pro and con, on several issues that strike deep for the Christian conscience, churchmen voted for Christian smugness as against the open road to God, for the relative ethics of Niebuhr rather than the universality of Gandhi, for the methods of war and militarism to gain the ends of peace, for supporting collective defense arrangements and armament as over against universal disarmament, for aligning the church with military expediency rather than the all-out effort at reconciliation and the attempt to change enemies into friends. . . .

The conference had just glibly asked our government, which is up to its ears in the cold war, to make its technical assistance programs free from subordination to military and strategic considerations, only to turn right around and bless NATO, one of the major instruments in the cold war. The commission report was asking for efforts toward universal disarmament and then called for a military program insisting on billions and billions of dollars, the conscription of millions of men and wielding the threat of hydrogen war as a deterrent to war. Church members have often castigated their government for talking out of both sides of its mouth at the same time, but here was a church conference doing it in the same breath. [7]

The last three conferences were not as prophetic and hard-hitting as they should have been. This was partly because of lack of time for discussion, partly because of lack of radical challenge from the speakers, partly because of the make-up of the membership of the conference. They did not speak out boldly against the Second World War, the Korean War, the H-Bomb, the whole nuclear build-up, and the basic injustices of our economic system.

On November 15, 1965, I wrote a four-page letter to Kenneth L. Maxwell and Leonard J. Kramer, executive director and associate director of the International Affairs Commission of the National Council, who had been in charge of the preparations for the Sixth World Order Conference in St. Louis. Evaluating the conference I said:

The conference emphasized consensus rather than prophecy, although many of the statements were ahead of the rank and file. Perhaps that was the purpose of this conference. On the other hand, we are still faced with the question of how we do get prophetic challenges. They are difficult to evoke from committees

---

[7]E. Raymond Wilson, "Hangover from Cleveland World Order Study Conference, 1953," in ERW Occasional Papers, Vol. VIII, SCPC.

and conferences.

> The Conference never did squarely confront the moral issue of the character and enormity of modern war. . . .

> The statements were very long on advice to the Government and very short on facing the inadequacy of the church (inadequacies of intention, machinery, finances, and vigor) in doing its part to build the public opinion necessary if the recommendations of the conference are to be achieved. . . .

> The conference was short on humility; I noticed in the reports that we were well into section five before there was much emphasis on humility and repentance for our selfishness in this society in which we live. In the section meeting dealing with the question of Vietnam, for example, the paragraph which attempted to state some of the effects of the war on the United States itself was deleted. . . .The Vietnam statement was achieved by cutting two corners sharply. One was any serious judgment of the war. The second was any adequate recognition of the great difficulties of settlement and reconstruction.

The very rules under which the conference was conducted conspired against the adoption of adequate statements. In the letter I wrote, "what is needed is a technique which moves away from Roberts' Rules of Order to the Quaker process of synthesis, a process admittedly difficult in so large and diverse a group." As an illustration of what I meant, Herman Reissig and Dean Griffiths both championed statements on Taiwan during the discussion of China policy, but neither was as adequate a statement as might have been written. I was sitting behind them and conferred with them about an alternative statement which they both accepted and which seemed to the three of us preferable to either that had been previously considered. I was standing at the microphone to present the synthesized version when Huber Klemme was recognized just ahead of me to move the previous question, and discussion on the issue was closed. There are a variety of techniques for achieving synthesis when it may be a matter of views which can be reconciled or language which can be clarified; but these can get short-circuited in the formal parliamentary procedure.

Unfortunately the recommendations which were adopted by the Sixth Conference on such issues as food for peace, and economic and social development, which were to be crucial issues in the ensuing Congress, were never even printed. The International Affairs Commission failed to present the proposals to the General Board in a form ready to be acted upon.

One problem which we often faced in these meetings was just how specific to make the resolutions. The General Board preferred not to endorse or oppose specific bills in Congress partly because measures were so often radically changed before coming to final vote. Thus the Board's statements tended to reflect general principles. The Christians have had the Ten Commandments and the Beatitudes before them for two thousand years. How often do they apply them and just what do they mean in today's world?

A similar dilemma we regularly confronted in the conferences was the choice between the ideal and the possible. The 1945 conference put this choice in these words:

> Christians must act in situations as they exist and must decide what God's will demands of them there. At all times they must keep the ultimate goals clearly in view, but they have equal responsibility to mark out attainable goals, and support them. An idealism which does not accept the discipline of the achievable may lose its power for good and ultimately lend aid to forces with whose purpose it cannot agree. [8]

While working on the achievable goals, however, the churches must keep proclaiming the ultimate goals toward which humanity must strive, and they must resist being easily satisfied with compromises.

As I reread now, years afterward, the reports of these six conferences, often hammered out by drafting committees in the wee small hours of the early morning, and often not subject to enough sustained discussions, I think that while they were often sketchy on the need for revolutionary social change and on the immoral character of modern war, they represented, on the whole, a remarkably solid effort on the part of churchmen to speak on the crucial issues of the time. They deserved more study and action than they received. While they did not always cry out with the blazing light of the prophetic, by and large they spoke earnestly, thoughtfully and courageously to their fellow churchmen about the complex issues to be resolved if peace and world order were to be achieved and maintained.

DETROIT CONFERENCE ON THE CHURCH AND WAR

One gathering I participated in which did strike a prophetic note

---

[8]"A Message to the Churches from the National Study Conference on the Churches and a Just and Durable Peace," Cleveland, 1945, pp. 9-10, DG 48, Series 1, Box 5, Folder "The Commission To Study a Just and Durable Peace," SCPC.

during this same period was the four-day Conference on the Church and War held in Detroit in December 1953. This representative conference of churchmen from eighteen denominations was sponsored by the Historic Peace Churches, the Fellowship of Reconciliation and a dozen denominational pacifist fellowships. It was a follow-up of a similar conference held in Detroit in May 1950, just before the outbreak of the Korean War.

The conference called on the church to "disentangle itself without reservation from violence and war, from allegiance to class or color or any narrow nationalism." The closing words of the conference message were: "We believe that it is God's will for his church that peace, with all that it involves of repentance, sacrifice, dedication and discipline, be the dominant witness of Christians amid the strife and violence of our time."[9]

THE THIRD ASSEMBLY IN NEW DELHI
OF THE WORLD COUNCIL OF CHURCHES

Picture more than a thousand participants marching four abreast with the bishops and other dignitaries in their white, black, blue, pink and variegated robes from the convention hall to the Shamiana, the big tent put up for the public sessions in the rear of the Vigyam Bhavan where the regular sessions were held. The various Orthodox delegations in their flowing black robes, their black headdresses, their resplendent chains and crosses, their long hair and full beards stood out in sharp contrast to the business suits or Sunday dresses which some of us un-ecclesiastical laity wore.

This was the lively spectacle which greeted us as churchmen convened for the opening worship service of the Third Assembly of the World Council of Churches on Sunday, November 19, 1961. This parade of colors and personalities took place under a sunny Indian sky and included men and women from every race and continent. There had never before been a Christian gathering representative of so wide a diversity both of historical background and of geographical extent. The nearly two hundred churches included some bodies that were the most ancient in Christian history and others that were the fruits of missionary work of the last century. Representatives came from sixty countries. It was estimated that the T.V. showing of the procession reached thirty-four million people in the United States alone.

---

[9]A fuller report of the conference can be found in Herman Will, Jr.'s, article, "Urge Church To Break with War," *The Christian Century* (December 30, 1953): 1532-33.

In speaking of the keen concern of Asian churches for unity, the Baptist delegate from Burma in his opening sermon said that the divided condition of the churches could no longer be excused on historical grounds: "The ecumenical movement has grown with great force in Asia because Christians have come to see that in Christ they really belong to each other as they belong to Him."[10] This opening sermon reflected the concern with ecumenical unity and cooperation evident throughout the seventeen-day conference.

The bonds of the spirit were stronger than the boundaries of language or nationalism. My neighbor on the left in the plenary sessions was from Germany and spoke virtually no English, but he sang the hymns in a strong clear German. Our common worship service, a blend of English, German and French, had been printed in advance and sent from Geneva. In addition to these three official languages, the simultaneous translation system included Russian and Spanish.

One of the high moments on the second day of the Assembly was the reception into membership in the World Council of twenty-three different churches including the Orthodox Churches of Russia, Bulgaria, Poland and Rumania which enlarged the Christian fellowship across deep political divisions. Unfortunately the representatives from the East German member churches had not been given visas to attend the Assembly so our representation was not complete. Two Pentecostal churches from Chile were admitted along with one church from North America, four from Asia, one other from Latin America, and eleven from Africa. The World Council in its membership, in its deliberations and in its outlook had a unique opportunity to transcend political and ideological barriers and to view problems and fellowship from a global standpoint.

The formal sessions were heavily freighted with theological verbiage and philosophical discussions which would have overwhelmed, if not outraged, the early Christians and the early Quakers. To them the living Christ was a vivid personal experience instead of a thick cloud of ecclesiastical wordage. That part of the sessions tended to leave a layman Quaker stone cold. In the plenary sessions the first three or four days there was no mention specifically of the problems of peace, and it remained for a nonchristian, Prime Minister Nehru, to speak most directly on the issue later in the program.

---

[10]W.A. Visser 'T Hooft, ed., *The New Delhi Report: The Third Assembly of the World Council of Churches, 1961* (New York: Association Press, 1962), p. 3.

When the Central Committee held an open hearing I appealed to them to make the issue of war and the establishment of peace a central priority in emphasis, staff, studies and finance. It seemed to me unfortunate that the suggestion was shunted to the Commission of the Churches on International Affairs rather than accepted as a central challenge to the World Council as a whole. I followed this effort up later with a personal appeal to Dr. Franklin Fry who was chairman of the World Council Central Committee, but without noticeable results.

Three of us, including Dr. Dahlberg, for three years president of the National Council of Churches in the United States, appealed to Mrs. Kathleen M. Bliss of England who was chairman of the Message Committee, to stress peace in the message to be drafted as the voice of the Assembly. Later we learned that the Message Committee decided not to receive statements from individuals — as if the Lord spoke only through committees.

For detailed consideration of the responsibilities of the church, the Assembly was divided into three sections on Witness, Service and Unity. In addition there were nearly twenty committees on specific concerns. I was a member of the Service Section.

When the drafting committee presented its preliminary report to the Service Section, many members were greatly disappointed in the paragraphs on disarmament and on the responsibility of the churches in peace and international affairs. The draft had about as much fire as the ice in the veins of a turtle. I felt the chairman had made a deliberate attempt to avoid serious consideration of disarmament and security by diverting the discussion and cutting short debate. Later Walter Muelder, dean of the School of Theology of Boston University, proposed a really strong statement which was considerably watered down by the drafting committee. The five improvements in the draft which I submitted apparently got lost in the shuffle and were never considered by the drafting committee. Even so, the final draft as printed was very much better than the original version.

Near the end of the Assembly a very fine "Appeal to All Governments and Peoples" was adopted after various referrals for redrafting. This appeal said in part:

> Today, war itself is a common enemy. War is an offense to the nature of man. . . .Let there be restraint and self-denial in the things which make for war, patience and persistence in seeking to

resolve the things which divide, and boldness and courage in grasping the things which make for peace. . . .

To halt the race in arms is imperative. Complete and general disarmament is the accepted goal, and concrete steps must be taken to reach it. . . .

To build peace with justice, barriers of mutual distrust must be attacked at every level. . . .

To enhance mutual trust, nations should be willing to run reasonable risks for peace. . . .

For the achievement of peace with justice, we pledge our unremitting efforts and call upon the Churches for their support in action and in prayer. [11]

After my experience at the Assembly, I felt very strongly that the Society of Friends should continue to be active members of the WCC. I have defended our membership in the National and the World Councils against proposals to withdraw support in sessions of the Iowa and Indiana Yearly Meetings. Friends have a good deal to contribute, with their ideas on peace, the laity, baptism of the spirit, their method of conducting meetings, and their emphasis on service.

I think, too, that we Friends have a great deal to learn from our fellow Christians, and that we should stand shoulder to shoulder with them on religious liberty, on aid and service to refugees, on protests against oppression, on the rights of all races and minorities — stands on which the attitude of the Assembly on the whole was forward-looking and instructive.

On August 15, 1969, defending active Quaker membership in the WCC and the NCC, I told the Iowa Yearly Meeting:

If we have nothing to learn from our Christian brethren in the other churches, may God forgive our spiritual blindness. If we have nothing to share with our Christian brethren, may God forgive our spiritual nakedness.

A Visit to Kenya

On the way back to the United States from the World Council

---

[11] Ibid., pp. 280-281.

Assembly I stopped for ten days in Kenya. This, with the exception of a brief stopover in Cairo once, was my first and only visit to Africa.

The trip was an exciting experience for two reasons. First, Kenya was to receive its independence from England the next year, and I had some instructive interviews with leading figures in Kenya on the principles which should be incorporated into the new constitution. Second, it was a joy to visit so many African Quakers in their homes and communities.

I talked with several members of the Legislative Council, a small unicameral body. Humphrey Slade, the speaker and presiding officer, told me that all the legislators had been invited to London for the drafting of the new constitution. He seemed a very fair-minded person and it was a pleasure to visit with him. Briefly I met with Mrs. Priscilla Abwao, a Quaker and, I believe, the only woman member of the Legislative Council. I was impressed by the high ideals of K.R. Shah, a legislator who had been born in India and whose great interest was in trying to overcome discrimination based on race or nationality. There was deep political rivalry between the Kikuyus and other tribes in Kenya and also resentment against many of the aliens from other countries — the English who owned much of the good farm land and dominated the government, and the people from India who were enterprising merchants and bankers.

A fourth legislator I talked with was Taita Towett, the Minister of Labour, Security and Land. He spoke quite frankly about the difficulties and necessity of establishing self-government.

Among many other interviews, I had a talk with W.B. Akatsa, whose job as Assistant Secretary on Localization was to get Africans into key posts in the government to replace the British as fast as qualified Kenyans could be found or trained. Of the 13,000 senior posts in the Kenya government, only about a thousand had thus far been filled with native Kenyans.

I did a bit of leisurely lobbying with John Porter, an English-born Kenyan who took Thomas Lung'aho, Walter Martin of the British Friends Service Council, and me to lunch in the Legislative Council dining room. His great interest was in agricultural development, but we raised questions of women's rights and of religious liberties in Kenya. He admitted that he had not given serious consideration to their place in the propsective constitution, but said that he should and would do so.

The second experience that made the visit to Kenya exciting and memorable was the opportunity to travel around the country for a

week with Thomas Lung'aho, administrative secretary of East
Africa Yearly Meeting, visiting some of the African Quakers in their
homes and offices, and attending a variety of conferences and
meetings.

The Sunday morning I was to go to the women's meeting at
Chwele, the Chevrolet truck taking me there got stuck in a mudhole
and Thomas rescued me. His faithful Volkswagen slithered around
the ant hills, mud holes and other obstacles and got us to the
meeting on time.

Quakers in East Africa Yearly Meeting numbered more than
thirty thousand, the largest number in any yearly meeting in the
world. Imagine being ushered to a seat on a little hummock about
three feet high and large enough to hold a half dozen people, and
looking out over a congregation of more than two thousand women
assembled for their annual conference. They sat on the ground like
the multitudes on the shores of the sea of Galilee. How they could
sing! Their voices shook the rafters of the heavens.

I had been invited to talk about twenty minutes on the Assembly
of the World Council of Churches and on my mission to Kenya. I had
come to Africa on behalf of the Friends World Committee to
encourage African Quakers to work closely with their government in
formulating their new constitution, and in other political ways open
to them. We hoped they would establish safeguards for political and
religious liberty and champion steps toward universal peace and
disarmament in an African counterpart to the FCNL.

As they passed baskets for the offering after my talk I saw how
generous these women were in their poverty. Into the baskets poured
the widow's mite, copper coins, and offerings of corn and oranges.

On December 18 I wrote, "Am thinking of changing my name to
Noah. It has rained for more than forty days and forty nights, and
the heavens really open wide in this country." Thomas Lung'aho
bore with outward fortitude the gradual destruction of his car's front
end alignment and ball joints as we lurched along ruts and over
various obstructions in Kenya's roads. An outgoing and cheerful
person with nine children and a small tea farm he was just getting
started, he showed great solicitude for me throughout the trip. Once
when three of us took a tiny second-class sleeper on the train from
Nairobi to Kasumu, Thomas Lung'aho insisted on taking the third
bunk, right next to the ceiling, where I'm sure the heat and the
motion of the train were the worst. Yet he was a good sport
throughout any discomforts, and I am grateful for the kindness and
companionship he showed throughout the trip.

It was the rainy season in Kenya, but the inconvenience of inching along muddy roads and getting stuck and unstuck during our 350-mile trek was nothing in the face of the cordial reception and the warm hospitality of African Friends. I attended sessions not only of the women's conference, but of the peace committee and the executive committee. I visited churches and schools, homes and farms, and listened to these people's hopes and aspirations and difficulties in a country undergoing a major transformation from colonialism to independence.

It was a great privilege to me to meet such a representative cross section of the yearly meeting leadership, and they almost overwhelmed me with their expressions of appreciation to the Friends World Committee for arranging my trip.

Some of the suggestions I made to the Friends in Kenya for their consideration either in the new constitution or in the transition to independence were the following:

First, they should be concerned about political and religious liberty in the new constitution and in the new independent government which would be forming the next year. I argued for a secular state which guaranteed freedom for people to hold any religion or none, and the right to change their faith and to carry on activities including religious education. I suggested that they review the U.N. Declaration of Human Rights to see that all applicable provisions were made part of the new constitution. I went over the Declaration point by point and believed that all but one article applied very appropriately to Kenya. In addition the section on religious and civil liberties in the charter which had been drafted by the British for Kenya just a few years before seemed to me excellent, and I expressed the hope that it could be incorporated into the constitution.

Second, I urged Friends to champion women's rights, including rights to hold property, to receive inheritances, to own or sell land, and to have fair opportunities in education and in employment. This point stirred up a lively discussion wherever I raised it. Often there would be an animated argument in Swahili which I couldn't understand, but in which I could sense the intensity of feeling in a country where women's rights were still quite circumscribed.

Third, I urged them to do all they could in the peace field, including sending able representatives to the United Nations, striving for world disarmament, and working for constructive leadership by Kenya in the Asian-African organizations. I emphasized the need for protection of the rights of conscience.

Fourth, I asked them to think through the problems of church and state which might become more complex as the government moved away from reliance on church-related schools and initiated universal compulsory education. The Friends with whom I talked did not anticipate any particular difficulty in this regard, and I hope they were right. But I reminded them of the long drawn-out controversy over government aid to parochial schools in the United States. At that time in Kenya a considerable share of elementary education took place in schools under Quaker auspices.

In following up my suggestion that Friends make official recommendations to the government on human rights in the new constitution, the yearly meeting sent a letter to each member of the Legislative Council in Nairobi in January 1962, urging consideration of the questions of: 1) Rights of Women, 2) Christian basis for rejecting the Death Penalty, 3) Redemptive measures in Penal Administration, and 4) Freedom of Religious Instruction and the right to maintain church-sponsored schools. The yearly meeting sent a small delegation to Nairobi to speak personally with members of the Council about these matters.[12]

During my visit I was especially interested in the efforts Rod Morris was making to lay out agricultural demonstration plots, to encourage the use of the God's little acre idea where farmers would set aside some of their crop land to be used for church financing, and to set up simple bookkeeping records to keep track of the money being handled by a local Friends meeting.

Kenya, which lies astride the equator, had, in some sections, good agricultural possibilities which were by no means fully realized. In addition to evangelistic, educational and medical work, the mission board of the Five Years Meeting of Friends (now the Friends United Meeting) had had for several years at least one trained agriculturalist working with Kenyans on the production and storage of food.

At Chevakali, after years of battling with government red tape in a country whose educational standard was the British classical model, the Friends, with the help of Earlham College, had started a technical agricultural school. Students came on foot or on bicycles from miles around to get this specialized training.

I visited Chevakali and soon after I returned to the United States I met Assistant Secretary of State for African Affairs, Mennon

---

[12]"African Quaker Witness for Right Government," *Friends World News* 66 (April, 1963): 10-11.

Williams, at a State Department reception. I told him that though I had been in Africa very briefly I was deeply impressed by the need for more secondary and higher education in Kenya and no doubt in the rest of Africa. I asked him why the United States didn't undertake a cooperative crash program to help build high schools and colleges and to train African leaders for their newly independent nations. "We don't have the money," Williams replied. At that time the U.S. was spending about forty million dollars on development in all of Africa while sending billions in arms or economic aid to other countries.

ONE COCA COLA PER PERSON PER YEAR

It seems to me that one partial measure of the attempt of the churches to relate their religious faith to major unsolved issues of the day can be found by asking what proportion of their national budget is spent on social and political action. In 1964 I made a preliminary study of the seven major Protestant denominations which were most active on current social and political questions excluding the Historic Peace Churches — the Mennonites, the Church of the Brethren and the Quakers. Were they tooled up for such a task by intention, by declaration, by organization, by program, by finance or by staff? The answer which I reluctantly came to was "No."[13] At that time the proportion of central funds devoted to support of departments in those fields varied from .05 to 4 percent of their central budgets and the average expenditure per member varied from four to fifteen cents, or roughly one Coca Cola per person per year! How can the sweeping changes in society demanded by our religious faith be accomplished with that limited investment of money and manpower?

These figures tell only part of the story of the outreach of the churches, but to me it was a shocking revelation, and showed the need for multiplying many times over their activities in the field of social and political action. This brief statistical study plus my experience over two decades in Washington led me to believe that the American Protestant churches were not exerting ten percent of the influence which they could or should in the fields of social and political questions. The churches did play a decisive role in the enactment of the Civil Rights Act of 1964, but only after many of them had practiced and condoned segregation for a century following the Civil War and the Emancipation Proclamation.

---

[13]E. Raymond Wilson, "Are We Serious About Social Action?" *The Christian Century* 82 (February 10, 1965): 169-71.

Today more is being done by the churches to influence government policy in Congress and other departments of the government than a decade ago. The Washington Interreligious Staff Council (WISC), a coalition of Protestant, Catholic and Jewish agencies in which the National Council of Churches has played a coordinating role, confers on information and strategy and puts out an excellent newsletter on Congressional legislation, *Mark Up*. They have built up a nationwide mailing list of key contacts in many Congressional districts. However, during the past five years there have been drastic cuts in the budgets for the central offices of the National Council of Churches as well as many of the denominations which have prevented the kind of expansion which I had hoped would characterize the churches at this time.

I would question whether there is within Protestantism a single social action department adequately staffed and financed for the job that needs to be done within its own constituency, let alone for its responsibility to influence and serve as leaven in the nation as a whole. I don't know of a single staff member in the churches set aside to work exclusively on international security and worldwide disarmament.

There is with all of us a temptation to confuse resolutions and pronouncements with social action. Such statements do serve to register a certain degree of consensus, but they are not self-executing. They can form a basis for action if they are forwarded to the appropriate authorities, or when they serve as the foundation for educational and study programs.

But all too often the people in the pews do not know what their denominations have said on peace and social action in their regional conclaves, and even when they do know they may act as if they were indifferent to the positions which have been advocated.

Or take another measure of the churches' activity. In 1964 the appraisal committee of the National Council of Churches' Division of Christian Life and Work reported that of the Council's thirty-one denominations at that time, only ten had agencies with one or more full-time staff members engaged in social education and action, while six others had voluntary commissions or committees at work on such questions. In other words, only one-third of the members had assigned any full-time staff members to the specific task of supplying congregations with pertinent information and helping them engage in social action endeavors. The church press is publishing more timely articles on current issues than they used to, but as a rule church members are not as well-informed or active as they should be.

In the important process of Congressional Committee hearings where legislation is being discussed and shaped, many denominations testify seldom if at all. Few churches have a clear-cut unequivocal mandate to do intensive interviewing or lobbying.

The dedication of the Church Center for the United Nations was a thrilling experience for me, yet now the National Council of Churches has closed its liaison offices there and denominational representation at the Church Center is at a low ebb compared to the expectations which many of us entertained at that time.

The Vietnam War has disillusioned millions of Americans, but it has still not led to entire repudiation of war by the churches. At the speed with which the churches move, I wonder if it is irreverent to hope that statesmen will abolish war before the theologians get around to fully renouncing it. It should be the churches' duty to make an all-out effort to bring peace. I covet for the churches a much more active and influential role in advocating better legislation on both the state and national levels, in opposing reactionary decisions by Congress and the Administration, in staunchly defending civil liberties and justice where threatened or denied, and in building a world where there is no more war.

CHAPTER 15

Glimpses of Wartime Europe

In the spring of 1940 after the Nazi invasion of Denmark and Norway, Errol Elliott and I were asked by the American Friends Service Committee to accompany Francis Pollard and Karlin Capper-Johnson, English Friends who had been visiting America, on their return to England. Our mission was twofold: first, to visit members and activities of the Society of Friends and to carry the loving concern of American Quakers to Friends under the strain of war; second, to search for any way to shorten or stop the Second World War. The story of some of our efforts in the search for peace has already been told in chapter 10. Here I want to give some impression of the mood of Europe as we saw it during the phony war, that period between the fall of Poland in September 1939 and the blitzkrieg which began May 10, 1940, when there was virtually no actual military combat, and to give some idea of what it was like to be a pacifist or a conscientious objector there in the months before total war engulfed the Continent.

It seemed unwise to make notes of my impressions at the time because censors searched our luggage at each frontier, so what I am writing is taken from notes I wrote on the boat coming back to the United States and from my recollections now of that trip thirty-five years ago.

The intention was for Errol and me to sail to Naples on the *S.S. Rex*, and then to travel to Rome, Geneva, Paris and London to interview key figures. We planned to return by the same route and sail home from Italy, but this itinerary quickly went by the board. As soon as we crossed a frontier a door seemed to lock behind us and we found we could not reenter any of the countries we left. Our only choice was to leave London, cross to Ireland, and take passage home from Galway on the *S.S. Roosevelt*, the next to the last boat evacuating American women and children from wartime Britain.

All these difficulties were unknown to us when we landed, however, and we traveled to Rome through country ablaze with the blooms of spring, hoping optimistically that something useful could be done to shorten the war. In Rome, while visiting my old friend Devere Allen, editor of the *No Frontier News Service*, we found ourselves under surveillance. As we sat down to talk the uniformed soldier who had been prowling the halls when we arrived actually walked into Devere's room unannounced. So we tried to be circumspect in what we said and did. That evening we walked down past the ruins of the Forum to the Colosseum with its jagged outline silhouetted against the night sky. In our imagination we could see the early Christians being thrown to the lions because they would not submit to the Emperor, and the gladiators squaring off for deadly combat.

In interviews with newspapermen and others in Rome that April we learned it was doubtful that the Pope would make any move to shorten the war. Indeed there was a strong possibility that Mussolini might lead Italy itself into the war very soon.

We left Italy threatened with the imminent spread of war and went on to Geneva. Rome had been brilliantly lighted at night in celebration of the founding of the city. But Geneva and all of neutral Switzerland had begun regular blackouts and air raid alarms during our stay. My first blackout was an overwhleming experience. Fortunately Karlin, who spoke French, was with me and helped me with taxis and changing trains in the dark. Even inside the trains the lamps were shaded so the light filtered downward. The only lights we saw were the tiny points of blue that marked pedestrian crossings and taxi headlights. Windows in the houses were all blackened with heavy drapes. I went out on the balcony at the Palais Wilson in Geneva after midnight, and the only light I saw was one on the mountain behind the city. The moon was rising, however, and since the city was just at the end of the lake it still would have made an easy target from the air.

In Geneva Errol and I had a small conference with four American Friends Service Committee workers, with Pierre Ceresole from Switzerland who had started the work camp movement known as the International Voluntary Service for Peace, and with Jim Lieftinck from Holland. We met to consider what more could be done about war refugees and to assess the probability of total war and what actions we might take to prevent it. The AFSC workers had planned a larger conference, but because of the war no representatives could come from Germany or Scandinavia, and because of visa restrictions none came from France or England. Percy Bartlett of the English Fellowship of Reconciliation and Corder Catchpool were denied exit visas, although the English Friends were inclined to believe this did not establish a precedent for all Friends.

Karlin Capper-Johnson and I tried not only to see and understand what was going on in the Allied countries at this time but to get as much information as we could about developments in Germany. This was difficult to do, but we did have a very useful conversation in Geneva with a man who had just returned from Germany. He told us of growing dissatisfaction there with Hitler, but indicated also that the dissatisfaction was not organized in any way that promised to dislodge Hitler.

I found Geneva, the crossroads and spy center of Europe, very depressing. People were fighting the war vicariously, and it was no surprise to learn that as early as April 1940 at least two of my American friends in Geneva were advocating immediate entrance of the United States into the war.

Our efforts to stop the war and to keep the United States out of it were motivated by a desire to save the lives of untold millions of combatants and civilians, and were in no sense reflections of any sympathy for Adolf Hitler or the Nazis. Hitler represented the antithesis of democracy, an overriding lust for power and for the expansion of German empire, a contempt and hatred for the Jews and an unconcern for human life. We hoped that if a truce could be signed, Hitler would no longer be able to play on the German feelings of insecurity and persecution, and that his control of the people would be undermined. We hoped to persuade world leaders to intervene morally to establish a cease fire or to initiate an early peace settlement as a member of the British Parliament had suggested that Roosevelt might do.

War presents cruel dilemmas for both the pacifist and the militarist. The pacifist knows peace requires fair dealings between countries and the submission of conflicts to a higher authority when they cannot be settled directly. It demands that peoples and governments place a high prioriety on peace. Had there been a fair settlement in 1918-19 after the First World War, had there been general disarmament and an encouragement of the new German democracy and of the League of Nations, the rise of Hitler might have been prevented.

The militarist believes that war may be the lesser of two evils when wrongs are to be righted, aggression stopped or when the basic liberties of a country or a people are threatened. With almost unlimited manpower, material and money, however, militarists have not been able to assure the maintenance of peace or a world of justice. As Quaker Stephen Cary has said, the pacifist believes there is more creative potential in massive efforts for human good than in massive efforts for destruction, and because he believes a choice must be made, he chooses to work on the side of justice.

PARIS BEFORE THE BLITZKRIEG

In Paris I was impressed by how natural the city seemed that April, ten days before the blitzkrieg. Many of the evacuated children had returned, and on Sunday the streets were crowded with hundreds of thousands of people. Though a shortage of manpower meant the parks had not been planted that spring with flowers, it was still possible to buy them in profusion from the stalls in the markets. Although the pastry and candy shops were closed the first three days of each week and butchers on some days sold only tripe, kidney, tongue and other variety meats, daily life seemed, on the surface, relatively unaffected by the war. To save labor and expense, few buses ran at night and half of the subway stops had been eliminated, but in the evenings taxis tore about in terrifying confusion, and men and women sat out in sidewalk cafes eating and drinking as usual. Movies and the opera were well attended. I could not speak the language to learn much about what people were actually thinking, but superficially life in Paris seemed much more normal than I had expected.

One of my most interesting interviews in Paris was with French economist Francis Delaisi, author of *Political Myths and Economic Realities*. Delaisi stressed the postwar problems of finance and economic reconstruction and told me that he hoped the United States would not extend military aid to Europe with which it could destroy itself.

In France pressure of public opinion and propaganda seemed directed toward stamping out dissenting opinions. Conscientious objectors were jailed for four-year terms. People were arrested for innocuous statements which could be construed as defeatist. Eric Brown, an English Quaker missionary on the way through France to Madagascar, for example, was imprisoned for three weeks for some pacifist remarks he made at the *pension* where his family was staying, remarks made to a relative of the owner, not even to a man in uniform.

France, of course, was sitting on a political volcano. With six million men under arms during the seven-month phony war, Frenchmen had plenty of opportunity to ask what they were going to get out of war besides a six-foot grave, and what kind of a world this was if the process had to be undergone every twenty-five years. One couldn't blame the French for their concern and fear of German invasion, although their determined hatred of Germany was a force which carefree Americans could scarcely understand. Whether France might undergo another revolution and whether it would become fascist or communist were real questions in the minds of serious Frenchmen.

We saw two posters displayed all over Paris. One showed a sailor on watch on a ship with the caption "On Guard — Subscribe to the War Loan." The other was a map of the world with the tiny German area in black and the far-flung British and French empires sprawling over the world in red. The implication was that the size and strength of the two empires couldn't be beaten. I couldn't imagine a poster better designed to infuriate the Germans or to play better into Hitler's psychology and his campaign for Lebensraum, living space.

THE PLIGHT OF FRENCH PACIFISTS

I spent an evening with Helene Schott, who was directing the office of the Fellowship of Reconciliation (FOR) in Paris. The small band of French pacifists had suffered prolonged and repeated imprisonment for their refusal to accept military service,[1] and she and I talked about some of them.

She told me about Francois Chevally, an FOR member who had been called up at the end of August and assigned duty as a military driver. He requested transfer to the *service sanitaire*, but since he had no diploma or special training in this field, his request was turned down. On February 5 he was officially refused appointment as a driver for the Red Cross, and the authorities ordered him to attach a machine gun to his assigned car and report for duty. He refused, was arrested, and disappeared into the prisons of France. Nobody knew where he was or when he would be tried.

---

[1] Their heroic story is told in detail in Vera Brittain's *The Rebel Passion* (Nyack, New York: Fellowship of Reconciliation, 1964).

In April police visited Helene to question her about Chevally and about the FOR. She assured them that though the membership declaration of the French FOR advocated the pacific solution of conflicts, not all the members had been conscientious objectors. She told them that Chevally had a great desire to serve his fellow men, and that he would harm no one. The charges against Chevally were very serious — refusal of obedience before the enemy. Helene did not know what would happen to him but felt his sentence would be more serious than those of Philippe Vernier or Henri Roser.

Philippe Vernier's difficulties began in June 1933 when he was sentenced to a year's solitary confinement for his refusal, on Christian grounds, to accede to Army demands. Fifteen days after his release in 1934 he was again arrested for refusal of military service and was sentenced to one year solitary confinement in a little cell measuring only six by nine feet. In July 1935 John Nevin Sayre, then International Secretary of the Fellowship of Reconciliation, presented a petition signed by people from forty U.S. States and from forty colleges and universities to the French *charges d' affaires* in Washington asking for Vernier's release. And in December of that year Vernier was freed and assigned hospital service in Morocco. There military authorities refused to allow him to minister to soldiers, and civilian authorities prevented him from preaching in church or conducting Sunday school.

Offered a missionary parish in Belgium, Vernier accepted but was recalled to France in September 1939 where, because he again refused induction, he was imprisoned along with his brother Pierre. Philippe nearly starved awaiting trial, and the brothers narrowly missed execution. In February 1940 they were tried and Philippe was sentenced to four years at Clairvaux where he was when Helene told me his story.

One afternoon soon after I had visited with Helen Schott, I drove about thirty kilometers out of Paris to where Henri Roser's wife was living in a little two-room cottage with her youngest child. Henri had been the first French Christian to proclaim his pacifism between the two wars. At the beginning of the war in 1939 he had been arrested and put into La Santa prison in Paris where he was allowed to work in the library and on the accounts. La Sante was a general prison then and was only later converted into a military prison.

Because of his popularity and suspected influence on other prisoners, however, he was transferred to a small prison at Rambouillet, not far from Maule, where there were only five inmates.

There his unsympathetic jailer spared no effort to make him uncomfortable.

To visit her husband Mme. Roser, who was not well, had to go into Paris, transfer, and go out to Rambouillet on another railway line. She could visit him only once a week for half an hour, and could talk to him only from behind bars and with a guard present. She was required to give the jailer the names of all her family and was not supposed to talk to him about anybody else. She told me she didn't know whether she could indicate by some indirection that I had come to see her or not, but she couldn't mention my name. In fact she was not allowed to say anything about conscientious objectors, pacifism, or, for some reason, about the Roman Catholic church. Aside from receiving one or two innocuous magazines, Henri was denied contact with the outside world except through his wife, his only visitor. He was even denied newspapers.

Mme. Roser was allowed to write her husband every day, but had to type her letters for the convenience of the censor. Henri could write one letter a week. She showed me a letter he had written to his little girl about his activities during one day, from the time he got up until he went to bed. Every mention of hours or time was blacked out.

I told Mme. Rosser as best I could of the widespread interest in the United States and England in the testimony which the two of them were making for their convictions, and I assured them of the prayers and love and sympathy of many friends. In America or England we had little knowledge of the price this devoted family was paying. Mme. Roser was lying down most of the time that she talked to me for she suffered from heart trouble, but she told me to tell her friends that her spirits were high and that she was determined to carry through. The faith and radiance on her face were a benediction I shall never forget.

WARTIME BRITAIN

The English channel was threatened by German submarines, so I flew from Paris to London instead of crossing by boat. The war in a way seemed closer in England. France had been putting its faith in the supposedly impregnable Maginot Line, which a few days later the Germans would circumvent through Belgium. England had no Maginot Line and prepared other defenses.

London was transformed for war. In the air overhead floated huge brown balloons like sinister cigars moored on steel cables above the city. I counted fifty-two from a spot in Hyde Park one day and later saw thirty-two more over the entrance to Bristol harbor. The steel cables could bring down a low flying plane, and at the beginning of the war they were quite effective along the east coast in preventing the Germans from laying magnetic mines by air and in forcing bombers to fly too high to see their objectives. Later, of course, the Germans developed V-2 rockets against which the balloons were powerless, and which did such widespread damage to London.

London at night was much blacker than Paris, but part of the time that I was there the moon shone brilliantly, and I will never forget the outline of Westminster Abbey silhouetted against the sky, or the curving majesty of Regent Street, or the outlines of the new London University buildings. By this time I had become rather used to blackouts. I carried a flashlight, and had learned to shine it straight down on the pavement while crossing streets so a taxi or bus wouldn't run me down.

Twice I had the privilege of lunching informally with about ten of the choice minds and spirits of Great Britain including Kingsley Martin, editor of the *New Statesman and Nation,* and David Low, the best cartoonist in England. We first met just after the collapse of the Norwegian campaign. Then for the first time it began to dawn on the English that the Allies might not win a decisive military victory and dictate the peace. The second luncheon was after the invasion of Holland and Belgium on May 10 when the prospect of a German invasion of England looked like an immediate and certain danger. These major leaders of public opinion were trying to face up to the implications for Britain of total war — the potential loss of life, and the uncertain future of England and Europe. They were people for the most part who had bitterly opposed the Chamberlain government and who represented English liberalism and culture at its best. If anything, the genuine travail of soul among these people was keener than I found later in London Yearly Meeting.

Still, when I first arrived in London on May 1, 1940, life seemed, as it had in Paris, more normal than I had expected. Rationing was in effect. At the first meeting with Low and Martin, for example, instead of a heavy business lunch we had a spartan plate with a tiny slice of meat that wouldn't have made a good snack. I went away almost as hungry as when I'd arrived. But the English laughed about the concern of Americans for the "starving British" and told me with glee about packages of food sent over to keep their English friends and relatives alive. My visit was at the beginning of the war, of course, before the import of food had been seriously curtailed, but the British seemed to feel they were getting along fairly well on their rations.

Sugar, bacon, meat and butter were rationed, and the government subsidized flour, potatoes and some other commodities to keep the prices reasonable. Most families got along pretty well on the eight ounces of sugar per person they were allowed in May, but the projected drop in ration to four ounces in June would have serious consequences for canning and preserving. Meat was rationed by price — one shilling ten pence (the equivalent of $.71 U.S. currency at the time) per person per week. Heavy laborers who needed greater quantity could buy more of the cheaper cuts for their money. Liver, heart and variety meats were not rationed, but bacon and ham were limited to a quarter pound one person per week.

For the lower class English family the high price of butter was even more effective in curtailing consumption than the ration. At the time I was there the ration was one quarter pound per person per week. With the invasion of Denmark and Holland butter became still more scarce.

The really pressing shortage, however, was of paper. The German invasion of Norway had cut off supplies, and printers were rationed to thirty percent of their 1939 paper usage. The government had an absolute whip hand on paper stocks.

The deeper effects of rationing had not yet surfaced. I met a Rhodes scholar specializing in bacteriology who told me that the Ministry of Health charts on tuberculosis and many other diseases were showing a sharp rise due to the effects of high food prices, shortages of fuel and so forth. While no major outbreak of disease had yet taken place, the ministry feared the possibility of something like the 1918 flu epidemic and the certainty of a sharp increase in deaths and illness due to lowered resistance of the civilian population.

England Girds for Total War: Shifting Tides of Public Opinion

May was an exceedingly fateful month to be in England. From the standpoint of public opinion it was by far the most important month of the war to that time. The month began with the continued grim determination to prosecute the war to a bitter but victorious end and to crush Hitlerism as a menace to the security of small states and to freedom in Europe. There was little enthusiasm for the war and no undue glorification of it. It was seen as dirty business forced upon a peace-loving Europe — a job that must be carried through.

After the Allied collapse in Norway the English were haunted by doubts. Perhaps the Allies weren't invincible after all. I heard bitter charges of gross military mismanagement and tales passed by survivors of the debacle that were disquieting in the extreme.

The invasion of Holland and Belgium on May 10 burst like a bombshell, and it was obvious that total war had been launched in earnest. Rage and biting invective against the Germans blared out over the radio, in the news reels and in the press. Any broad distinction between Hitlerism and the German people began to fade rapidly. There was fear that England might be invaded in a matter of days. The English felt that not only the life of the British Empire, but all it stood for was now at stake — its political tolerance, its haven for refugees, a leisurely and satisfied outlook on life, a broad confidence in a certain goodness in humanity that couldn't quite comprehend Nazi ruthlessness, the centuries of accumulated culture. Any sense of responsibility the English might have felt for the conditions which led up to the war began to disappear. They began to believe the Versailles Treaty had been too generous, and that England's part in the collapse of European stability was negligible. Citizens began to direct all their energy to winning the war. No sacrifice was too great. A coalition cabinet was formed; munitions factories were asked to work a seven-day week; and the busy hum of workshops almost drowned out the observance of the solemn day of prayer called by the King. Yet the English still balked at complete military retaliation, and could not justify to themselves the bombing of open unfortified towns. I heard one woman on a bus say, "They bomb London, we bomb Berlin, and where will it all end?"

Up to May 10th and the beginning of the blitzkrieg, the freedom of expression in wartime England was almost unbelievable. Communists were selling the *Daily Worker* on the streets. Sir Oswald Mosely was still publishing his Fascist sheet, *Action*, until he and his lieutenants were clapped in jail about the middle of May. The pacifists had almost complete freedom from the authorities. The Peace Pledge Union was holding meetings all over England. Pamphlets were still being circulated suggesting ways to conduct oneself before the military tribunals which granted C.O. status. Petitions on "Stop the War Now" were still being issued by religious and political groups; harangues continued in Hyde Park against the war. Up to May tenth the churches had been reluctant to justify British participation in the war as the will of God.

After May tenth pressure increased on the pacifists. Nearly every day the papers carried some story of a city council or other organization refusing to have any conscientious objectors, or "conchies" as they were called, on their staffs. C.O.'s began to lose their jobs. Printers who, under English law, were as liable for the material that they printed as the publisher, were afraid to continue publishing peace materials. The printer of the Peace Pledge Union's *Peace News* quit and, though another was found to put out a very small four-page issue, he gave no promise to continue.

The increasing intolerance of public opinion was reflected in the growing harshness the C.O.'s experienced in the military tribunals. I attended a tribunal for conscientious objectors in London where only one young man was granted complete exemption, and he was supported in an excellent statement by his father. The young men claimed exemption on grounds ranging from communism to extremely fundamentalist religious objections, and though there was great variety in the way the tribunals dealt with the men before them, they were getting less and less lenient in their decisions.

Four national officers of the Peace Pledge Union were on trial while I was in London. They had been arraigned for the circulation two years before of a poster which read, "Wars will cease when men refuse to fight. What are you going to do about it?" The attorney general himself prosecuted the case, and the government showed great interest in its outcome. Before the case came up for final decision on June 6 the Council of the Peace Pledge Union withdrew the poster, denied that it had been directed primarily toward the armed forces, and instructed the officers on trial "to exercise due care in the issue of future literature with a view to avoiding this kind of misrepresentation."[2] The court eventually released the defendants with suspended sentences and proclaimed publicly that there was nothing political in the conduct of the trial, but the message was not lost on English pacifists.

I had collected quite a number of Peace Pledge Union publications which I planned to bring back to the Swarthmore College Peace Collection for its historical files, but practically all of them were taken away from me by the censor as I left Britain. Censorship was quite strict in England, and carrying out books, papers, written materials and cameras was difficult. Censorship of mail was accomplished not so much by actual destruction or blacking out but by delay. The last letter I got from Miriam came through in nine

---

[2]*The* (London) *Friend* 98 (June 14, 1940): 370

days, but the average for ordinary mail from the United States was a month to six weeks. If the censor could hold the mail up long enough, the news was stale and did not need censoring.

I had many interviews with leaders of thought in England about the war and its implications and the possibility of rational peace afterwards. We spoke of America's possible participation in the war and the hope of many Americans to avoid being drawn into the conflict. I was at a luncheon of the National Peace Council Executive Committee and twice attended the meetings of the Council of Christian Pacifist Organizations when there were between thirty and forty present. I visited with Percy Bartlett, secretary of the Embassies of Reconciliation, and Canon Raven, professor of divinity at Cambridge, an outstanding scholar and chaplain to the Queen. And I talked with Dr. G.H.C. MacGregor of Glasgow, author of the *New Testament Basis of Pacifism*, who had planned to come over to America for our Institutes but was denied an exit visa.

Karlin Capper-Johnson and I had lunch with Gilbert Murray, chairman of the League of Nations Committee on Intellectual Cooperation and president of the British League of Nations Union, and his wife, Lady Mary, at their home near Oxford. Later that week we talked with Provost Hodgkins of Queens' College, Oxford, as we walked along the banks of the Cherwell River.

On my weekend at Oxford I wandered through century-old cloisters and colleges, feeling a kinship with historic England and absorbing a bit of the atmosphere of this intellectual center of the British Empire. During the warm and sunlit days bombers, fighter planes and military aircraft zoomed overhead incessantly. How impotent, I thought, how futile education had been in overcoming war. Oxford, too, was being transformed by the war. Government offices evacuated from London were taking over more and more of the larger buildings in Oxford, and an increasing number of wounded were housed there.

I talked with a group of Friends one evening in Oxford on "America's Attitude Toward the War," which was, at that time in large part, a determination to stay out of it. In the psychology of the moment, as England looked with horror on the invasion of Holland and Belgium, the discussion which followed my talk, while polite, was stiff and difficult. I felt that I had not built bridges of fellowship and understanding in this wartime crisis. That weekend was one of the most depressing experiences of the entire trip.

As I reviewed my month in wartime England I became more aware of some of the intangible effects of war on the human psyche. The spiritual costs of war are incalculable. People develop blind spots about the effects of their nation's policies on other people. I doubt that the British and Americans have ever realized the full psychological impact on the German mind of the Allied blockade during the First World War nor the injustices of the Versailles Treaty and its part in creating a willingness to follow Hitler in his moves to make Germany impregnable against invasion by land or by sea. Americans have never been able to sympathize with the French terror of German invasion. Most of the German Nazis were not able to understand how they outraged the sense of decency and fairness of the entire world.

Not only do people develop blind spots, they lose their trust in means of settling disputes without war. Only a small minority in either France or Britain believed any peace would be possible before the Allies inflicted a crushing military defeat of the Germans and paraded their arms in Berlin. I suppose propaganda had led as large a percentage of Germans to distrust England and to believe that the French and British empires were determined to encircle and strangle the emerging German nation.

Another result of war was the bitterness it engendered. I was shocked at the people listening to the radio and counting up gains and losses in aerial warfare day by day as if they were baseball scores, instead of human lives. On the boat back to America I heard bloodthirsty demands that Berlin be bombed immediately if Paris were bombed.

Then, too, there were the false hopes which war arouses. I watched the profound disillusionment with which the English took the Norwegian collapse, which opened the North Sea to German warships and cut the source of important supplies of timber and fish. England had hoped that Norway would form the northern bulwark of Allied defense. Many in England had come to stake their hopes on American intervention, and I trembled at the repeated question, "When is America coming into the war?" I was appalled at the amount of wishful thinking both regarding the war and the peace. People hoped that peace could be based on military occupation, Federal Union of the democracies,[3] or other unrealistic plans. They hoped that somehow the problems left by the war would be swept

---

[3] A proposal of Clarence Streit, former *New York Times* League of Nations correspondent and author of *Union Now* and other books, to unite the North American and European democracies.

aside as if by some miracle. There was the same personification of the war in Hitler that there was of the Kaiser in the First World War, but we should have discovered in the twenty years that separated the wars that the causes of conflict are always more fundamental and harder to eradicate than just one person.

In late May as we prepared to leave England we saw our worst fears being realized. The phony war was over, and since no formula for a negotiated peace had been found the war would spread across the face of the world. It seemed unlikely that there would be an opportune time for a negotiated peace since the political and military initiative had been taken by Germany from the beginning of the war. Even in May 1940 we could see that it would be years before Europe knew peace again.

One might ask if the trip, short as it was, served any purpose. In the first place it allowed Errol and me to assure European and British Friends of the love and concern of American Friends. We were the first Americans to visit the Friends in France since the war began, and in England I was showered with expressions of cordiality and appreciation for having come. I saw again the value of the Friends World Conference held in Swarthmore in 1937, for time and again people entertained me for lunch or dinner or helped me however they could, saying, "I had such a wonderful time in America and everybody was so hospitable to us, that any little thing which I can do in return is nothing." I felt strongly then that Friends should not relax their efforts to keep channels of communications open, to maintain fellowship and common thinking and to cultivate contacts to decide if and when they might take an initiative for peace.

The trip also allowed me to visit major peace organizations in England and to meet their leaders and become acquainted with their programs. It also gave me the unique opportunity to study the British tribunals and their way of handling C.O.'s, and to use this information in efforts to obtain adequate legislation for the protection of American C.O.'s on my return.

While I did not see the physical ravages of war firsthand, I did see many of the spiritual problems for governments, for the civilian population, for the Christian and for the conscientious objector. Sharing the fellowship and the agony of soul as British Friends searched their hearts and consciences was a humbling experience.

As I left England, the British army was being evacuated from Dunkirk, and France was falling to Germany. Allied Europe was girding itself for what would be four more years of bloody war —

years that would take the lives of thirty million people and which would shackle the world with the task of rebuilding a shattered civilization. America, from its isolation, was to be drawn into the conflict the next year. Far from bringing true peace, this war would create the conditions for more wars and leave political and economic questions still unsolved thirty years after the close of the conflict.

CHAPTER 16

The Sweetest Girl I Ever Saw

A few days after her death, Kent wrote the following tribute to his Mother:

MIRIAM DAVIDSON WILSON
February 17, 1899 — December 16, 1965

After a full and joyful life, sustaining her husband, raising two sons, and teaching school, Miriam died on December 16th in Washington. Her virtues were many; she was loving, giving, hard-working, humble, joyous even in suffering: her faults were but virtues in excess.

She was born in 1899, the oldest of five children, to Mark and Mary Davidson on their farm in Iowa, near Stanwood.

Miriam began her education in a one-room school house adjoining the farm and completed it in 1922, graduating from Monmouth College in Illinois. There she was Queen of May, president of her class, president of her Dormitory Council, and at the top of her class academically.

She taught school first in Iowa and Illinois, and then for three years at the United Presbyterian Pressly Memorial Institute in Assiut, Egypt, spending her summers traveling in the Middle East and in Europe.

After serving for three years as Dean of Freshman Women and teaching English at Monmouth College, Miriam married Raymond on August 4, 1932. They left immediately for Europe where Raymond spent four months studying the League of Nations in Geneva. It was here they started their annual Thanksgiving-Christmas letter. They traveled through seven countries by car. On their return to the United States she often accompanied him on his travels as Field Secretary of the Peace Section of the American Friends Service Committee. It was a busy life; she often commented that during her first 18 months of marriage they packed up and moved on the average of once every four days.

After they moved to Philadelphia in the mid-thirties, Miriam and Raymond joined the Society of Friends, and in 1937 Kent was born.

In 1939-40 with a group of friends they helped start the Bryn Gweled Homesteads, a cooperative community near Southampton, Pennsylvania. There the land is owned in common by the more than 80 member families, the woods and streams are set aside for joint enjoyment, the community affairs are run by a "town meeting" type of government, and much of the development of community facilities from surveying to building a swimming pool has been done by family members working together.

In 1944 Miriam and Raymond adopted Lee, who, 21 years later, is now a student at Penn State University. In 1945 the Wilsons began a seventeen-year migratory life, moving south for the school year to Washington, where Raymond continues to work with the Friends Committee on National Legislation, and then back to their friends at Bryn Gweled for the summers. This was interrupted in 1956 when the family, minus Kent, who was in college, went to Japan where Miriam taught at the Friends Girls School in Tokyo and Raymond traveled and reported for the American Friends Service Committee.

For many years the Wilson home was a little International House. For six and a half years it was home for Eppie Umeki soon after she came out of a Japanese relocation center, and later her sister Toshi lived there while serving as a visiting nurse. Among the other students who lived with the Wilsons were Masayo Yamamoto, Masaji Suzuki and Takeshi Amemiya from Japan; Melissa Farley whose parents were with the AID program in Korea; and Philippe Padin from Mexico.

Miriam continued home activities while teaching seventh grade at Sidwell Friends School [accumulating 26 years of teaching on three continents in every grade from second through college], bringing up two sons, taking care of the housework for two houses, and canning and freezing fruits and vegetables [770 quarts one summer] much of which she had grown herself, happy in giving to those around her.

For five years she knew she had cancer, but continued her life as before, cheerful and uncomplaining, telling only a few, forgetting herself in service to others.

Knowing her family needed her, she lived many months beyond any expectations but her own, and died without a long period of intense suffering after talking with her sons, holding her husband's hand.

Memorial services were held at the Florida Avenue Friends Meeting House on December 19, and at Frankford Friends Meeting in Philadelphia on December 20. Burial was in the Frankford Friends Cemetery in Philadelphia.

After Miriam's death more than five hundred notes and letters of sympathy and tribute poured in. It seemed everybody who met her loved her. The most common theme was how radiant her life and spirit had been, even in her last sickness during which I never heard her complain.

"There is no word in the English language so priceless as the word 'radiant,' " wrote Stephen Cary, associate general secretary of the American Friends Service Committee, "and to earn it from so many, lifts her to a pinnacle that few attain.

"Her smile was the kind that lights a room, her values — wrapped up in a contagious personality — made her the kind of a teacher I covet for my children, and her unflagging support of you contributed mightily to the leadership you've provided for so many Quaker enterprises. . . . You were married to a great and gracious lady, and I know her influence is still much with you, and will remain with you."

At the memorial service at the Friends Meeting House in Washington, Martha Weyl said: "I am one of the friends of Miriam Wilson who loved her very much. It always seemed to me that she had a special quality of living and loving. But the miracle of Miriam Wilson was to me that during all those long months just passed, when she knew that she could not recover, this rare quality of living and loving went on unchanged and the miracle was that she got strength to minister to her family and friends. I know she got this strength from the people she loved, from her family, and from the things she read.

"After she went to the hospital the last time, Raymond found some notes in her handwriting beside her bed including these words from J.P. Caussade: 'The passive part of holiness is far easier still, for it merely consists in accepting what most frequently cannot be escaped, and in suffering with love, i.e., with consolation and sweetness, what is too often endured with weariness and disgust.' "

I Meet the Farmer's Daughter

In the summer of 1922 to earn money for college, I sold Cram Atlases in Cedar County, Iowa. I drove around Cedar County in an old tin Lizzie that had to be cranked to start. Practically no roads were paved at that time. One of the big arguments in those days was whether the transcontinental Lincoln Highway, or Route 30, would be paved and on which side of the Chicago and Northwestern Railroad tracks it should run. The dirt road zigzagged across the tracks to run through the small towns on either side of the railroad. Some farmers made a pretty penny pulling cars out of mud holes with a team of horses or a tractor if they had one.

Many of the farmers were suffering from the effects of wild speculation during the First World War and also from the depression which started in 1921 among the Midwest farmers. Some had bought blue sky stock like Atlas Wheel which turned out to be worthless. One day I climbed up into a haymow where the farmer was putting away hay as it came up to him on the fork. I was selling an atlas with roadmaps of every state — now easily available, but quite a scarce commodity in those days before filling stations gave them away.

As I made my pitch about the atlas while the sweating farmer pushed hay back under the eaves with his pitchfork, he said, "That sounds like a good proposition. But I lost a lot of money on Atlas Wheel and I resolved that I wouldn't buy anything until I earned that money back. A feller was in here a few days ago wanting to sell

me *The Farm Journal* for five years for a dollar and I told him 'no.' "
Needless to say he didn't buy an atlas either. I didn't make much
money that summer, but I still counted the season profitable for I
met Miriam Davidson and her fine family. Though a confirmed
bachelor at the time, I was impressed by her friendly and outgoing
nature. She was practical and sensible, and having been raised on a
busy farm, knew what hard work meant. I was delighted by her
charm and her many fine qualities.

After a few dates including the County Fair at Tipton and a ride on
the homemade Ferris wheel which Miriam found rather scary, and
some picnics, I went back to Iowa State College and she started to
teach school at Washburn, Illinois. On the second day of teaching
she wrote me, "I certainly enjoyed getting acquainted with you this
summer. It does one good to meet people with somewhat the same
ideals and ambitions though you have succeeded in attaining so
much more nearly the goal set. I wish you the best of everything in
the coming year's work."

It was a long decade later before we were married and I have felt
many times that we missed very much by not marrying earlier. But
for me that decade covered four more years of graduate study, a year
in Japan, my father's death followed by two years' struggle by my
brother and me to hold the farm together in the depression, two
years campaigning against compulsory military training for the
Pennsylvania Committee and then the National Committee on
Militarism in Education, and finally a year of almost constant travel
for the Peace Section of the American Friends Service Committee.

For Miriam those years included two years as a high school
English teacher in Washburn, Illinois, and a year teaching in Tipton,
Iowa; three years at the Pressly Memorial Institute, a mission school
in Assiut, Egypt; and three years as dean of Freshman Girls and
teacher of English at Monmouth College. In those troubled
depression days we weren't even engaged until 1931. Settling down
in the usual sense didn't seem to be in the cards. But we kept in
touch by correspondence.

On October 22, 1928, about a year after my recall from Japan
because of my father's last illness, I wrote Miriam,

> I had another chance to return to Japan — a cable a few days ago
> — but the situation at home isn't unravelled yet and I replied that
> I couldn't go. Sometimes I am in two worlds — my head and heart
> in a stream of men and women and events and places and ideas —
> my feet and hands in a land of mud and taxes and pigs that don't

know enough to come in out of the rain and where there are at least nineteen things every day that should have been done day before yesterday.

A few months later I was commenting, "About the time I get well into the psychology of slaughtering the military mind then I change to the extraction of consolidated school taxes from a ration of corn silage and soy beans."

Soon I was writing, urging Miriam to come to Morning Sun to the young people's church convention. "If so I hope you can come out to Cloverdale Farm. . . .Wish you might have seen the peonies last week — they were glorious. The color scheme now is weeds."

In a later letter I wrote Miriam that at a church program a few days previously we had a summary of the major problems of achieving peace, and:

> Yours truly as a benediction pointing out some things out of step with the above program. I was wound up for fair and had hoped for twenty minutes, but the chairman limited the last two speeches to ten minutes — for which I was very glad considering the length of the program and the time — So I did all I could to play havoc with compulsory military training, the Legion universal draft bill, and the sixteen cruiser bill, trying to sink each one in three minutes.

In 1931 I, at last, had what looked as if it might become a permanent job as field secretary of the Peace Section of the American Friends Service Committee, and I felt my life settled enough to ask Miriam to marry me. On August 4, 1932, we were married in a lovely ceremony on the ivy-covered porch of the country home where Miriam had been born near Stanwood, Iowa. Miriam's uncle, the Reverend Walter C. Davidson was assisted in the ceremony by the Reverend W.H. Hemphill, the minister of the local United Presbyterian church of which Miriam was a member.

That day Miriam gave me a tiny card on which she had written:

To My Best Beloved on Our Wedding Day

Where our trails join
There will be joy,
A sudden coming as
From shades of densest forest
Into the open sunlit spaces.
Your love to me is like the glints of gold
Before us on the hills
Which gives the life and beauty to the whole.

My love for you is
The swift channel of the stream
Which gives direction
And meaning to the swirls
And eddyings along the shore.
There will be joy
And happiness and faith
Where our trails join
Because together we face the upward path.

We left immediately on the *S.S. Bremen* for more than four months in Europe, taking round-trip passage for $120 apiece plus a U.S. tax of $5. We were helped along by a small Biddle Fellowship to study the League of Nations during that critical period when the Lytton Commission Report on the Manchurian conflict was to be debated by the League Council. This is referred to in more detail in chapter 10.

On our way to Geneva we stopped at Bad Pyrmont for the German Yearly Meeting. This was the first Friends Meeting which Miriam ever attended. Since my first experience had been at Shimotsuma, Japan, we used to say that we were initial members of the International Society of Friends. These German Friends were rebuilding an old meetinghouse which would be the only building owned by the small group of 199 Quakers scattered throughout Germany. The rafters had just been raised when we arrived. They made us feel very welcome. During the worship services we could hear in the distance strains of music from the Dresden Orchestra which was playing in Bad Pyrmont at the time.

These Quakers were an inspiration to be around. A Berlin engineer, seeing two men approaching along the tree-lined avenue, turned to us and said, "They must be some of your party of Friends — they have the look of God in their faces."

That fall we had the good fortune to be loaned a brand new four-cylinder Ford by the Hinrich's of Brown University, in which we drove 2900 miles through seven countries in Europe. Our objectives were to attend the International Conference of Friends at Amsterdam, visit the work of Quakers in Europe, and get some insight into the economic and political situation in Central Europe.

On our wanderings through Europe we drove much of the way through avenues of trees — apple, cherry, pear, poplar, maple and evergreens. For nearly thirty miles in Holland we swept down a majestic avenue of beeches with small golden-brown leaves showering down on the road as the car passed. We drove by

hundreds of men planting tulips near Haarlem and wished we could
return to see the plants in bloom in the spring.

What grim reminders of war we saw. At Verdun we visited the
battle fields where a million men lost their lives in the hardest fought
battle of the First World War. Thousands of acres showed the utter
desolation of that terrific bombardment and our guide told us that
only a quarter of the men lost there were ever identified. We saw the
imposing new French memorial at Douamont and another memorial
built over the trench where a company was buried alive with only the
tips of their rifles showing. At Bras we visited the large French
cemetery and a German cemetery nearby. Finally, we saw the
American memorial and cemetery at Romagne on the edge of the
Argonne forest where 14,500 white marble crosses — row on row —
mark the resting place of some of the men who never came back.

In Geneva we lived at the Quaker Student Hostel where
Thanksgiving Day we sat down to dinner with twenty-two young
people from ten countries. Christmas Day 1932, found us rolling and
tossing on the Atlantic as the *S.S. Ballin* brought us back to
America. Miriam regaled me with the story of being terribly seasick
on a Mediterranean crossing and lying flat on her back on her bed.
Looking up she saw scribbled on the bottom of the bunk above her,
"Whoever would go to sea for pleasure, would go to hell for a
vacation!"

We returned to face the life of newlyweds in the depression. In
February 1933 Miriam wrote her family that eggs were fifteen and
seventeen cents a dozen and milk cost nine cents a quart. "We didn't
spend more than a dollar each day last week for the two meals and all
the supplies like crackers, flour, sugar, potatoes, salt, soda, baking
powder, cocoa, tea, breakfast foods, etc."

The depression kept deepening. In April 1933 we stopped in
Dayton, Ohio, to visit Elizabeth Nutting. Dayton was the place
where the year before I had made a speech to about a hundred
Sunday school teachers and had been approached afterward by a
man who asked, "Does anybody ever tell you that what you say is
socialistic, bolshevistic, destructive and anarchistic? If you've never
heard it before, you are going to hear it now!" But Elizabeth Nutting
was one of the more liberal elements in Dayton.

She was a social worker who, while helping distribute relief, had
become convinced there was a better way to help people. She read,
asked advice, borrowed money, and moved very carefully to set up
ten production-for-use units. These were small businesses that

helped people make some income with which to survive.

One group set up a shoe repair shop, another a canning project, one ran a bakery and several had small farms or gardens to raise food. The groups made their own decisions about their specific operations but sent delegates to central meetings of all the groups to decide matters of general policy. Their purpose was to become self-sufficient and then to direct profits toward other groups just starting.

We spoke to one man who had fourteen men under him repairing shoes. He told us that at one time he had supervised 18,000 men in a factory, but when the firm cut back on management he had looked everywhere for work and, unable to find any, had suffered a nervous breakdown. Now, he said, he was happy in this work. For while he wasn't making much money, his family was warm, clothed and fed.

Another leader in these groups had been in his basement making two bombs — one to blow up the bank that had refused to lend him money to save his house and another to kill himself — when a delegation had come to talk to him about going into this venture. Now he was working with Elizabeth Nutting to help these units solve their problems, and he had found other ways to use his ingenuity.

At nearby Antioch College we found the president, Arthur Morgan, and his wife feeding fifty-eight students in their basement for $3.50 a week apiece. They were encouraged that Antioch had been able to place about fifty percent of its students. Many other colleges found jobs for only ten to thirty percent.

Until Kent was born Miriam and I traveled a good deal together. In 1933 we left our apartment the first of August and didn't get back until the day before Thanksgiving, spending much of that time on a field trip through Iowa. In 1934 we packed up the last week in July when the temperature was 106°. Our Christmas letter that year reported that in three years of travel we had averaged two thousand miles a month for a total of more than seventy thousand miles. Miriam said then that if we ever had a home of our own we should call it "Dunrovin."

Miriam shared my ideals for a peaceful world and was always supportive and helpful. Each year at Thanksgiving we would prepare a Christmas letter summarizing some high spots of the year. In 1933 we wrote:

> Under the New Deal, much of which we heartily approve, we are solemnly asked to borrow ourselves rich, drink ourselves sober, blast our way to peace through new tanks and armor plate, all of

which is the height of insanity and the depth of folly.

On Christmas we gather round the Christmas tree and sing about Peace on Earth, Goodwill to Men, and the other 364 days carry on the war on our campuses, in our legislatures, by economic barriers, racial discrimination, military propaganda, naval races, aeroplane demonstrations, preparedness campaigns, institutional poison gas and nearly every other way short of bayonets.

Miriam shared not only my travels and ideals, but was a gracious and ready hostess. Each year she had the FCNL staff over for a Thanksgiving dinner which she cooked and served herself. Lee once paid tribute to her abilities by naming her "the goodest cooker in Washington." In 1936 alone there were 133 names in our guest book of those who had been to the house for a meal or longer, and this didn't begin to indicate the number of friends who went zooming through Philadelphia and didn't have time to come out to the house or the scores who called on the telephone.

To me our marriage was an extremely happy one but tempered with frequent and often long absences from home. While Miriam and I had the normal differences of opinion that two people might have who had married in middle life (Miriam was 33 and I was 36 when we married), I do not remember one violent or vigorous disagreement. Our life wasn't so easy for Miriam who sacrificed a lot of companionship because the life of a peace-worker and later a lobbyist was wide ranging and often irregular and unpredictable.

After Kent was born there were fewer trips for Miriam and more separation for us. In 1937 my vacation at home with her lasted only three days. These absences left Miriam with more than her share of work in raising the children, gardening and taking care of one and later two houses.

One low time for her was during the weeks I was traveling in wartime Europe in April and May 1940 with its constant uncertainty. On my return I had only a few fleeting days at home until my schedule took me across country to Institutes of International Relations and to Washington for lobbying on the conscription bill. She wrote me on June 15:

> Wish you *were* here. I feel pretty flat today. I anticipated your coming so long and worked so hard that last week to get things ready — and have been going so fast with you this week — and now it seems so long until you will be back again. . . .I hope you won't be run ragged at the Institutes. It was grand having you here a few days but I certainly don't want to go on like this forever. Life seems so pointless.

There ought to be a Nobel Peace Prize for peace widows like Miriam. Sometimes I wonder, as Levi Pennington did who wrote once, "What have we done to merit such wonderful wives as we have been blessed with?"

Miriam was a woman of amazingly varied skills. Not only was she a fine teacher and mother, a woman able to meet great numbers of strangers with such warmth and aplomb that they quickly became her friends, she was also impressive at the more mundane aspects of life. Daughter of a farmer she became, among her other responsibilities, a skilled amateur farmer herself. Absentee husbands are almost a total loss as gardeners, and much of the care of the garden — its cultivation, dusting and fighting off insects and night visiting animals, picking and canning and freezing — fell on her arms and shoulders. I still ache when I think of the day we squeezed and canned seventy-five quarts of grape juice between sunrise and sunset.

In 1942 Miriam began a small poultry industry at Bryn Gweled. We bought one secondhand chicken house for $30 and had another built for $357. Both were soon paid for by the profits from the sale of eggs and chickens. Beginning with 258 day-old chicks in 1943, she raised 252 of them old enough to be sold for meat.

During the war six Bryn Gweled families formed a hog cooperative to augment the meat supply. Out of secondhand lumber we built a hoghouse and corncrib on the Bergstrom lot, and purchased five squirming, squealing pigs. Elliston Morris, a member of the cooperative, used to give a vivid account of pigs in a sack struggling to get their freedom on the way home. One day they did get their freedom, briefly, when they broke out of their pen. For a time we were hard pressed, chasing them around the grounds of Bryn Gweled, capturing one in a flying tackle, cornering others, until they were rounded up again. Our hog cooperative would have been far less successful, however, if Miriam, an experienced amateur veterinarian, had not nursed two of our founding pigs in our basement for a week and overcome their early reluctance to live.

CHILDREN WHO MAKE HOMES HAPPIER AND LOVE STRONGER

In 1937 our life was changed by the birth of our first son, Kent. What a joy children are (with some trouble, expense, care and concern thrown in)! Porter Miller, Miriam's colleague in Egypt, once wrote her about the little visitor who "makes homes happier, love stronger, patience greater, hands busier, clothes shabbier, the past forgotten, and the future brighter." Life has never been the same since Kent and Lee arrived. I wonder if there were ever two more strong-minded, independent boys.

One morning three-and-a-half-year-old Kent woke as usual with the chickens, and came bouncing into the bedroom where his father was trying to sleep. "Can't you keep still, you little earthquake?" I asked sleepily. "You're a Quaker yourself," replied Kent, which silenced even his loquacious father for a moment.

Kent was always curious. One day when Miriam and he were walking over to the Sears and Roebuck store about a mile away, Kent asked 110 questions in less than an hour. As he approached five, he asked one day,

"Mommy, does God have any children?

"Yes, a Son —".

"Doesn't he have any daughters?" And then, "The children of Adam and Eve didn't have any grandfather and grandmother, did they?"

For a time Kent was deeply puzzled by the war. He said grace thanking God for "things we have and things we don't have, for things all around the world, for bread and butter, dishes and chairs, buttons to hold up our clothes," and so on. One day he included, "We thank you God, the war isn't any worser than it is —," and another day, "We thank you for a few guns." Then by way of explanation afterwards he said, "I thanked God for a few guns to kill animals, because I don't like meat very well."

For a while during the war, Miriam's sister Carol and her two children, Roderic and Marcia, lived with us at Bryn Gweled while Roderic, Sr., was serving as a Navy chaplain in the Pacific. When he would visit he would say a lovely verbal grace. One time when I came home and bowed my head quietly for a silent Quaker grace, Kent spoke up crisply, "Say it loudly, Daddy, say it loudly!"

Kent and Lee each displayed strong propensities early — Kent for science, Lee for working magic with his hands in wood or metal. Kent's idea of a perfect eighth birthday celebration was to take his father to see the science exhibits at the Franklin Institute.

In his senior year at Sidwell Friends School, marked by honors in math and science, Kent rebuilt a Ford coupe and got the car through inspection. The day after school closed he and his classmate John Terbough drove 1300 miles in two days to South Dakota to work on a ranch there. After arriving at 4 a.m. they were wakened by the farmer at 6 a.m. to enjoy the ardors of life in the wide open spaces and demonstrate their prowess in the gentle art of early morning agriculture. Whatever enthusiasm Kent ever had for farming did not survive the summer.

Kent graduated from Harvard in physics and chemistry, then spent a year at the University of Strasbourg under a French government fellowship and a Fulbright grant. He wrote his thesis in French on the economic and political aspects of the production of electricity through nuclear sources by the European community, the United States, the U.S.S.R. and Great Britain. In his fourteen months away from the United States he traveled thirty thousand miles by foot, bicycle, hitchhiking, motor scooter, mortorcycle, car, train and boat.

His graduate work at Berkeley and Harvard in physical chemistry was under the leadership of Dudley Hershbach. On his transfer from Berkeley to Harvard Kent rode his BMW motorcyle seven thousand miles through parts of twenty-eight states, spending thirty nights in a sleeping bag on the journey. His thesis dealt in part with the crossing of molecular beams and other esoteric subjects which his father can neither explain nor understand. Today he teaches chemistry and studies environmental problems at the University of California at San Diego, at La Jolla, and speaks frequently at professional conferences at home and abroad. He and Lana and their two daughters, Tasha, five, and Maya, one, are householders at Del Mar, just north of the University of California campus.

Lee joined the Wilson family when he was a little over two weeks old. With his curly hair and boundless energy, life has never been totally quiet since. Lee's curiosity led him into all sorts of scrapes. One year we had just arrived at Bryn Gweled on our annual move from Washington and were unpacking when young Lee drank some rather deadly nicotine sulphate. We called the doctor who told us to pour him full of soapy water. We fed him soapy water until his little tummy was round as a basketball but we couldn't get him to throw up. When he seemed all right we continued unpacking. Soon Lee, never quiet with so much activity going on around him, picked up some simonizing preparation about the consistency of very thick gravy and poured it into the gas tank of the lawn mower. After that he went over to a neighbor's and collided with a little homemade merry-go-round and knocked out his two upper front teeth. His parents thought that was enough excitement for the first day at home.

When he was young Lee showered his affection on two defenseless kittens. One day he painted one kitten's face with lipstick in an artful fashion, and then proudly told his mother, "Now, see, she's a lady!"

Lee has always been very skilled with his hands. One year in grade school at the Sidwell Friends School, he had more exhibits in their science fair than any of the other 800 students, including mobiles, a little table top and several other things he had made.

On Lee's sixteenth birthday Kent found a Chevrolet for him with only 17,000 miles on it which Lee paid for with money he had earned. His father has never had his hand on the wheel. In a variety of ways he souped up the car and won twenty-eight drag racing trophies with it in supervised drag racing competitions. He not only has a huge shelf of drag racing trophies but a number of bowling trophies including one inscribed, "Greatest Imp." He explains that this does not mean the greatest imp in bowling, but the greatest improvement.

Lee spent almost three years at Penn State in architectural engineering. He had nourished some interest in building houses since he was five years old, but his interests finally turned to computers. When he was drafted Lee was studying data processing at the Temple School in Washington, D.C. He did his alternative service as a conscientious objector during the Vietnam War by working at the Washington Hospital Center. His first assignment was in the business office trying to help collect some of the five million dollars in bills owed the hospital. Later he was put on the graveyard shift and for fourteen months ran a computer from midnight to eight-thirty in the morning helping the hospital turn out bills, payrolls and the other jobs which computers perform today. He seemed to thrive on this nighthawk arrangement of ten nights on and four nights off. Today he is back on daylight hours as a computer programmer in a business firm in Silver Springs in suburban Washington.

Though I was frequently away on work for the AFSC or the FCNL, Miriam, Kent, Lee and I enjoyed many good times together. One of the most memorable events was the centennial of Piney Knoll Farm, Miriam's birthplace. Miriam's grandfather had bought the farm from the government in 1851 for $1.25 an acre, and Miriam's brother, William, an outstanding farmer who had been named in 1947 by *Wallace's Farmer and the Iowa Homestead* as one of six Iowa Master Farmers, and his wife, Lois Jane, were proprietors of the farm at the time of the centennial on June 29 and 30, 1951.

The celebration included a centennial tea the first day, and a pot luck supper, jamboree and square dance in the haymow on the second. Three carloads of William and Lois Jane's college friends drove from Ames and farmers flew their own planes in from all over the state.

Miriam's mother was the life of the party, recounting exploits of the Davidson and Hoyman families and reminiscing about the history of the farm. Bill and Lois Jane regaled us with stories of their experiences in the AID program abroad. Miriam's brother, Arthur, a veterinarian in the race horse country of Lexington, Kentucky, could make a horse sound like the most interesting thing in the world. It was one of those heartwarming nostalgic occasions of family and friends getting together to celebrate an historic event in the friendliest fashion. Lois Jane wrote us afterward: "I am sure our centennial brought us all together and gave us all a glowing feeling about each other and made us realize that tradition, religion, family and friends are indeed important."

Lois Jane had made a major renovation of the house and its furniture and the place was filled with lovely antiques she had restored herself. Ethel Blythe Penningroth wrote about the William Davidson home, verses which are reminiscent of old houses everywhere:

An Old House

Something so permanent in its brick walls,
Something so mellow about its long halls;
Many a pioneer tale it could tell,
Many a story of moderns as well.

I like to pass just to see its quaint grace.
(Houses grow lovely with age like rare lace),
Five generations have watched time unroll —
Don't ever tell me a house has no soul.

Miriam taught for sixteen years at the Sidwell Friends School in Washington. I wish she were here now to write of the joy and satisfaction she found in teaching and the warm relations she had with her students. One of her pupils was Craig McNamara, son of the Secretary of Defense, Robert McNamara. Mrs. McNamara was an active patron of the school and visited it frequently. One day Miriam was talking with her and asked her if she knew what I did for a living. Mrs. McNamara said she hadn't the slightest idea. "Why, he works over in Congress for peace and total disaramament," Miriam told her. "More power to him!" was Mrs. McNamara's earnest reply.

When Miriam ended her teaching career many of her students sent her notes of appreciation. One girl wrote:

They say that a student is supposed to feel happy when his teacher goes away, but I don't feel that way. I mean I'm not exactly crying, but I do miss you, and the rest of the class does too. I am not much for sentimentality, or for writing letters, but I hope you recover soon, and maybe come visit us sometimes. I hope I don't seem too formal, because this is supposed to be a friendly letter, but as the saying goes "Get Well Soon!"

In the Wilson Christmas letter two weeks before her passing, my wife could write, "Life on the reduced schedule of the retired has been easily accepted by Miriam. Each day is faced with joy and faith, leaving the worrying to the careful and sympathetic and excellent doctors who share her belief in miracles."

Kent wrote in his Christmas letter just a few days before his mother's death, "My mother has continued to amaze us by living joyfully under the shadow of prolonged and serious illness — loving, sweet, always thinking of others. Her secret for strength and joy seems to turn outward, giving to others instead of dwelling on her own problems."

After her death Pat Nixon, whose daughters Tricia and Julie were in Miriam's seventh grade home room at different times, wrote a beautiful letter in which she said in part,

> We were sad to learn that Miriam is no longer with us in person, but she will always live in our hearts.
>
> Tricia and Julie always recalled her precious friendship during their days at Friends School where many storms, not of their making, hovered.
>
> Your family can be proud of the beautiful tributes paid to a noble member who enriched the lives of people throughout the world.

Florence Gosnell, who also taught in the grades in Sidwell Friends School, expressed her feelings about Miriam:

> I feel that she was a wonderful example to all of us to be living her faith through great joy and humility and gentleness. I feel this example will stay not only with us but with the children she taught and with her own family. She was one of those rare women the Bible talks of in the truest sense of the word.

During the last ten years, while I have missed Miriam's love and companionship very much, I have tried to rejoice and be thankful for the wonderful thirty-two years we had together rather than mourn over a decade of separation. I try to keep a zest for life as it comes and for work which needs to be done.

To Live in Your Heart Is Not To Die

A high school classmate of Miriam's had a hobby of translating Latin. He paraphrased some lines the Roman poet Catullus, who lived in the first century B.C., wrote to comfort his friend, Calvus. The last four lines have been precious to me:

> You vainly yearn to lift to her your love;
> And — could it be? She watches from the sky,
> And seeks to tell you all is well above,
> And to live in your heart is not to die.

CHAPTER 17

Thus Far on My Journey

On a tomb in St. Pancras:

Godfrey Hill, aet. 46.
— Thus far am I got on my journey:
READER
Canst thou inform me
what follows next?

Thus far on my journey should merit a few reflections and a few glances forward. There have been many changes for the better in my lifetime — women have gained the suffrage, segregation has been struck down by a Supreme Court decision although much discrimination still exists, opportunities for education have been broadened, a whole cluster of international institutions have grown around the United Nations, modern communications have put us in instant touch with much of the world. But I have lived through five wars in which the United States has been involved and each has left its train of death and destruction and created the conditions for more hostility and more wars. How far the human race still has to go to build a world of peace and justice and freedom!

I do not find in the gospels any assurance that if a man seeks to follow the will of God and the life and teaching of Jesus Christ in his activities as a citizen in trying to make his faith relevant to the world in which he lives, that he will necessarily achieve success or victory in the popular sense in his lifetime. His obligation is to follow the light as it is given to him, do the very best he can to make his actions suitable and effective, and leave the final judgment to time and to God.

The critics of the early Christians accused them (Acts 17:6) of having turned the world upside down. Their manner of personal and communal life, their wholehearted dedication to their ideals, and their defiance of arbitrary Roman authority brought down the suspicion and wrath of many of their contemporaries.

How many Christians today are Christians in this revolutionary sense? How energetically are we working to transform a world of war, exploitation and injustice, or are we standing astride that world accepting and even benefiting from its inequities? How many far-reaching changes in our national and world society are needed and how much time and effort it will take to achieve these changes!

Time is running out. We must strive to be responsible and effective world citizens in a growingly interdependent world. At best, one person can only do so much. To be genuinely productive he must cooperate with other people and organizations in building a better world of tomorrow.

Of all the unsolved problems that threaten the future of the human race today — such as racial hostility, illiteracy, disease, poverty and pollution of the environment — two in particular demand our attention as concerned world citizens because they affect so many people so deeply. The first is the problem of food and population; the second, the question of war, the arms race and disarmament. These are issues which have troubled me for more than thirty years, and to whose resolution I shall continue to devote myself as far as time and strength permit, recognizing that these are only two parts of a wide range of interrelated issues confronting mankind on which substantial progress should be made in the next few years.

Some of the activities on relieving hunger in which the FCNL has been involved during the last three decades are summarized in chapter 9.

THE RACE BETWEEN FOOD AND FERTILITY

Today nearly one-half of the human race is either undernourished or malnourished or both. It is estimated that some four hundred million people — nearly twice the population of the United States — are starving or chronically hungry.

In December 1974, a writer in the *U.N. Forum* accused the affluent countries — the United States, Canada and Western Europe — of eating a hundred thousand children in the recent past in places like the Sahel and Bangladesh. These children died because the grain which could have been sent to them to save their lives was fed to livestock instead.

In the developing countries of Asia, Africa and Latin America the per capita availability of grain is only about 400 pounds a year, or a little more than a pound a day, most of this consumed directly. But in North America the average person consumes almost one ton of grain per year, about eighty percent of which is in the form of meat, milk and eggs. In the United States about ninety percent of grain is fed to livestock. If beef consumption alone in the U.S. were reduced one-third, the grain saved would be enough to feed one hundred million people.

It is not only food but fuel, fertilizer and water to produce food that is in short supply. The use of energy such as gasoline and electricity in the U.S. food supply system of production, distribution and storage has trebled between 1940 and 1970. In countries like India, Pakistan and Bangladesh, wherever farmers relied on petroleum for pumping irrigation water or running small agricultural power machinery or depended on petroleum-based fertilizer, the rise in the price of oil over the last three years has been a calamity of major proportions.

The land base for growing food is also shrinking. While some additional land could be brought into production worldwide, about a million acres a year in the United States, often quite productive land, has been diverted to urban sprawl and housing, industry and roads. Population pressure is causing deleterious ecological effects on the earth including overgrazing, deforestation, desert expansion, soil erosion, siltings of irrigation reservoirs and increased flooding.

Water is becoming a major limiting factor in agricultural expansion. Some years ago it was hoped that the new lands in Siberia would greatly enhance the food supply in the Soviet Union, but production proved disappointing because of the northern latitude and the light rainfall. The Sahara desert has been creeping southward. There is a real struggle for water among California, Arizona and Mexico. The hoped-for bonanza of the green revolution depends upon adequate fertilizer, abundant rainfall or irrigation, and there isn't enough water in many places for the hoped-for green revolution.

Then, too, the number of grain-exporting countries has been shrinking to where the United States, Canada and Australia are now virtually the only countries with significant grain surpluses. The United States and Canada control a larger percentage of exportable grain than the Middle East does of oil. U.S. exports of agricultural products have risen from 56 million tons in 1970 to nearly 100 million tons in 1975. Just picture what a severe and prolonged drought in the United States would do to the world food supply! In spite of a bumper wheat crop in the United States, the world's carryover in reserves in 1975 was only about a thirty-three days' supply.

The prospects for closing the world's hunger gap are not bright. Mexico, Venezuela, Algeria, Pakistan, the Philippines and Thailand were among the countries which between 1965 and 1972, according to the World Bank Atlas, had a population growth rate of three or more percent per year. A three percent rate of population increase if maintained means that the population would multiply nineteen times in a century. Vannevar Bush has written that "the world's population is increasing at a rate which renders distress, famine and disintegration inevitable unless we learn to hold our numbers within reason. Man is headed for catastrophe unless he mends his ways and takes thought for tomorrow."[1]

The world raced from three billion people around 1935 to more than four billion people at the present time. Since with only about six percent of the world's population, the United States consumes nearly forty percent of the world's resources, some population experts argue that it is the affluent countries beginning with the United States which should first achieve zero population growth (ZPG). This would materially conserve food and natural resources for wider distribution and use.

With a net gain of about 270,000 new mouths to feed every day, or about 80 million a year, the world is in a desperate race between increasing population and slowly increasing food production. Some population experts believe that if we were to define optimum population as a level beyond which further increase would no longer improve the quality of life, then world population has already passed the optimum level.

CAN THE WORLD BE FED?

Is it possible to abolish world hunger? Only if there is a sustained crash program to slow down and eventually halt world population growth while increasing agricultural production. If the United States government were as interested in seeing that hunger was abolished as it is in arming people, it could play a dominant and perhaps a decisive role in that struggle.

There are no easy, immediate or simplistic solutions. On the other

------

[1]Quoted in the magazine *Good News*, December 1975.

hand it is not an inherently insoluble problem if peoples' minds and policies will change. But it will require a world revolution in thinking and action.

Lester R. Brown, one of the outstanding leaders of thought in the field of food and population, has recently published two very helpful books: *In the Human Interest: A Strategy To Stabilize World Population*[2] and *By Bread Alone.*[3] He argues that it is urgent to stabilize world population at least under six billion not later than A.D. 2015.

For an expenditure of approximately two billion dollars a year, half of which might be supplied by the nations with high birth rates, Lester Brown estimates that family planning services could be brought within the reach of every one needing them. Compare that with the almost ten billion arms sales by the United States in 1975 or the currently projected military budget of $114+ billion. Such a stabilizing of population, he says, would imply changes in human fertility behavior more comprehensive than any before in history.

Of course, it would take much much more than the mere availability of family planning services to check population expansion. For example, it would require a major change in the official attitude of the Catholic Church which has condemned artificial methods of birth control and abortion.

At the World Food Conference in Rome in 1974, great emphasis was expressed that for family planning to succeed it must be an integral part of a comprehensive program of economic and social development. Where children are wealth or life insurance or old-age security for the parents, and where only one child in three may grow to be an adult, severe limitation of births has no appeal. Adequate economic and social development would involve a much greater commitment not only on the part of the more developed nations but also on the part of the least developed countries. It would require enormous amounts of capital and numerous skilled personnel, both in notoriously short supply in most countries. The countries of rapidly increasing population will have to give agriculture and land reform and social development the priority and emphasis which they deserve if food and population and the good life are brought into equilibrium.

A contributing factor to the population problem is illiteracy. If people can neither read nor write, it is difficult for them to learn of

---

[2]Norton, New York, 1974.

[3]Praeger, New York, 1974.

new scientific advances, or to benefit from instruction about better ways of living, spacing births or raising better crops and livestock. It is tragic that five centuries after the invention of the printing press, two-fifths of the human race lack the capacity to take advantage of this basic invention. According to Lester Brown:

> In the sixties, UNESCO estimated the cost of enabling a person to become literate in a developing country at about $8, slightly less for an adult, slightly more for a school-age child. Given the nearly 1 billion illiterates in the less developed countries, the elimination of illiteracy would require an outlay of $8 billion. [4]

Even if the cost were multiplied several times the outlay would be peanuts compared to the world's investment in war and militarism.

Georg Borgstrom, professor of food science, Michigan State University, says: "Our future is at stake in this century, and food is the key issue. . . .As a human race we are heading for Supreme Disaster, and the great challenge to our generation is to avert this calamity. We need to declare the Great War for Human Survival — but it is getting late. Time is running out on us. It is five minutes to twelve." [5]

Some Things Which the United States Could Do

1. Take the lead in helping develop a more workable world order, adapted to present and future needs. This would involve much greater use and development of the United Nations, the specialized agencies, and other existing international institutions and the creation of new supranational organizations where needed. Adequate solutions of complex world problems require global institutions and global programs. For the first time in history, the resources exist to extend some of the basic social benefits of modern civilization to all of mankind and that is the vision we should keep before us.

2. Enlarge its economic aid and technical assistance increasingly through UN and international channels rather than bilaterally. There are several hundred U.S. technicians abroad plus many Peace Corps volunteers working on the whole complex of enlarging agricultural production. Compare these few numbers with about 485,000 men and women, plus dependents, stationed abroad in military service. The goal recommended by the U.N. for public and

---

[4]*By Bread Alone*, p. 186.
[5]Quoted in the magazine *Good News*, December 1975.

private investment abroad of a developmental nature is two percent of GNP. For the United States this would be over $20 billion a year. More rapid economic and social development is imperative if comprehensive family planning is to succeed.

As far as possible, people ought to be fed by food raised near where they live rather than by vast grain imports. The severest deprivation today is in the Indian subcontinent and Africa where the poorest of the poor exist. These regions particularly call for heroic measures on the part of the more affluent countries. The goal we want is a productive society where nations and peoples earn their way when they can and trade the products of hand and brain for what they need. This emphasizes the importance of world trade keeping in mind ecological considerations and the necessity of protecting the environment.

3. Make a considerable shift from feeding grain to livestock, place more reliance upon grass and silage for beef, and encourage a reduction in per capita consumption of beef. It takes seven or eight pounds of grain to produce one pound of grain-fed beef, about four pounds of grain to yield one pound of pork, and about two pounds of grain for one pound of poultry. However, farmers must be assured of a fair return on their labor and investment if they are to be expected to produce efficiently.

4. Encourage great simplification of life styles in order to cut down on consumption of food, energy and natural resources, and to eliminate waste. We face the cruel problem of compound arithmetic when infinite appetites compete for finite resources. One desirable step would be to cut out fertilizers on golf courses, lawns and cemeteries until the world catches up with its fertilizer shortages for producing food.

5. Increase the specific allocation of grain to the most needy nations under the Food for Peace Program. In President Ford's proposed budget for FY 1977 the Food for Peace recommendation was for an increase of $79 million to $1,169 million while asking for the appropriation for three B-1 bombers to be increased $871 million to a total of $1,532 million.

6. Develop a grain reserve program as part of a world system to accumulate a carryover reserve in order to meet contingencies in years of less than average crops or to help countries suffering from drought or floods.

7. Multiply the allocation of funds, personnel, supplies and services for birth control and family planning and for maternal and child care around the world. Work for the goal where each child that

is born, is wanted, is loved, and has a decent chance for food, shelter, health care, education and employment.

8. Strive for an adequate and balanced diet for all, including protein with balanced amino acids, vitamins, minerals, fruit and vegetables, and not just a given quantity of cereals.

BEATING SOME SWORDS INTO A FEW PLOWSHARES

I have already said that world disarmament has proven to be about the most difficult political step which the human race has ever undertaken. Perhaps we might more accurately say, which it has not undertaken. This is partly because of the vested interests in the arms race, and partly because of the fears, real or imagined, engendered by rivalries in arms. In spite of our massive expenditures on the military in recent years, as this chapter is being written, we are being bombarded by assertions of how strong the Russians are and how weak is the United States. I have listened to such propaganda for nearly fifty years when appropriation time comes around in Congress. World disarmament is imperative if the human race is to avoid bankruptcy and mutual destruction.

During the past thirty years I have worked with the FCNL on many campaigns designed to reduce U.S. involvement in the arms race, and to protect the individual citizen from abridgement of his civil rights by military conscription. Our successful eight-year battle to defeat universal military training, the series of national conferences on disarmament, appeals to political leaders here and abroad for moves toward drastic disarmament, and the thirty-year struggle against the draft, are all detailed in chapter 9. The projects I have listed in that chapter and others in which I have been involved, reveal the glacier-like progress toward a disarmed world which has characterized the last three decades.

As early as 1925, Professor Morris R. Cohen of the City College of New York said, in regard to the controversy at the college over compulsory military training, that "to compel men to do things against which they have moral scruples is generally recognized as politically inefficient and morally evil."[6]

INVESTMENTS IN THE PRECARIOUS BALANCE OF TERROR

It is estimated in the publication, *World Military and Social Expenditures 1975,* published by the Arms Control Association,

---

[6]City College *Lavender,* December 8, 1925.

Washington, D.C., that world military spending in 1975 was approximately $300 billion a year for arms and military establishments in a desperate gamble for maintaining peace by a balance of terror. In reality the world was preparing for possible war by ever increasingly brutal and inhumane methods.

There are more than 25 million men and women — largely conscripts — in military service or para-military units around the globe today. This is almost the current population of Denmark, Finland, Norway, Iceland, Ireland and Albania. The world spends on arms approximately as much as the disadvantaged half of the human race in the developing nations of Asia, Africa and Latin America receive in total income.

The Library of Congress Legislative Service calculates that the United States has spent since the end of World War II in 1945 a total of more than one trillion seven hundred billion dollars on military and defense activities, including the Korean and the Vietnam wars. This stupendous expenditure has brought us neither peace nor security. President Ford has asked Congress for $114.9 billion for defense-related expenditures and obligational authority for fiscal 1977. That is about equivalent to the total incomes of the 54 countries of Africa which in 1973 had a GNP of approximately $114 billion dollars, according to the *1975 World Bank Atlas.*

For the period 1963 to 1972, the federal government received $681 billion dollars from federal income taxes and spent $680 billion on the military. So far as federal income taxes were concerned, the whole country worked the year round for those nine years to maintain the U.S. military establishment. At the FCNL we have estimated that roughly 75 percent of the current national debt of $594 billion is either war or defense related. Interest alone on the national debt for the fiscal year beginning July 1, 1976, is calculated at $45 billion a year.[7] Both the national debt and the interest are rising rapidly. Excessive military expenditures are a primary source of inflation in the U.S.

Another menace to peace and stability are the skyrocketing arms sales. According to a *Washington Post* story,[8] the Defense Department estimates that sales orders from foreign governments for arms and backup equipment will be about $9.8 billion for the fiscal year ending June 30, 1976, not counting credit sales. This is

---

[7]Figures on the national debt as of February 29, 1976 and interest on the national debt from the U.S. Treasury, March, 1976.

[8]December 31, 1975

somewhat below the previous record of $10.8 billion in 1974. But how fast arms sales have risen is indicated by the fact that the projected figures are more than nine times the amount sold in 1970. These yearly figures top the fifteen-year total of $8.5 billion in the period 1950-1965.

To these government-to-government figures must be added arms sales in the private market. These commercial deliveries which are outside Congressional control, but require State Department approval, are projected by the Ford Administration to reach $2.1 billion in 1976, more than triple the sales of the previous year. Congress is now trying to bring these arms sales under their review. One of the anomalies is the extensive military aid and sales to Israel on the one hand, and to Iran, Saudi Arabia and Kuwait on the other hand. This is going on in the still explosive Middle East situation where after four wars between Israel and some of the Arab states there is still no final peace settlement. The U.S. has furnished $10 billion in arms to Persian Gulf nations since 1973.

Do arms sales prevent wars or foment wars and national hostilities? The United States supplied arms to India and Pakistan who fought two wars, in part with American weapons on both sides. Arms were furnished to both Turkey and Greece who fought in Cyprus.

Our far-flung military commitments in late 1975 were indicated by the stationing of about 485,000 troops abroad, plus dependents, in addition to troops in U.S. territories and possessions. The United States has military pacts with forty-two countries, and maintains military missions, or their equivalent, in fifty-two countries.[9]

The Center for Defense Information[10] in its publication, *The Defense Monitor,* for August 1975, claims that the U.S. has some kind of military arrangements including treaties, executive agreements, arms sales or various kinds of military grant assistance with 92 nations. The Center also estimates that the U.S. spends at least $62 billion each year to maintain these "commitments." Military costs are becoming astronomical. The center estimates the overall cost of the projected B-1 Bomber force, if it is finally approved by Congress, at $92 billion. Their estimate for official U.S.expenditures on Korea from 1946 to 1976 totals $189 billion.

The cost of the Vietnam War to date has been variously figured at

[9]Arms Control and Disarmament Agency by telephone.

[10]122 Maryland Ave. N.E., Washington D.C. 20002. Rear Admiral Gene R. LaRocque (Ret.), Director; Brig. Gen. B.K. Gorwitz, U.S. Army (Ret.), Deputy Director.

$130 billion or more. However, the extended cost including veterans benefits, interest and other cumulative charges may amount to two or three times that amount.

Another rising cost is for around one million military retirees or their survivors. The estimate for the cost of military retirement for fiscal 1977 is $8.5 billion as against $1.6 billion ten years ago. A member of the armed forces can retire after twenty years of active service. A typical retiree leaves the service in his early 40's and can expect to receive total annuities greater than the basic pay which he received during his active duty.[11]

As this is being written, revelations are coming out almost daily about alleged bribes, payoffs and kickbacks by nearly forty large American corporations to secure business with foreign firms or foreign governments. Some of these were huge American defense firms seeking to sell American weapons or products abroad. Lockheed Aircraft Corporation which received a $256 million loan guarantee from Congress admitted to giving $202 million in commissions, payoffs and bribes to foreign agents and government officials in the Netherlands, Italy, Japan, Turkey and other countries during the last few years. The company admitted that $22 million of this sum went for outright bribes. McDonnell Douglas Corporation paid $2.5 million in commissions and consultant fees between 1970 and 1975 to foreign government officials. Northrop Corporation admitted in part SEC charges that it paid $30 million in commissions and bribes to government officials and agents in Holland, Iran, France, West Germany, Saudi Arabia, Brazil, Malaysia and Taiwan.[12] A sizeable share of the business community defends these practices as justified and necessary to promote sales abroad. Whether these revelations will lead either to punishment or reform is not clear at this time.

The cost of armaments might conceivably be justified if they really assured peace. Actually they tend to divert the attention of nations from the difficult task of creating the conditions of peace. There is always the temptation to use them. It is doubtful that the U.S. would have gotten into the Vietnam War if there had not been a very sizeable military establishment plus military conscriptions so the President did not need to go to Congress for specific authority to become militarily involved.

Sir Edward Grey, British Foreign Secretary, who committed

---

11 *Washington Post*, December 15, 1975.
12 *Newsweek*, February 23, 1976

Great Britain to the First World War, wrote in his memoirs:

> More than one true thing may be said about the causes of the war,
> but the statement that comprises most truth is that militarism and
> armaments are intended to produce a sense of security in each
> nation — that was the justification put forward in defense of them.
> What they really did was to produce fear in everybody. Fear
> causes suspicion and hatred; it is hardly too much to say that,
> between nations, it stimulates all that is bad, and depresses all
> that is good. [13]

From observing the actions of our government in Washington for
nearly forty years and visiting Russia three times, I think I do not
underestimate the difficulties of securing agreements with the Soviet
Union, which is our chief arms competitor. Both the Russian people
and the American people are in the grip of their hardliners. The
Pentagon and the Kremlin think a good deal alike on arms. Both
want military superiority. Neither are ever satisfied with what they
wring out of the taxpayers at the expense of crucial human needs.

But the Russian people have suffered infinitely more from the
devastation of war than the American people have, and for the most
part desperately want peace. The Soviets have proposed budget cuts
and some other steps toward reduction of arms which have been
refused by the United States partly because of the dispute over
verification and inspection. The use of spy satellites has reduced but
not eliminated the desirability of on-site inspection.

The Americans intervened in Vietnam. The Russians have
intervened in Angola with Cuban troops and substantial military
supplies. Congress stopped the U.S. intervention in Angola taking
place with money and military supplies. These developments have
clouded current negotiations in the SALT talks.

A joint statement was worked out by John J. McCloy for the
United States and V.A. Zorin for the USSR, and issued on
September 20, 1961. This statement said in part

> 1. The goal of negotiations is to achieve agreement on a
>   programme which will ensure:
>   That disarmament is general and complete and war is no
>   longer an instrument for settling international prob-
>   lems. . .

---

[13]Sir Edward Grey, *Twenty-five Years* Vol. II, (New York: Frederick A. Stokes Co.,
1925), p. 53.

The negotiators did not reach agreement on control and the promises and goals of that agreement were never carried out. But both countries recognized the desirability of general and complete disarmament. Did they do it with tongue in cheek?

In spite of deep political and ideological differences, the United States should seek to build on the limited detente which has already been achieved with the Soviet Union and the People's Republic of China, and make an all-out effort by agreement and example to reverse the arms race. Our dwindling and limited resources are now wasted on a suicidal competition in arms which is threatening us with bankruptcy.

Risks have to be taken for peace as they are all the time in war. Sometime the world must come to its senses and use the precious manpower, money and resources for meeting the basic needs of God's children everywhere. If sometime, why not now?

SOME THINGS THAT SHOULD BE DONE ABOUT DISARMAMENT

1) Recognize that political settlements need to precede or accompany disarmament agreements. The mediation and peace-making and peacekeeping functions of the United Nations should be strengthened and really used. Part of the problem is that our world is characterized largely by the anarchy of nations which are more concerned with wielding power than promoting justice. A limited world government should be evolved that can promote justice and prevent wars.

2) Halt the nuclear arms race and begin the destruction of nuclear bomb stockpiles. The history of the SALT talks so far has mostly been ratification of existing or projected levels of arms rather than any serious reduction of strategic weapons. Reverse the current doctrine of first strike capability and the possible first use of nuclear weapons.

Dr. Harold C. Urey, who helped create the atom bomb, was quoted in *Collier's* for January 5, 1946, "as a scientist, I tell you: *there must never be another war. . . .*I have never heard — and you have never heard — any scientist say there is any scientific defense against the atomic bomb."

3) Elect a President who really believes in pushing hard for general and complete world disarmament both by international agreements and by unilateral initiatives. We need a President who will appoint a Secretary of State who will exert strong leadership

toward that objective. Such leadership, in my judgment, is imperative.

There has not been such a combination since World War II — neither a President nor a Secretary of State who made any all-out drive for ending the arms race. I even heard Secretary of State John Foster Dulles argue in a Senate hearing that the rearmament of Germany was a step toward general disarmament.

4) Replace the leading hawks in Congress with members of Congress who will strive for a more peaceful foreign policy and for far-reaching reduction of armaments. It is incredibly difficult to get Congress to cut out expensive weapons systems because of the pressure from defense lobby groups, from constituents in districts with large military installations or defense contracts, and from campaign contributors who favor heavy defense expenditures. Most Congressmen play it safe instead of voting against military appropriations.

5) Work out a program of rapid-phased withdrawal of U.S. troops from other countries.

6) Reduce the U.S. military establishment drastically.

7) Undertake an all-out effort for promoting peace among nations. Seek an end to all arms sales to all countries. There are many suppressed people who long for more democracy and freedom. The opportunities for peaceful change must be encouraged. President John F. Kennedy said, "If we make peaceful revolution impossible, we make violent revolution inevitable."[14]

8) Abolish the CIA and clandestine actions by the Internal Security Division of the FBI usually in the name of national security. Covert CIA operations have included the Bay of Pigs invasion of Cuba, the Phoenix program in Southeast Asia which murdered untold numbers of people, the subsidizing of the military junta which overthrew the Allende government, various assassination plots which were never carried out, and other such reprehensible actions.

In the United States we have seen illegal wiretapping, mail interception, burglaries, cover-ups, surveillance and infiltration of lawful groups, political dossiers on individuals and groups exercising legitimate rights of citizens and other violations of freedom under the excuse of preserving national security.

---

[14]President John F. Kennedy in an address to Latin American diplomats, March 13, 1962.

9) Abolish military training in high schools and compulsory military training in colleges and universities. Use the money saved for intensive courses in ways to establish and maintain peace by nonmilitary means.

10) Establish by Congressional and Executive action the appropriate organizations to deal effectively with the problems of conversion from military spending to constructive civilian programs for the benefit of the country directed toward cushioning unemployment and enhancing the general economy. Many economists believe that, if the appropriate political decisions were made, such transfers could be accomplished without a serious depression and that spending on civilian needs would employ more people than spending the same amount of money on military projects.[15] The production of war material endangers our economy by concentrating the skills of scientists and technicians in the production of weapons rather than toward the solution of our economic and social problems.

A Closing Personal Word

As this sketchy story draws to a close about my life thus far on my journey, I am humbled when I think of the many, many people and events which have influenced and enriched my life and which have left me in their debt. I was fortunate to have had parents whose teaching and example emphasized integrity and responsibility. Country school developed a love of nature and of flowers and a spirit of self-reliance and independence. Even though I grew up in the country I did not sufficiently understand the delicate balance of our environment and the importance of protecting it.

College helped me learn to work with people, to enjoy the companionship of books, to understand some of the lessons of history, the clash of ideas, and an interest in doing something about unsolved problems of the human race. I came to know a number of the great spiritual leaders who swept through the colleges in my student days.

Although I did not follow up professionally my technical training in agriculture, yet my years at Iowa State College have strengthened my concern that a hungry world should be fed. Nor did my studies in

---

15See *The Empty Pork Barrel*, by Marion Anderson, Public Interest Research Group in Michigan, Lansing, Michigan, April 1975. This publication claims "an analysis of the years 1968 through 1972 indicates that the net annual job loss nationwide, when the military budget averaged about $80 billion, was about 840,000 jobs.

agricultural education and in religious education lead me either into teaching in high school or college or into religious education in the churches. But that training was an important factor in preparing me to try to educate the public on citizen responsibility in a democratic society and in seeking to win the assent of reasonable minds in Congress for advancing justice and protecting liberties.

Nearly forty-five years work with the Society of Friends has been an intellectual joy and a spiritual association of inestimable worth to me. I have felt a maximum of intellectual and spiritual freedom. While one is never able to say or do everything which he would like to, I have never had to say something or do something which I did not believe. That doesn't mean that in working politically one does not have to accept compromise or defeat — those are inherent in the political process. But it did mean that I did not have to be torn apart intellectually or spiritually by internal conflicts because of regulations, or restraints, or dogmas externally imposed.

The American Friends Service Committee and the Friends Committee on National Legislation gave me an opportunity as a staff member for wide travel at home and abroad, for meeting personally thousands of Friends and non-Friends around the globe, for participating in interminable committee meetings and conferences, and in concentrating on questions which seemed important for the welfare and the survival of the human race. Serving on the Governing Board of the National Council of Churches has brought me in touch with many of the leaders of the churches in the United States. Attendance at the Third World Assembly of the World Council of Churches in New Delhi, India, was a fellowship of Christians from almost every corner of the globe as they met to worship and think together about their common tasks and problems.

My friends have often heard me say that if speeches would save the world, it would have been in good shape a long time ago. I have no idea how many speeches on how many topics I have inflicted on how many audiences. There is something thrilling and perhaps intoxicating about facing an eager audience on some urgent question of mutual interest. But we are witnessing a considerable change for the better in conferences with various techniques to increase audience participation, including breaking up into smaller groups and buzz sessions, rather than relying just on formal speeches, debates, panels, and questions from the audience. The spoken word still has an important role in informing and arousing people to their opportunities and responsibilities although it plays a lesser part in forming attitudes and crystallizing action than it used to because of radio and television.

My life has been spent on controversial questions — the only ones worth investing one's life in. The resolutions of conflict demand our best endeavors. We can never eliminate conflict in a crowded, competitive, sinful, selfish world but we can improve our methods of solving conflict, and we can abolish war as the method of meeting conflict.

The search for peace must be accelerated. Mankind has to quit destroying the treasures of the past and the prospects of the future by mass mutual suicide. Our allegiances, our institutions and our loving concerns must be worldwide.

I used to describe myself with a touch of irony — as a champion of "lost causes." But a friend of mine interrupted me and said, "No, as a champion of causes not yet won."

The association with hundreds of colleagues in scores and scores of organizations has been very rewarding. Lobbying has brought me into contact with a great variety of men and women in the House and Senate on a wide range of issues. I regret that I haven't taken the time to develop much closer personal ties with more elected and appointed officials who were struggling with difficult and far-reaching decisions, and who would disappoint and grieve many people whatever decision they made on a given issue.

Too often I have been given credit for things which my colleagues have done. Too often I have been silent when I should have spoken out. Sometimes I've spoken when I should have listened. But I am thankful that my life has been led by God into various crusades for ending war and promoting peace and cooperation, for ministering to the hungry and disadvantaged, for upholding the rights of those discriminated against, and for trying to speak in behalf of men and women and children around the world who have no voice in Washington except that of their concerned fellow men, about the decisions of our government which affect their welfare and may determine their lives. May our minds and hearts be dedicated to those causes not yet won but whose time has come.

At the Swarthmore College Commencement on June 2, 1975, I was awarded an honorary degree of Doctor of Humane Letters. Each honoree has an opportunity to make a brief charge to the graduating class. Looking to the future, my remarks were as follows:

CHARGE TO THE SWARTHMORE COLLEGE GRADUATING CLASS

I look out on this class of 1975 with a great mixture of awe and envy because you have the majority of your life ahead of you to invest in building a better world than my generation has left to you.

You've listened to hundreds of lectures. In three or four minutes I cannot add to your knowledge. You are already overbrimming with it. I can't add to your wisdom because that is a much more elusive and scarce commodity. What I would like to do would be to challenge you to deepen your motivation to do what you can as an individual and as a member of whatever group you can associate yourself with, in building a world without war, without walls and without want.

War is the ultimate obscenity of today. It is the job of your generation not to glorify it but to abolish it. You and I are suspicious of simplistic solutions and all I can do in these few minutes is to give you a little shorthand on these three questions. I am speaking this morning as a veteran of the First World War which started when I was a student. I hope that will not be the case with generation after generation in the future. What you tend to get out of one war is another one.

There are four imperatives, among others, for the elimination of war. One is effective world organization. If the United Nations is weak, the United States has helped to make it weak. What we need is a strengthened United Nations and a whole web of international organizations to carry on the intellectual, political, social and economic and other aspects of cooperation in solving of conflicts before they break down into war.

Second, is drastic world disarmament. The United States spends more on armaments than the entire income of the total continent of Africa. The world spends on an unresolved arms race just about the equivalent of the entire income of the underdeveloped one-half of the human race. That is one measure of the cost of the failure of humanity to learn to live together.

A third imperative of peace is world development. The resources of the world ought to be used to abolish world hunger, to narrow the gap between rich and poor, and to slow down and stop population growth. We should try to see that every child that is born, is wanted, is loved, and has an opportunity for food, for shelter, for employment and for a decent and dignified life.

Fourth, is world reconciliation. Understanding must be built between East and West, between Communist and non-Communist, between rich and poor, between Arab and Jew, between North and South, so that the whole world moves forward to use the resources with which the world is so abundantly supplied. What bridges are you ready and willing to build across these frontiers?

In the second place, a world without *walls*. The human race ought to be one family under God. What can you do to lower the walls of nationalism, of racial prejudice, of religious intolerance, of riches and poverty, the strong and the weak, or discrimination because of religion or race or sex?

And last, a world without *want*. In a country as affluent as the United States we could abolish dire involuntary poverty in part by a system of guaranteed minimum income. Since from the economic point of view we could do it, our failure to do so is a moral responsibility for which we as citizens are responsible. To do it on a world scale would, of course, be very much more complex. We need a world of equitable distribution of income, and equitable opportunities.

You can make a significant contribution as individuals. But as individuals we can only do a little bit compared to what needs to be done. You can't change the world without effective organization of people around the interests and achievements that need to be made. So I hope you will be movers and shakers, not only as individuals, but as members of organizations like the Friends Committee on National Legislation and a hundred more that I could name, which are working for the goals we are talking about this morning.

Now when you toddle back to your fiftieth reunion I am not going to be here, because I would be 127 at that time and between you and me, I don't think I am going to make it. The best I know a Wilson has done was an aunt of mine who died earlier this year at 107. A few years before that she said to her daughter who was a teacher, "We must go down and vote. There is a particular candidate that I want to see elected." So they went to the polls and voted. The next day when the votes were counted, her candidate had won by one vote. My aunt had swung the election and she was 101½ years old. So don't give up yet!

No, when you get back in fifty years, I hope you can clasp the hands of your classmates and say with the Apostle Paul, but in the Quaker sense, "I have fought a good fight. I have done my part as an individual and my part as a citizen, and my part as a part of organized society to build effectively — there is no use being good without trying to be effective — toward a world without war, without walls, and without want."

E. Raymond Wilson Chronology

September 20, 1896	Born, Cloverdale Farm, Morning Sun, Iowa.
September 1903	Entered Honey Creek Country School.
May 28, 1914	Graduated, Morning Sun High School.
1914-1915	Helped father on the farm.
1915-1916	One year at Monmouth College, Illinois.
September 1916	Entered Iowa State College, Ames, Iowa.
April 7, 1917	United States declared war on Germany; left school soon after.
July 10, 1918	Enlisted U.S. Navy; entered service July 27, 1918.
December 24, 1918	Mustered out of U.S. Navy.
January 1919	Re-entered Iowa State College.
1921	President Student YMCA.
June 15, 1921	B.S. Animal Husbandry, Iowa State College.
1921-1923	Associate secretary, Iowa State College Student YMCA
June 11, 1923	M.S. in Vocational Education, Iowa State College.
1923-1926	Three year Lydia C. Roberts Fellowship, Teachers College, Columbia University, New York.
1924-1926	Lived in International House, New York City, the first two years after it was built.
June 3, 1925	M.A. in Religious Education, Teachers College, Columbia University.
1925-1926	Part-time Executive Secretary, National Committee on Militarism in Education.
1926-1927	Japanese Brotherhood Scholarship, Japan. Traveled 6000 miles in Japan, including Hokkaido, Saghalien and Taiwan.
December 10, 1927	Death of Charles B. Wilson, Raymond's father.

1927-1929	Home on the farm in Iowa.
1929-1930	Secretary, Pennsylvania Committee on Militarism in Education.
Summer 1930	American Seminar in Europe with Sherwood Eddy — England, Germany, France, Poland, Soviet Union and Switzerland.
1930-1931	Associate Secretary, National Committee on Militarism in Education, New York City.
September 1931- November 1943	Field Secretary and later Educational Secretary, Peace Section, American Friends Service Committee, and Dean of Faculties for eleven Institutes of International Relations.
August 4, 1932	Married Miriam Davidson, Stanwood, Iowa.
August-December 1932	Biddle Scholarship to study the League of Nations and attend Council meetings in Geneva on the Manchurian conflict.
October 1932	Miriam and Raymond drove through Switzerland, Austria, Czechoslovakia, Germany, Holland, Belgium and France.
1936	Joined Frankford Monthly Meeting, Society of Friends, Philadelphia, Pennsylvania.
January 14, 1937	Kent Raymond Wilson born.
September 1-8, 1937	Attended Second Friends World Conference, Swarthmore College.
Summer 1938	Second American Seminar in Europe with Sherwood Eddy — Berlin, Vienna, Paris, Geneva, London, Denmark, Sweden, Finland, Germany, Russia, Czechoslovakia. Italy with Russell Freeman and Andrew W. Cordier.
April-May 1940	Trip to wartime Europe with Errol Elliott — Rome, Geneva, Paris, England and Ireland.
January 2, 1942	Moved into Wilson home at the Bryn Gweled Homesteads, Bucks County, Pennsylvania.

November 1, 1943	Helped launch the Friends Committee on National Legislation — 1943-January 1962, Executive Secretary; 1962-1975, Executive Secretary Emeritus, full-time.
September 22, 1944	Lee Roy Wilson born.
1948-1951	Chairman, National Civil Liberties Clearing House.
1951-1966	Member, Board of Trustees, Wilmington College.
Summer 1952	Delegate, Friends World Conference in Oxford, England; traveled in England, Germany, Austria, France, Switzerland, Holland and Denmark.
1953-1961	Chairman, National Conferences on Disarmament, Washington D.C., 1953; New York City, 1954; Chicago, 1955; Washington, 1959 and 1961; Friends National Conference on Disarmament, Germantown, Ohio, 1958.
March 11, 1955	Death of Anna Jane (Willson) Wilson, Raymond's mother.
July 1956-June 1957	Quaker International Affairs Representative in Japan for AFSC; also visited South Korea, Okinawa, Hong Kong, Taiwan and the Philippines.
1957-1962	Chairman, Disarmament Information Service, Washington, a clearing house of representatives of nongovernmental organizations.
June 6, 1958	Honorary Degree, Doctor of Laws, Haverford College
August 22-September 6, 1961	Consultant, AFSC East-West Reciprocal Seminar at Poughkeepsie, New York.
November-December 1961	Observer at the meeting of the Commission of the Churches on International Affairs in Bangalore, and delegate from the Friends General Conference to the Third Assembly of the World Council of Churches, New Delhi, India.

December 1961	Ten-day visit among East African Friends in Kenya.
1963-1975	Member from Philadelphia Yearly Meeting on the Governing Board, National Council of Churches.
September 1964	Delegate to Christian Consultation on Approaches to Defense and Disarmament in Friedenwald, West Germany; visited London, East and West Berlin and Geneva.
December 16, 1965	Death of Miriam Wilson.
1966-1971	Member Board of Directors, American Friends Service Committee.
June 7, 1970	Honorary Degree, Doctor of Human Reconstruction, Wilmington College
October 1970	T. Wistar Brown Fellowship, Haverford College, to start work on *Uphill for Peace*.
July 15- August 5, 1971	Jerome Davis' Eastern European Seminar, Poland, Soviet Union, Bulgaria and Hungary.
January 22- February 12, 1972	Visit to South Korea, Japan and Okinawa.
March 3-23, 1973	Visit to El Salvador, Costa Rica and Guatemala.
1973	Thirtieth Anniversary celebrations, Friends Committee on National Legislation.
June 2, 1975	Honorary Degree, Doctor of Humane Letters, Swarthmore College.
September 1975	Moved into Friends House, Sandy Spring, Maryland.

Wedding snapshot of Raymond and Miriam Wilson, August 4, 1932.

Raymond Wilson's maternal grandparents, James R. and Myrilla Willson.

His paternal grandparents, James X. and Martha Wilson.

Raymond Wilson's parents, Charles B. Wilson and Anna Jane [Willson] Wilson.

The Charles B. Wilson farmhouse, Cloverdale Farm, Morning Sun, Iowa, where Raymond Wilson was born. Photo taken before Raymond planted shrubbery around the house.

Honey Creek Country School which Raymond Wilson attended for eight years.

Raymond Wilson in sailor suit with his younger brother, Russell, 1900, and as seaman second class, U.S. Navy, 1918.

Imperial University YMCA. Dormitory group including staff. Professor Yoshina and the Y Secretary, Mr. Fujita, in the foreground.

The party that traveled around Formosa in 1927. L to R. Sam Crathwell, E. Raymond Wilson, Gordon Bowles, Arthur Rinden, Clarence Griffin, C. Koshimura.

Women weaving china grass fiber, Formosa.

Bunun men in Formosa with headhunting knives.

Paiwan chief and his daughter welcome us at Rikiriki, 1927.

Ainu couple, Hokkaido.

Japanese middle school boys drilling with wooden guns at Hondo, Western Saghalien, 1927.
Left, Mt. Asama, highest active volcano in Japan.

*The Mark Davidson farmhouse, Piney Knoll Farm, Stanwood, Iowa,
birthplace of Miriam Davidson Wilson. It was on the ivy-covered front porch
that the Wilsons were married.*

*Raymond Wilson's mother, Mrs. Charles B. Wilson, Raymond and Miriam,
Miriam's father and mother, Mark and Mary Davidson, 1932.*

Raymond and Miriam Wilson visit the tall corn country in Iowa for the AFSC.

Two tons of literature packed for the Institutes of International Relations.

*Staff of the Institutes of International Relations, AFSC Peace Section. L to R:
E. M. Best, E.L. Harshbarger, Ray Newton, Joseph Conard, Guy W. Solt,
Alfred Cope, Tom Sykes, Raymond Wilson, and George Selleck.*

*Part of the FCNL staff at 104 C Street, Washington, May 1966. Back row:
Allen Treadway, Edward F. Snyder, Caroline Treadway, Mary Jane Simpson,
Alice Stout. Middle: Patricia Parkman, Jeanette Hadley. Front: Antoinette
Simmons, Wilmer Cooper, Joan Gibbons.*

Raymond, Miriam and Kent beside the Carl Mackley Houses wading pool, 1940. Photo by Don Honeyman.

The Wilson house at Bryn Gweled soon after it was built.

Lee, Kent, Miriam and Raymond Wilson, 1959.

Raymond Wilson visits the Committee on Appropriations on one of his many lobbying rounds.

Raymond Wilson with Friends in Africa, 1961. Thomas Lung'aho is on Raymond Wilson's right.

Swarthmore College awarded Raymond Wilson an Honorary Doctorate of Humane Letters at the Commencement exercises, June 2, 1975. Here he is giving his charge to the Senior Class to do all in their power to "build a world without war, without walls and without want," a speech which brought a standing ovation.

STUDIES IN
POETIC DISCOURSE

MERIDIAN

Crossing Aesthetics

Werner Hamacher
& David E. Wellbery
Editors

Translated by
William Whobrey

Translations from
the French and Latin by
Bridget McDonald

Stanford
University
Press

Stanford
California
1996

STUDIES IN
POETIC DISCOURSE

Mallarmé, Baudelaire,
Rimbaud, Hölderlin

Hans-Jost Frey

Originally published in German in 1986
as *Studien über das Reden der Dichter*
by Wilhelm Fink Verlag
© 1986 by Wilhelm Fink Verlag

Stanford University Press
Stanford, California
© 1996 by the Board of Trustees of the
Leland Stanford Junior University
Printed in the United States of America

CIP data are at the end of the book

Stanford University Press publications are
distributed exclusively by Stanford University Press
within the United States, Canada, Mexico, and
Central America; they are distributed exclusively
by Cambridge University Press throughout
the rest of the world.

Contents

STUDIES IN
POETIC DISCOURSE

Foreword

READER: What is this book you've written all about?

AUTHOR: I can't explain it to you. Why don't you just read it? I said what I had to say as well as I could and I can't say it any differently now.

READER: You're not getting off the hook that easily. You claim to be a scholar of literature, and I don't think it's asking too much to ask you to explain what you're doing. What would happen if everyone just started talking without being responsible for what they said? You have to be able to explain what you're talking about and how you relate to your subject. That's the only way to create useful secondary literature.

AUTHOR: That may be true, but hopefully the damage is minimal. And besides, I'm only marginally concerned whether what I do is scholarly or not, and whether it is useful or not. Instead, . . .

READER: Do you really think that anyone would want to read your book after hearing what you just said?

AUTHOR: Whoever hears this, as you just said, has already begun to read our discussion and has therefore declared a willingness to listen to us. It may be possible to create an interest in the unexpected. Those who cling too much to their own expectations can't listen. That holds true for those who read a text for its usefulness as well.

READER: Do you want to be read the same way you read?

I

AUTHOR: That's not for me to say. Everyone reads the way they best know how. How do I read texts, anyway? I wanted to comment on this when you interrupted me a minute ago.

READER: That may have been for the better.

AUTHOR: Perhaps. Our relationship to a text constantly changes. You could almost say that we get closest to a text when our relationship to it seems most endangered. Finding and losing are close bedfellows in reading. The most important discovery is all the closer the less we can firmly hold on to it.

READER: That's just another one of your paradoxical formulations that sounds intellectual but doesn't help at all. Said more plainly: they remain incomprehensible.

AUTHOR: I'm sorry. I would like to speak plainly and clearly. But it's still hard for me to talk about literature. I have tried several times to say something about it in this book. In trying to understand a text, it seems to me that the question of my relationship to a text, for example, is a question manifest in the text itself.

READER: Not a very original thought! Nonscholarly readers have always tried to insert their own questions into the text. The text as a mirror, as the forest that echoes what is shouted into it and that can't be seen anymore for all the trees.

AUTHOR: What you're describing is appropriation. If we read this way, we reduce the text to ourselves. It fulfills our own expectations in that we find in it what we already have. But I'm talking about something else when I say that the question of my relationship to a text is the same as the question of the text itself. A text is discourse, and I speak about it. By speaking about it, I do what I am speaking about, and therefore, whenever I speak about a text, I also speak about what I'm doing. The question of my relationship to a text is always the question of my relationship to my own speaking about it.

READER: If that's your question, then it's a long way from being the text's question, which, after all, doesn't concern itself with other texts.

AUTHOR: Perhaps it does, if whatever is said always means something. But I'm really concerned about something else. Imagine that you're riding on a train. Most of the seats are occupied, and the people are talking. No matter why they're traveling, people always have something to say that they think is important and that they think other people have to know about. They are completely engrossed in what they are doing, and they speak with a single purpose, just like the train staying on the tracks. You sit there and listen because you can't do anything else. But suddenly you stop listening. You don't hear what the people are saying, but only that they are talking. And you notice that they only talk so much and so loud and for so long, because they aren't aware of what they're doing. They don't even notice that they're talking. They're much too caught up in what they're saying. But you sit there and hear talking, without paying attention to what's being said, and wait for the train to derail. You feel like a rock on the tracks.

READER: I really don't know what you're talking about anymore.

AUTHOR: Then we have reached our destination—literature, I mean, a speaking that is no longer concerned just with what is being said, but with itself. Authors are conscious of the fact that they are speaking. This kind of discourse need not concern itself only with speaking, and even if speaking becomes a topic, we fail to exercise any control over it, since discourse is something that only exists through speaking. We have to speak to have discourse. Even if you sit silently in the train and only listen, discourse takes place inside you. If you listen in a way that what is said is less important than the speaking itself, then you are listening literarily, and you speak literarily whenever you are aware that what you say is being spoken. You will then speak differently and speak about different things. Literature is, among other things, the admission of its own linguistic nature. This is why politicians' speeches are not literature, even though they could be read in a literary manner, something that would not necessarily increase their effectiveness.

READER: Now I see what you're getting at. If literature concerns itself not only with communicating this or that but also with discourse, something that makes communication possible in the first place, then it develops a relationship to itself that is similar to the relationship that you have to it. You are concerned with a discourse that is concerned with itself. In this way, you find your relationship to a text within the text itself.

AUTHOR: That's pretty good. But now the difficulties involved in my relationship to my own discourse and that of others start to become clear. If both are concerned with discourse, that is to say, with themselves, how can they be kept apart?

READER: The literary text is not concerned with itself the same way you are. It is a self-referential discourse, whereas you say this or that about it as self-referential discourse. Why can't speaking *about* the text be considered instrumental discourse?

AUTHOR: I thought I had already answered that. But perhaps this is one of those questions that must constantly be asked without ever being answered. Whenever I talk about literature, I am concerned not with a discourse that says something but that says itself, that is, a noninstrumental discourse that goes beyond its own subject. An instrumental speaking about literature would be a discourse that remained completely untouched by the insight that causes it to be communicated to begin with, even though such an insight opens up the possibility of a discourse that is both objective and self-referential. How can I speak about the self-referentiality of discourse and at the same time forget that I'm speaking?

READER: That doesn't seem to me to be so improbable, if you allow me to follow your train of thought for a minute, but seems unavoidable. Why do you even want to talk about the special relationship of discourse to what is spoken and to itself? Only because literature doesn't explicitly talk about this relationship itself, and because it couldn't possibly do so, because it is it. To describe this relationship, you have to be able to keep your distance to it. You might not be speaking literarily, but it then becomes possible to speak of the literary. But that's only something I read in your book.

AUTHOR: That won't stop me from contradicting you. Your solution is a weak compromise in which literary discourse is unable to speak about what it is in order to be literature, whereas speaking about literature avoids being literature in order to be able to say what it is. I'm afraid I can't be that easily appeased. Can't we imagine a speaking about literature that is itself literature?

READER: A literature that says what it is? Now you're asking me to do more than you yourself have done. Why don't we just trade roles? It would be fun to be an author. You're imagining some kind of literature that would no longer require any secondary literature, because it could say everything itself. Or said another way: secondary literature would be the highest form of literature both by being self-referential discourse and still being able to speak. This utopia is just too imprecise. The way your question is worded, it can only be answered with yes. Nothing prevents speaking about literature from being literary discourse . . .

AUTHOR: If that's the case, then we can do away with literary criticism. Literature is all we need.

READER: . . . but speaking about literature is not literature. You said that literary discourse always says something but is at the same time concerned with itself. A literary discourse is possible whose subject is the self-reference of literary discourse. But this spoken self-reference does not communicate the special way in which that special discourse refers to itself. This reference presents itself as the discourse that speaks of self-reference. But the premise of what is said within this discourse remains out of reach and unspeakable. It is possible to talk about the self-reference of literary discourse, and it is possible to express how discourse refers to itself in a text, but no discourse can accomplish this on its own, because it always exists as something greater than what it is able to say. All discourse would require interpretation if we want to understand how a text speaks about itself through itself. But this is not always a beneficial undertaking. Literature on literature: perhaps these are texts in which what is spoken can be read as a figure for its being spoken. Texts like those that have engaged your efforts. Interpretation—what I read your book to mean—is the attempt to recognize the figure as such and thereby to resolve it, so that it is applied to the unique way in which a special text constitutes discourse as self-reference.

AUTHOR: I'm grateful to you for this somewhat tedious production that I encouraged you to pursue. Now I have a better understanding of the kinds of texts I have written about, and how everything that is written relies on the reader. Would you mind if I used our discussion as a foreword to my book?

READER: I prefer the middleword or nowword to the foreword or afterword.

AUTHOR: Sayings like that guarantee an effective ending. But they are less effective than one might hope. There really isn't anything that can be said against what you've just said, but the fact that you have said it allows it to become what it would least like to be: the foreword or afterword.

H.-J. F.

Mallarmé

THE UNDECIDABILITY OF TEXTS

According to an often professed characteristic of literary discourse, expression cannot be separated from its being expressed. This inseparability of being expressed and expression, if it is to be taken seriously, precludes all attempts at determining a text's meaning and at making this meaning available to others. The burgeoning business of meaning determination, which to some extent always lives off the claim of saying the same thing but in a different, better, simpler, clearer way, runs the risk of atrophy. What remains is the task of reading texts differently from the way in which communications are received. Texts cannot be understood if we stop short at a presumed meaning. They must be allowed to continue their discourse. Only when they continue speaking can they survive as the expression of what has been expressed and as the irreducible relationship between the two. A reader is not primarily a receiver of content. A reader enables a text to speak. This is quickly forgotten, however, if the reader is too intent on discovering what the text has to say. Hunger for information is deadly to language. Information always attempts to suppress language in favor of what it can convey. Literature is created when we realize that information is dependent on language. By contrast, if we imagine what is expressed to be the thing itself, forgetting its

7

dependence on language, then referential illusion takes over. This can be observed in the most elementary form of linking expression to expressing, whenever everything that is expressed is represented only by its having been expressed. No human discourse can, by itself, prove the existence of what it says. The potential for lying is based on the fact that discourse alone cannot verify an extralinguistic reference. Whether someone is telling the truth or not cannot be determined by discourse, and the smooth flow of the exchange of utterances in human intercourse is based not on the recognizable truthfulness of the utterances but either on a mutual trust that grants the discourse partner some degree of trustworthiness or on the fact that the referential illusion has become a convention.

If referential illusion is the assumption that whatever is expressed has some extralinguistic correspondence, then simply ignoring this correspondence cannot result in unveiling the illusion, since by doing so we would fall prey to the object of investigation. The illusion is not based on assuming an extralinguistic reference but rather on overlooking the uncertainty of this assumption. The simple negation of this assumption would lead to the same mistake. It is therefore impossible to come to grips with referential illusion by asserting a lack of referentiality. The realization that texts are undecidable is the only solution. What is expressed remains linked to discourse, not because there is no correspondence outside of discourse, but because it is uncertain whether or not these correspondences exist. Certainty about what is expressed exists only within the discourse in which it is expressed and only for as long as it remains dependent on the fact that it was spoken. This limitation of expression to the discourse that transmits it contradicts a common, even dominant concept of language as an instrument of mediation, leading to the assumption that what is expressed exists outside of language before and after its transmission and is therefore no longer something that is expressed but an extralinguistic given. Language is degraded to an available means, used whenever needed. But suppression of the importance of discourse as such does not extinguish that importance. Discourse is allowed instead to break out all the stronger in other ways. Whoever believes that language is an instrument believes that he can control it and use it in any way he desires. But in refusing to acknowledge the dependence of what is expressed on its being expressed, he subjects himself to the effects of discourse without being able to defend himself against it. He is dominated by discourse because he is vulnerable to everything it says without considering its linguistic status. Given that the utterance gains such power as soon as it is forgotten, it is not redundant to speak about it in terms of itself. Literature is this kind of discourse.

Whatever literature may be cannot be determined from its contents. It is less an arbitrary speaking about special things than a special speaking about arbitrary things. Literature is a manner of speaking. It speaks in such a way that it contradicts referential illusion. A literary text is never primarily information, but discourse. This is not to say that this discourse remains within itself and says nothing, but that it works against the tendency to decouple the expressed from the being expressed, and that, by saying what it says, always reminds us both of itself and the foundation of the expressed. By always drawing attention to itself as discourse and thereby to the linguistic foundation of what is expressed, literature attains the power that other forms of discourse claim to have when speaking beyond themselves and over themselves. It is less mystified and mystifies less. Sometimes literature suffers from being itself by denying itself the chance of having any direct effect. If it becomes untrue to itself, then it loses itself. If literature remains true to itself, then the chorus of ephemeral voices refuses to take it seriously. This does not compromise literature's importance, however, because when literature is taken seriously, it is misunderstood. Literature's task is to question the fact that what is expressed is always taken seriously, a fact that characterizes everyday relations between people. This questioning reveals the unbreakable link of what is expressed to its being expressed. This can only take place by putting obstacles in the way of referential reading, making it more difficult for what is expressed to transcend discourse. Literature is reserved. It avoids assertions or identifies them as such. It does not easily grant meaning from within itself but offers several meanings without enabling a choice between them. Since literary texts are undecidable, they remain present in speaking, and they speak continuously. Their reservedness is the reserve from which they draw the strength to have meaning and out of which they never really lose themselves if their message is not to fall silent.

The opinion that texts are not reliable, namely when answers, not questions, deeds, not words, are called for, has to do with their reservedness. But too many evil deeds take place in the name of a discourse that is taken seriously to justify ignoring discourses that do not claim to take themselves seriously. If taking seriously what is expressed equates to suppressing its language, then literature deserves to be taken seriously as a disruption of seriousness, but in such a way that it questions itself as well. This is prompted by texts that do not allow themselves to be pushed into the backwater of undecidability. The suspension of information characterized by the insolubility between expressing and expression is disrupted by the fact that extralinguistic reference is absent not because it does not exist, but because we cannot know whether it exists or not. A literary text is not a text that has no reference but a text whose referentiality is uncertain. Therefore literature should not be misunderstood as a speaking that is satisfied with the irreducible language of what it says. In its undecidedness, it talks about whether its saying is the only reason for what it has expressed, or whether this has any correspondence that would allow a transcendence of language. Literature is not only a speaking that cannot be founded in the extralinguistic, but it also fails to recognize this impossibility. It is therefore not enough to say that the literary exists within the insoluble relation between expressing and expression or in the transcendence of referential illusion. The literary also refuses to be satisfied with this definition. Literature distances itself from itself and finds itself through self-denial. The literary is therefore not accessible through a theory that could define it as what it is. Literature always questions whatever it threatens to become, not to negate it but to bring it back to undecidability. The undecidable text has an undefinable status, because it constantly calls itself into question. The doubt in referentiality is always preferable to referential illusion, especially when it counts.

Mallarmé's texts distinguish themselves by a particularly high degree of restraint. They are never informative and don't present themselves as what they seem to say. Since they don't communicate anything tangible, they are considered to be dark. Where darkness is a reproach, the concept of language as means predominates. Whoever speaks darkly does not know how to use language properly and therefore expresses himself unclearly. Clarity is defined as the flawless transmission of a message. If discourse had no other function than to act as a transmitter, then it could properly be found lacking. There is, however, a kind of restraint with regard to communication that is not lacking. The darkness of discourse, the fact that it does not directly lead to something definite, counters referential illusion and moves discourse itself into the spotlight. This is discourse's own clarity, lacking in communication that merely seeks to inform, remaining hidden from itself in shadows of self-deception. Because darkness disrupts direct communication, it blocks the unambiguous path of communications and creates a realm where discourse is freed from its instrumental bonds.

Communications are disrupted if what is being communicated is uncertain, that is, when a single meaning is lost and the multiple meanings of the dark text challenge the linearity of discourse. Ambiguous discourse leads to a fork in the road with several options. It is impossible to choose between them because each is the right one and none can be ignored. For Mallarmé the image of a bifurcated fish tail sometimes represents the suspension of this hopeless uncertainty. It appears in his *Coup de dés* (Throw of the dice) in connection with the indecisive Hamlet figure as the "impatient final bifurcated flakes" (*Oeuvres complètes*, 470) and is always meant wherever sirens surface or disappear. In the prose *Solitude*, the fish tail characterizes indeterminate discourse and becomes a metaphor for undecidability. "When a speaker affirms, in one sense more than its opposite, an aesthetic opinion, generally beyond eloquence, which seduces, the result is nonsense because under sinuous and contradictory blows to the rump, it is not at all unhappy to end in a fish tail; only refuses that this be displayed and spread around like a public phenomenon" (408).

Mallarmé distinguishes between the assertion of an opinion that leads to something stupid and the idea that brings oppositions together, terminating in a fish tail that points to unavoidable duality. The impossibility of taking one path or the other obviates the requirement to choose one over the other. Opinionated discourse is instrumental because it serves as a means of saying something to someone. This scheme of communications is challenged as soon as the message can no longer be linked to a point of view, which is to say, to a speaker. All opinion depends on a point of view, thereby rejecting undecidability. The opinionated decide when no decision can be made. This results in absurdity ("the result is nonsense"). The word *défalquer*, "to cut off with a sickle," points to the absurdity inherent in cutting off one end of the fish tail, that is, in the decision that enables the assertion of an opinion. The decision is a mutilation of the undecidable idea, which can only be determined in one particular direction if the opposing direction is suppressed. The problem of ambiguity cannot be solved by force. The decision must be suspended between the available possibilities, and the discourse that cannot be attached to one or another meaning must remain suspended. This suspension of discourse is a darkness grounded in undecidability. To characterize the discourse that cannot be determined, Mallarmé uses the concept of vagueness. In a late poem, we read: "Le sens trop précis rature / Ta vague littérature" (The too precise meaning, erases / Your vague literature [73]). In the contrast between vagueness and precision, the metaphor of cutting off, also present in the etymology of decision (*décision*), is effective. Precision destroys vagueness by surrounding it with clear, cutting lines. The limits of the precise and unequivocal seek to protect it from the limitlessness of vague ambiguity. Turned around, the opening to vagueness renounces an aesthetic that could define works of art as final forms. Vague discourse hovers in language, by which it is carried and which it employs. It does not rush purposefully toward a statement but remains suspended in the tension between expressing and expression, in which it receives itself as a potential of the statement.

Vagueness is an unsatisfying condition because the possibilities of discourse are blurred by undifferentiation. Insofar as the experience of vagueness is equivalent to the experience of lost differentiation, there always exists within it the desire to break out. If ambiguity is recognized as irreducible, then it is so only through a differentiation that is not also a decision. The end of Mallarmé's sentence, in which he refuses to spread out the fish tail and display it publicly, seems, however, to reject any such attempt. It is not enough to renounce the reduction of ambiguity by choosing one or the other meaning, but it is also not enough to want to spread out ambiguity through the display of individual meanings. This kind of spreading out and rolling up (*dérouler, étaler*) is only made possible by sacrificing the simultaneity of meanings. As meanings in the clarifying dissection of vagueness are presented, one after the other, ambiguous discourse is transformed into a series of single meanings. Every single phase of this series is an equally inadmissable and unavoidable determination of the undecidable and therefore, if only temporarily, a precise reduction that can only be challenged in the next phase of the unfurling process, in turn subject to the same indictment. The unfurling of the simultaneous within the sequential makes different meanings available, but it also invalidates ambiguity because it is not a succession but a coincidence of meanings. Mallarmé refuses to unfurl the fish tail because a list of meanings would destroy the many possibilities of vagueness. This presents what might be unavoidable in the attempt to explain a dark text. It seems unavoidable to take apart what is in simultaneity still rolled into one. We must ask ourselves, however, what essential part of the ambiguous text is lost in the transformation of the simultaneous to the sequential. If nothing were to be lost, then the clear text could easily replace the dark text, whose darkness becomes nothing more than a reparable deficiency. If darkness is necessary, however, then it must be understood as such, as something that never can be translated into clarity. The transformation of the simultaneous into the sequential opens itself to the accusation of being a reduction of the ambiguity of the text, from whose recognition it proceeded in the first place. As soon as unfurling the meanings of a text is understood to be a reductive act, then one must be able to show in what way this act misses the text. It should therefore be possible to grasp the irreducibility of the ambiguous text in its positivity.

Something always remains unspoken in ambiguous discourse. It does not unfurl itself and therefore always contains more than it specifically states. Discourse restrains itself in indecision, which is not just insufficiency, because it is only made possible by the fact that a decision is absent. The totality of unrealized possibilities is the prerequisite for the decision that destroys the indecision upon which it relies. Both relate to each other as actuality toward virtuality. Decision makes actuality possible but also destroys all possibilities brought together in virtuality aside from the one that was chosen. Thus decision is always impoverishment. Speaking, however, is deciding. Whoever speaks says something to the exclusion of everything else. If ambiguity eliminates the decisiveness of discourse, then virtuality is preserved in actuality by ambiguous discourse. Ambiguity is the actualization of virtuality as virtuality. This actualized virtuality is incapable of being a statement in which it would simultaneously be nullified. It is accessible as the unspoken within the ambiguous discourse in which the statement is suspended. This accessibility of the unspoken is difficult to understand. It must be connected to the way in which the ambiguity is experienced. This cannot occur in a way that allows for different ways of reading a text, since this would mean that what may not occur has already occurred. When we read a discourse twice, the unfurling of the ambiguous text into a sequence of singular meanings would already have taken place, by which the undecided balance, the main element of ambiguity, would migrate to the poles between which the ambiguity hangs suspended. If there is to be another way of experiencing ambiguity, then it must precede any such unfurling and allow for the simultaneous acceptance of a plurality while recognizing the singular sequence of words. The ambiguity that lies in the unviolated unity of discourse is its density. The experience of the density of a text is the motivation for the analytical explication of meanings. The varied meanings are present in the experience of ambiguity as density, but this unity makes it impossible to separate the different levels of meaning. The undecidability of meanings in the experience of density is the same vagueness that Mallarmé claims for literature. If density is experienced independently of the unfurling of ambiguity, then it is something more than the sum of distinguishable meanings. Density is what is unspoken in discourse, where virtuality is constantly effective as an unyielding foundation and as the eternal fountain of meaning, beyond grasp in individual meanings and their sum. The force of meaning is most active when it does not rest in the acquired meaning but when it can be read as an eternal promise. This promise lies in the irretrievable deferment of the spoken in the clarity of undecidable speaking.

The dense text is not explainable, because any explanation is a dilution of the density and thereby misses its mark. Understanding in literature is not the determination of meaning, because ambiguity prevents discourse from ever being replaced by something that has been determined from it. In every attempt to fix discourse to this or that possible meaning, we are thrown back to the discourse itself, which will not allow itself to be reduced. Discourse is ambiguous not because it means more than one thing, but because it presents itself as the potential of its own meaning. The power of discourse lies not in what it expresses but in its speaking. An unresolvable tension exists between the two, by which speaking manifests itself as the unspeakable potential of what has been spoken. The unspoken part of discourse is what makes it possible to say anything at all. But discourse as its own unspoken is made accessible in the multiplicity of meanings as its inexpressible simultaneity. Discourse speaks in undecidable ambiguity, always focused not only on the external or what is to be expressed but also on itself as the source of all that is expressed. Mallarmé says that in poetry the initiative is given to words (366). This is to say that they are no longer used by someone to communicate something already known but begin to gush out. Out of their relationship to each other, words gain the ability to pour out their hidden and repressed potential for meaning. The texts that allow this force of words to be active are no longer unequivocal or equivocal, meaning this or that. They are carried by the pure ability of words to have meaning. Speaking regains its virtuality through them (368).

THE FOAM

A la nue accablante tu
Basse de basalte et de laves
A même les échos esclaves
Par une trompe sans vertu

Quel sépulcral naufrage (tu
Le sais, écume, mais y baves)
Supréme une entre les épaves
Abolit le mât dévêtu

Ou cela que furibond faute
De quelque perdition haute
Tout l'abîme vain éployé

Dans le si blanc cheveu qui traîne
Avarement aura noyé
Le flanc enfant d'une sirène.

By the crushing cloud stilled
Shoal of basalt and lava
Down even with the enslaved echoes
By a trumpet without force

What sepulchral wreck (you
Know, foam, but babble there)
Supreme, one among the derelicts
Abolished the stripped mast

Or that which furious failing
Of some high perdition
All the vain abyss spread wide

In the so white hair trailing
Avariciously will have drowned
A siren's childish flank.

As obscure as this poem may be, it observes convention sufficiently to permit an attempt to read it for meaning. This sonnet consists of a single sentence, the subject of which is *naufrage*. Belonging to this are certainly the verb *abolit* and perhaps *cela*, either a form of *celer*, "to hide," or the demonstrative pronoun. The *ou* offers either two objects to *abolir* (*le mât, cela*) or two activities (*abolir, celer*). In both cases, the two tercets are to be read as a dependent clause introduced by *que* with the subject *l'abîme* and the verb *aura noyé*. The entire first strophe should be linked to *naufrage* as an apposition, the link being established by the participle *tu*. Finally, the word *quel* at the beginning of the fifth verse marks the sentence as a question constructed as follows: "What wreck, stilled by the crushing cloud by a trumpet without force, abolishes the stripped mast or that which the abyss will have drowned—the siren's childish flank?" In addition to this is the inserted parenthetical sentence, an address marked by the otherwise absent punctuation. Within the parenthetical sentence, the word *écume* is delineated by commas and thereby clearly marked as the addressee.

The poem speaks to the foam but doesn't know what about. What the discourse intends to incorporate is the question that is the poem. The foam has knowledge that would answer this question but is unwilling to part with it. The foam hints at some event, but what this event might be is left to speculation. Perhaps a shipwreck, but this remains uncertain. By attempting to read a shipwreck out of the first strophe, the syntax leads us to read the second verse ("Basse de basalte et de laves") as an apposition to *naufrage*. Since the reef (*basse*) is not the shipwreck but rather the cause, the effect (*naufrage*) is used as a metonymy for the cause (*basse*). The rocks as a cause for the shipwreck remain hidden (*tu*) because they are hidden under the water's surface. Only the foam knows of their existence but is content with its own foaming (*mais y baves*). If a ship were wrecked, the cause remains uncertain. The reef is only made suspect by the foam. If *sépulcral naufrage* is assumed to be a metonymy for the basalt reef, then the completely groundless relationship between reef and shipwreck has another aspect, the invisible tombstone for what was lost in the shipwreck.

It is a reminder of what has died but is hidden and visible only insofar as the foam hints at its existence, if not at something else.

It is not only uncertain if there was a shipwreck, but what, if anything, went down with it. Perhaps it is a ship (*le mât dévêtu*), but maybe it is a siren that has drowned in the ocean. Whatever it might have been, it cannot be discovered except through the mediation of the foam. Since everything has disappeared, there is no way to determine what it was. This presents us with the central importance of the foam. It is the only given. Everything else must be gleaned through it. The foam is language. But it speaks in a way that fails to lead to any affirmative communication. In that the foam never speaks explicitly but only presents possibilities, it possesses the virtuality of ambiguous discourse. It might point to a reef that caused a shipwreck, in which a ship, but maybe a siren, was lost. All of this remains suspended in the virtual meaning of the foam and is relegated to the uncertainty from which the poem constitutes itself as a question.

This is not the only place where foam is used as a metaphor for language. In the poem *Salut*, written only slightly later, foam in a wine glass is equated with the discourse of the poem:

> Rien, cette écume, vierge vers
> A ne désigner que la coupe (Vv. 1–2)

> Nothing, this foam, virgin verse
> denoting only the cup

There is nothing that prevents us from interpreting the foam as poetic discourse in *A la nue accablante tu* (By the crushing cloud stilled), understanding the parenthetical sentence as a self-address, unless we were unwilling to accept the very far-reaching consequences of this equivalence. If the poem addresses itself as foam, then it thematizes itself as ambiguous discourse. The poem is a discourse of a particular kind. It is no longer ambiguous but has as the topic of its discourse its own ambiguity. The poem is caught in the problematic situation created whenever ambiguity is no longer just an event but a topic in and of itself. Ambiguity requires the simultaneity of meaning. If meanings are presented simultaneously, however, then they can no longer be kept apart. The determining factor for the density of ambiguous discourse also determines its vagueness. This vagueness can only be overcome by the uncovering of meanings in succession, whereby the density is diluted. If the poem is more than just ambiguous discourse but also speaks about that ambiguity, then it must deliberate on the meanings of the foam. This is indeed the case, since the poem is constituted as a deliberative explication of what the foam refers to. The alternatives of ship and siren ("Quel naufrage abolit le mât dévêtu ou cela que . . ."), vaguely alluded to by the foam, are unfurled, presenting clear possibilities. The poem's structure in its entirety is the unfurling of the fish's tail, to which its last word so aptly alludes.

Such a reading of the poem shows it to be a unification of what cannot be united. It not only has the density of ambiguity but also unfurls the multiple into an understandable sequence. Ambiguous discourse unfurls ambiguity, that is, it speaks implicitly and explicitly at the same time. What must be understood here is the simultaneity of simultaneity and succession, the concurrence of concurrence and sequence, the unification of ambiguity and explication in one single event. (Additionally, the ambiguous word *cela* reestablishes ambiguity within its own unfurling.) It should be assumed that whenever the vagueness and darkness of ambiguous texts fail to present themselves as correctable faults, this simultaneity cannot be replaced by an explicating text but becomes irreducible. Any explication is, by nature, reductive. What is gained in clarity is lost in density. When a text becomes more dense, darkness must be accepted. If Mallarmé's text combines these two opposite tendencies, we are left with the question whether or not some form of explication is possible that is not reductive and that, at the same time, retains the darkness of the text. The differentiation of simultaneous meanings within a succession can be achieved in various ways. With Mallarmé we find neither the preference of one potentiality over another nor simple tabulation. This differentiation occurs instead as a true alternative. The elements of succession are bound by the conjunction *ou*. Things confront each other in the alternative that cannot be combined because they are mutually exclusive. Their simultaneity as the either-or of the alternative is therefore precarious and demands resolution. The alternative includes the demand for a decision that excludes one or the other element. As the alternative *or* requires a decision, it expresses the fact that a decision has not been made. The compulsion to decide is only possible in indecisiveness, which itself leads to the formulation of the alternative. The *or* is the suspension of the decision by which ambiguity would be reduced. In that the possible meanings of the foam are bound together in the unfurling of the *or*, the decision has been postponed. Simultaneity is maintained as the untenable sequence within the alternative's concurrence. The alternative demonstrates the tendency towards clarity by demanding decisions. Insofar as no decision is made, the undecidability of ambiguity remains.

Mallarmé's poem unfurls the ambiguity of the discourse of which it speaks (*écume*) in such a way that it succeeds in circumventing any decision. But the undecidability of the unfurling discourse differentiates itself from ambiguous discourse in that it sways back and forth between explicitly different and enumerated possibilities, whereas the foam has the undifferentiated virtuality of implicit and vague discourse. If the alternative can provide meanings of the foam, and if it has within itself the need for decision, what then prevents a decision from being made? All criteria are lacking. To make a decision, the foam would have to surrender its knowledge and share its meaning. In view of its silence, all attempts at interpretation only result in fictitious meanings that cannot be compared with anything else and are therefore all equal. The interpretation of the foam is therefore in no way decisive but is instead groundlessly arbitrary. Many other possibilities offer themselves aside from ships or sirens. The arbitrariness of what is evoked by the explicit discourse of the poem leads at the same time to the renunciation of what is elicited in the interpretation of the foam. What does not yet exist in the undifferentiated vagueness of the foam is created in the unfurling discourse as something that no longer exists and perhaps never did. The interpretation is the story of the disappearance of what appears within it. The ship appears in order to be shipwrecked, the siren surfaces in order to drown. By renouncing explications of the foam, the poem returns to the vague ambiguity it is. In that the poem reads itself on a circular track and in doing so returns to itself through the rejection of this reading, it prevents its speaking from being forgotten, and its speaking continues to have meaning by never arriving at any meaning.

This interpretation of the poem remains disappointing. It seems now to say that ambiguity is not reducible and that its dense discourse can only be unfurled in such a way that the decision between its possible meanings remains suspended. The poem, seen as discourse explicating the foam, constitutes itself as an alternative and demonstrates undecidability. But in this way the poem is read in exactly the way in which it refuses to be read through what it expresses. Undecidability has now become the meaning to which it has been reduced. Instead of being undecided, the poem now states undecidability and loses it by being forced to do so. As a discourse on undecidability, it returns to the decidability of communication. And yet it should be read as the foam to and of which it speaks, because the undecidability of which it speaks is its own. This is not to say that any attempt at interpretation becomes untenable. The diversity of meanings in the unfurling discourse provides the impetus that causes the poem to foam.

This divergence is evident not only in the undecidability of possible meanings for the foam, ship, and siren. The word *basse* must, if the sentence is to be constructed coherently, be taken as a noun, denoting a reef hidden just under the surface. Nevertheless, the supposition that the word comes from the adjective *bas* is not off base. Not only are these the same words, but in the tenth verse we find the word *haute*, and height and depth are united in the word *basalte*. *Basse* and *haute* are the unfurling of *basalte*, just as in the greater structure of the poem, *écume* is dissected into *mât* and *sirène*. This repetition of the unfurled structure is not only a confirmation but also brings something into view not heretofore noticed. The origin of the word *basalte* does not have anything to do with height and depth. This connection is established in the confrontation with the words *haute* and *basse* and associated with them through sound. The word is not used here in its conventional meaning but according to its sound value, which in French provides the word, based on its phonetic proximity to other words, certain possibilities that are here put to good use. But if *basalte* contains the opposition of *bas* and *haut*, this by no means eliminates the conventional meaning. Basalt is confirmed as a volcanic rock by the lava that appears in the same verse. The verse "Basse de basalte et de laves" comes to represent the double meaning of words in Mallarmé's text. *Basalte* is phonetically coupled with *basse*, semantically with *laves*. The words are to be read two ways. On the one hand they fulfill their normal function of meaning, from which we would not want to free them, and on the other hand they bring new meaning to their surroundings with their phonetic relationship. The word *basalte*, in its internal opposition, stands for the word that flows high and low and is important both as something meaningful and as meaning. This contrary effectiveness of the word—away from itself and towards itself—is represented in the verse by the reversal of sounds that makes the word *basalte* a symmetrical axis from which the verse goes out in opposite directions to the phonetic association *basse* and the semantic association *laves*:

The normal and the poetic meanings of *basalte* are not randomly placed side by side but are meaningfully related to one another. The basaltic crystallization of the linguistic lava, uniting height and depth, gives the word the volcanic qualities it signifies. The movement from the depths to the heights is the eruption in which the furibund abyss rises. This is countered from up to down by the sinking of the ship and the drowning of the siren.

This unfurling can be seen in the text in another way, most noticeably in the word *éployé*, present not only for its conventional meaning, but also because it embodies in the letter *y* the bifurcation of the fish tail. The text of the eighth page of the *Coup de dés*, in which the fish tail of the siren appears, comes together in the letter *y*. A similar form is evident in the letter *v*, especially prevalent in *A la nue accablante tu*. The split from below is contrasted with the split from above in the inversion of the *v* to the ^ . The *accent circonflexe* (*circonflexe*: "Turned from one side to the other . . . orthographic sign in the shape of an inverted *v*" [Littré]) and the letter *v* relate to each other in the same way that both parts are related. Where they converge, a basaltlike structure is formed, such as in the word *dévêtu*, whose graphic structure represents its relationship to the word *nue*, which means not only the cloud but is also the positive expression for being unclothed, whereas *dévêtu* describes being naked in a negative way. The same suspension between up and down is visible in the verse "Tout l'abîme vain éployé," where the white hair of the foam whirls between heaven and sea as the unfurling of the abyss.

This passage is suspended in another way. The twelfth verse can be linked to either *éployé* or *noyé* as a more precise determinant. The abyss, which is inherent in the white hair, drowns the siren, but she is drowned in this hair, which, as the foam of the sea, is also the discourse of the poem itself. Indeed, in the verse "Dans le si blanc cheveu qui traîne," the siren drowns as "si . . . traîne" and even carries the crown of foam of the *accent circonflexe*, to which she is entitled as *reine*. If read this way, the verse itself, appearing as black on white, is the white hair, unless the hair is taken to swim between the lines. Then the drowned would only be accessible to those able to read between the lines. It is what the *trompe sans vertu* keeps secret, without keeping the verse secret (*sans vers tu*), because it speaks without virtuality. In contrast, reading between the lines recognizes language as black on white and experiences it more as an elemental establishment of meaning than in its given symbolic function. The poem, which makes the uncontrollable possibilities of language possible, is not only discourse that repeats what is given. It is also productive in that, according to Mallarmé, the initiative is left to the words themselves (366).

A speaking that allows language to thrive is no longer easily determined. A speaker can no longer be made responsible for what is expressed. The language speaks without his even knowing it. Nothing is expressed that might precede its being expressed or that is not given through it. Discourse is no longer the transmission of something to someone, nor is it the communication of something between two people. Discourse is no longer understandable when viewed as based on communication, and it does not gain its meaning from some purpose. What kind of discourse is this, and how can it be understood aside from what it is not? It is the discourse in which language foams, and for which the word *baver* stands in the poem.

Baver is the babbling of children and the speaking of those who have trouble sticking to the subject. In the older language, the word primarily means "to chitchat," "to speak nonsense." *Babiller* and *bavarder* are variants. The blabbermouth talks so much because he says so little. Precisely because chitchat is so meaningless, it is always found lacking. Its fault lies in the fact that it remains incomprehensible because it says nothing. Chitchat is speaking for speaking's sake. Those who have nothing to say, chitchat. Chitchat is stingy with messages. This stinginess is reflected in the French word *bavard*, just as the word *avare* is only slightly less stingy to become *bavard*. *Baver* is noncommunicative as a discourse that says too little. The foam has knowledge but speaks in such a way that it remains concealed. *Baver* generally has a negative connotation. It could very well denote the kind of hermetic, secretive style of speaking of which Mallarmé has always been accused. A journalist used these words in 1898:

> [This] poet, he composed, in all sincerity, never with the intent of mystifying his contemporaries, these extraordinary logographies which forged his fame, and whose key he carefully kept to himself. By what cerebral aberration did this scholar and finely lettered man, appreciator of our best classics, misrecognize, with his mind made up, pen in hand, one of the primordial characters of the genius of the French language—clarity? Mystery! He could even, if necessary, dis-

cern his own thoughts among the heavy darknesses in which he liked to envelop them. (*Documents Mallarmé* II, 39)

If one accepts the negative tone of *baver*, and we have nothing in the poem that speaks against this, then these sentences can be read as a paraphrase of "tu / Le sais, écume, mais y baves." The poem anticipates later criticism by ironically presenting its own discourse from the perspective of those who do not understand. Incomprehension is manifest when communications are expected where none are intended. Comprehension begins when *baver* is no longer understood as a negative thing. This revaluation requires the renunciation of instrumentality and the recognition of a discourse that does not communicate or that does so in another way. If one breaks the chains of convention, then it becomes questionable whether the foam conceals any knowledge at all. The word *naufrage* contains the first-person pronoun, so that the assignation of this knowledge becomes unsure: "you / Know, foam, but babble there." If the speaker in the poem had this knowledge, he could share it. If, however, it foams at the mouth, then it is either unimportant to know the extent of this knowledge, or it relates directly to the manner of speaking of *baver*, shared by you and me. *Baver* is the discourse of the poem, which can no longer be criticized from the viewpoint of instrumentality but should be understood in its positive aspects as the foaming of language.

The words *écume* and *baver* serve not only to characterize the poem's manner of speaking, they also belong to the same speaking they characterize. They not only point to the foam, they *are* the foam. The poem is the foaming of these two words, from which the predominant sound groups of the text can be derived. *Baves* is used several times as a rhyme but also belongs to *basse, basalte*, or to *abolit, abîme*, in which its initial sound appears in reverse, as well as to the many words with *a* and/or *v*. *Ecume* finds its echo in *échos esclaves* and *accablante*, but also in *suprême, abîme*, and the common *u* and *é* sounds. The entire poem seems to swirl out of *écume* and *baves* like foam. It shows itself to be an unfurling of a new kind. We are no longer concerned with unfurling the possibilities of the foam's meaning; instead we let the foam froth up, the language run rampant. The foaming of the language is the unfurling in the verse "Tout l'abîme vain éployé." The abyss is not only what reveals itself in the foam but also the foaming itself. The word *abîme* contains elements of *écume* and *baver*, and in the middle *î*, the foam comes to a head and sprays out language. Perhaps the song of the drowned siren rings out in this *î*, a relatively rare sound in the poem. This frothing of language has nothing to do with onomatopoeia, which always presumes a given meaning assigned to a certain sound. The linguistic foam is not representative but productive. The poem speaks not of the foam itself but of foam as an attempt to say how it occurs.

Whenever language foams, its message is endangered. The poem *A la nue accablante tu* can be construed as a sentence. It is therefore linear according to a discourse ruled by logic. But the difficulty in determining the parts of the sentence and the uncertain assignment of others points to a threatened grammar and to a force that counteracts it. Foam does not foam linearly. It sprays like fireworks. Everything is illuminated and becomes dim at the same time. The movement of foam is purposeless, eruption from a predestined and regulated scheme, volcanic eruption, not forward, but up from below, as with basalt, claiming a space wherein the relationships run helter-skelter and no longer respect convention. Words for Mallarmé are not closed entities with precise meaning, something they have become in everyday discourse. They have a depth that allows them to speak in noninstrumental ways. In this way, *accablante* contains *blanc*, *écume* plays on *écrire*, and *abolit* on *lire*. But the borders between words also become permeable: in *blanc cheveu*, the adjective is put in the feminine form *blanche*. This frothing of linguistic function cannot be forced into the structure of a coherent communication. Word bubbles are blown within the framework of the poem and create billowing constellations, reflect each other, permeate one another, and pop. What pops, breaks apart and disappears. What is to be communicated sinks in the foam of the linguistic gale, leaving language to speak alone. The superfluous arises out of the foam, frothing up from the broken crust of functional language. Where the superfluous takes over, it can no longer be controlled and becomes troublesome. The superfluous is by no means unimportant because it is not used. Its presence without being used makes it so worrisome. The useful is gotten rid of by being used up. The superfluous makes itself known because it is not used up as the scandalous presence of the useless. The foam is abysmal in its lack of foundation. The distressing and uncontrollable part of literature is its foaming, in which instrumental discourse is dissolved and dispersed, and in which language begins to unfurl its abysmal character. The linguistic play of words is unjustifiable within the structure of the poem. Since they have no justifiable foundation, they become doubtful guarantors of their own order. So too the dream that, according to one of Mallarmé's early insights, constitutes itself in its lack of referentiality as *men-songe* (*Correspondance* I, 207f.). Foam is dream, and the poem is a place of dreams wherein the norms of the waking world are set aside and normal relationships are confused. These dreamlike cross-connections, unconcerned with grammatical order, enable widely dispersed parts of the poem to be illuminated. Thus, lying and deceit (*mentir, tromper*) are conjured in *trompe, faute,* and *avarement* without being derived from their common usage or injected into a statement that could be attributable to the sentence. These allusions, uncorralled by grammatical structure, are the bubbles of foaming language. Linguistic foam is the play of words that remains irreducible and must remain within the confines of the poem because it is unjustifiable. The poem does not say nothing but foams over what it says with the superfluity of its allusions. In the play of allusions, language is superfluous and without foundation. It is no longer subsequential in its superficial bottomlessness but is a suspended outgrowth and sublimation of itself.

The foam stands for language. It characterizes the poem's manner of speaking. It is therefore a metaphor: the poem speaks in the same way that foam foams. But nothing is gained. The similarity between language and foam is not grasped at any conceptual level. The "understanding" of this metaphor assumes that the poem is experienced as something foaming. This is possible to the extent that the poem happens, since it is, in the broadest sense of the word, spoken and heard. This is to say that the metaphor represents the speaking of the poem, accessible only through its being spoken.

What happens when the poem is spoken? Not only is the poem spoken, but the poem expresses *something*. Speaking the poem is expressing *something*. This thing that is expressed is removed from the speaking. All speaking is concerned with making itself more dark and forgotten. As speaking gravitates towards what is expressed, it remains unexpressed. Nevertheless, whenever a poem is spoken, somehow speaking is present as the enablement of what is expressed. Not only is something expressed; language occurs, enabling something to be expressed in the first place. The transpiring language remains unspoken as the spoken, but it can be experienced in speaking as its enablement, as long as what is expressed is experienced linguistically and is not confused with what it stands for. The experience of expressing something attaches the experience of what was expressed as something that is expressed without having been articulated.

Does expressing something have to remain unexpressed? If it is expressed, then it is no longer expressing but something that has been expressed. The word *expressing*, which I am constantly using, means the expressing that is expressed. What I'm doing now, speaking about the act of expressing, which makes the having been expressed of expressing possible, is far removed by the very fact that I transform it into something expressed. To avoid this unavoidable demise of expressing, we would have to fulfill the seemingly contradictory requirement of expressing the expressing of something without letting it become something already expressed, or: expressing it without expressing it. This is perhaps less hopeless than it appears. If expressing something is not to become something expressed and thereby lost, then it must be replaced by another something that has been expressed that expresses the unmentioned expressing indirectly. This potential is fulfilled by metaphor. In metaphor, expressing is not expressed but meant. What is expressed is something else, fashioned in such a way that it makes what is meant but not expressed accessible. Expressing something can thereby be expressed without becoming something already expressed: when it is what is meant by what is expressed.

This accessibility of expression via what is expressed is bound to the intransferability of the metaphor. Since expressing never becomes what is expressed without forfeiting the expression that it is, what is meant by what is expressed must not become something that is expressed. The nature of the metaphor, which does not say what is meant, must be kept viable. Waiving the hardly obligatory limitation of the metaphor, it can generally be said that discourse can make expression accessible when what is meant does not coincide with what is expressed, which is to say, whenever it does not name, but speaks figuratively.

How is expressing something made accessible in figurative discourse if it is never what is expressed but only what is meant? The step from expression to meaning must be made without reducing the metaphor. The metaphor must not be translated but must take place. Expressing something cannot be made accessible as something expressed, because it would no longer be what it was. But it is only what it is in the act of expression. If the metaphor is to make expressing something accessible as its unexpressed meaning, then it can only do so by provoking the act of expression as the occurrence of the metaphor. The unsolvable metaphor produces the expression that is its meaning.

Something else must be added. It is a special kind of expression that is to be made accessible, namely the expression that is concerned with expressing itself. It is, therefore, the expression of a discourse that speaks with a reluctance to lose itself in what it expresses. We are therefore concerned with the expression of a particular manner of discourse, with an expression that is negatively defined by the fact that it cannot be reduced to the expressing of something. This becomes accessible in Mallarmé's poem as the meaning of the foam. The foam is a metaphor for the expression of the poem. But expression as what is meant by the metaphor is not made accessible by its translation but is accessible only to the extent that the metaphor produces the act of foaming discourse.

The transition from the preceding discussion of the irreducible metaphor to the metaphor of the foam in Mallarmé's poem has certain problems. It is easy to talk about the irreducibility of the metaphor as long as we are not exposed to it. Being exposed to it means: to experience its uncontrollability. The controllable metaphor would be the translatable metaphor. Any attempts to say what the foaming of language is are attempts at control: attempts at determining the expression of the poem through definition, banishing it to the safe realm of what has been expressed. If the metaphor relies on the impossibility of making expression into something expressed, it becomes untranslatable. The foam as the metaphor of expressing is not understood unless the expression of this understanding becomes itself a foaming discourse. In this way it falls prey to the metaphor that it brings forth in order to express itself.

The expression that is provoked by the metaphor as its meaning is initially the expression of the poem itself, since the poem says itself via the roundabout way of what is expressed. The poem speaks in such a way that what it expresses leads back to its being expressed as its unexpressed meaning. Isn't it possible that the metaphor triggers another expression? The metaphor is untranslatable, and what it means cannot be expressed without retreating from itself. On the other hand, the demand for translatability lies in the metaphoricity of the metaphor. All metaphors demand that their meanings be expressed. What happens—now in reference to Mallarmé's poem—when we submit to this compulsion? The foaming of expressing something is expressed as the meaning of the expressed foam. It is thereby possible to make the nature and stillness of the metaphor speak. The foaming of language can be described and understood at the level of what can be expressed. But the expression of the foaming poem does not participate. It is an expression that is lost in what it has expressed, that is, it succumbs to exactly the manner of expression from which the expressing removes itself. It may be that the discourse that expresses the foaming of the expression starts to foam itself. This means that the expressed meaning of the translated metaphor becomes a metaphor for its own unexpression becoming expressed. There is a gradual, not fundamental difference between this secondary metaphoric discourse and the primary metaphor. The meaning of the primary metaphor becomes what is expressed by the secondary metaphor. But in this problematic transformation of expressing into being expressed, as occurs in the translation of the metaphor, the secondary expression becomes the metaphor of the unexpressed secondary expression, and the primary situation is restored.

THE TREE OF DOUBT

In Mallarmé's later texts, the subject becomes more and more obscure, replaced by word games, a phonetic and orthographic ballet. The words are not restricted to their conventional use, but assume new relationships whose potential is provided by the alphabet, the origin of everything. This independence of language, which, instead of mediating, actually creates relationships, eludes the grasp of a reader who is looking for a message and in doing so rushes past the poem that exists as an expression and reexpression of itself. The dilution of the message and the undecidability of meaning is the flip side of an expression that understands itself less as making reality into language than as a realization of language. But not all of Mallarmé's texts are as marginal with regard to their message as his last poems. *L'après-midi d'un faune* (The afternoon of a faun), even in the late version of 1876, is a poem characterized by an unusual amount of action and narrative passages, something uncommon for Mallarmé. If the message is given more weight here, then this in no way excludes the play of words. It does confine this play somewhat, however, and allows instead a thematization of discourse in the poem no longer possible in the extreme texts that hardly *express* anything. *L'après-midi d'un faune* expresses the undecidability of discourse realized in the foaming discourse of *A la nue accablante tu.* This is not to say that *L'après-midi d'un faune* can be reduced to a message, only that the discourse of this poem is more closely tied to an object and can therefore be more easily read for content.

There is already an indication that the theme of undecidability is close at hand in the title. Mallarmé had the words *favne* and *églogve* printed with a *v* instead of a *u*. This could be an allusion to Roman orthography and brings the poem more closely into the realm of mythology. More importantly, we see here a graphic realization of bifurcation, the fish tail of the unsolvable alternative. The theme of decision is also stressed in the word *églogue*, which can be read on several levels. First there is the poem over which it stands, recognizable as a pastoral. According to its etymology, it means "the chosen," a chosen piece or a collection of such. This could also be interpreted as an allusion, considering that the poem is only part of a planned work that Mallarmé never gave up. The word also radiates from the poem itself:

> arcane tel élut pour confident
> Le jonc vaste et jumeau dont sous l'azur on joue: (Vv. 42–43)

> as confidant such arcanum chose
> the great twin-reeds one plays beneath the azure:

The chosen is selected out of many and is thereby distinguished as unique. Here the unique is a double, something that requires a choice. I will show that this propagation of indecision is actually the theme of the poem. It unfurls in the discourse of the Faun, as he reflects on his relationship to two nymphs. We are not only concerned with a dual object but also with a dual relationship, bringing both the erotic and the artistic side of the Faun to the fore. The importance of duality in this poem justifies the attempt at a more precise reconstruction of these relationships.

In the opening verses, the Faun speaks of the nymphs. They are no longer present, and he wants to provide them with some sort of immortality. He is overcome by doubt:

> Aimai-je un rêve?
> Mon doute, amas de nuit ancienne, s'achève
> En maint rameau subtil, qui, demeuré les vrais
> Bois mêmes, prove, hélas! que bien seul je m'offrais
> Pour triomphe la faute idéale de roses. (Vv. 3–7)

> So I loved a dream?
> My doubt, a mass of ancient night, concludes
> in many a subtle branch, which, since the real woods
> remain, proves, alas, what I offered to myself
> as triumph was the ideal lack of roses.

These verses have invited little comment, probably because, despite difficulties in certain parts, the argumentation of the whole seems to be fairly straightforward. According to the current interpretation, the Faun wonders whether the nymphs were real or only a dream. The proof that he only imagined the nymphs is that the trees, under which he believes to have seen them, remain. Robert G. Cohn writes: "The most direct meaning is that the reality of the woods—as opposed to the nonexistent nymphs (represented perhaps only by roses which he mistook for them)—proves his 'fault' (love-act) was only an 'ideal' or unreal one, with a sort of 'specter of a rose,' as in Gautier's familiar poem" (16). Such a proof should not be attributed to Mallarmé, even if put into a faun's mouth. The fact that the trees are still there could prove that the nymphs are no longer there (something not requiring proof), but not that they were not present earlier. Their current absence does not exclude their prior presence. That the trees, which the Faun now sees, are real, is not only not proof but not even an indication that the nymphs were not real. The question of reality cannot be answered in this way, and uncertainty persists. The Faun speaks in a way that makes it doubtful whether this uncertainty will ever be resolved. The verb *s'achever* not only means that the doubt is removed, but also that it is realized in the branches of its own uncertainty. This possibility is supported by the fact that in an earlier version, Mallarmé allows this doubt to sustain (*se prolonger*) itself in the branches.

Even if previous argumentation falls apart, we are still left with a proof. We are also left with a question: what is proven and how is it proven? It is proven "que bien seul je m'offrais / Pour triomphe la faute idéale de roses." This sentence seems to say that the Faun feels certain that the nymphs were an illusion. This would support the traditional interpretation. Aside from the fact that this does not disprove the reality of the nymphs, we are left with problems in understanding the later parts of the poem, where the Faun remembers his encounter with the nymphs in great detail. This casts doubt on whether everything was just made up. If this question remains unanswered, then the sentence that provides proof cannot be reduced to its answer. The Faun is not only concerned with the status of the nymphs but also with his own relationship to them. Words like *s'offrir, triomphe,* and *faute* relate to the emotional state of the Faun. He not only wants to know if the nymphs were real or not, but also to understand what they mean to him. His completely affective relationship to them is defined as love in the opening question, "Aimai-je un rêve?" The question whether the nymphs were dream or reality is motivated by this love and does not arise from an academic need to know. The actual presence of the nymphs only interests the Faun insofar as they mean something to him. Something is not loved just because it exists but because it becomes personally meaningful. This meaning is the basis for the Faun's relationship to the nymphs, and this relationship is not affected by the uncertainty concerning its status. The question "Aimai-je un rêve?" raises the possibility of loving a dream. The love of the Faun is therefore independent of the nymphs' reality or irreality because, in both cases, it is based on their meaning. Insofar as they have meaning, the nymphs are language, regardless of whether they are referentially real or not. Referential reality is unimportant until it begins to mean something. Even if the nymphs are real, the Faun does not love them as they are but as the image he has created. As long as this image, be it reproduction or representation, has meaning, then love has substance. It is not based on something external, something beyond control, but on the linguistic nature of the image. The opposite of this independence from the external is loneliness. The person for whom the other is what he means does not relate to the other in his otherness. He transforms the other into a language of his own, a language with which he then remains alone. Seen in this way, the Faun is lonely even in the presence of the nymphs. Whether they are present or not, it holds true that "que bien seul je m'offrais / Pour triomphe la faute idéale de roses." The word *faute* must not be interpreted as a love act (cf. Cohn, 16) (for why should this be a moral liability?), nor does it refer to the guilt of the roses, which trick the Faun into believing they are girls (Austin, 25). What can be gleaned from this passage is the deception and absence contained therein. The Faun's mistake, the reason for his loneliness, is turning his surroundings into language, thereby causing them to become unreal. This is described by a sentence from *Crise de vers* (Crisis of verse) as: "I say: a flower! and, outside the forgetting to which my voice consigns any contour, as something other than known chalices, musically rises, same idea and suave, the one absent from all bouquets" (368). As things begin to have meaning, they no longer remain what they once were. They receive their meaning from those for whom they are meaningful and who put this meaning in place of what is. This transformation of the other in language causes it to lose its otherness. It becomes a possession. Turning his surroundings into language is the cause of the Faun's loneliness. It pokes holes in the presence of his surroundings, which gives way to the notion he creates. In this "idealization," existence is replaced by language, recedes in its meaningless factuality, and is dissolved in meaning. The duality of this turning into language allows for a lasting relationship to the image, one independent of an external but sacrificing a real presence, and is represented in the verb *perpétuer*, which says what the Faun intends to do with the nymphs. It not only means perpetuation by preservation, but with *tuer* also infers the transition from presence to absence, the price for the appropriation of the other. Proven is the loss of presence in reality's acquisition of meaning.

The question is, how is this proof provided? The critics who want to prove the irreality of the nymphs point to the reality of the trees. Mauron (112), like Cohn, reads the previously quoted passage in this way: "Meanwhile, the shadow of past sleep evaporates; but the branches persist, remain 'the real woods.' Thus no more doubt. The Faun learns he was alone, alas, and that he was dreaming." But the syntactic structure of the text does not permit this reading. In the sentence "maint rameau subtil, qui, demeuré les vrais / Bois mêmes, prouve . . . ," *maint rameau subtil* is the subject of the proof, and *les vrais bois mêmes* is only an apposition. The proof is therefore not given in the real woods but comes from an insight into the special relationship between *maint rameau subtil* and *les vrais bois mêmes.* This relationship can be seen as a similarity, that is, a mixture of likeness and difference. We can assume that *maint rameau subtil* is a metaphor for doubt, represented by the branches of a tree that reach nowhere and protrude into nothingness, as a suspension between undecidable possibilities. The tree stands for what Mallarmé describes in other texts as a fish tail. In the prose poem *La gloire* (Glory), he speaks of "many a wavering idea floating away from chances as branches do" in connection with a visit to the forest of Fontainebleau, and Mallarmé calls the branches "flying arms of doubt" (289). If the tree is used as an image for doubt, it acquires meaning. It represents the Faun's uncertainty. This meaning does not depend on the factual presence of the tree but is made possible by the internal imagining of its structure. On the other hand, the real tree is unaffected by the fact that it now represents the Faun's uncertainty and remains what it was ("demeuré les vrais / Bois mêmes"). The Faun is caught up in the relationship between the real and the metaphorical tree, and insight into this relationship provides proof. The tree as such has no meaning. To the extent to which the Faun gives it meaning, it becomes language and is no longer a real tree, the meaningless object that it always was. This insight, gained with the help of the tree, into the relationship between the real object and the object that has gained meaning as metaphor is now transferred to the nymphs, providing proof of the nymphs' linguisticality regardless of their factual presence or absence. The question whether these are real or dreamed nymphs remains unanswered. The Faun is in any case alone with what they meant to him. Insofar as they have meaning, the nymphs have no extralinguistic existence but are only the Faun's language. The act of giving meaning leads to isolation. Meaning is not inherent in things but given by us. What is outside does not have meaning, and what has meaning is no longer outside. The external other disappears as it is given meaning and rescued from its exile to the availability of the known.

The tension between language and extralinguistic reality is not solved in the poem. In contrast to his counterpart, Hérodiade, the Faun refuses to recognize the disappearance of presence in connection with the turning into language. No matter how much he talks himself into solitude, he is speaking against language, which constantly takes away whatever he says. On an anecdotal level, the conflict is shown as the Faun's oscillation between art and sensuality. His art is playing the flute, and the process of turning into language is presented as the creation of the flute. This is Mallarmé's interpretation of the Syrinx myth. The nymph, transformed into reeds, becomes the material from which the Faun carves his flute, its sound driving the nymphs away:

> "Et qu'au prélude lent où naissent les pipeaux
> "Ce vol de cygnes, non! de naïades se sauve
> "Ou plonge . . ."
>   Inerte, tout brûle dans l'heure fauve
> Sans marquer par quel art ensemble détala
> Trop d'hymen souhaité de qui cherche le *la*:   (Vv. 30–34)

> *"And to the slow prelude whence the pipes*
> *are born, this flight of swans, no! of Naiades*
> *goes scampering off or dives . . ."*
>   Inert, all things
> burn in the tawny hour, not noticing
> by what art together fled this too much hymen
> desired by who seeks for *la*:

The Faun's story concerns the creation of music and the disappearance of the nymphs, from which the story originates. The tone of the flute as the most extreme expression of the transformation of the nymphs coincides with their disappearance. Physical presence dissolves in artistic expression. One excludes the other. The necessary, but in the case of the Faun completely involuntary, decision between the two is indicated in the word *prélude*, which contains *élu*, echoing not only artistic calling but also the choice of art over sensuality. The irreconcilability of meaningless reality and unreal meaning appears in the text as the contrast in which the indolence of nature and art find themselves. Etymologically, *inerte* means the absence of art and is here used as a direct negation of *art* to illustrate the irreconcilability of the Faun's art and surrounding nature. Its inactivity is based on the fact that it cannot carry out the request to speak ("CONTEZ," v. 25) and remains discourseless. The Faun's story is indirect discourse put into nature's mouth and dictated without being confirmed (*sans marquer*). Nature does not speak unless it is transformed into language, in which case it ceases to be what it was. This is what the Faun's art accomplishes. It makes reality, which it transforms within itself, disappear. The relationship between *inerte* and *art* corresponds to that between the meaningless reality of the tree (*les vrais bois mêmes*) and the meaningful, but unreal, branches of doubt. The special thing about the figure of the Faun in Mallarmé's poem is that he constantly experiences the exclusivity of presence and meaning but still tries to deny this and bring the two together. This is indicated in the expression "chercher le *la*," because *la* is not only the tone upon which music is built but also the sign for the feminine that the Faun seeks. Both together are "trop d'hymen souhaité."

And so the Faun reluctantly experiences over and over again that the linguistic appropriation of things is at the same time the loss of their real presence. What becomes meaning distances itself (as a meaningless reality) from the one for whom it has meaning. Mallarmé represents putting something into words as dissolution by using the extreme example of music. The melody, as "sonore, vaine et monotone ligne" (v. 51), contains nothing of the nymph, but is her loss and replacement by something completely different. This is why the transition from the visual image to its purely musical realization is expressed in the word *évanouir* (v. 49). This not only points to hearing (*ouïr*) but also defines the path from seeing the representative image to hearing the self-referential sonority by the *vanus* it contains as an emptying. This strong accentuation of emptiness, created by the Faun with language and music, only shows one side of his speaking. This expression does not come from wanting everything to disappear but is supposed to make present what has been lost. This is evident not only in the initial formulation of the intent as *perpétuer* but also in the decision to renounce music and rely only on words that can assume a representative function. This use of language to "paint" something is what the Faun employs in the second half of the poem to counter its destructive effect. Language should re-present that which, by becoming language, has lost its presence.

But before these evocative discourses can be traced, the process of becoming language must be defined more clearly. The sentence where the nymphs become language can and must be understood in two ways. On the one hand it states that the nymphs are language to the extent that they have meaning for the Faun. On the other hand they are only language insofar as the Faun speaks of them. They are language not only because they mean something but also because they are spoken. They are what has been expressed in discourse. The relationship between the nymphs as language and speaking about the nymphs is thematic in the Faun's discourse:

> Réfléchissons . . .
> > ou si les femmes dont tu gloses
> Figurent un souhait de tes sens fabuleux! (Vv. 8–9)

> Let's think it over . . .
> > if those women you describe
> Figure a wish of your fabulous senses!

The nymphs are interpreted here as the figure for the Faun's wish. But they are not only figures for the Faun but also something about which the Faun speaks. They point to the wish of the one who speaks of them as the object of his wish. Since the Faun speaks of something which in turn speaks of him, he characterizes his activity as glossing, that is, as an expression that refers to another in an elucidating manner.

The duality of the nymphs' being language is understandable through this wish, the motif of their being expressed. The Faun's discourse is the representation of what he wishes. What is expressed, however, is not only a representation of the desired object. The object as represented refers back to the wish, itself the basis for the representation. The wish, based on what is expressed, is not directed toward possession of what is desired but initially sees it as something represented in order to become inflamed. The one who wishes depends on language. The wish is based on the absence of what is desired, something present only in the imagination of the one who wishes. Representation is the linguistic anticipation of the presence of the desired object. The linguistic structure of the wish in Mallarmé's poem illuminates two problems that determine the Faun's attitude and discourse. The first concerns the already questioned importance of what is desired. The object of desire, insofar as it has meaning for whomever wishes, a meaning gained only from this relationship, has no real correspondence but is only defined linguistically. Insofar as the desired object is not a true image of something real, it becomes a figure. The desired object is a fiction of the one who wishes and remains without extralinguistic confirmation. This brings about the second problem. Representation of the desired object does not happen for its own sake. It is a substitute for a time when the wish is fulfilled, a time that comes when the represented is present and the representation becomes unnecessary. The discourse of the one wishing is therefore always directed against itself and occurs with a view to its own dissolution. The wish cannot manage without representation, but it seeks presence. If the object of desire lacks extralinguistic correspondence, then its fulfillment is at the same time a loss. What is gained is insufficient for the representation of what is desired. The one wishing falls victim to a dilemma. On the one hand, as the one who has the wish, he can only want its fulfillment. On the other hand, since fulfillment does not provide the desired object, if only because it is no longer desired, the fulfilled wish is accompanied by the desire to keep the wish alive, maintaining the representation and lack of correspondence of the desired object. The attitude of Mallarmé's Faun is characterized by this necessary contradiction.

His discourse can be read with a view toward the wish after fulfillment and the wish after the wish.

The Faun has, against his will, experienced that things lose their reality when they become language. He then rids himself of his flute with the ironic demand that it turn back into the plant it once was and decides henceforth to rely only on language. Language is recognized and employed as potential representation. Representation is a replacement for what is in fact missing. Whether it is called *feinte* (v. 58) or *souvenir* (v. 62), the story of the Faun basically makes present what is not. The events as they are told can be related to the representational role of the story, allowing it to be understood as the allegorical representation of its own telling. The Faun remembers having found two closely entwined nymphs. He overpowers the couple, wanting to satisfy his desire, but is forced to separate them. Since he can't decide between one or the other, both escape. He finds, possesses, and loses. A distance is overcome for a time but then reestablished. This structure not only determines what is narrated but appears again in the relationship between the Faun as narrator and the narration. This can be deduced from the typography of the final version of the text, which adds a level of meaning to the earlier versions by changing the relationship between the one who is speaking and his discourse. Mallarmé had the beginning and ending of the story printed in italics and placed in quotes, whereas the middle part retains a normal typeface. From the beginning, the story is expressly represented as something remembered, and the Faun as narrator is distinct from the figure in the narration. The Faun is aware of this distinction in the cursive passages. He knows that the past is only present as something linguistically represented. The quotation marks that designate the discourse as discourse confirm the awareness of the linguisticality of what is expressed. Here the story is, like the inflated grape that has no more juice, a linguistic replacement for a suggested missing reality. But only the replacement, no longer recognized as such, can count as complete. The Faun speaks to replace what is absent, but he speaks against the language he is forced to use, because he yearns to transcend it to win back what is expressed as reality. But this is precisely the goal of his discourse. He is "avide / D'ivresse" (vv. 60–61). The word *avide* contains the emptiness from which greed is fed, whereas in *d'ivresse* this emptiness is turned around in the intoxication of fulfillment. The Faun's only intoxicant is his own discourse. His intoxication is forgetting the narrator's language. For a short time in the middle of his story, he actually believes that he is experiencing what he is expressing. This ecstasy of forgetting language is marked in that the middle section is not set off as a quotation. The transition points are especially telling. The forgetting coincides with the moment the Faun possesses the nymphs. Sobriety sets in when he separates the nymphs and they escape. Here we see a parallel between the narration and the narrator's changing frame of mind. Where distance is overcome, the narrator succumbs to the illusion that what is narrated is also real. Where the loss of the desired object occurs, the narrator regains the distance created by an awareness of the narration as something transmitted by language. The relationship between the narrated Faun and the nymphs acts as a metaphor for the relationship of the narrating Faun to the act of narrating the story.

The Faun's discourse seduces him into believing what he says. The discourse is determined by the desire to repress language, allowing the making of the present to count as the present. The fulfillment of this wish is granted in the illusion of forgetting language. But it would be one-sided to characterize the Faun's attitude to his discourse as the wish for self-deception and illusionary fulfillment. We can easily recognize the joy of fable-telling (v. 9) and invention (v. 58) while fully acknowledging language. This is also recognizable in the capitalization of "CONTEZ" (v. 25) and "SOUVENIRS" (v. 62), which stand over the Faun's narration as a mark of confessed language. The other—artistic, playful, ironic— side of the Faun manifests itself in this joy in discourse, not for the sake of some extralinguistic goal, but from the creative force of need. This too has its correspondence in the story, hardly reducible to a failed erotic adventure. If the Faun were concerned only with the satisfaction of sexual urges, then it is difficult to understand why he doesn't hold on to one of the nymphs. Nothing in the interpretation to this point explains why there are two nymphs in the story. This duality is important because it presents the Faun with a choice he is incapable of making. He loses both nymphs because he would like to satisfy himself with one without having to give up the other. If union with the one nymph is fulfillment, then the refusal to give up the other means that the Faun wants to maintain his wish even at the moment of fulfillment. But the simultaneity of wish and fulfillment is contradictory, the wish being the absence of fulfillment, and fulfillment negating the wish. By experiencing both at the same time, the Faun is suspended between wish and fulfillment. This suspension is a persistence in language different from the persistence of the one making the wish. He anticipates the fulfillment linguistically but is still intent on transforming what is only represented in the present. For the one who wishes, wishing is a condition of wanting that requires alleviation. This is different for the one suspended between wish and fulfillment. Wishing for the wish works against longing for fulfillment. Language is no longer devalued in relation to actuality but is a positive element that balances the language of fulfillment and cannot be sacrificed. It is no longer possible to distinguish between wish and fulfillment. Just as fulfillment is lacking for whomever wishes, so too is the wish lacking for whomever is satisfied. Lacking in fulfillment is need, just as abundance is lacking in the wish. Neither wish nor fulfillment can adequately capture the frame of mind of those suspended between the two. The Faun is trapped in language, because on the one hand he tries to go beyond language in order to achieve what he does not have in it and on the other hand must stay in language in order not to lose what he cannot find outside it.

If the story of the encounter of the Faun and the nymphs demonstrates his indecision between wish and fulfillment, then it becomes questionable whether the nymphs represent the Faun's wish. This assumption, which was the foundation for the preceding discussion, is based on a reading of verses 8–9, in which the uncertainty at the heart of the relationship between the nymphs and the Faun's wish went unnoticed.

Réfléchissons . . .

ou si les femmes dont tu gloses
Figurent un souhait de tes sens fabuleaux!

The sentence, which hypothetically represents the nymphs as a figure for the wish, is the second half of an alternative. It is therefore not an assertion but rather a possibility to be considered. The *ou si*, which introduces the sentence, shows that the Faun is torn between several explanations. His thoughts (*réfléchissons*) are supposed to make him choose. But initially there are no other possibilities. The alternative is thereby rendered undecidable, since it is presented as an inadequately formulated alternative. The nothingness, the discourseless emptiness of the white spaces, to which only the *ou* can refer, stands between the possibility mentioned in both verses. The most elementary way of understanding this alternative lies in the contrast between silence and discourse. In the Faun's situation, he can either have nothing or he can have what he says. Not only is this alternative decided by the fact that language takes place, but it is also too general to do justice to the special form of the fragment at hand. What stands opposite lack of discourse is not just language in general but a specific kind of statement. This restricts our room to find contrasts for the formulated possibility. Strictly speaking, only two opposing suppositions are possible when assuming that the women represent the wish. One would question the act of representation (*figurer*), the other would question the wish as what is represented (*souhait*). The first would contrast the real women with the women as the figure for the wish, whereas the second would accept them as representative but would change what is represented by them. This provides us with two possible reconstructions of the incomplete alternative. The question that must be answered is either: are the nymphs real or a representation of the wish? or: do the nymphs represent the wish or something else? From the fully formulated second half of the alternative, both supplements are possible. Since the first half is missing, there can be no decision between the two questions. The first undecidable alternative is the choice between two possible alternatives. Since this remains unresolved, the two conflicting alternatives are also undecidable. This means that both the question of reality and the question of meaning remain unanswered. We cannot decide if the nymphs are real or not, and we cannot decide if they stand for the wish or for something else. The meaning of the nymphs remains—like everything else—completely uncertain. But the suspension of this uncertainty is not a balance in which all movement comes to a halt. The wish as a possible meaning for the nymphs is privileged in that it is expressed as a possibility. It is therefore within our rights to pursue this possibility, even if only as a proviso to a hypothetical consideration. But the investigation of the nymph episode has shown that the wish in itself is another undecidable alternative. The nymphs may represent the wish or something else. If they represent the wish, then our uncertainty is only displaced one step. The wish goes back and forth between the wish for fulfillment and the wish for the wish, giving it the structure of an undecidable alternative.

In every situation, the Faun finds himself in the hopelessness of the undecidable. We are concerned not only with a procrastinator's inability to make a decision but also with the impossibility of allaying the doubt in which everything is suspended. The question "Aimai-je un rêve?" determines the status of what is loved as the object of this uncertainty. To the extent that we cannot determine whether this is something dreamed or real, any extralinguistic correspondence to what is linguistically present remains uncertain. This uncertainty is also important for the complex structure of the wish. Its goal, on the one hand, is the realization of what is wished for and linguistically anticipated. The hesitation linked to this realization is based on the uncertainty of its correspondence to the linguistic image. This leads to a maintenance of the wish, which in turn prevents its fulfillment. On the other hand, if this fulfillment were to occur, it could no longer be measured according to the image of what is wished for, which would disappear, and the uncertainty would remain unresolved. Uncertainty results from the fact that things receive meaning and value through language, but it remains unknown if they really are what they are understood to be, wished for, or loved as. The discourse of the Faun transpires as a continued confirmation of the impossibility of stepping out of language towards things. The language of opaque reality is the possibility of a transparent order to the world, as it appears in music as a pure system of relations. But the doubt always remains whether this order, which is a transposition (366) of the reality of things, is confirmed in this reality or remains suspended in ground-less fiction. This uncertainty is perennial. It prevents the mind from providing its own construction with any foundation other than an internal harmony.

Lack of determination should not be seen as a character flaw that turns the Faun into a comical figure, but it touches the relationship of the speaker to the world in its essence. When there is speaking, it presents itself as the search for the foundation of what is expressed in reality. The speaker is left dangling between a reality that cannot be accessed without language and language that cannot be determined without reality. This is why Mallarmé's speaker is a faun, which is to say, a mixed being suspended between nonlinguistic nature and human spirituality. The Faun in Mallarmé's poem is in no way the extralinguistic being to which discourse can be traced back and in whom it is founded. He is, instead, language, and as such takes part in the uncertainty that characterizes everything linguistic. In *Les dieux antiques* (Ancient gods), Mallarmé considers the creation of the Faun in terms of the mysterious nature of the forest: "We cannot not see in the Satyrs the phenomenon of life that seems to animate the woods and make the branches of the trees dance, down to the knotty trunks that frighten travelers" (1254). The Faun is the tree, the metaphor for mankind's fear of a nature untamed. The process of the Faun's creation described here corresponds exactly to the metamorphosis of the tree that the Faun considers in his discourse. The Faun's meaning-giving act uses the tree as a metaphor for his doubt and is also the act by which the

Faun becomes the metaphor for human fear. The Faun has meaning by becoming language in the same way that everything real has
meaning for the Faun. As language he stands for the relationship of
a speaker to a reality that is otherwise inaccessible, just as the
nymphs cannot be comprehended as an irreferential reality but
only as figures for the Faun's wish. Only meaning, never the
meaningful reality itself, can be given in language. "Abolished, the
pretension, aesthetically an error, though it directs masterpieces, of
including on thin paper anything other than for example the
horror of the forest, or the spare silent thunder in the leaves; not the
intrinsic and dense wood of the trees. Some bursts of intimate pride
truly trumpeted awaken the architecture of the palace, the only
livable one; outside of all stone, on which the pages close poorly"
(365f.). The Faun is not to be left unquestioned as a real being but
should be questioned with regard to his existence in language.
Mallarmé's constant connection between the fabled Faun and the
tree is important. In *L'après-midi d'un faune*, the tree is less frightening because of its movement than as an image of branching
uncertainty. It is in this sense that we should read Mallarmé's
dedicatory verse to a friend:

> Pan
>
> tronc qui s'achève en homme (113)

> Pan
>
> trunk that finishes as a man

With the tree and the word *s'achever*, we have a clear reference to
the opening lines of the poem. Undecidability is shown on several
levels to be the Faun's nature. Not only is he suspended between
tree and human, but the human who grows out of the tree is the
crown of the branching tree. This is completed (*s'achève*) in the
person who branches out from nature in the uncertainty that
spirituality and language bring into the world. The Faun not only
doubts, he is the figure for the doubting nature of man, not
knowing where he belongs. The world is foreign to the extent that
it becomes meaningful and therefore important to him. The fact

that the Faun is to be read as a metaphor for undecidability is
confirmed by the spelling with *v*, which Mallarmé maintained in
the title. Here the Faun does not speak but is written and is to be
read as the speaker. Certain passages of the text itself, read from a
distance, can be taken to refer to both the Faun as speaker and to
that about which he speaks. If the Faun is the tree made language,
then the Faun is also the metaphor constituted as his own discourse. *Mon doute* (v. 4) is then not only the doubt I have but also
the doubt I am. And *fabuleux* (v. 9) does not only mean that the
Faun is full of the fables he tells, but also that he is himself a fable
told. This breaks through the fiction that the poem's discourse
refers back to the Faun as its narrator. The poem is not only the
language of the Faun, but it also expresses the Faun as language.
The speaker as the last possible foundation of discourse proves to
be made of language himself. In his own undecidable uncertainty,
he himself becomes the metaphor for what his discourse unfurls.

DOUBT AND FICTION

Allusions, vagueness, ambiguity, and undecidability keep Mallarmé's text suspended in permanent uncertainty. The doubt that is
at work is not to be misunderstood as an expression of wavering
temperament. Mallarmé's letters from the 1860's, which tell of the
experiences that form the foundation for his later poetics, are, on
the contrary, witnesses of great determination and show a break-
through to certainty. Doubt is connected to this certainty. Doubt
belongs to certainty and is, so to speak, uncertainty based on
certainty. But uncertainty can only be released from a kind of
certainty that concerns the total lack of any foundation upon
which certainty could be based. It is a certainty that overcomes
itself. In a letter dated March 14, 1867, the removal of that foundation appears as the murder of God. Mallarmé at first formulates the
result of his endeavors ("my Thought has been thought and has
reached a pure Conception") and then goes on to describe the
experiences connected with this.

Unfortunately, I arrived at this point through a horrible sensitivity,
and it is time that I wrap it in an external indifference, which will

replace my lost strength. I am, after a supreme synthesis, in this slow acquisition of strength—incapable, as you see, of amusing myself. But how much more was I, a few months ago, first in my terrible struggle with that old and mean plumage, fortunately, felled, God. But after this struggle had occurred on his bony wing, which by an agony more vigorous than I would have guessed in him, had carried me into the Shadows, I fell, victorious, madly and infinitely—until finally I saw myself again one day in my Venetian mirror, such as I had forgotten myself several months previously.

I admit, moreover, but only to you, that I still need, so great were the affronts of my triumph, to look at myself in that mirror in order to think and that if it were not in front of the table from which I write you this letter, I would again become Nothingness. This is to make you understand that I am now impersonal and no longer Stéphane whom you knew, —but an aptitude that has the spiritual Universe to see and develop in itself, across what was me. (*Correspondance* I, 241f.)

God's existence is not questioned in this text. It is contested and overcome. What does this kind of victory mean? God guarantees thought and language. He ensures truth. As such a guarantor, God is an authority outside of language, something only He can establish because He is superior to it. The victory over God is the removal of God as the extralinguistic foundation of language. To kill God is in Mallarmé's thinking to recognize Him in his being language and thereby to subordinate Him to that which He would have to establish. The supposed foundation of language is language and can only be raised to its creation by forgetting its existence as language. This existence as language is restored when Mallarmé talks about the invention of God in another letter (*Correspondance* I, 207). The invented God is nowhere else but in the language that posits Him. The fact that the guarantor of language is uncovered in His existence in language cancels any guarantee that there is some extralinguistic correspondence to what is expressed in discourse.

The referentiality of discourse is uncertain, but it is not negated. A negation would suppose that God, having been eliminated as the guarantor of certainty, could be replaced by the certainty of His absence. But this certainty becomes untenable the instant it is posited, for if the foundation of all certainty crumbles, then the certainty that there is no certainty dissolves, plagued by the uncertainty of which it is certain. The victory over God cannot lead to the negation of His existence, only to its suspension in undecidability. If God is fiction, then His negation is no less fiction. It must consciously remain such to avoid becoming a hardened and arbitrary atheistic doctrine. Claim and negation are both shaken by the elimination of the guarantee of language, and every Yes and every No stands in the shadow of As-If. The uncertainty, now unleashed, disallows all certainty but, at the same time, is incapable of negating it, because it is radical enough to be uncertain even of itself.

Nothing is safe from the uncertainty the victory over God brings with it, least of all the victor. This, according to the passage in the letter on the destruction of God, is equivalent to self-destruction. Mallarmé says that this battle took place on God's wing, which is why, having gained the upper hand, he and his victim plummeted into a bottomless pit. The fallen sees the end to this descent in the mirrored image of what he had been months before. This image is not to be understood as the reproduction of the original, but it has all the characteristics of Mallarmé's fiction. Whoever sits in front of this mirror has no ontological priority over the image that is reflected. He has lost himself in a bottomless descent and can no longer form an image of himself. It is the copy that sustains the possibility of positing the original. The original exists by virtue of the copy that represents something that would otherwise not exist. Without the mirror, says Mallarmé, "I would again become Nothingness." The representation of what does not exist is fiction. What fiction presents exists only in this representation and through it. What is presented has the status of the linguistic with uncertain referentiality. As with all things linguistic, the mirror image lacks the guarantee of correspondence. It is not devalued by this fact but gains its irreplaceability because of it. The image is not simply a repetition of what exists without it but leads to the supposition that what is represented could actually have some existence outside the image. For Mallarmé the subject can no longer be certain that it exists in a way different from that of a linguistic fiction with uncertain referentiality. It is telling that this uncertainty is linked to the experience of thought, which thinks itself, which comes as close to self-certainty as is possible: "my Thought has been thought and has reached a pure Conception." The self-thinking of thought can no longer ensure any certainty of existence. It too has lost the foundation that formed a basis of trust. There is definitely a self-certainty of self-thinking thought, but its validity is limited to fiction, which thought—perhaps—is. Whether thought reaches something beyond itself, and whether there is someone who thinks, remains suspended in uncertainty.

Mallarmé's doubt is the doubt in the referentiality of language. The temptation of wanting to make a certainty out of this uncertainty remains. If the referentiality of language were simply negated, then this negation could be set as an affirmative statement forming the basis for a doctrine of language, even though, but also because, it lays claim to what it negates by virtue of its affirmative character. If, however, referentiality remains uncertain, then no determination is possible. It is then one-sided to talk about Mallarmé's radical break with instrumental, everyday language and his complete refusal to communicate. It is also improper, however, to want to limit him to an instrumental use of language, as one does when one tries to reduce the texts to a communicable content. Mallarmé's fiction is not an invention without external correspondence but rather a discourse whose external correspondence remains uncertain.

As ambivalent as the position of language may be, we are given nothing else. This is also true for the subject, which can no longer be seen as an independent element that might be available to language but rather as something linguistically represented as a reflection of the possibly unrealizable postulate of itself. Since language cannot be referred back to something outside itself, it gains the initiative. No one writes when something is written. Language employs the writer for the creation of fiction. The writer only represents the capability of language to unfurl itself into fiction. Mallarmé knows no other place than fiction. Writing is "claiming you are fine in the place where you have to be (because, allow me to express this concern, an uncertainty remains)" (481). If fiction is the only place in which the writer can exist, it is certainly not a firm foundation. It constitutes itself in freely suspended language without the guarantee of extralinguistic support, whose postulate it represents: "a summation to the world that it matches its obsession with richly ciphered postulates, as its law, on paper blemished with so much audacity" (481). The structure of the mirror image repeats itself here, not representing a given, but presenting something as a copy and therefore as a postulate of an original. We are still uncertain if this has any correspondence outside the mirror. In its construction, fiction is suspended in the undecidability of its own status.

This uncertainty also applies to the relationship of fiction to the external. Certainty is possible within fiction. Here we have what Mallarmé called the proof. The proof is not the elimination of doubt in the referentiality of language but the self-confirmation of fiction, as can be read in the following sentence: "The book, total expansion of the letter, must draw from it, directly, a spacious mobility, through correspondences, institute a game, one knows not which, that confirms fiction" (380). Since language has no foundation outside itself, it is not subject to dependences or limitations but can unfurl itself in the free combinations of the alphabet. The possibility of variable combinations of letters is transferred to higher elements or parts of a book. These can be words, pages, or poems. They are no longer bound to the rigid chronology in the traditional idea of the book but can refer to each other in different ways. This emancipation of the book from the singularity of a fixed progression has consequences that are discerned in the key words of Mallarmé's sentence. The mobility (*mobilité*) of the book, whose elements are no longer sentenced to an unchangeable sequence but can follow each other in various orders, is given with the multiple referentiality of its parts. The temporality of the book is questioned by the possibility of several sequences. Every chosen order is a progression, but none of them is equal to a book, since all have equal value. The book can therefore only be understood as the space (*spacieux*) in which these variations come together. This sequential variety is the game (*jeu*) that confirms fiction. This confirmation does not come from the truth of fiction, since this would assume that what confirms—an extralinguistic reality—has a markedly different status from that of fiction. In this game everything is always already fiction. The different versions of the game are mutual confirmations. Fiction is confirmed as fiction. The confirmation only plays within fiction, which remains in an undecidable relationship to everything that is external to it. The following quote refers to the irremovable doubt concerning the referentiality of language: "a game, one knows not which, that confirms fiction." The "one knows not which" leaves open the question whether the game is only a game, for it could be that fiction hits upon a reality. Fiction may confirm itself within this game, but we don't know whether what is proven is referentially supported or not.

The uncertainty concerning the place of fiction as a whole is very important for the understanding of fiction itself. Were it to be disregarded, it might seem as if we have in fiction reached a place of possible certainty, where discourse could unfurl itself as a purely linguistic game, unconcerned with prescribed sequences. Mallarmé's texts are indeed readable as expansions of the letter and as self-confirming fiction. The dissolution of logical and grammatical relationships and the free rein given to language, which makes words speak outside of conventional fields of meaning, characterize a speaking that no longer expects sanction from a superior entity. The dissolution of this entity causes the uncertainty to which everything succumbs. If fiction is defined as an area in which language reigns freely without regard for anything else, then we find ourselves in danger of forgetting that everything that takes place in fiction is without foundation. We could be tempted to define fiction as a kind of alternative world, constituted according to its own rules. To avoid this illusion, the recognition of the uncertainty of fiction must be valid for everything that happens within fiction. Fiction must have within itself the tendency towards its own disassembly to the same degree that it is in danger of defining itself as reality, the reality of fiction. Fiction is what it is only by virtue of the fact that it contradicts itself. It confirms itself by refuting itself. To the extent that it destroys the conventions of everyday communications, it must in turn respect them, so as not to harden in negation. No matter which way the pendulum swings, fiction's suspension of doubt must always be restored.

If Mallarmé's poetry is fiction, then it cannot be read for a specific meaning, something it refuses to represent from the beginning. It is also not enough to point out the necessary one-sidedness of every commentary and then proceed to surrender to this very same one-sidedness. Instead, it should be possible to read these texts with a sense of their undecidability. We should try to sense how, in their constant uncertainty, they come to be something undecidable and how they maintain their insight into the doubtfulness of their own status. Insofar as the poem is concerned with the problematic situation of its own discourse, it is neither descriptive nor communicative but speaks of itself along the necessary route around as few objects as possible, a route that must be reversed as well. The following attempt to understand the sonnet *Une dentelle s'abolit* (A lace curtain is abolished) as discourse, which reflects and speaks its own uncertain referentiality, forgoes the search for anything but the poem itself. The desire to avoid any determination prevents an interpretation that would construe the poem as a completed whole. The poem's contradictory character, necessary to prevent a cover-up of the uncertainty of discourse with affirmative statements, prevents any conclusion. It is therefore unjustified for a series of equally ordered ideas, which always circle the self-referentiality of the poem, to take the place of a leveling interpretation.

> Une dentelle s'abolit
> Dans le doute du Jeu suprème
> A n'entr'ouvrir comme un blasphème
> Qu'absence éternelle de lit.
>
> Cet unanime blanc conflit
> D'une guirlande avec la mème,
> Enfui contre la vitre blème
> Flotte plus qu'il n'ensevelit.

Mais, chez qui du rêve se dore
Tristement dort une mandore
Au creux néant musicien

Telle que vers quelque fenètre
Selon nul ventre que le sien,
Filial on aurait pu naître.

A lace curtain is abolished
In the doubt of the supreme Game
Half-open like a blasphemy
Only eternal absence of a bed.

This unanimous white conflict
Of a garland with its like,
Having fled onto the pale window
Floats more than it buries.

Yet, with him who is gilded by dreams
Sorrowful a mandola sleeps
In the void musical hollow

Such that toward some pane
Along no womb but its own,
Filial one might have been born.

The first line concerns an abolished lacework. Something is posited only to be immediately negated. But what is said to disappear appears by being said and is expressed in the word *dentelle*. Not only is the lacework linguistically established, despite its negation, but the act of negation must be considered incomplete. If it were complete, nothing would remain, and neither itself nor what it includes could be named. We can talk about disappearance to the extent that it is something in progress. If it is in the act of disappearing, then it is still present, and the negativity of negation can be felt in its gradual retreat. The process of elimination occurs in the area of undecidability between Yes and No. The movement is clearly directional, but it follows on and as a reaction to the determination that precedes negation. This corrects the affirmative tendency towards determination and functions as its counterweight. This is only possible as long as the process of negation is in progress. If it were to be completed, then the statement would congeal into a hard and fast No. The statement "s'abolir dans le doute" shows that this is not the case. Doubt is first the context in which the elimination takes place, since doubt in the determination of the lace is supposed to gain validity. It is secondly the goal toward which the movement flows. This would be contradictory if one were to view the negation as complete, since whatever is negated is not doubted. Doubt does not eliminate, it suspends. Only the negation itself is negated as a completed act in not allowing either Yes or No. Negation, because it merges with and is subordinate to doubt, can only be a never-ending act in progress. Just as negation destabilizes determination, doubt questions negation and prevents it from getting the upper hand. Although the sentence "A lace curtain is abolished in the doubt" presents itself as an affirmative statement, it undermines any attempt at determination through the sequence of its elements and is constituted as a constant questioning of its own discourse. This process begins with the linguistic positing of the lace. At the same time, however, the lace posits the language by which it is posited, since it can be read as a metaphor for writing, of which Mallarmé speaks elsewhere as "this fold of somber lace, which infinitely detains" (370). In that the poem speaks about lace, it is concerned with itself. It is itself what concerns itself, the meaning of its own expression. The two opening verses, referring to the poem, represent a self-questioning. They identify the poem's speaking as a determination eliminated in doubt. The poem enters into opposition to itself the moment it begins to speak. It constitutes itself as a questioning of itself. The self-reference of discourse takes priority over its reference to other things. Language does not appear here in contrast to what is not language, as Mallarmé indicates in the statement "man follows black on white" (370), but appears to be struggling with itself: "This unanimous white conflict / Of a garland with its like." This self-reference is conflicting because the poem is forced to fight its own positivity in order not to disavow the doubt from which it is created.

This conflict is also evident in other passages of the poem where what is said conflicts with the act of saying it. The verse "Tristement dort une mandore" contains the word *mandore* twice. If we were to explain this as onomatopoeia, imitating the sound of the instrument (Noulet, 162), then we remain caught up in the kind of mimetic concept of language that Mallarmé's texts overcome. The discourse's point of departure is not an external reality that can be imitated but rather language itself, the letter, whose total expansion is the book. The wordplay points to the absence of an objective relationship between the sound sequence *mandore* and its meaning, since the same sounds in (*triste*)*ment dort* have a completely different meaning. On the one hand the relationship between the word and the object it signifies is called into question, and on the other hand the verse justifies the consonance it points out. The repetition of the word *mandore* is not simply ornamental. It allows us to read the verse as a metaphor of what is happening. It not only tells us of a slumbering lute, but slumbering in *tristement dort* we have the word *mandore*. The development of the resulting double stratification of the verse leads to a contradiction. The verse talks about a lute that sleeps, which can only mean that it is not being played, just as the music, inherent within it, does not sound out. But the sleeping of the lute is expressed in such a way that in the words "tristement dort une mandore" the word *mandore* sounds as something itself asleep. In that the sleeping word is awakened from its latency and brought into our consciousness by the express naming of the lute, the opposite of what the verse says occurs: the word *mandore* can only be discovered as something hidden in *tristement dort* by becoming the instrument that is played. The poem is created as this playing on the instrument of language and, at the same time, refutes itself by *being* the playing which it says is not taking place. Here we see again that discourse refutes itself as something in progress by what it says. The act of speaking and what has been expressed neutralize each other. The poem speaks in such a way that it refutes the negativity of its own statement. Insofar as it holds up the positivity of its own discourse, it must confront this negativity to maintain the suspension of doubt.

If the poem is to be understood not only as communication but also as actual speech, then it must be something incipient. Not only what is expressed is important, but also that the poem constitutes itself as the expression of what has been expressed. The second half of the poem is about a missed birth. In the verse "Filial on aurait pu naître," what could have been born is "one." The first question is not who this one is, but if one *exists*. If one could have been born, then the birth did not take place. But even though one was not born, one *exists* in the discourse of the poem, unborn as what could have been. Every potentiality, whether its realization is yet to come or has already been missed, is linguistic. One takes place linguistically as what could have been born. The birth would have taken place in the motherly hollow of the lute, had it been played. One becomes by playing the lute. It is true that one must already exist to be able to play, but only in play do we playingly create what is born. The lute, with which we create ourselves, brings us out as players. What we playingly create as ourselves is only possible in and through music. It is said of music that it was not created. Birth was therefore absent, but sounds, including those of language, are the instrument whose music is poetry. In poetry we are the language players who appear not as persons but as nonpersons. We are only born out of the discourse we create. We are not an element outside of discourse, superior to and users of it. We are first born as speakers. We are born out of the music we make. The poem as language act is the self-incarnation of the speaker. This kind of creative discourse deals with foregone birth and negates what it does through what it says. In that it happens and allows the speaker to come into being, it contradicts what it expresses. The poem as something that comes into being is completely incompatible with what it expresses. If what it expressed were actually true, then it could not have come into being. In this way, everything that is expressed is questioned by the fact that it is expressed, just as, on the contrary, the positivity of expression is itself questioned by what is expressed.

The ontological status of the poem, born as discourse from a foregone birth, is doubtful, not only in the questionable nature of what it expresses, but also in the positivity of its own speaking. It constitutes itself as its own annulment. This is apparent at the end of the poem, which relates to the past of its own birth. The past that is recalled by the conditional of the last verse is now the completed discourse of the poem itself. The poem states that the birth, which would have been possible, did not take place, at the same moment that its own birth is complete. Therefore, not only could what does not exist have existed, but what already is, that is, the poem itself, could not have been. The poem uses this tension in its expression by finishing within an aporetic ambiguity: *naître* is also *n'être*. The poem pays homage in this wordplay to the division into which it fell by coming into being while still speaking of foregone birth. Not only has the chance for birth been missed, but, insofar as the poem has become, so has the possibility of nonbeing. The ambiguity cannot be reduced. It states that the birth has taken place and that it has not. If, however, both statements are true at the same time, then neither is true. We are left stranded between being and nonbeing. We can therefore neither say that Mallarmé's poem is nor that it is not. It no sooner becomes than it is already past. But by dealing with its own past, it receives this past in its own discourse. It expresses itself as the missed opportunity to be and not to be.

The poem, which neither is nor is not, eliminates itself in doubt. Only in this way does it appropriately address the uncertain status of its own language. "Le doute de Jeu suprême" is now accessible in its relationship to the poem. The play is the fiction's constant referral to itself, preventing its reassurance in the claim and maintaining itself in the modulation between Yes and No. The highest form of play is what no other forms can go past. This boundary is reached not only when all of fiction's invention becomes questionable, but also when even the act of invention itself is objectified and recognized in its positivity, which can only be encountered by negation. Otherwise the act of invention would suppress its doubting itself. Not only is the referentiality of everything that is expressed in this extreme play in doubt, but even the expression of doubt is doubtful. For Mallarmé, self-reflection no longer forms the basis for certainty, which would again require a divine guarantor, but gets sucked into a doubt which is no longer methodical.

Mallarmé's doubt is a doubt in language. Language, in speaking of itself, is made doubtful because it slips away from itself and at the same time posits itself as the very thing that slips away from itself. When the poem, where every possible position is playfully resolved, allows this tension to go unresolved, then it transpires as the place of doubt.

Baudelaire

Imagination and Memory

CRITIQUE OF IMITATION

Images of the mind are reproductions. Imagination, then, is the ability to have an idea of something not present, of something that can no longer be directly experienced. The possibility of such an idea presupposes an earlier experience, and this experience is then pictured, stored, and reproduced. Imagination is recollection. There seems thus to be little difference between imagination and memory. Imagination can deliver nothing but imagination. It is itself the image of the experience, the existence of which results from a productive imagination, unifying sensual data into the whole of an idea. Considered in this way, the image does not remain a reproduction, however, but becomes productive. The question of the image's creation is more fundamental than the reproductive nature, since it can only reproduce something insofar as it can constitute itself as an image. The imagination, as something productive, can then no longer be lumped together with memory, since it no longer renders something already present but creates something new.

Seen from an artistic perspective, the transition from a reproductive to a productive imagination represents the replacement of a

reproductive aesthetic with the attempt to understand art as a
creative act. Baudelaire's writings on painting represent such an
attempt. His discourse on imagination in the *Salon* of 1859 follows
a detailed rejection of photography, which has no other function
than mimetic recollection, and leads to a critique of imitation. This
is discussed in the context of the phrase "copiez la nature," which
proceeds from an official aesthetic (Baudelaire later calls it the
realistic or *positivistic* [*Oeuvres complètes* II, 627]) as a challenge to
the artist. Baudelaire examines the demand to imitate nature in two
ways. First he is concerned with the motivation for imitation, second he questions in what way the imitated subject is represented.

The question of motivation involves arguments that speak for or
against the reproduction of what exists. According to Baudelaire,
nothing speaks in favor of repeating what already is: "To these
doctrinaire people, so satisfied with nature, an imaginative person
certainly would have had the right to respond: 'I find it useless and
tedious to represent what is, because nothing of what is satisfies me.
Nature is ugly, and I prefer the monsters of my fantasy to positive
triviality' " (II, 620). The criterion for the imitative value of what
exists is the satisfaction it gives the viewer. Imitation is the activity
of the satisfied. Only those who find pleasure in what is want to
reproduce things the way they are. Those who are unsatisfied, on
the other hand, have no reason to reproduce something full of
imperfections. They are instead intent on countering imperfections with completeness. But in that everything that exists is
unsatisfactory because it is imperfect, they are unable to repeat
what already is and must create something new. Imagination is an
asset of the unsatisfied. Dissatisfaction assumes that there is something better to replace what already is. The exercise of imagination
is motivated by deficiency. This is, in the final analysis, also true of
imitation, since there is little need for copying what exists if its
presence alone were deemed adequate. We might find the motivation for imitation in the desire to hold on to the transitory, that is,
to prevent the desire for what is anticipated in the idea. It is not
satisfaction, but rather the notion of its imperilment, that causes
imitation. Baudelaire's text does not concern itself with this issue

because he is not concerned with the motivation of the satisfied but with the fact that the unsatisfied have no desire to imitate what already exists.

Something else is inherent in the dissatisfaction with what already exists. If the extant does not satisfy, then this supposes that it is accessible to us as the thing that it is. The phrase "I prefer the monsters of my fantasy to positive triviality" only makes sense if the monstrosity of the fantastic can be measured in terms of what is, if the accessibility of the extant is not questioned in what it is. The demand to imitate the extant is based on the assumption that what already exists is accessible as what it is.

It is precisely this assumption that is undermined by Baudelaire in the second part of his critique of imitation. "It would have been more philosophical, however, to ask these dogmatists, first whether they are really certain of the existence of external nature, or in case this question seemed too well calculated to please their caustic nature, whether they are quite certain of knowing *all nature*, all that is contained in nature" (II, 620). Of the two questions posed here, the first asks whether there can be any certainty of the existence of external nature, whereas the second questions the possibility of knowing all of nature with all that it contains. It is important to see that this passage says absolutely nothing about the status of nature but only undermines the certainty that the embattled doctrines of the beautiful have with regard to this status. The question, whether external nature is real or imagined, is undecided. But its irresolution is the important thing. For those who use the phrase "copiez la nature," the status of nature remains unproblematic; it is inherent as what it is. If this objective character of nature is questioned, then it becomes impossible to decouple it from its relationship to the observer or copier. The consideration of this relationship leads to the collapse of the naive concept of imitation exposed by Baudelaire's text. Whoever looks at nature as an object to be imitated forgets that he is himself a part of that nature. The artist is not outside of but in nature, and in him nature confronts itself. With this the second part of the quoted passage becomes accessible: "whether they are quite certain of knowing *all nature*, all

that is contained in nature." Any knowledge of nature that claims
to possess nature as an object is incomplete to the extent that it fails
to consider the observer as a part of nature. Whoever believes that
he is in possession of all of nature falls victim to an illusion insofar
as he forgets his own existence in and his own relationship to
nature. Nature cannot be thought of as an object distinct from the
subject. The subject and its relationship to the object is itself a part
of nature.

We should ask ourselves how Baudelaire's discussion of nature's
imitation can be understood after he dismantles the naive concept
of imitation. The conclusion of the first part devotes itself to this
question, presenting Baudelaire's own interpretation of the criticized doctrine.

> The artist, the true artist, the true poet, must paint only in accordance
> with what he sees and what he feels. He must be faithful in a *real* way
> to his own nature. He must avoid, like death itself, borrowing the eyes
> and feelings of another man, however great that man may be; for in
> that case the productions he would give us would be, so far as he is
> concerned, lies and not *realities*. (II, 620)

Accordingly, the artist does not paint what is, but what he sees. His
object is not only what is seen but also the seeing of what is seen,
that is, his own relationship to what is seen. The proponents of
imitation seek out the objectivity of the object, which is supposed
to exist in a state free from the traces of the seeing eye. A later
passage formulates this doctrine as follows: " 'I want to represent
things as they are, or rather as they would be, supposing I did not
exist.' The universe without man" (II, 627). Baudelaire counters
this with the statement that the imitation of nature can only be
accomplished by rendering one's own relationship to nature. My
way of seeing what is seen is my nature, and a work of art must be
made accordingly. It should also be noted that my relationship to
nature is the only certainty—Baudelaire calls it reality (*réalité*)—
left. Whatever the disposition of what I am seeing may be, my own
seeing is not questioned. Reality is not what I see, but my seeing.
Since what is seen only exists as it is for me because I see, it cannot

be separated from its being seen. It can only be understood as something seen and as dependent on the seeing entity. If we can only have certainty vis-à-vis what we see but not what is, then it remains open whether we see what is as it is. If we believe to see a thing as it is, this usually only means that we do not see it with our own eyes but within a tradition or as the majority has determined it to be. Everything we encounter is already in some way predetermined, and the abandonment of our own determination is the acceptance of the previously determined. Baudelaire says: "borrowing the eyes and feelings of another man." The imitation of nature in the doctrine which Baudelaire disputes is nothing more than this kind of seeing with others' eyes. We do not copy nature as it is but instead as a predetermined conventional image. The imaginative painter does not paint what others see, but what he himself sees. He is distinguished in that he remains true to his own vision. This presupposes understanding that access to a reality independent of its own being seen is a false pretense. The artist is not supposed to render something that exists outside of him as it is but as he sees it.

How is this critique of imitation connected to imagination? We must assume that the critique addresses the predetermination of the predetermined. In the phrase "copiez la nature," nature is assumed to be a predetermined original, whose likeness is to be created. Baudelaire's critique undermines this assumption. If nature is not rendered as it is but as what we see, then it is not predetermined. It does not constitute itself as predetermined until it is seen. Since what is seen is dependent on seeing, it can no longer be understood as something that precedes it. The relationship between original and likeness, as every imitation must be defined, is therefore threatened. The original does not have priority, nor is the likeness secondary to the original. The original is dependent on the likeness, because it can only exist as its likeness. If the original is no longer predetermined, then it can no longer be imitated but must be imagined. Imagination is creative because it creates an image without the predetermination of the original. The problem of imagination must therefore be put in the following terms: how is an image created without being a likeness of the original? As soon as imagination creates something not previously extant, the predetermination of the original becomes indefensible. Every theory of creative imagination conflicts with the theory of imitation. Since Baudelaire's text introduces imagination in connection with imitation, we are faced with the question of how this conflict is decided.

LIKENESSES WITHOUT ORIGINALS

It can be demonstrated that Baudelaire's texts, which seem on the surface to remain true to an aesthetic of imitation, always transition to a concept of image that is irreconcilable with the usual relationship between original and likeness. I would like to show Baudelaire's refutation of the mimetic model using three examples from the *Salon* of 1859. The first text is concerned with the relationship of the painter to nature. Baudelaire refers to conversations he had with Delacroix, who was wont to say, "Nature is only a dictionary." This sentence from the painter Baudelaire most admired and quoted on several occasions is discussed in the following text:

> To properly understand the full meaning implied in this statement, one should keep in mind the many ordinary uses of the dictionary. In it one seeks the meaning of words, the genealogy of words, the etymology of words; in short, one extracts from it all the elements that compose a sentence and a narrative. But no one has ever considered the dictionary as a composition in the poetic sense of the word. Painters who obey their imagination seek in the dictionary the elements which suit their conception; yet, in adapting these elements with a certain art, they give them an altogether new physiognomy. Those who lack imagination copy the dictionary. The result is a very great fault, the fault of banality. (II, 624f.)

We are concerned here with the effect of imagination. Three things seem to play a role: the dictionary (*dictionnaire*), the concept (*conception*), and the composition (*composition*). The dictionary seems to provide material. It contains elements that are then arranged in the composition in some sort of order. In another passage, Baudelaire speaks instead of a dictionary of "a storehouse of images and signs" (II, 627). The sequence of events seems to be that the artist first has a concept of his work and, with the help of material given him by the dictionary, realizes his concept, that is, creates a composition. This would then be the way to interpret the passage "Painters who obey their imagination seek in the dictionary the elements which suit their conception." But this linear sequence, emphasized by the text, is not unproblematic as soon as one is willing to more closely examine the elements involved. In the just-quoted passage, it is worth noting that the painters seek out the needed elements in "their" dictionary ("dans *leur* dictionnaire"). This could mean that nature is the dictionary of painters, but it could also mean that every painter has his own dictionary. How can this be reconciled with the fact that we are always talking about nature? The question, then, of what a dictionary is, is unavoidable. The dictionary makes it impossible to speak of an unordered pile of material as the artist's starting point. The dictionary represents order, not because it lists words alphabetically, but because the words it lists are the words of a particular language and have meaning only within the order of this language. The dictionary represents the language we speak. But language is not something that exists to be used at will. It is never present outside of individual speech. The meanings of words can only be determined by their usage, provided that a certain consensus exists between them. There is neither language without individual speech, nor is there speech without language. The interaction between the two is important for an understanding of the dictionary metaphor. If nature is a dictionary, then its elements have meaning. But they do not have meaning in and of themselves. They are given meaning. Nature can only be a dictionary insofar as its interpretation has become set in a substantially accepted convention. Nature as a dictionary represents a conventional interpretation of nature.

In that the dictionary maintains generally accepted meanings, it promotes the tendency to misunderstand language as an available commodity. It is the misunderstanding of those who lack imagination. Their speech can only be dependent on previous speech.

"Those who lack imagination copy the dictionary." It is they who, without compunction, stay within the bounds of convention and accept the interpreted world without any need to reinterpret it. To "copy the dictionary" (II, 625) as an acceptance of existing interpretations is therefore equivalent to "borrowing the eyes and feelings of another man" (II, 620). Contrasted with this is the imaginative person, whose relationship to the dictionary can now be examined with the help of another text. "The entire visible universe is but a storehouse of images and signs to which the imagination will give a relative place and value; it is a kind of fodder that the imagination must digest and transform" (II, 627). At first, this sentence seems to offer nothing new to the passage quoted above. Conspicuous are the metaphors related to two distinct areas. The first part of the sentence invokes the image of a set of building blocks containing elements from which an ordered whole can be constructed. This construction-set metaphor is contrasted in the second half of the sentence with the digestion metaphor. Baudelaire made use of this metaphor in relationship to the dictionary in other places, such as his essay on Victor Hugo: "I do not know in what world Victor Hugo has previously consumed the dictionary of the language that he was called upon to speak; but I see that the French lexicon, coming from his mouth, has become a world, a colored universe, melodious and moving" (II, 133). The difference between the metaphors is important. With the construction set, everything stays in the realm of the mechanical. The building blocks are present and remain what they are even when used in different combinations. In contrast, digestion is a transformation (*transformer*). What is digested is no longer what it was but something new. The elements are not only arranged in a new way, they are changed. These two ideas seem to contradict each other. Still, the understanding of Baudelaire's text is dependent on seeing both together, since both metaphors obviously represent the same thing. If we make this assumption, then we arrive at the necessary conclusion that the ordering of elements is also the transformation of elements. Transformative digestion is based on ordering. The building blocks, with which the construction is built, do not always remain what they are but change according to their relationship to other things. The element becomes what it is through these relationships. One such element is the word. It does not have meaning independent of its relationships, and its meanings change with these relationships. Ordering words means changing them.

From these considerations comes what we can call the imaginative use of words, when a speech cannot be reduced to a dictionary's convention. What Baudelaire calls "copier le dictionnaire" is the speech of those who have no imagination. The imaginatively employed word is, on the other hand, one that is, strictly speaking, not in the dictionary. Every imaginative speech goes beyond convention and requires that the dictionary be corrected. Where imagination begins, words stop being predetermined elements. This is not to say that the one speaking (or painting) stops using these elements, but it does mean that, in his composition, they are not what they were determined to be in the conventional order. Elements only become what they are by virtue of the order in which they stand. They are not predetermined and later given order but infer this order as the thing that gives them meaning.

Imagination questions the idea of the dictionary as something predetermined. The composition of the artist is not simply put together from existing material. The material from which it is made comes into being with the composition. What was previously present is not as it is now. The creativity of the imagination does not encompass the being of things but their meaning. It does not create things but meanings. Its creation is interpretation. It has been demonstrated here that the creativity of imagination always emerges when the predetermination of something seemingly predetermined is overcome. The reception of conventional meanings ("copier le dictionnaire"), understood as imitation, is contrasted with interpretation as an act that gives meaning. Interpretation occurs as an ordering, and meaning is given through order. But how and by what is order given? As a work of art or as a composition, the result of the creative process seems only to be present at the end. But it cannot come into being without somehow being anticipated, even if only as the idea of a goal towards which the movement is directed. The anticipation of order in the mind is its predetermination. The word *conception* is used in Baudelaire's text as the predetermination of order. It seems that the mimetic model, believed to have been overcome, is introduced again with a pre-determined order. The original is no longer external nature but an internal concept. This does not change the fact that the picture being painted is the likeness of an original determined in the concept. We might argue that imagination is already at work in the concept's predetermined order, but this only sets the entire prob-lem back to where it would have to be examined anew.

Instead we can examine the nature of order's predetermination in the concept. It is said of painters who follow their imagination that they look for those elements in the dictionary of nature that fit their concept. The creation of a picture is accordingly the concept's realization in a composition, given the aid of the elements of the dictionary. To find the elements that fit the concept, their order must already be present in that concept. It has been shown that the elements only become what they are through their determined order. If the elements of this order are undetermined, then the order cannot be determined. An architect cannot design a house if he doesn't know what building materials are available. The concept is the anticipation of the order. What does not yet exist is already present in its anticipation. But how can something that does not yet exist already be determined? We could surmise: as an image. But what kind of image is it that is the image of something that does not yet exist? It can't be the likeness of an original, because this does not exist. But it can also not be the original, because it would then be the same thing. The assumption that what is anticipated in the anticipation is present as an image is therefore untenable. The difficulty lies in the fact that what is anticipated would have to already be present to be represented, and that the representation is no longer an anticipation as soon as it becomes possible. This difficulty can only be resolved if we stop looking for what is anticipated in the anticipation as something rendered. Something anticipated is present neither as itself nor as an image but rather as something absent. What does not yet exist can neither be present or represented but is inherent in the anticipation as something that does not yet exist, that is, as absence. Order in the concept is therefore not anticipated as itself but as the lack of order. It would be wrong to want to understand the concept as the anticipation of order and the composition as the mimetic imitation of this internal image. The concept is first of all nothing more than the empty idea of an absent order. The order inherent as absence characterizes the dissatisfaction in light of the given, which Baudelaire attributes to the imaginative person. Satisfaction is inherent to the unsatisfied as absence. The concept as an empty idea of a missing connection does not have the status of an original. A composition as the realization of this absent order cannot be thought of as the imitation of the determined in the concept. The sequence of conception and composition in the sense of a mimetic model is thus dissolved. A composition cannot be built on the predetermined. It is a creative, not an imitative, process. This implies that imagination does not create an image as the painter's original that is then copied. Rather, imagination determines the compositorial act itself to be a creative act.

The compositorial act is not the imitation of nature, even though it results in a picture. This picture is a picture of something, but this something is not a copied original of the picture. A picture is the likeness of an absent original. This is the starting point for an understanding of the compositorial process. This is the self-constitution of the original as something that is copied in the compositorial process. Composition is not the copying of an inherent original but the creation of the original as a likeness. This clarifies the relationship of the concept to the composition. The concept is at first nothing more than an empty idea of order that does not yet exist. The process of composition is the gradual realization of this empty idea. The concept as something realized is therefore not inherent but is created in the completion of the composition. With this, everything that could have preceded the act of the creation of the image is dismantled. What remains as inherent is only the absence of order, that is, the absence of what must be created as the composition. The fact that nothing else precedes the completion of the composition results in the increased importance of this completion, that is, in the act of execution (*exécution*), as opposed to the role it is granted in a mimetic concept of art. With the imitation of something already present, the act of execution becomes instrumental, since it occurs in relationship to matter created outside and independent of it. In contrast, the nonimitative composition in Baudelaire's sense has a creative character, because it creates its own original of which it is the likeness. For Baudelaire, everything is shifted to the activity of painting (speaking). Painting is imagining.

All passages in Baudelaire's text that have to do with execution can be read from this perspective, even if they seem to be subordinate to a mimetic model. This is true of the following text from the chapter "Le gouvernement de l'imagination" (The government of imagination).

> A good painting, faithful and equal to the dream that conceived it, must be produced like a world. Just as creation, as we view it, is the result of several creations whose preceding ones are always completed by the next, so a harmoniously conducted painting consists in a series of superposed paintings, each new layer lending more reality to the dream and raising it one degree closer to perfection. On the contrary, I remember seeing in the studios of Paul Delaroche and Horace Vernet huge paintings, not sketched out, but begun, that is, absolutely finished in certain parts, while others were not yet even marked except by a black or white outline. One might compare this type of work to purely manual labor which must cover a certain quantity of space in a determined time, or to a long route divided into a large number of stages. When a stage is finished, it no longer has to be done, and when the whole route is traveled, the artist is freed from his painting. (II, 626)

What in other places is called concept appears here as dream (*rêve*). Emphasized is the relationship between dream and image (*tableau*), whereby we are to understand image as composition. We are dealing with the relationship between concept and composition with a view towards the creation of the image. When we read: "A good painting, faithful and equal to the dream that conceived it," then the dream seems to be the intrinsic essence to which the image must liken itself as faithfully as possible.

The image is not related to the dream in only a mimetic way but also genetically. The dream creates the image. The image comes out of the dream. This brings to mind our earlier understanding of the concept. The dream creates the image so that the absence of the image in the dream can be rectified. This is confirmed by the later passage on the realization of the dream. Baudelaire speaks of the creation of the image by overlapping several layers. Of these, he says, "each new layer lending more reality to the dream and raising it one degree closer to perfection." Here we are tempted at first to understand the image as the imitative visualization of the intrinsic as an internal dream image. But the sentence is ambiguous. It not only says that the image realizes something inherent in a dream, but also that the dream only becomes real in the creation of the dream's image. It constitutes itself in the image that is created as its own intrinsic essence. The dream is created with the image both as what the image refers to and as what it was created from.

But how can an image be created if it must first create the very thing from which it was created? With the elimination of the original/likeness relationship, the accustomed sequence of steps in the creation of an image has become impossible. The creation of the composition must now be thought of as a process that aims towards its own precedent, faced with the impossible task of enabling itself. The image must always already exist in order to be created, but still it must be created in order to exist. We must examine an image's creation, as described in Baudelaire's text, in connection with this paradox. The picture is created in such a way that a series of images overlap. This method of composition, advocated by Baudelaire, is contrasted with another method in which the painter begins to paint a canvas in a corner and proceeds to the next spot only when the first is completed. Baudelaire calls this process a beginning (*tableau commencé*), whereas the process of the imaginative painter is called drafting (*tableau ébauché*). The metaphor that illustrates beginning and drafting connects the two methods of painting with the original/likeness problem. Beginning is proceeding along a linear path in which each step enables another: "When a stage is finished, it no longer has to be done." The picture is created according to the building-block principle by a simple assembly of elements. The image that is created in this fashion can only be a unified whole if the order, which it is, is determined from the beginning, that is, if the relationship between the parts is predetermined and the execution is nothing more than the repetition of the extant. This is completely different with drafting. Each of the many images that overlap is somehow already the whole, even though the whole is only created by overlapping the different layers. There is no simple assembly of parts and no linear progress. Every step is not only a step towards the whole but is also already the whole itself. No order is predetermined, and yet the order is given from the start as a network of relationships that becomes ever more refined and precise. The image is not created as a sequence of elements but by the gradual division and filling of a space. The individual and the whole are simultaneous. The individual only exists as a part of the whole, and the whole is inherent as the relationship of its parts. The smallest detail is inaccessible without the whole, of which it is a part, and yet the whole is only achieved by a combination of its parts.

I will try to examine the relationship between concept and composition, made more complicated by the rejection of the mimetic model and the resulting elimination of the simple succession of original and likeness, in another part of the text. One could object that the preceding discussion is based on an overinterpretation of the text, and that it is by no means certain that the ambiguity of the passage that speaks of the dream's realization is intentional. This might be countered with the observation that this ambiguity is independent of any intention beyond the text and is therefore to be taken seriously, even if only as a reminder that texts say more than they want to say. In the preceding case, however, it seems possible to go further and to show that Baudelaire is by no means a stranger to playing with several meanings. This conclusion is supported by the following text:

In a similar method, which is essentially logical, all the personages, their relative arrangement, the landscape or the interior which serves as their background or horizon, their clothes, everything finally must serve to illuminate the generative idea and continue to bear its original color, its livery so to speak. Just as a dream is placed in an atmosphere appropriate to it, a composition, once it has become a composition, needs to move in a colored atmosphere that is particular to it. There is evidently a particular tone attributed to a certain part of a painting that becomes a key and governs the others. Everyone knows that yellow, orange, red inspire and represent ideas of joy, wealth, glory, and love; but there are millions of yellow or red atmospheres, and all the other colors logically will be affected and in proportionate measure by the dominant atmosphere. (II, 625)

The first sentence of this passage deals with a relationship similar to that between concept and composition. Everything that is part of the image serves to illuminate the idea that created the image in the first place: "everything . . . must serve to illuminate the generative idea." *Everything* here is equivalent to the composition; *the generative idea* is the concept. We might want to assume some sequence. The idea would then be the inherent, the creative. But the idea is apparently not independent of the thing from which it is created. The image created through the idea must illuminate the idea it has engendered, that is, make it visible. This does not make a great deal of difference, since something made visible still needs something that makes it visible. It appears to be something that is thought, something already inherent prior to its visualization. But then the relationship between image and idea is described differently: "everything . . . must . . . continue to bear its original color [= of the idea], its livery so to speak." "Porter la couleur" is a set phrase. By wearing someone's colors, one shows that one serves that person. This is true of the knight who wears his lady's colors and of the lackey's clothing, for which the French *couleur* is used metonymically. If the color of the idea carries everything, then this is to be read as a metaphor for *servir*: everything must belong to the idea in that it contributes to its illumination. But the connection makes it probable that Baudelaire is not using color only metaphorically.

This entire passage is concerned expressly with color and the relationship of colors to each other. What unifies the many colors in an image is called atmosphere or *milieu coloré*. This is created out of a dominant color tone, which, from a part of the picture, influences the whole. It seems legitimate to take the "original color" (*couleur originelle*) literally. Read this way, a color is no longer a sign that refers to an idea. The idea is from the beginning a color idea. This is reminiscent of what Baudelaire expresses in another part of the text in reference to Delacroix: "It seems that this color, if I may be pardoned these subterfuges of language to express my quite delicate ideas, thinks by itself, independent of the objects it clothes" (II, 595). If the idea is color, then it is no longer inherent but is transferred to the immediacy of the painter's activity. This activity makes the idea visible using atmosphere. The atmosphere is formed as the referentiality of everything to the idea. The atmosphere is impossible without the idea, and the idea is never inherent as anything but atmosphere. The atmosphere is composition under the aspect of color. The self-creation of the idea unifies the whole in its creation and postulates this as its foundation with reference to the idea created along with it. The idea is the subsequent inherent element. It is only inherent in the image, but the image presents it by referring both to it and to that from which it was created. The idea constitutes itself in the composition as the reference to its own inherence.

This clears up the ambiguity of the sentence, according to which an idea's color conveys everything in the picture. It holds true that color refers to the idea. But it is also true that the idea is color. If it were true that color only *refers* to the idea, then the idea would be independent of color, and color would only be the means to make it appear. If it were true that the idea *is* color, then the distinction between the two, and therefore the image as image, would be untenable, because the image cannot be what it shows. If, however, both are true, then the image is not what it shows but instead shows what it is. The image that refers to an idea and is at the same time that idea refers to what it already is. It does so not by claiming to be the idea, because this reduces the ambiguity, but by showing itself to refer to the idea it is. But what, then, is the image? To the extent that it is a reference to the idea, it is more than the idea. To the extent, however, that it is the idea, it is more than the reference to it. It is therefore the nature of the image not to be able to be what it is, because it is always at the same time something else.

The image that simultaneously is and is not what it is, is the image being created. The image is the activity of its own creation. As the likeness of an original, the image is a fixed presence and likewise something determined as the predetermined thing it reproduces. If the image were no longer a likeness, then it could also no longer be understood as an object. It cannot simply be taken to be inherent but presents itself as the self-creation of the image. The elimination of the sequence of original and likeness focuses attention on the activity of image creation as the nature of the image itself. Baudelaire's interest in the creative process of an image is not the anecdotal curiosity of those who look over the shoulders of giants but is based on the understanding of the image as a creation of itself. This implies that the "finished" image, insofar as it is not simply understood as the likeness of an original, must be seen as the image of its own creation. The image is the image of its own creation. The creation of the image as what the image shows is the self-constitution of the original as likeness.

CREATION OF THE IMAGE

Baudelaire deals with the creation of the image in detail in his chapter "L'art mnémonique" (Mnemonic art) in *Le peintre de la vie moderne* (The painter of modern life). This title is surprising because memory, which seems to be contrasted with productive imagination as a reproductive force, is given some degree of importance. On the surface, the text seems to present itself as a reversion to an imitative theory, as Baudelaire says of Constantin Guys: "He draws from memory and not from the model" (II, 698), and generally: "As a matter of fact, all good and true draftsmen draw from the image written in their brain and not from nature." This forces us to examine the function of memory and its relationship to imagination more closely.

The conflict is between drawing from memory and drawing from a model—the remembered image (*image écrite dans le cerveau*) and nature (*nature*). This relationship gives us some indication of the function of memory: the image the artist maintains in his memory is not the exact reproduction of the object. If simple repetition were the main concern, then it would make little sense to prefer drawing from memory to drawing from a model. What is observed is therefore not only stored in memory but also altered. We should ask ourselves what kind of change we are dealing with. The text provides clues, especially where it is argued that the memory's image is preferable to the extant object:

> When a true artist has come to the point of the final execution of his work, the model would be more of a *burden* than a help to him. It even happens that men such as Daumier and Monsieur G. [Constantin Guys], for long accustomed to exercising their memory and storing it with images, find that the physical presence of the model and its multiplicity of details disconcerts and as it were paralyzes their principal faculty. (II, 698)

Most disconcerting about the model is the variety of details. This variety is the distinction between the present and the remembered model. In the transition from one to the other, a reduction to the essential occurs, a valuation of the elements and a discarding of those that are unnecessary for the preservation of the whole. Baudelaire speaks of the painters, "whose gaze is synthetic and abbreviating" (II, 698), and he calls their accomplishment "this *legendary* translation of external life" (II, 698). The legendary contains what is most important. Baudelaire formulated his understanding of legends with the help of Victor Hugo's *La légende des siècles* (The legend of the centuries). He acknowledges that Hugo only borrowed from history what history could legitimately give to poetry: "I mean legend, myth, fable, which are like concentrations of national life, like deep reservoirs where the blood and tears of peoples sleep" (II, 140). Legends generalize, abbreviate, or concentrate life. In that they extract the general out of the individual, they take on an exemplary character. Baudelaire is completely willing to see the legendary together with simplification and stylization, something unique to certain exotic cultures, and something he calls the barbaric: "What I mean is an unavoidable, synthetic, childlike barbarousness, which is often visible in a perfected art (Mexican, Egyptian, Ninevan), and which comes from a need to see things broadly, to consider them above all in their total effect" (II, 697). All of these passages give some indication of the changes that take place in the transition from the present model to the image of memory: sketching, simplifying, generalizing, emphasizing the whole versus the individual. If an artist draws from memory rather than from a model, he seems to do so because his task is to divide the essential from the unessential, to glean the special from the general, to get away from the individual, and to see the whole. If this were the case, then the special and the individual would be devalued in relationship to the general and the whole. It would become the unessential and could therefore be discarded. But how can the special and the individual be unessential, if the general cannot exist without the special and the whole without the individual? Synthesizing cannot lead to an abandonment of detail. Rather, the threatened loss of the individual must be countered by a tendency to maintain it.

The painter with whom Baudelaire's text is concerned, Constantin Guys, is not a classicist fixed on the timeless and the general. As an illustrator for newspapers and a journalist in the Crimean War, he was intent on capturing reality in pictures. In this enterprise, great weight is given to the accidental, the transitory, things that seem to be without lasting value, such as fashion or the way women dress and make themselves up. But it is precisely these trivialities that are important to Baudelaire, because they constitute half of beauty, the other half of which is the eternal, the permanent. This dual aspect of beauty, which, among other things, forms the basis for its historicity, does not need to be discussed here. It is sufficient to state that the artist's task consists of extracting the permanent from the fleeting and impermanent: "He makes it his business to extract from fashion whatever it contains that is poetic in the historical, to distill the eternal from the transitory" (II, 694). This means, however, that the permanent depends on the transitory. The transitory is not important in and of itself, but only because the permanent is given in and through it. The eternal is not an inherent thing to be recalled at any time, rather it must always be acquired as what shines through as the temporal. The permanent must be captured *in* the fleeting. The fleeting, the individual, the specific must be captured. It is therefore not enough to speak of the simplification of the object, of the translation of life into legend. We are left with the view that the sketchy overview might exist at the expense of the individual that makes it possible in the first place. The tendency towards the general and the whole is therefore countered by the tendency towards the specific and the individual. Both struggle with one another, and yet both are necessary. The resulting conflict is characterized in "L'art mnémonique" as follows:

> In this way a struggle is launched between the will to see all and forget nothing and the faculty of memory, which has formed the habit of a lively absorption of general color and silhouette, the arabesque of contour. An artist with a perfect sense of form but one accustomed to relying above all on his memory and his imagination will find himself at the mercy of a riot of details all clamoring for justice with the fury of a mob in love with absolute equality. All justice is trampled under foot; all harmony sacrificed and destroyed; many a trifle assumes vast proportions; many a triviality usurps the attention. The more our artist turns an impartial eye on detail, the greater is the state of anarchy. Whether he be long-sighted or short-sighted, all hierarchy and all subordination vanishes. (II, 698f.)

The ability to set an object in the realm of the legendary ("of general color and silhouette, the arabesque of contour") is contrasted with the opposing need to maintain all details ("the will to see all and forget nothing"). This opposition does not permit a decision in the sense that the one side or the other would win out. Either result would be fatal. The suppression of detail leads "in the emptiness of an abstract and indefinable beauty" (II, 695) to a generality that is empty because the tension between it and the specific no longer exists. Equally undesirable is the victory of the detail, because the whole threatens to be lost in focusing on the detail. The inclination towards detail leads to anarchy. It destroys hierarchy as the order toward which an image should strive. This dual threat can only be dealt with in that both tendencies balance each other out, and the contest remains undecided. The image is created as this contest. It is the activity of its own creation and must be accessible in the act of painting (*exécution*).

The execution of painting is burdened with the dual require-ment that it achieve the whole of the order to be established and that it do justice to the specificity of the individual. The problem lies in that the detail tends to be lost in the overview of the whole, and the inclination to detail destroys the whole. To the extent that the whole is seen, the individual grows pale, and when the individ-ual predominates, order is lost. These alternatives must be over-come by turning the either-or into a not only–but also. It is memory that accomplishes this. If I turn towards detail, I must simultaneously have the disappearing order present as something remembered, and if I look at the order of the whole, I must store the threatened details in my memory. No matter which way I turn, I need memory to keep the other. Memory prevents the one from being lost by the focus on the other, and it thereby prevents me from losing myself in the one or the other. It permits the return to what might disappear by its preservation and allows for a constant back-and-forth between detail and the whole. This back-and-forth is the creative process of the image, which is supposed to establish the simultaneity of the detail and the whole.

It is not easy to understand what is meant by *art mnémonique*. Contrary to popular belief, the simple notion that the painter paints an image according to the image of the model stored in his memory is insufficient. Rather, memory has its function within the imaginative process itself. This is accomplished in the tension between the detail and the whole. So that neither one is lost, even though both cannot be present at the same time, the missing part must be remembered. Memory prevents the connection between the whole and the detail from ever being severed.

This raises another point in Baudelaire's text, which is not comprehensible based on what has been said up to now and that should be seen together with the role of memory. Whenever speaking of the activity of painting and the importance of technical ability, it is emphasized that the execution must be carried out as quickly as possible. We should question the need for this hurry. This haste is based on the fear that what is to be captured in an image could disappear before it is captured. We should not be satisfied with thinking of certain objects as unstable and therefore only available for short periods of time, even though this may often be the case for a painter, such as Guys, trying to capture the contemporary. But even these unstable objects are remembered, and it is telling that speed is also important to the painter who paints from memory, even though the state of the object is less precarious. This haste must be explained another way, but even the differentiated way is of little help in understanding the role of memory. It has been shown that the painter is at all times in danger of losing the whole, whenever he concentrates on the detail, and the reverse is true when the detail is lost by focusing on the whole. This could explain the fact that one must be abandoned in favor of the other as soon as it is achieved. The constant fear that the detail could be lost in the whole and vice versa should encourage a constant and hasty back-and-forth between the two. It remains to be proven that such a movement really does exist. But right now we are at a loss to explain it. If memory takes over the task of making available whatever might be forgotten, then haste should be unnecessary. If, on the other hand, Baudelaire constantly seems to demand this rush, then whatever might disappear before it can be turned into an image is apparently not something that can be preserved by memory. We must therefore ask what it is that this rapid execution is supposed to save from destruction.

There are several passages that deal with haste. With the exception of *Le peintre de la vie moderne*, they all refer to Delacroix. This is already the case in the 1846 *Salon* (II, 433). The two excerpts that will be discussed come from Baudelaire's later writings. The first quote is from the *Salon* of 1859:

> If a very clean execution is necessary, that is because the language of the dream must be very cleanly translated; if it must be very rapid, it is so that nothing is lost of the extraordinary impression that accompanied the conception. (II, 625)

The second quote is from *L'oeuvre et la vie d'Eugène Delacroix* (The work and life of Eugène Delacroix):

> He once said to a young man of my acquaintance: "If you have not sufficient skill to make a sketch of a man throwing himself from a window in the time it takes him to fall from the fourth floor to the ground, you will never be capable of producing great machines." This enormous hyperbole seems to me to contain the major concern of his whole life, which was, as is well known, to achieve an execution quick and sure enough to prevent the smallest particle of the intensity of action or idea from evaporating. (II, 763f.)

Both texts explain why the execution must be quick. Both passages state that something is lost without haste. In the first case, what should be preserved is called "the extraordinary impression that accompanied the conception." In the second case, this is "the intensity of action or idea." The parallel is obvious. Not the object or its image are threatened but a certain way of experiencing the object. This is not simply a matter of perception. Instead, one's relationship to this object is emotionally charged. It is characterized by what Baudelaire calls intensity. This intensity is introduced as the thing that memory cannot preserve and that can be lost without quick painting. Apparently only the act of painting itself is able to save this intensity in the image. But we still do not understand this intensity nor its relationship to painting.

When a man jumps out of a window, how is what Baudelaire calls "the intensity of action or idea" related to the spectator? Certainly the impression of whomever witnesses such an event is related to the expected outcome. This expectation anticipates the outcome at the beginning. In the middle of the jump, the fall is already present. This presence of the whole in each moment of movement is the intensity of the experience of the fall. If I see the man at a height of three stories, then the intensity of the impression lies in knowing, at that same instant, that he has already jumped out of a window and that he will land on the ground. No single moment of the fall is witnessed in isolation; rather each part constantly refers to the whole of which it is a part. The intensity is based on the presence of the whole sequence in each of its phases. Baudelaire is no stranger to such an understanding of intensity, and it can be found again in other relationships. The intensity as just characterized appears in conditions of the mind that result from drug use but generally belongs to the realm Baudelaire calls *surnaturel.* In his diary we read: "The supernatural comprises the general color and accent, or intensity, sonority, limpidity, vibravity, depth, and reverberation in space and time" (I, 658). Radiation from a point into a breadth or depth is part of this *surnaturel.* Shortly after this passage, there is a sentence that relates exactly to the connection made here, even if it does introduce entirely new terminology: "In certain almost supernatural states of mind the depth of life is revealed in its entirety in the spectacle, as ordinary as it is, which you have before your eyes. It becomes the symbol" (I, 659). The same sentence can be found again with slight alterations in *Le poème du hachisch* (Hashish poem; I, 430). The symbol is the individual that represents the whole. The symbolism of the individual in which the whole is present determines the intensity of the frame of mind with which Baudelaire is concerned ("certain almost supernatural states of mind"). Accordingly, the intensity of the experience is determined by the fact that the experience of the individual does not stop there but goes on to a whole of which the individual is a part.

We must understand the transfer of intensity to an image in light of this definition. Although Baudelaire never seems to expressly develop this transition, our question can certainly be clearly posited from the realities of the texts. The goal is the preservation of intensity, and we may assume that this intensity can be lost, that memory is apparently not capable of preserving it, and that finally the loss of this intensity can be prevented through quick execution. This essentially anticipates the solution to our question, even though it is not yet understood. The preservation of intensity is made possible by its immediate transposition in the act of painting. Nothing besides the movement of the brush can prevent the disappearance of intensity. We must now examine this transfer of intensity in action.

Intensity is defined as the experience of the whole in the individual. Important is how the relationship between the individual and the whole is constituted in an intense experience. This is, without a doubt, a referential relationship, as the appearance of the symbol in this matter clearly shows. It is clear, however, that it is not enough to see in the individual a symbol for the whole. This symbolic relationship would be emotionally neutral, and it would be hard to understand wherein the intensity of such a relationship would lie. It would be equally difficult to fathom how such a relationship could be threatened, since the fact that one stands for the other can very easily be remembered without compromising the reference in any way. Intensity is the experience of a different kind of referential relationship than exists between a sign and its signified. To better understand this relationship, I return to the fall from the window. Each individual moment of this fall is related to and stands for the whole of the fall in my experience, not the way a sign stands for a signified, but in such a way that I experience the single moment as one that pushes past itself towards a whole. The whole is inherent in the individual that strives to complete itself by going beyond itself. Reference in this case is not a standing for something else but a striving beyond oneself. The individual is less a representative of the whole than something driving towards the whole. The intensity of this experience of the individual as something striving beyond itself is at the same time its downfall. The experience of the individual requires a completion of the movement that leads from the individual to the whole. The intensity of the experience of the individual is based on the individual's reference to the whole. But in this reference, the individual points to the whole through movement. The experience of the individual moment is therefore neces-

anticipation

sarily converted into movement and aims for the realization of the
whole. It can be said that the spectator who watches the fall has
already realized it in his imagination, and that the transformation
of perception in the imaginative act is what is called the intensity of
his experience.

This illustrates the transformation of an experience in an act, but
this is by no means the same as the act of the painter who retains
something in an image. What I have tried to describe is what
happens to everyone, and what everyone who witnesses an event
does. More happens with the painter, because the experience of the
individual is not only realized in the imaginative act of the movement's whole, it also causes the movement of the brush, the act of
painting. How is this done, and how does this act preserve the
intensity of the experience? I ask the question based on the example
that Baudelaire takes from Delacroix. We will assume that whoever
sees a man jumping out of a window also draws this man, and that
the intensity of the experience of this spectator is preserved in this
act. The intensity of the experience consists of the fact that in each
moment of the fall the whole of the fall is given, that in each
moment the movement is already completed in thought. If the
falling man is to be drawn, then this can only mean that such a
moment is retained. Movement can only be drawn in that a
particular moment is taken and presented in such a way that allows
the movement to be deduced. The task of whomever draws the
falling man is to fix the given situation in one isolated instant. He
must not draw a sequence of moments but a concurrence of the
contemporaneous, which, in the chosen instant, stand in a particular relation to each other. Primary for the drawer is no longer a
sequence of events but rather a spatial construct of relationships.
He is concerned with the correct position of body parts and the
situation of the falling man in his surroundings. This spatial coincidence is the drawing, which can only be created through the
movement of the pen. The spatial simultaneity therefore presumes
a sequence. This is the result of the act of drawing. The movement
of the pen is experienced in a way that is similar to the movement
of the fall. It is not an event removed that is simply watched, but a

guided movement. For the artist, the whole is the final order of the elements in the simultaneity of coincidence to which the movement of the pen must lead. Wherever the pen is, it strives from this single point towards the whole, because every line must be directed towards the whole. Every line contains the whole. We could call this the intensity of the act of drawing, and we would understand what is meant by the preservation of intensity if we recognize that an analogy exists between the experience of the falling man's movement and the experience of drawing with regard to intensity. We are therefore not concerned with fixing the intensity by reproducing what was experienced. Instead the intensity is transformed in the act of drawing. To understand this relationship we must accept that there is no causal connection between the intensity of the experience of falling and that of drawing. This is also true with regard to the quickness of the movement. There is no need to draw quickly just because the man to be drawn is falling quickly. The intensity of the experience of drawing excludes any delays in the drive of the individual beyond itself towards the whole. The speed of execution is based on the nature of the act of drawing itself and not on the object to be drawn.

One might argue against all that has been said by pointing out that it is based too much on the rather extraordinary example of a man who jumps out of a window and can therefore only be of rather limited value. This argument does not stand if one considers the importance given the example by the result of the investigation. It has absolutely no determining influence on the act of drawing but is used to show the movement Baudelaire calls *exécution* with the help of a movement that is analogously experienced.

How can we relate these thoughts concerning intensity and the speed of execution to what was said earlier about memory? The most important result of our examination of memory was that the task of memory was not to preserve something that had preceded a productive process, such as an original, but that it has its function within the productive process itself. This process is required to prevent what can be called the individualization of the individual, and what Baudelaire himself called anarchy in the *Salon* of 1859.

Memory assures us that we will not become lost in the details of the detail and that the connection between the individual and the whole is maintained. In that memory retains the presence of the whole, it allows the ordering of the individual. The whole is not preserved as something present in memory, since it is the very thing that is supposed to be created by the compositional act. The whole is therefore remembered as what is absent. It can only constitute itself in the ordering of the individual. Memory of the whole as something absent is therefore created by the act of ordering; in other words, it keeps us from remaining with the individual and drives the movement towards the whole. The movement of the pen rushes towards the whole, remembered in memory as something absent. This makes the desired connection accessible. Memory of the absent whole, a part of the experience of the individual, is the intensity caused by the movement of the pen as it aims beyond the individual.

THE SWAN

We might ask ourselves if the function of memory in the imaginative process, as it is presented in Baudelaire's writings on art theory, can contribute to an understanding of his poems. This seems at first unlikely, based on the verses that come most readily to mind in connection with Baudelaire and memory. In lines like "Je sais l'art d'évoquer les minutes heureuses" (I know the art of evoking happy minutes [I, 37]), or

> Charme profond, magique, dont nous grise
> Dans le présent le passé restauré! (I, 39)

> Deep charm, magical, whose restored past
> Renders us gray in the present!

memory is celebrated as an act of realization and must be understood as mimetic memory insofar as it reproduces past things the way they were. In the writings on painting, however, the topic of evocative speech is always key, and it requires a certain interpretive effort to construe the memory of something absent as the mover of imaginative movement. The question of why this link to evocative memory remains is not easy to answer. Leaving this aside for a moment, we can investigate whether some other kind of memory is at work behind the explicit evocation in the poems. This will be discussed using the example of *Le cygne* (The swan; I, 85–87).

The poem is about a series of figures, all of whom have lost something they remember and who, in turn, are remembered by the speaker. All these figures are nostalgically bound to their past. They mourn their loss and want to recover it. This is most clearly demonstrated in the character of Andromache, taken from the third book of the *Aeneid*, who rebuilds a miniature home in exile ("I recognize a small Troy, and a simulated great Pergamus" [3, vv. 349–51]) and makes offerings at Hector's empty grave ("At the shores of a false Simoïs Andromache sacrificed to the remains" [3, vv. 302–3]). The mimetic character of evocative memory is unmistakable. The lost past is replaced by its likeness so that the illusion of its presence can be created. Baudelaire's verse "Auprès d'un tombeau vide en extase courbée" (Beside an empty tomb in bent ectasy [v. 39]) might refer to the copy being confused with the real grave, because its nature as an image is forgotten, and the boundary between original and likeness is blurred. This is also made clear by Virgil: Andromache seems confused when Aeneas suddenly appears ("Are you coming toward me, a real form, a true messenger, goddess-born?" [3, vv. 310–11]). Forgetting the past tense of the past would represent its successful and complete representation as the restoration of the lost present. All nostalgic memory has the desire to completely restore the past, even when this desire can only express itself as lament in the knowledge of its unattainability. This is true of all figures who appear in the poem, for the swan whose heart yearns for the waters of his homeland, and for the African woman who searches for the palms of her home beyond a wall of fog.

Despite all the examples of the never-ending desire for an evocative realization of the present, it would be wrong to declare the roll of memory in this poem to be self-evident. We must above all try to understand why so many cases of the same behavior are presented. The story of the swan does not add anything to the story of Andromache. It remains a complete mystery why the second half of the poem adds a list that, for the most part, simply recounts very general situations ("to whomever," "to the captives," "to the conquered"). The reason for this aggregate of examples is to be found by examining their relationships. The connection lies in the fact that all the figures are present as remembered by the speaker. "I am thinking of . . ." is the phrase that, throughout the entire poem, demonstrates the correlation between what is evoked and the remembrances of the poet. What kind of memory is this, and what kind of relationship is established between the individual episodes?

The memory of the poet also seems at first to evoke the past, and the text tells us how this process proceeds: the thought of Andromache calls to mind the image of the swan, encountered by the poet where the carousel now stands. The transition from Andromache to the swan is easy to follow, since both episodes are analogous and can therefore refer to each other metaphorically. Thanks to this similarity, the Andromache story is able to trigger the memory of the swan:

> Ce Simoïs menteur . . . ,
> A fécondé soudain ma mémoire fertile (Vv. 4–5)

> This lying Simoïs . . . ,
> Suddenly impregnated my fertile memory

The one functions as a substitute for the other and can elicit its realization. The relationship between Andromache and the swan is therefore not much different from the relationship that exists within the Andromache story between the make-believe and the real Simoïs. Andromache would be the means by which a past is made accessible through evocation. But Andromache is a memory, and it is fair to ask how it is that Baudelaire thinks of her at precisely this moment. If we are unsatisfied with anecdotal chance and don't want simply to forego an explanation, then we must assume that he thinks of Andromache while crossing the carousel. This is only clear if the place has acquired some meaning in connection with this memory. The place in its new form is experienced as having changed (*le nouveau Carrousel*). This awakens the memory of its previous condition, that is, of the old Paris (*le vieux Paris*) and of the swan that belongs in this context. The swan, as exile, reminds us of Andromache. This contradicts the just-established sequence. The consequence of this contradiction is simple but of considerable significance for the understanding of the text: the relationship between Andromache and the swan is interchangeable.

This memory is different from nostalgic memory, where such a reversal would be impossible. Troy and Epirus cannot be exchanged in Andromache's mind, because one is a lost reality and the other is only an image. These priorities are no longer valid for the speaker in *Le cygne*. He is concerned with the relationship between memories that are equal. It doesn't matter whether the memory of Virgil's text evokes the memory of the swan or whether the swan reminds us of Andromache. What does matter is the relationship between memories and the relationship between memories and the one remembering. This relationship is not nostalgic. The swan as the object of memory does not have the status of something lost, which we lament as the swan laments the lost lake. The attempt to read the poem as an elegy of old Paris does not get us very far. The reversibility of the relationship between what is remembered and the one who evokes the memory leads to a neutralization of the chronology. The nostalgic's time is irreversible and experienced as a constant losing. The past is a lost presence. This is true of all the characters who appear in the poem with the exception of the one who remembers them. He does not lament something lost but instead thinks about having lost, the situation of the others. Andromache, the swan, and their relatives all lament something they have lost and that lives on in their memories as a lost presence. The one in whom all these memories gather does not invoke a specific loss but loss as the one thing common to all. None of the situations listed can make accessible the particular kind of

memory the poem represents, because any memory of loss, to the
extent that it remains concentrated on the objectivity of the loss,
covers up the loss as such.

We can only become conscious of loss as such if the bond to the
loss is loosened. In the poem this is achieved by piling up examples
of nostalgic obsession with loss. The resulting inventory of examples produces something decidedly new. The constancy of loss
shines through the manifold possibilities of experiencing loss. In
the grand movement of losing into which the one and then the
other withdraw, loss remains constant. The constancy of the experience of loss is what Baudelaire calls melancholy:

> Paris change! mais rien dans ma mélancolie
> N'a bougé! (Vv. 29–30)

> Paris changes! yet nothing in my melancholy
> has budged!

The melancholic appears here as the opposite of the nostalgic. He
is characterized not by lamenting a specific loss but by the obsession that everything must be lost. He is no longer concerned with
the past but rather with passing. With this, the objects of loss
become fairly arbitrary and interchangeable, of equal value, and
even indifferent, simple elements of enumeration. The past is no
longer lamented as a lost presence but represents through its being
past the passing of what is transient. In light of this transience, each
passing or past falls victim to an arbitrariness that makes the
attempt to hold on seem useless. The nostalgic bond to the lost is a
revolt against a transience of which the melancholic is no longer
capable. He is prevented by his own indifference from clinging to
this or that. He is no longer in danger of losing himself in each
object, as is a nostalgic. Instead he is threatened with the complete
loss of objectivity and sinks into an objectless abyss.

Objects don't disappear in Baudelaire's poem, they become alle-
gories. The allegorization of the world is very closely linked to
melancholy. It presents to the melancholic the possibility of a
constructive behavior. The melancholic neither clings nostalgically

to what is lost nor loses himself in emptiness but experiences the permanence of transience in the impermanence of the transient.

This allegorization overcomes the nostalgic bond to objects. One might be tempted to see the loosening of this bond in *Le cygne* as present in what is remembered, since what is remembered is not arbitrary but rather a series of examples of nostalgic memory. This remembering is thereby somewhat removed and becomes itself the object of remembering. But therein lies the danger that nostalgia will remain uncontested. The person remembering can assume the attitude of his characters, whose nostalgic memories become his own, and thus fall prey to nostalgia instead of overcoming it. It is important for an understanding of Baudelaire's poem that the poet does not, or does not exclusively, identify himself with these nostalgics, the objects of his remembering. The sense of the poem would be lost if we were to take Andromache or the swan as adequate representatives of the speaker. The speaker shares in the objects of his memory to the extent that nostalgia is by no means finally defeated, but he also accomplishes a critical separation from them in that he refuses to accept the lament of loss.

Nostalgia, or falling victim to what is remembered, is overcome by enumeration. The function of this enumeration and its dominance in the second half of the poem must be questioned. The transition from one to the other creates a distance to the individual. This individual is no longer employed only by itself and lamented for its own sake but, in conjunction with the enumeration of all like things, represents a generality for which it serves as an example. The fact that things are no longer considered in their simple presence or absence but rather in their meaning is what Baudelaire calls allegorization. Everything becomes allegory: that is, nothing is exhausted in its being here, but everything has something missing within itself and therefore has meaning. What is meant is the other to which we point, that which the meaning lacks. Meaning is always a hollowing out of presence. It remains hidden as long as things are considered only in terms of current or lost presence, thus hiding their internal hollowness. This is the case with nostalgics, who only know what is present and what is lost but are unable to anticipate loss in the present. In contrast, the present always holds up its own emptiness for those who see allegorically and is experienced not as something present but as something passing. If the experience of things is always accompanied by the memory of their transience, then the possibility, if not the desire, of holding on to the transient must also be recognized as transient. The fixation on the presence of the present is avoided. Instead of clinging to the present, losing it, and becoming nostalgic, one can avoid loss by accepting the present as always passing and then leaving it. Enumeration is such a leavetaking. In the transition to the subsequent, the previous is accepted as untenable. This transience is now no longer something suffered forcibly but construed and produced in the rhythm of enumeration. Instead of suffering loss, we effect renunciation.

Memory is effective in enumeration. This memory is not mimetic and evocative, since its function is to prevent falling victim to images. Important is not the memory of the list but the need to list, the constantly repeated renunciation of what is listed. The need to enumerate exists as the danger of lingering in the individual threatens. Only those exposed to the lure of memory must be reminded of its transience. The movement of enumeration lasts as long as the danger of the individual's nostalgic stagnation prevails. As this danger is never totally overcome but is resurrected at every step of enumeration, the movement becomes never-ending and merges at the end of the poem with an undetermined continuation: "a bien d'autres encor" (to still many others). The tension between nostalgic obsession with things and allegorical escape from them does not find a solution in the sense of a resolution. It is instead what results from the movement of enumeration, its mover, and cannot be reduced by any decision. This tension is palpable in the first strophe of the poem's second part, where allegorization is starkly confronted by the material weight of memories, something understandable only in the context of a nostalgic relationship:

> tout pour moi devient allégorie,
> Et mes chers souvenirs sont plus lourds que des rocs. (Vv. 31–32)

everything for me becomes allegory,
and my precious recollections are heavier than rocks.

The same conflict between the temptation to hold on to the memory and distancing oneself from it also makes the difficult verses of the final strophe, those dealing with memory, more accessible:

> Ainsi dans la forêt où mon esprit s'exile
> Un vieux Souvenir sonne à plein souffle du cor! (Vv. 49–50)

> Thus in the forest where my spirit takes exile
> An old Memory rings in full force from the body!

It is at first difficult to see how these verses fit the list, which continues in the last two lines of the poem. We might surmise that the person remembering has placed himself in the series of his own examples. Just as all others have lost something to which they cling, so (*ainsi*) the mind of the speaker, too, reflects his loss in exile. The poet would then be included among those of whom he speaks. But the fact that he does speak makes it impossible for him to be in the same category. It is not incorrect, but certainly inadequate, to read these verses on the same level as the others. The I is not, like the other characters of the poem, only one element of a list, but the enumerator himself. What happens here affects the enumerator. What has up to now been said of exile and memory is true of him as well. The two verses must be seen as a characterization of what occurs in the poem as enumeration and must be read in this sense.

The forest represents the many memories that have been gathered in the list. In each of these memories, the mind is in danger of losing itself in the loss. To the degree that he succumbs to this danger and the fascination of the memory, he estranges himself and forces himself into exile. But this is exactly what the list should prevent. The list's task is to undo the fixation on the individual. This requires the memory's trumpet call in the forest of enumeration. This memory recalls the wandering mind to itself, reminds it of itself, as the hunter's horn calls an end to the hunt and a return home. What is forgotten in nostalgic memory under the burden of memory is here recalled to memory: the act of remembering as the possibility of an evocation based on the transience of the transient, something that must always be present to form the nostalgic bond. *Un vieux Souvenir* must be understood as the memory of the act of remembering.

This expression shows a curious internal tension. The capitalization of *Souvenir* indicates that the memory appears here as a personified allegory. A distancing from all objects of individual memories has already taken place, and remembering becomes itself the possibility of remembering what has been remembered. This is contradicted by the indefinite article, indicating that an individual memory might be meant. *Un vieux Souvenir* represents both the generality of remembering and the specificity of a single memory. Baudelaire's understanding of memory depends not on the reduction of this tension but rather on its unfolding.

An attempt at this unfolding can proceed from the fact that remembering is only accessible through individual memories. *Something* is always remembered, and the realization of this something is memory's achievement. But in looking to individual memory, remembering itself can be lost. To regain it, we must distance ourselves from what is remembered. This must occur in such a way that does not abandon memory along with what is remembered. The memory must live on but in a way that overcomes the fixation on what is remembered. This is accomplished by substituting one memory for another, that is, through enumeration. Remembering is accessible through the constant withdrawal from everything remembered or listed. This is why the memory of the act of remembering sounds out in the forest. The act of remembering can never become a remembered object, in which the memory could quiet itself. It can only appear or sound out in enumeration as a never-ending distancing from the remembered or the listed. Positively speaking, this means that each single memory becomes an allegory of that memory to the extent that each is a part of the enumeration. The nostalgic memory (Andromache, the swan) has meaning in that it is listed along with other, similar things. The remembered nostalgic memory signifies the act of remembering, which, taken as a single instance, has been forgotten. It does so when it becomes part of an enumeration. *Un vieux Souvenir* is individual memory in enumeration. But it is also the act of remembering as it is enumerated that is given meaning by individual memory. It is this that sounds out in the list (*dans la forêt*) from the single memory (*un souvenir*), and it is the general act of remembering that makes this possible.

Memory of the act of remembering is also a memory of the fact that what is remembered is something past and that remembering itself depends on transience. If the nostalgic turns memory against transience and by doing so hopes to fight off the transience of the transient, then he negates the prerequisite that makes all this possible in the first place. This is opposed by a memory that makes not only the past present. The transience of the transient reminds him, yet attempts to hold nothing, because it reminds him of his own impermanence and also makes any sojourn impermanent.

A sojourn with the remembered is rejected in enumeration, the constitution of the poem's speech. Enumeration is a means to construe the sequence of speech. What was said earlier about the creation of images, comparable to enumerating speech, intrudes into our discussion. Movement is always what is prevented by staying and resting. In the first instance, it is the intensity that drives the individual toward the missing whole, of which it is a part. Movement goes to the construct that ties sequence to simultaneity and then comes to rest. In enumeration, on the other hand, the individual is abandoned, because it is itself transient. Movement here does not go to the stability of the construct's whole, and integration of the individual is not even attempted. Enumeration as a construct is the rhythmic realization of transience and is unopposed. But the renunciation of the individual enumeration's self-satisfaction must always be kept alive with the memory of its own transience. The danger of forgetting, that is, deference to the individual, still exists where the memory of the transience of the remembered is put into words. This occurs in the image of the trumpet call in the forest, something that demands attention for its own sake and is difficult to ignore. Nevertheless the image prevents us from succumbing to it. As the image of a sound that fades away, it recalls a memory and thereby effects a disengagement from itself and maintains the movement of enumeration.

A Renunciation of Understanding

Baudelaire's prose poem *Chacun sa chimère* (To every man his chimera) tells about an encounter with several men who are carrying chimeras on their backs. They trek through a desert with this load not knowing where they are going. After the caravan disappears, the observer wonders what it all means but soon gives up his attempt to uncover their secret and sinks into apathy. Given a story not understood by the very person telling it, we must ask ourselves what interpretation can do in such a situation. We should certainly not attempt to understand the story where the narrator fails, ascribing to it some unrelated meaning, no matter how believable. This would miss the very point that makes this text so special and which we should consider first: the speaker claims to understand nothing of what he says. His nonunderstanding is what must be understood. The narrated story should not be examined for this or that meaning, but we must ask how this incomprehensibility for the speaker might actually be its meaning. We are not so much interested in the content of the story of the chimera carriers but rather in the special way that Baudelaire's text speaks about the narration of the story. If the narrator of the story cannot find meaning in his tale, then it is not altogether clear why he chooses to tell it. In questioning the meaning not only of the story but also of its telling, the rejection of understanding can be seen as the distinguishing characteristic of this text.

CHACUN SA CHIMÈRE

Sous un grand ciel gris, dans une grande plaine poudreuse, sans chemins, sans gazon, sans un chardon, sans une ortie, je rencontrai plusieurs hommes qui marchaient courbés.

Chacun d'eux portait sur son dos une énorme Chimère, aussi

lourde qu'un sac de farine ou de charbon, ou le fourniment d'un fantassin romain.

Mais la monstrueuse bête n'était pas un poids inerte; au contraire, elle enveloppait et opprimait l'homme de ses muscles élastiques et puissants; elle s'agrafait avec ses deux vastes griffes à la poitrine de sa monture; et sa tête fabuleuse surmontait le front de l'homme, comme un de ces casques horribles par lesquels les anciens guerriers espéraient ajouter à la terreur de l'ennemi.

Je questionnai l'un de ces hommes, et je lui demandai où ils allaient ainsi. Il me répondit qu'il n'en savait rien, ni lui, ni les autres; mais qu'évidemment ils allaient quelque part, puisqu'ils étaient poussés par un invincible besoin de marcher.

Chose curieuse à noter: aucun de ces voyageurs n'avait l'air irrité contre la bête féroce suspendue à son cou et collée à son dos; on eût dit qu'il la considérait comme faisant partie de lui-même. Tous ces visages fatigués et sérieux ne témoignaient d'aucun désespoir; sous la coupole spleenétique du ciel, les pieds plongés dans la poussière d'un sol aussi désolé que ce ciel, ils cheminaient avec la physionomie résignée de ceux qui sont condamnés à espérer toujours.

Et le cortège passa à côté de moi et s'enfonça dans l'atmosphère de l'horizon, à l'endroit où la surface arrondie de la planète se dérobe à la curiosité du regard humain.

Et pendant quelques instants je m'obstinai à vouloir comprendre ce mystère; mais bientôt l'irrésistible Indifférence s'abattit sur moi, et j'en fus plus lourdement accablé qu'ils ne l'étaient eux-mêmes par leurs écrasantes Chimères. (I, 282f.)

TO EVERY MAN HIS CHIMERA

Under a vast gray sky, on a vast and dusty plain without paths, without grass, without a nettle or a thistle, I came upon several men bent double as they walked.

Each one carried on his back an enormous Chimera as heavy as a sack of flour, as a sack of coal, as the accoutrement of a Roman foot soldier.

But the monstrous beast was no inanimate weight; on the contrary, it hugged and bore down heavily on the man with its elastic and powerful muscles; it clutched at the breast of its mount with enormous claws; and its fabulous head overhung the man's forehead like those

terrible helmets with which ancient warriors tried to strike terror into
their enemies.

I questioned one of these men and asked him where they were going
like that. He replied that he did not know and that none of them
knew; but that obviously they must be going somewhere since they
were impelled by an irresistible urge to go on.

A curious thing to note: not one of these travelers seemed to resent
the furious beast hanging around his neck and glued to his back;
apparently they considered it a part of themselves. All those worn and
serious faces showed not the least sign of despair; under the depressing
dome of the sky, with their feet deep in the dust of the earth as desolate
as the sky, they went along with the resigned look of men who are
condemned to hope forever.

And the procession passed by me and disappeared in the haze of the
horizon just where the rounded surface of the planet prevents man's
gaze from following.

And for a few moments I persisted in trying to understand this
mystery; but soon irresistible Indifference descended upon me, and I
was more cruelly oppressed by its weight than those men had been by
their crushing Chimeras.

HOPE

The chimera, according to French usage, is not only an ancient
mythological animal but also represents illusion, the unfounded
vision. The men who carry chimeras across the desert are bent over
with the weight of illusion. If we ask ourselves what this consists of,
then it seems only natural to look for a connection with the journey
which the men have undertaken. Asked where they are going, one
of them answers that he doesn't know. They are apparently going
somewhere, however, since they are driven by an irrepressible force
to go on. This line of reasoning is based on an understanding of the
journey wherein movement is motivated by the wish to arrive at
another place. Movement is seen as directional, that is, towards a
goal which gives it meaning. This understanding of movement is
maintained in the above argument even though the relationship
between movement and goal is notably different from normal,
because the goal is unknown. Those who know their goal travel to

arrive there. This is impossible for those who don't know where they are going. It is not the intended goal that motivates travel. Travel first postulates a goal. Since I'm traveling, there must be a goal towards which I am heading. If the meaning of movement is seen in the goal, then aimless movement would have no meaning. But since a goal is at least postulated, meaning is only deferred. I may not know where I'm going, but when I arrive, the journey will prove to have been worthwhile. Meaning is given retrospectively to the future arrival. This explains what keeps the chimera carriers going. Their travel to reach a destination from their currently meaningless journey will be given meaning. The meaning of their movement is not present but hoped for. They are driven by the hope for meaning, that is, by the hope for a place that legitimizes the journey which leads to it. The justification for this hope is not doubted by the man who tells about his travels: "but that *obviously* they must be going somewhere since they were impelled by an irresistible urge to go on." This is why they carry with them the hope for meaning, their chimera. They are traveling under an illusion, not because their hope is futile, but because they don't seem to notice its uncertain prospects.

This simple interpretation of hope and chimera does not withstand the sentence that renders the final and complex character of this strange procession: "they walked with the resigned look of men who are condemned to hope forever." The connection that is made between the two contradictory concepts of hope and resignation is difficult. Whoever hopes is not resigned, and whoever is resigned to a given condition does not hope to change it. Baudelaire's chimera carriers hope and are at the same time resigned. The unification of the seemingly disparate is achieved in that hope is the condition to which these men are resigned. The men are content to be condemned to hope. This resignation presumes, however, some distance from their own hope. Those simply hoping would never be able to simultaneously possess the knowledge that hope is a destiny that can never be fulfilled. This is what being condemned to hope means. Hope is instigated by the unsatisfactory conditions in which one finds oneself. Hope is the reference to the future of the unsatisfied. The region through which the hopeful travel is a desert that can only be described by listing what is absent ("without paths, without grass, without a nettle or a thistle"). Those condemned to hope are subjected to eternal desire. Hope is constant, because no satisfaction can quench it. This would be the commutation of the sentence. The chimera carriers are conscious of the unremitting dissatisfaction of the present and their resignation is grounded in this realization. They are content to constantly hope, because there is no point along their path in which need turns into plenty. Their hope is a resigned hope. It is without any positive expectations. The chimera carriers are not traveling towards a definite goal but to somewhere (*quelque part*), to an arbitrary place of which they have no concept except that it is somewhere else. We should therefore not try to understand this hope from the viewpoint of a specific wish. It is not based on future fulfillment but on present need. It is not a hope for what has not yet come to pass but a hope that what is will not always be. It is less a hope for something than away from something. The chimera carriers are not traveling to arrive but to get away. The carrier of their hope is not the to where but the from where. Their world is like the hospital in Baudelaire's *Any Where Out of the World*, where all patients are obsessed with the desire for another bed. "It seems to me that I would always be fine where I am not" (I, 356). Baudelaire's patients and travelers could find a traveling companion in the protagonist of Kafka's story "Der Aufbruch" (The departure), who, asked by his servant about the goal of his imminent journey, answered: "Away from here—that is my goal."

This examination of resigned hope leads to an interpretation of the journey of the chimera carriers that is somewhat contradictory to the previously attempted interpretation. Whereas the movement was at first focused on the goal, it now seems necessary to see it from the perspective of the starting point. The two are complementary, as are hope and resignation. This hope is the hope of getting away; this resignation is the resignation of not arriving. The hope of getting away is necessarily connected with the belief in the possibility of reaching a place that is different from the present one. This rather ill-defined expectation of change is the hope for some future justification of one's own journey. The resignation, on the other hand, depends on this moment's never arriving. Everything always stays the same, and one place is the same as any other. But what else can the motivation of this movement be? We can certainly understand the decision to leave based on the intolerability of the given. We go away because we can't stand it anymore. But somehow the idea is present in our departure that we can stand it somewhere else better. The chimera carriers, who "go on their way with the resigned expression of someone who is condemned to hope eternally," content themselves in the fact that this hope can never be crushed, even though there is absolutely nothing to support it. This unsupported hope for change is the chimera, which drives the travelers on as the unquenchable desire to travel. What is impossible to understand is that, even when we have contented ourselves with the fact that what is hoped for will never be fulfilled, we continue to hope and go our way.

INDIFFERENCE

The procession of travelers is the observer's vision. The observer does not take part in the movement but stands apart and looks on. His distance to what he sees is so great that the earth appears curved. "And the procession passed by me and disappeared in the haze of the horizon just where the rounded surface of the planet prevents man's gaze from following." This could at first be interpreted as the unknown that lies beyond the horizon. We do not know where the chimera carriers' journey will take them. If this were the view of the observer, he would have to hope along with the others, and he would have to go with them to get out of the desert of need. But the picture of the curved earth leads us to another interpretation. The spherical shape of the planet shows the travelers' path to be circular, eventually leading them back to where they started. There is, on the other side of the horizon, nothing new, just the same desert. The perspective encompassing the entire globe is a disillusioned perspective without hope, not full of curiosity. It does not assume that one will forget that one travels in a circle. We come across it again in *Le goût du néant* (The longing for nothingness; I, 76):

> Je contemple d'en haut le globe en sa rondeur
> Et je n'y cherche plus l'abri d'une cahute.

> I contemplate from above the globe in its roundness
> And I no longer seek the shelter of a hut.

In the same poem, the rider Hope and the horse Spirit find each other, and their travels come to an end:

> Morne esprit, autrefois amoureux de la lutte,
> L'Espoir, dont l'éperon attisait ton ardeur,
> Ne veut plus t'enfourcher!

> Gloomy spirit, once in love with battle,
> Hope, whose spur pricked your ardor,
> No longer wants to mount you!

Hope is the force behind movement. The observer stands motionless, because he is without hope.

This hope is a hope for change. Whoever does not have it no longer believes that it is better somewhere else. It makes no difference if he is here or there. The observer in *Chacun sa chimère* is indifferent. Indifference is the absence of difference. Where there is no difference, there is no movement, because in the lack of difference in all things, the difference between here and not here becomes meaningless. The observer stands still. There is no path away from here, because here is the same as there. There are other places, but they are the same as this one. The one for whom here and there are the same is indifferent. Yet this still does not adequately describe indifference. The difficulty of Baudelaire's text lies in the fact that indifference is not just the absence of difference, but that in a certain sense it creates difference. Indifference itself is what distinguishes. The observer is different from the others in that he is indifferent. Indifference is what distinguishes him and makes him different from the chimera carriers. The observer has, in place of the chimera, indifference. In that everything is the same to him, he becomes different. His indifference situates him. This shows that indifference is not all encompassing, because it is itself different from others. Total indifference would be given if the difference between the hopeful and the apathetic did not exist. This would then mean: it makes no difference if I go or stay, if I am condemned to hope or to indifference. The unconquerable drive to go ("l'invincible besoin de marcher") and irresistible indifference ("l'irrésistible Indifférence") would be the same. But this is not at all the case. The distinction between indifference and the chimera remains. In the last sentence, the two are compared but not equated: "I was more cruelly oppressed by its weight than those men had been by their crushing Chimeras." The comparison confirms the difference. Indifference is weightier than the chimera. This means that the observer has not reached a state of complete indifference, but still sees himself in his own indifference as different from the chimera carriers. Recognizing this difference is questioning apathy. Wherever apathy is questioned, however, there exists some interest. The difference between the observer and the chimera carriers is the surviving interest of the apathetic. It appears as a desire to understand that is quickly overcome by apathy. Insofar as the observer is indifferent, he renounces understanding; insofar as indifference makes him different, however, he wants to understand. What he would like to understand is the difference between him and the chimera carriers, who are in the same desert and are driven by an unfounded hope he seems to lack.

At the end, the story and the apathy of the observer become one, but to the extent that the apathy is compared with something else, it recognizes another and is therefore incomplete. It is said of apathy that it is a burden heavier than the chimera. Its greater weight is the difference of apathy towards others. The observer does not succumb to his burden, but he nevertheless sees it as a burden in comparison to other burdens. The heavier something is, the more difficult it is to carry. To the extent that the burden increases, it becomes more unbearable. The observer, who measures the weight of his apathy, does not completely succumb to this weight but experiences in it the unbearable. There is something active in apathy that undermines it. It is accompanied by the sense of not being acceptable and is experienced as a feeling that must be overcome. Those who experience apathy as a burden are already entering into a relationship with it and are therefore already outside it. No matter how apathetic he may be, he is not apathetic towards his apathy. The desire for difference is given to indifference as a heavy burden.

Whoever is no longer apathetic is someone who is interested. Interest highlights certain things and thereby makes them different. The apathetic, however, is incapable of this kind of preference of one thing over another. His lack of interest prevents him from aiming for a certain goal. The desire within his apathy to overcome his apathy has nothing to counter it but is only intent on getting out. Getting away from apathy is instinctual. Each distinct interest is disqualified from apathy. But the fact that apathy can have no interest stirs its interest. Its interest is therefore not directed at this or that but rather at interest itself and the difficulty of having it. Interest is being in the middle. The interested person is caught between where he is and where he is not. His interest lies in establishing the difference between here and there, linked with the desire to get to where this object of interest is. The interest of an apathetic person, on the other hand, is not directed at a thing but at the interest in this thing. Interest as an in-between is the difference of a something and therefore of what separates it. This separation lasts as long as the interest. This is why the person interested in interest as difference never gets anywhere. His interest is endless because it maintains itself as something interested in itself. Those interested in interest are always in between, neither here nor there but on the go. Baudelaire, in his prose poem *Les vocations* (Vocations), uncovered the difference between an interest in something and an interest in interest. The three children, who become what they believe they are supposed to become, are contrasted with a fourth child, who is unable to choose a goal. He would like to travel with the gypsies, who also have no goal. His starting point is *ennui*, which for Baudelaire is the same as apathy, and the purpose of his interest is the interest that keeps him going: "Il m'a souvent semblé que mon plaisir serait d'aller toujours droit devant moi, sans savoir où, sans que personne s'en inquiète, et de voir toujours des pays nouveaux. Je ne suis jamais bien nulle part, et je crois toujours que je serais mieux ailleurs que là où je suis" (It often seemed to me that my pleasure would be always to go straight ahead, without knowing where, without worrying anyone, and always seeing new countries. I am happy nowhere, and I think I will always be happy elsewhere than where I am [I, 334]).

The observer in *Chacun sa chimère* would have to be going somewhere if the interest in interest were a secret force pulling him away from apathy. He would have in himself this incomprehensible, groundless hope that gets the chimera carriers moving, and, contrary to our initial impression, would be one of them. This seems to be contradicted in that the story ends in a disinclination to understand, that is, in indifference.

DISCOURSE

Nothing in the text points to overcoming this indifference, the terminus towards which it flows. But the story does not end there. The text includes not only the story but also its being told. We know of the observer not only what is said about him but also that he is saying it. It is the distinguishing characteristic of first-person narration that the narrator is always a character in his own narration. If the story is told in the past tense, as is the case here, then the narration is subsequent to the narrator. It begins after the story and is its continuation beyond the story's end. The last thing we know about the narrator of *Chacun sa chimère* is not that he succumbs to indifference, but that he becomes a narrator. This leads to the question of how this transition takes place. What makes him talk? One likely incitement to narration might be the need to understand what has happened. The desire retrospectively to provide the past with cohesion and meaning is one credible motivation for such an autobiographical undertaking. But as the narrator begins to tell his story, this motivation becomes obsolete, the attempts at understanding having already been exhausted. The renunciation of understanding may be a part of the story, but nothing supports the assumption that anything has changed in this regard for the narrator. The narration is expressly presented as something not understood. The only thing left is to assume the narration to be a discourse born of indifference. The discourse of the indifferent, unlike the discourse of the interested, serves no purpose. It is not meant to achieve anything beyond itself. Discourse out of indifference is nothing more than discourse away from indifference. As a movement away from . . . , it has no other purpose than to create its own opportunity. The driving force is the interest in the movement itself, that is, the interest in interest, effective in indifference as the sense of its own intolerability.

This detour has not yet made the narrated discourse of *Chacun sa chimère* comprehensible as a discourse born of indifference. It is difficult to understand, based on the manner of discourse, that the story does not gravitate towards a particular purpose, since it is concerned with the transmission of a specific content. What is uncommon about this narration's story is that it is said to be incomprehensible, and the story expressly refuses to understand what it tells. If we want to better understand the uniqueness of this narration born of indifference, then we must ask ourselves what purpose is served by the communication of the incomprehensible. It is difficult to accept that nothing more is to be gained from the text than the incomprehensibility of what is said. We can pose the question from the perspective of what is communicated, that is, from the standpoint of the chimera carriers, the story's main subject.

The reader's first and most urgent question of *Chacun sa chimère* concerns the meaning of the chimera carriers. It is also the narrator's question, a question he cannot answer and finally refuses to try. This not only does not answer the question, but makes it even more troubling. Considering the text's refusal to answer, the question becomes to what extent the meaning of the chimera carriers can be understood. The comments already made on this subject have shown the internal contradictions of the chimera carriers, whose attitude bespeaks both hope and resignation and who, in the end, remain an enigma in the simultaneity of the irreconcilable. Regarding the meaning of a story whose content is incomprehensible, we must first question the meaning of the failure to understand the meaning of the chimera carriers. The chimera carriers lose none of their effectiveness through the obscurity of their meaning. The reader's sense of the chimera carriers is obviously based on something other than a definite meaning. This other can be better viewed from the perspective of contradiction, given considerable weight in the text. This contradiction is not only expressed in the opposition of hope and resignation but also in the contrast between the appearance of the chimeras and the facial expressions of the men who carry them. The head of the chimera, as it appears over each man's head, is described in terms of the intimidating headgear of ancient warriors: "its fabulous head overhung the man's forehead like those horrible helmets with which ancient warriors tried to strike terror into their enemies." Baudelaire's interest in helmets is based not only on Manet's sketch, in which the poet is barely recognizable under a huge top hat, but also on his plan for an "elègie des chapeaux," which appears as one of his unrealized projects for prose poems. A draft version speaks of the relationship between hats and heads: "The hats remind one of heads and seem like a gallery of heads. For each hat, by its character, calls for a head and reveals spirit to the eyes" (I, 373). The hat points to the face that best suits it, just as each face demands a suitable hat. In *Chacun sa chimère*, the face under the frightening chimera helmet is characterized by fatigue and resignation. Hat and face act as hope and resignation, visible in the dichotomous appearance of the chimera carriers. But hope is the absence of resignation and vice versa, so that hope and resignation both point to their own absence, even though both are still present. This internal contradiction of the chimera carriers is their incomprehensibility. It is impossible to separate the chimera and the men as contradictions. Both must expressly be seen as a whole ("they considered it a part of themselves"). The question of the meaning of the chimera carriers is the question of the meaning of this whole. The whole is a reference, but since it is itself made up of a contradictory referential structure, the reference can never achieve its purpose but remains suspended in the openness of contradiction. The reference cannot be a reference to . . . but must be understood as a reference from. . . . The chimera carriers have meaning in that they point away from themselves, that is, they never achieve meaning in the sense of something signified. Their meaning is their signification.

The story tells about chimera carriers. The narration is a discourse of indifference. Its relationship with what it expresses is now apparent; it is not a discourse that wants to understand. Its purpose is therefore not the discovery of meaning. If what is said were to be given this or that meaning, then the discourse would be one that understands. Here it is born of indifference as the renunciation of wanting to understand. This discourse does not speak the meaning of the chimera carriers themselves but the chimera carriers as carriers of meaning. Something is said that has meaning, but the meaning remains hidden. What is spoken in the discourse thereby becomes a metaphor for its expression. The expression of the poem is like the chimera carriers as something said, a signification not given by the meaning. Its meaning is not what it means but the distance from . . . , its meaning. Giving meaning as the meaning of the expression can only be expressed so that the expressed in turn becomes a signifier without arriving at a meaning. The chimera carriers are this expressed signifier, which can be considered as the self-representation of the indifferent narrative discourse. That the chimera carriers move at all is as incomprehensible as the narrator's discourse. Both are attributable in the end to the compelling grip of the chimeralike, from which no manner of lucidity can protect us. The highest lucidity is not what claims to eliminate the chimeralike but rather what recognizes it. This is the lucidity of those resigned in hope and speaking in indifference.

UNDERSTANDING

If this has brought us a certain understanding of Baudelaire's text, this understanding itself is the least understood because in the poem itself, understanding is not reached. It is most disconcerting, especially in the reading of this prose poem, that all attempts at understanding prove fruitless. Before we ask about ways to understand the text, we must question the understanding that confronts us in the text. The narrator, concerned at first with understanding, sinks into apathy. Understanding would have consisted of discovering the meaning of the chimera carriers. The indifference in which the will to understand is extinguished is the indifference to the meaning of the meaningful. A reduction of what gives meaning to something meant through it is avoided. It is, however, not altogether certain that all understanding is thereby denied. If it is true that the chimera carriers do not mean this or that but are signification itself, then we might come closest if we reject any determination of their meaning. This approach can also be seen as a form of understanding. The text provides answers as to how this understanding comes about. The desire to understand is replaced with narration. In realizing the impossibility of communicating the meaning of the chimera carriers, the narration becomes an understanding of them as signifiers. This understanding is not, however, an expression of some thing. The meaningful, whose meaning remains inaccessible, is understood in the conversion to the act of narration, whose signification remains as unreducible as that of the narrative. Signification, as the chimera carriers are to be understood, occurs in narration. The interpretation and expression of the meaning of what we encounter as meaningful is rejected. The narration, whose signification remains as irreducible as that of the discourse in the sense that within it occurs the act of signification, that is, what is to be understood. Narration out of indifference to the signified, as occurring signification, is as close as we can get to the elusive signification it narrates. The understanding of signification occurs as the signification of narration.

This understanding, as it occurs in the text, can be better defined if it is related to our present attempt to understand the text. This attempt has up to now concentrated on the determination of meaning. From this we have seen that what the text communicates cannot be defined as a determinable meaning but is to be seen as something meaningful. This interpretation defines signification as the meaning of what is communicated. This is the common understanding that is denied us by the text, because it cannot succeed. What we found as the meaning of the communicated is nevertheless noteworthy. The special thing about this meaning is that it is signification. The text thereby shows itself to be a special kind of discourse. What it expresses does not refer beyond itself but back to itself. It is self-referential discourse. This reference is not accomplished in that the discourse expresses itself. Instead, the discourse expresses something that refers back to itself. The story of the chimera carriers is told. They are, as what is expressed in the discourse, a figure for their own expression. But why such a roundabout way via figurative speech? The discourse can only express itself as something expressing by turning itself into its own expression. In that it becomes its own expression, it slips away from itself as something expressing. It loses itself in the expression it becomes. It can regain itself if it expresses something that simultaneously refers away from itself, without having the reference resolved in a particular. The reference that is unresolved in its own reference refers back to the discourse of which it is the expression. Self-reference is therefore necessarily figurative, because only a figure allows the relationship between expressing and expression to be expressed as a whole, without having the expressing slip away completely in what has been expressed. The text accomplishes the reference to itself as expressing something about a common communication. What is thereby communicated prevents, through the suspension of its own meaning, the act of signification and expressing from being forgotten. In that what has been expressed in the discourse refers back to itself, it avoids the danger of losing itself in what it expresses.

Given this kind of textual understanding, we must ask ourselves at this juncture if there is still room for the interpretation that has led us to this understanding. The text seems to create its own understanding as discourse in self-reference, requiring no further interpretation. Nevertheless, the self-understanding of the text is made possible through interpretation. The function of interpretation might be seen in the necessarily figurative character of self-referential discourse not being recognized as such. Nothing in the text protects it from a reading that is hungry for meaning and fixes a discourse's expression and signifying. The proposed interpretation would like to prevent such a misunderstanding by showing expression and signification to be the meaning of the text. It can only do this by reducing the figurativeness of the text and expressing directly what the text expresses indirectly. Interpretive discourse then runs into exactly the same trouble that was avoided by the interpreted text through figurative speech. Interpretation can only speak of discourse and signification to the extent that it objectifies the discourse, losing it and itself in the act. Insofar as interpretation forgets its own active character, it becomes inadequate for the text at hand, itself concerned with avoiding this falling into the expressed. To be adequate, interpretive discourse would have to speak figuratively, in which case it would be prone to the same misunderstandings that it sets out to clear up.

If literary discourse can be considered as a discourse concerned with itself, then the conflict that raises its head becomes valid for all discourse on literature. This discourse can itself be literature. It then understands the discourse to which it refers in that it realizes the discourse in the very same act. This is the understanding realized in *Chacun sa chimère*: the transformation of the signification of the chimera carriers in the act of narration. The narrative act, which represents itself in the narration, understands in that it is what it narrates: narrative and its narration in one. But this understanding cannot, although it takes place through some communication, end in the communication of what is understood, because the discursive act is never available, only realizable. This would mean that literature is only comprehensible in that we create it. We can understand it to the extent that we avoid saying what it is. An understanding of literature can only exist *within* literature. This is opposed by the other kind of understanding that is always forced to some degree into objectifying literature. It is the kind of understanding that the narrator of *Chacun sa chimère* rejects but that the interpretation uses to be able to express signification as the meaning of what has been expressed. Interpretive discourse thereby distances itself from the text and contradicts itself. It is bound to express what the text in question is prevented from expressing. Its legitimacy may lie in the fact that it succeeds. But it succeeds at the cost of its own self-understanding, something the literary text already has. Interpretive discourse does exactly what it attempts to prevent. It wants to save the text from being fixed to a specific meaning and preserve in the text the productivity of continuous meaning. But to express what the text does, it must do precisely what the text avoids doing to do what it cannot express. Signification was understood in that it hardened into meaning, because it had to be expressed and made accessible to the kind of understanding that the text avoids, allowing the act of signification and expression to take place. Conversely, interpretive discourse, in that it illuminated the discursive act in contrast with what has been expressed, was also the negation of its own insufficiency. The emphasis of the discursive act on the level of what has been expressed is contrary to the discursive style of communication, where the expression disappears in what has been expressed. The content of what is communicated was the questioning of communicative discourse. Here we seem to see glimpses of a relationship between Baudelaire's text and interpretive discourse. In both, what has been expressed refers to the act of its being expressed. In *Chacun sa chimère,* this self-reference results from the incomprehensibility of what is communicated. In interpretive discourse, this results from the contradiction between what is communicated and the communication. But this similarity remains illusory. In *Chacun sa chimère,* the renunciation of understanding, as the indication of the impossibility of ever reducing the meaningful to a specific meaning, is built into the text. The contradiction in interpretive discourse between communicating and what is communicated is not reflected in such a discourse unless it were to step outside itself, as it has in this case. Interpretive discourse is prevented from continuously being concerned with itself by its fundamental focus on the object. If it were able to show more concern for itself, it could more closely approach its object—the text as the relationship between discursive act and content—but at the cost of being able to make any assertions concerning the text. It would then no longer be interpretation but literature. That it might be able to unify the two: that is, each beyond itself and away from itself—but to where?—is the chimeralike hope it carries.

Rimbaud

"JE EST UN AUTRE"

Disputed Aesthetics

The letter containing the phrase "JE est un autre" is polemical, and the phrase is intended to be shocking. The phrase challenges the domination of the subject as the foundation of an aesthetics that celebrates works of art as free products of responsible authorities. "Legally, art can only be defined as a product of freedom, that is, of a choice whose actions are based on reason" (Kant, *Critique of Judgment*, § 43). The I is not a romantic aesthetic, but in a romantic aesthetic the I is itself and in control. Conversely, the subject, aware of its otherness, loses control and remains at best a perceptive observer of events. But the disempowerment of the subject in the phrase "JE est un autre" goes along with its employment in an elevated self-awareness. The idea of the I as a preeminent authority is precisely the illusion that the phrase shows to be untenable. A better insight into the process of poetic discourse cannot be the basis for the same domination it rejects. But it does make it—but what does that mean?—more accessible in its uncontrollability. The poet's self-awareness is the awareness of his own discourse's detachment.

Context

The phrase, in which I is another, stands in contrast like a colored dot on a gray background. It has always been preserved by its readers in isolation. It exudes a power not shared by its surroundings to which we succumb before we understand. This phrase overpowers us, and the experience it reports becomes the experience of the report. We are justified in asking from where this phrase gains such power. It is also justified to ask what kind of understanding this surrender to its fascination allows. Is there any guarantee that this phrase will have this effect, and wouldn't we have to examine this passage in the context of the letter to determine what it says? The need to read in context stems from the question of "how it might be meant." The opinionated authority is a speaker who has access to language and uses it to express his opinion. The question of meaning conflicts with the cited phrase, because it presumes a control of discourse that this phrase destroys. The isolation of the phrase corresponds to its sense and allows it to take effect without questioning what it is *supposed* to say. "JE est un autre" is not meant one way or another but occurs as the transformation of the speaker, whose opinion is lost. Even though the force of the phrase lies in its expression, it is nevertheless a statement whose expression explains the correlation as well as being explained by it.

Change

That I is an other is expressed in a discourse on poetic discourse. Disputed is the primacy of the speaker over what is spoken. When I speak, then it is not I who am speaking. We are concerned here with the discursive authority. This cannot be solved by the replacement of I by an other. If an other were to speak in my place, then it would simply be a different I. We are not questioning this or that person as the discursive authority but rather the subjectivity of discourse in general. Whatever speaks is not a different I but is different with regard to every I. Whenever speech takes place, it speaks not without me, but the I is transformed to the other in speaking. The I is, whenever it speaks, always already the other. I does not precede the discourse; it is within it. There is no decidable I that is present and that begins to speak. In speaking it gives up control and surrenders to language. I transpires as something speaking. As something taking place in discourse, the I would have to be able to gain control over itself in discourse, to understand itself as speaking, and to find itself in speaking. I does not find itself as something that it always was and perhaps didn't know, because it wasn't itself before it began speaking. I only becomes itself in that it transpires in speaking, and it can therefore only find itself as what it has yet to become in speaking. In speaking, the I consigns itself to language as something uncontrollable. It finds itself by leaving itself. It finds itself in change. This is not an arbitrary process, in which I remains the same although it changes itself. The I is the changed, and what effects this change is the other. The one who wants to change himself is not the one who says I am an other but rather the one who experiences himself most strongly as himself when he feels himself slipping into the other. Discourse is the experience of this slipping away. My speaking changes me, because what is supposedly mine is effective as the other, to which I belong, although it is not essentially the I in which I must lose myself to become myself.

Uncontrollability

The phrase "JE est un autre" speaks of the speaker's crumbling domination of his own discourse. The controlled discourse would presume an independent authority from which it could be derived. As something controlled, it would be secondary to whatever is in control. It would be available, would be used, and would therefore always be instrumental. Should there be a noninstrumental concept of language, then we must abandon any authority primary to discourse. Noninstrumental discourse is uncontrolled. Language is not used in it, but the speaker exposes himself to it. The speaker does not know what uncontrolled discourse expresses, because its expression is neither subordinate to him nor can it be traced back to him. The uncontrollability of what is expressed is not only valid for the speaker but also for the receiver, who, to understand the discourse, must make it his own. In the attempt to do this, he encounters the impossibility of possession. The uncontrollability of what has been said prevents the determination of discourse. Any determination of discourse to something expressed would make the expressed impotent. Conversely, the more original expression, in contrast to all the speaker's attempts at communication, is felt in the unavailability of what is expressed. Whoever attempts to speak surrenders to this expression. The need for the controlled statement comes from the fear of surrendering to language. We don't know where it will lead us, abduct us, or seduce us. The poet is the one who endures the risk of the unknown by changing himself in speaking, letting language do the talking. "He reaches the unknown, and when, crazed, he was about to lose the intelligibility of his visions, he saw them! May he collapse in his boundings from things unnameable and unheard of" (*Oeuvres complètes*, 271). The unheard and unnameable is what has always been the lost and disavowed, although active, expression and is effective in the unpremeditation in all its discourse.

Expression and Expressed

The phrase "JE est un autre" is an insight into the detachment of speaking. But isn't detachment, in that it is expressed, controlled and thereby eliminated? The attempt to express the uncontrollability of discourse aims to control it. It is to be silenced in the solidification of what is expressed. As something expressed, uncontrollability is brought under control. The phrase "JE est un autre" contradicts what it expresses, unless it were a discourse that admitted its own uncontrollability. We must ask how this phrase relates to what it expresses. Does its expression of the speaker's I hold true for anyone expressing this phrase? Is the subject of the sentence (JE) also the subject—the discursive authority—of the discourse in which the phrase occurs? Does the statement "JE est un autre" take place in the illusion of being controlled, or does it lose itself in the uncontrollability it expresses? If the phrase does not understand itself to be a determining statement, then it must unexpress what has been expressed. This unexpression, as the rejection of control over discourse, would be the speaker's personal task as the discursive authority. But the discourse is not uncontrolled when the speaker expressly forgoes controlling it, rather, when it slips away from him. Rejection is not the speaker's accomplishment but his subjugation by language. This is evidenced as the undecidability of discourse that cannot be fixed in a specific expression. The opinion of the speaker dims in the face of undecidability, and discourse opens itself to the unpremeditated expression that makes it possible in the first place. The phrase "JE est un autre" is not decidable in one important respect. JE is distinguished above all other words through capitalization. What does this emphasize? If I were the speaker, then the phrase would have to be: "je suis un autre." If I were the object of the phrase, then we would expect: "le moi est un autre." Both versions lack the tension of Rimbaud's phrase. I am an other: this is the private determination of the speaker's otherness. Nothing in this manner of speech points to the difficulty of a statement that conflicts with what it says. The person who claims to be someone else does so as someone saying *I*, thereby reversing the claimed change in its pronouncement. Conversely, if an other is meant by "the I," then no one comes forward to be recognized as the speaker. The I in this sentence is the objectified subject that allows itself to be spoken of. The suggestion that everything that is said has to be attributed to a silent *I*, which enables all discourse, cannot be claimed for a discourse that strives to subordinate expression to the expressed. The sentence speaks differently: "JE est un autre." JE is associated in such a way—and this must be emphasized—that it is both the speaker and the object and neither of them. The phrase remains suspended between both versions, defines it one way or another, and thereby deflates it. Someone appears in the phrase as the speaker (JE) but then fails to speak. The first person is combined with the third person in such a way that makes it impossible for us to decide for one or the other. The discourse proceeds in such a way that I, which posits itself and is recognizable as the speaking authority, slips away from itself, errs and changes from "I am" to "I is." It is detached from itself and undermines itself as the speaking authority. This undermining is not the expressed of the phrase. It is what the phrase occurs as. "JE est un autre" is neither my discourse nor discourse about the I but discourse that is realized as the change of JE. The phrase speaks in a

way that robs me, who speaks it, of power over it. Its power is based
on a privation of power, and what I was falls headlong into it.

Theater

No one speaks. JE is not the speaker, because it is no longer the
first person and no longer I. I as the first person of the verb is always
doubly determined, on the one hand by what the discourse says
about it, on the other hand as the one who says it. I, with whatever
verb it may join itself, always means: I say. I am an other includes: I
say, that I am. "JE est . . ." is the rejection of "I say." JE is, contrary
to its placement before the verb, not the I that says. Here JE is said,
without having defined the discursive authority as the discourse's
reduction. The renunciation of the speaker is not his negation,
something still bound to a viewpoint and forced to reintroduce the
negated in the act of negation. JE in "JE est un autre" is not negated
but is blurred in the haze of its own ambiguity (I am / the I is).
There is no other viewpoint, such as that of the other, to counter
that of the "I say." It dissolves midway, there where the speaker
languishes, and lets language happen. This letting happen in the
middle of viewlessness is the theater in Rimbaud's text. "I attend
the hatching of my thought: I look at it, I listen to it: I release my
bow: the symphony makes its rustle in the depths or comes from a
leap onto the stage" (270). I is not only the audience in this theater
("j'assiste," "je regarde," "j'écoute"), but also the piece that is being
played ("l'éclosion de ma pensée") and the stage ("la scène") on
which the production takes place. The mind produces the thinking
which it then watches and observes. This watching oneself is self-
awareness. But according to the theater's explanation of our phrase,
I am an other. To be self-aware does not mean that one possesses
oneself through consciousness. I myself is not a first and final
authority that guarantees consciousness. There is a hole in the
seemingly sound system of self-reference through which the uncontrollable other streams in and destroys the self-assurance of I.
The play that I watch is my thinking, but what appears in my
thinking as my thought is not I. I may be my own play, but the one
I see as myself is an other. I walk next to myself and encounter

myself as a stranger, whose actions, whether they surprise, enter-
tain, or astonish me, are not subject to my influence. Self-awareness is the observer's awareness of the self, knowing that what he
sees is himself but that it all happens without him. Self-awareness is
the awareness of being an other, of being isolated from oneself; it
is the awareness of the other in me. The other is isolated in
this awareness as something inaccessible. To the extent that with
this self-awareness goes the awareness of what cannot be reached
through awareness, the I cannot be reduced to an awareness. Self-
awareness is not only an awareness of an awareness. It is also the
realization of the I in the impossibility of self-containment within
the framework of this awareness. I can only be itself in that it lets
itself go, opening itself to something more fundamental than the
inclusive awareness of itself. Rimbaud's theater is therefore not a
self-production of something in control of itself but an encounter
of something that changes itself with the other within.

Conversation

Within me is the other, experienced as something withdrawn.
Rimbaud's text speaks of "my thinking," whose unfolding I witness. It is not clear, however, to what extent my thinking is withdrawn from me. Should we consider here things from the dark that
step into the light as thought? Something thought becomes accessible by being thought. What was previously detached becomes
conscious and accessible as thinking unfolds. The detachment of
what is thought is therefore inconsequential, because it can be
remedied. There is no real control over what is brought into the
light of thinking, but whatever comes into that light is established
in a comforting objectivity. Not the contents of thinking are
withdrawn, but rather the thinking itself. "It's wrong to say: I
think. One should rather say: they think me" (268). The fact that
thinking occurs is what is beyond myself, within me. Rimbaud
believed openness to the impossibility to influence the thought
process to be the poet's distinguishing characteristic. The poet not
only has a sense for the content of thinking and discourse but also
for the incomprehensibility of the origin of thinking and discourse,

isolated from his own grasp. Again and again, thinking and expression are buried under the rubble of what is thought and expressed. Letting it shine through nonetheless is the accomplishment of a discourse that does not fall victim to instrumentality. It remains open to the unvanquished within itself and allows it free rein. The conversation in Rimbaud's poetry is often realized and appropriate to his theater, because in it everything is said with a view to letting the other have its say.

CONVERSATION ABOUT A CONVERSATION
(Myself, the Other)

L'ETERNITÉ

Elle est retrouvée.
Quoi?—L'Eternité.
C'est la mer allée
Avec le soleil.

Ame sentinelle,
Murmurons l'aveu
De la nuit si nulle
Et du jour en feu.

Des humains suffrages,
Des communs élans
Là tu te dégages
Et voles selon.

Puisque de vous seules,
Braise de satin,
Le Devoir s'exhale
Sans qu'on dise: enfin.

Là pas d'espérance,
Nul orietur.
Science avec patience,
Le supplice est sûr.

Elle est retrouvée.
Quoi?—L'Eternité.

C'est la mer allée
Avec le soleil. (133f.)

She is rediscovered.

What? Eternity.
It's the sea gone down
With the sun.

Sentinel soul,
Let's murmur the wish
Of nothing night
And day on fire.

From human approvals,
From common impulses,
Here you free yourself
And fly in accordance.

Since from you alone,
Embers of satin,
Duty is breathed
With no one saying: at last.

Here no hope,
No *orietur*.
Science with patience,
The torment is sure.

She is rediscovered.
What? Eternity.

It's the sea gone down
With the sun.

MYSELF: She is rediscovered.

THE OTHER: What?

MYSELF: Eternity.

THE OTHER: Why didn't you say so to begin with?

MYSELF: I ask myself why it isn't said right away, I mean, in the poem, where our conversation takes place. In any case, our conversation would never have gotten started if I had said at the beginning what *she* meant. You wouldn't have had to ask. Our conversation would have been superfluous. It would only have been necessary if my account were incomplete. You were obviously angry when you reproached me for not having said everything right away. Your question was meant as a criticism, wasn't it?

THE OTHER: You always seem to be primarily concerned with how something is meant. But I must admit that I don't understand my own question anymore. If your explanation of our conversation is right, then I shouldn't have posed the question. I would like to think that my first question arose out of curiosity: to find out what is rediscovered. But after you informed me on that account, the conversation should really have been over, because then I knew what it was you wanted to say. We had arrived at the same place, just as if you had told me from the beginning that eternity is rediscovered. And yet—this is what concerns *me*—we hadn't both arrived at the same place. The phrase "eternity is rediscovered" could have given me cause to ask you a number of things (which I might still do later). For example, how eternity is lost and how it can be rediscovered. I could never have asked the way I did: why didn't you say so to start with? This question really doesn't belong to our initial conversation anymore but actually starts another one that is connected to the first. We're not talking about eternity anymore and what happens to it—and somehow I'm glad about that—but rather about the conversation we had about it. And that's why, you see, we are not at the same place, as we otherwise would have been. It could have changed with a single bit of information. But because your statement was incomplete and required an exchange of words, we've gotten away from what you thought you were saying and have concentrated on the saying itself. Is that what you wanted?

MYSELF: Now you're asking how it was meant. I don't know. I would like to know how to interpret the dialogue in Rimbaud's poem: "Elle est retrouvée / Quoi?—L'Eternité." We would have to pass your question on to the poem. It would sound something like: why does the first person in the conversation hide what he has found?

THE OTHER: You're making it too easy on yourself. You are this first person, and your question is directed at him.

MYSELF: You're being difficult. I'd rather be alone. Secondary literature would be better served. But since you're here, I'll fill you in on why I hid what I had found: I didn't want to tell you because . . .

THE OTHER: But you did say it.

MYSELF: But only after you had asked me. I have to admit I changed my mind and decided to tell you.

THE OTHER: At least this gives our conversation some purpose. It doesn't happen every day that someone changes his mind. It's even rarer when he admits it, even begrudgingly. But why begrudgingly? Because we are, after all, primarily someone based on our opinions, that is, we are what we appear to be. We don't like to question ourselves. That's why I wonder if you're telling the truth when you claim that you didn't want to disclose what was found. That way, you still have the chance to disclose it if you want to. Since you really did disclose it, you have to admit to having changed your mind, but at least you had an opinion. You seem to think that's better than not having one at all, because there was nothing on which it could be based. Isn't it true that you didn't even know what had been rediscovered?

MYSELF: But I said what it was.

THE OTHER: Only after I asked.

MYSELF: But I couldn't have said "*She* is rediscovered" if I didn't already know that what had been found was feminine.

THE OTHER: Since we're not talking about eternity, we don't need to be concerned with her gender. But wasn't this feminine gender the only thing that was certain from the beginning?

MYSELF: Nothing gets past you, does it?

THE OTHER: It's not hidden at all but clear as day. Just think back to your own words: "She is rediscovered." We only need to stick to what the sentence tells us. It isn't eternity but a feminine pronoun. We don't have anything else at the beginning of the poem. It doesn't start with the name of a thing but rather with a word that stands for the missing thing that isn't discovered until later on in the conversation. Everyone who takes in what Rimbaud wrote and what we have said has to see that what was claimed to be found in the first sentence is in reality what was searched for, and the conversation is its discovery. Only because we're used to accepting pronouns as standing for something else, and we assume that what they stand for is already present, do we then assume that *she* stands for something known. But this isn't getting us anywhere. If the speaker knows what the pronoun stands for, then why doesn't he just say it? It seems to me much more likely that he doesn't know what he's talking about.

MYSELF: Then I have to ask myself why you asked me something that you assumed I didn't know.

THE OTHER: To let you find it. The question was unavoidable. It didn't just arbitrarily follow your sentence. If I hear that *she* is rediscovered, then I have to ask what it is that is found. *She* is rediscovered: this provokes a question, it is said with the question in mind. To such an extent that the question is more yours than mine. The necessity that lies in the pronoun *she* is expressed. This pronoun is not something after the fact, but something that looks ahead. It is an agenda that must be satisfied without already knowing how. It questions what it stands for. This question is the driving force behind the incomplete statement and is what started our conversation. By asking the question that was inherent in your sentence, I gave you the chance to disclose what the pronoun referred to.

MYSELF: It isn't easy to follow your train of thought, and I have to abandon notions I would like to have of myself. I would always have liked to have been known as someone who only speaks when he has something to say. You are implying that I speak not because but rather in order to have something to say. Only by speaking do I become someone who might in retrospect be able to say about himself that he had something to say. But even if I content myself with that, plenty of problems remain. You define our conversation as a search for what is found. If, however, we proceed from my first, albeit incomplete, sentence, "She is rediscovered," and see in it the question you consequently asked, then the answer to this question is given and limited only to a very broad framework. What is found could be my watch or my girlfriend. Any feminine noun would do. Why does it have to be eternity? We can't get that from the flow of the conversation.

THE OTHER: It seems that we do finally have to talk about eternity. I was always a little afraid that it would come to this. It's true that I can't explain eternity.

MYSELF: How would it be if we assumed that I knew from the very beginning what I was talking about?

THE OTHER: That's fine with me.

MYSELF: You're going to give up your position that easily?

THE OTHER: That's why we're here. Have you considered why the one who lets us speak is writing a dialogue instead of an essay? I think he needs us to help him get by without a viewpoint. He realized that there is always speaking before anything is spoken and that one can't approach a discourse that does more than just make statements with more statements. This is only possible in giving up the position from which statements are made. In a dialogue there are at least two viewpoints that question one another, and it's difficult to attribute a dialogue like ours or the one in Rimbaud's poem to an author, because we never really know where he stands. If, however, we are thought of as viewpoints that undermine the other, then nothing prevents us from doing away with a determination and questioning our own positions. That's why I don't mind at all suddenly admitting that you always knew what the pronoun in the first sentence stood for. But you have to explain to me why you kept it a secret.

MYSELF: The last time I tried, you interrupted me. But I'll be happy to try again. I said that I didn't name what was found, because I didn't want to. I didn't want to give it a name because it seemed to me that by doing so I would lose it. Since I've long since lost eternity again, I don't have to be afraid of finally talking about it. Eternity is not something you have, but something you are in. Finding is becoming. This is why, in a text I would gladly explain to you, Rimbaud talked about his "eternal life." "A cette [période, c'était] c'était ma vie éternelle, non écrite, non chantée, —quelque chose comme la Providence [les lois du monde un] à laquelle on croit et qui ne chante pas" (At this [time, it was] it was my eternal life, unwritten, unsung, —something like Providence [laws of the world one] in which one believes and which does not sing [249]).

THE OTHER: That's a draft of *Une saison en enfer* (A season in hell). Ignoring the fact that it's a discarded draft, it seems to me to be one of those texts that everyone does with what they want, because they speak so undecidably that a lot can be read into them, and very little can be refuted.

MYSELF: Is that so bad? The fact that we're talking about a draft doesn't prevent us from taking it seriously. It doesn't undo the fact that something was spoken, but it does give what is said a preliminary nature that can never be recalled and that protects it from solidifying. You really ought to have some sense for this, since you wanted to read the sentence "She is rediscovered" as a draft.

THE OTHER: I'd like to come back to that later. Right now, let's stick with eternity.

MYSELF: Gladly. I believe that, in the text I read, Rimbaud tries to describe or circumscribe what he calls his eternal life. But it is this writing that contradicts an eternity that is unwritten and unsung. Whoever speaks of eternity has already lost it, is no longer in it, but rather at a distance that allows him to talk about it. Any amount of speaking is too much here. When I said "It is rediscovered," I not only said too little, as you thought, but too much, because whoever claims to have found eternity loses it by saying so. I was cautious because I sensed this. I didn't want to identify eternity, so I could preserve it.

THE OTHER: Then I guess I shouldn't have asked . . .

MYSELF: On the contrary. I needed your question. Only I took it differently from what you apparently intended. I don't know that I said too little, but I think I said too much. That's why I don't take the question as a desire for additional information but as questioning the statement I made in spite of everything. The question raises doubts about the assertion. It reestablishes the openness that the assertion closed off. In that your question eliminated the excessive-ness of my discourse, it allowed me to rediscover what might have been lost, what I said I had rediscovered: eternity. "L'Eternité": this was not simply an answer to a question; it was the scream I let out as I ran through the hole you made in the linguistic concrete. I discovered eternity in the dissolution of the sentence, in the blurring of boundaries, and in the disappearance of appearance: "C'est la mer allée / Avec le soleil."

THE OTHER: I didn't think you had that kind of rhetoric in you. May I nevertheless ask the sobering question whether you now think my interpretation of our conversation is refuted?

MYSELF: I don't want to make it that easy. I just found out from you that it doesn't do much good to insist on viewpoints and opinions. Each of us has explained our dialogue in his own way. Our opinions confront each other, and now they question themselves. We can't go back past the stage we have reached. We shouldn't argue over who's right. Since both explanations are possible, we're both right. The amazing thing is not that we disagree, but that our conversation—or, if you prefer, Rimbaud's poem—which we would like to understand, allows for our disagreement. It is, so to speak, the higher unification of disunity, since it is, in the end, a single word that is the cause of our disagreement. It seems to me that we should try to see our differing interpretations in light of the unity of the interpreted conversation, instead of talking ourselves apart again.

THE OTHER: I hope that doesn't lead to our convergence. It would be unfortunate if our conversation were to end so suddenly. But since the text in which we are supposed to converge is still the conversation from which we were created, we might be granted some additional time. Be that as it may, our explanations of the dialogue undeniably have something in common. The conversation is a discovery for both of us. What else could a conversation be? The fact that it takes place only makes sense if it cannot be replaced by a simple statement, such as: eternity is rediscovered. The conversation is the discovery that might later result in a statement but that cannot be replaced in the actuality of its transpiration. Maybe this will bring us back to the draft.

MYSELF: We seem to be constantly changing roles. We should probably be content with the fact that we belong together. But you wanted to say something about the draft.

THE OTHER: Right. It occurred to me that foresight comes into play. You didn't say anything about it, but foresight is employed in, even equated with, "eternal life." But isn't foresight primarily a draft? We tend to think of it as premonition, which we, since we don't have it ourselves, tend to ascribe to some divinity. Our human foresight is no less foresight just because it isn't divine omniscience. It is not the knowing foresight of the draft. This is the distinguishing characteristic of the draft: we don't know how it will turn out, but still we work to realize it, because somehow we foresee it. Without this foresight, nothing would ever be drafted; and no draft would take the risk that a real draft does if foresight were certain. If we knew from the beginning how what has yet to be created would finally turn out, we wouldn't have to create it. And so I take our conversation to be a draft. It is not the refashioning of some statement into dialogue form. It takes the risk of a not-knowing, searching foresight. Only because the conversation searches can we understand it as discovery.

MYSELF: Maybe now we understand the foresight in the draft better, which incited you to yours. Rimbaud says that his "eternal life" is "something like Providence in which one believes and which does not sing." This means that eternity is discovered by whomever believes in this nonsinging foresight. Foresight doesn't sing because it is the foresight of song. Song is the draft made possible by foresight. Rimbaud's eternal life is the belief in the unlimited ability to draft, the carefree openness to the unforeseen in one's own foresight. "De joie, je devins un opéra fabuleux" (What joy! I myself became a fabulous work [249]). In this way, whoever lets himself speak presents himself as himself—as the other.

THE OTHER: That must be me. In me you go beyond yourself. Eternal is the life that is, in the foresight of itself, no longer itself, but the potential and the draft of the other's song, which it is not.

MYSELF: You were right in not wanting to talk about eternity. But let's think about the draft again. If it is what you say it is—and I must admit, I can't imagine it as anything else—then what is created if we complete our drafts is never quite what we wanted, unless it was from the start not quite subject to our will. The unforeseen always lurks in the draft and participates in the creation of the nascent. But then none of our work is really quite our own. Since our foresight is not knowing, we are not authors. "JE est un autre."

THE OTHER: That's me again, if I may say so myself. The fact that you open yourself up to me and I to you makes our conversation a draft. Each one of us is the inestimable in the foresight of the other. It is rediscovered. What is? Eternity. Each of us understands it differently. *You* believe to possess something that you lose in speaking and regain in the dissolution of discourse. *I* believe that nothing is already present and that discourse brings out what it offers. Holding a conversation both ways shows that neither of us is master of a conversation in which the other is unforeseeably active. You discover what you say in speaking, and you lose it by saying it. Then you're forced to dissolve the present discourse. Our conversation has taught us that much. It doesn't matter so much that we interpret the dialogue differently, but rather that each one discovers the other's interpretation by doing so. Each of us is the risk in the other's draft. That he takes the risk and puts it into words allows him to discover in his discourse what he didn't want to say but is still said as the contribution of the other. We are always together as draftsmen.

Hölderlin

Hölderlin and Rousseau

Pausanias: O Sohn des Himmels!
Empedokles: Ich war es! ja! und möcht es nun erzählen.

— Hölderlin, *Sämtliche Werke* (4, 106f.)

Pausanias: Oh son of heaven!
Empedocles: I was the one! yes! and want now to tell it.

TEXTUAL REFERENCE

Halbgötter denk' ich jetzt
Und kennen muß ich die Theuern,
Weil oft ihr Leben so
Die sehnende Brust mir beweget.
Wem aber, wie, Rousseau, dir,
Unüberwindlich die Seele
Die starkausdauernde ward,
Und sicherer Sinn
Und die süße Gaabe zu hören,
Zu reden so, daß er aus heiliger Fülle
Wie der Weingott, thörig göttlich
Und gesezlos sie die Sprache der Reinesten giebt
Verständlich den Guten, aber mit Recht
Die Achtungslosen mit Blindheit schlägt
Die entweihenden Knechte, wie nenn ich den Fremden?

Die Söhne der Erde sind, wie die Mutter,
Allliebend, so empfangen sie auch
Mühlos, die Glücklichen, Alles.
Drum überraschet es auch
Und schröckt den sterblichen Mann,
Wenn er den Himmel, den
Er mit den liebenden Armen
Sich auf die Schultern gehäufft,
Und die Last der Freude bedenket;
Dann scheint ihm oft das Beste,
Fast ganz vergessen da,
Wo der Stral nicht brennt,
Im Schatten des Walds
Am Bielersee in frischer Grüne zu seyn,
Und sorglosarm an Tönen,
Anfängern gleich, bei Nachtigallen zu lernen.

Und herrlich ists, aus heiligem Schlafe dann
Erstehen und aus Waldes Kühle
Erwachend, Abends nun
Dem milderen Licht entgegenzugehn,
Wenn, der die Berge gebaut
Und den Pfad der Ströme gezeichnet,
Nachdem er lächelnd auch
Der Menschen geschäftiges Leben
Das othemarme, wie Seegel
Mit seinen Lüften gelenkt hat,
Auch ruht und zu der Schülerin jezt,
Der Bildner, Gutes mehr
Denn Böses findend,
Zur heutigen Erde der Tag sich neiget.
　　　　　　—(*Sämtliche Werke* 2, 146f.)

Of demigods now I think
And I must know these dear ones
Because so often their lives
Move me and fill me with longing.
But he whose soul, like yours,
Rousseau, ever strong and patient,
Became invincible,

Endowed with steadfast purpose
And a sweet gift of hearing,
Of speaking, so that from holy profusion
Like the wine-god foolishly, divinely
And lawlessly he gives it away,
The language of the purest, comprehensible to the good,
But rightly strikes with blindness the irreverent,
The profaning rabble, what shall I call that stranger?

The sons of Earth, like their mother, are
All-loving, so without effort too
All things those blessed ones receive.
And therefore it surprises
And startles the mortal man
When he considers the heaven
Which with loving arms he himself
Has heaped upon his shoulders,
And feels the burden of joy;
Then often to him it seems best
Almost wholly forgotten to be
Where the beam does not sear,
In the forest's shade
By Lake Bienne amid foliage newly green,
And blithely poor in tones,
Like beginners, to learn from nightingales.

And glorious then it is to arise once more
From holy sleep and awakening
From coolness of the woods, at evening
Walk now toward the softer light
When he who built the mountains
And drafted the paths of the rivers,
Having also smiling directed
The busy lives of men,
So short of breath, like sails,
And filled them with his breezes,
Reposes also, and down to his pupil
The master craftsmen, finding
More good than evil,
Day now inclines to the present Earth.

In Hölderlin's Rhine hymn we encounter the name Rousseau. The mention of Lake Bienne makes the reference less general than, for instance, in the ode titled *Rousseau*, where clear references to specific works are lacking. In the Rhine hymn, Hölderlin evokes the fifth promenade from the *Rêveries du promeneur solitaire* (Reveries of the solitary walker), where Rousseau tells of his stay on St. Peter's Island. Since one text refers to another, we might ask what kind of relationship exists between the two. Every previous attempt to illuminate the role of Rousseau in Hölderlin's poem answers our question without really considering what happens when one text refers to another. In this particular case it is important to note that these references belong to a later draft of the poem, both "Rousseau" and "Lake Bienne" being penciled in the manuscript (2, 727). This raises questions about the reference to Rousseau. On the one hand it seems to complete the last step of the poem, that is, it adds the last missing part. On the other hand it seems to be nothing more than a simple supplement that provides another illustration of what was already there. Accordingly the name Rousseau is either essential or superfluous. All interpretations expressly or implicitly represent one or the other view.

If the name, as an afterthought, stands for something already present, then the attempt to create a bridge between Hölderlin's and Rousseau's text is pointless, since whatever the name Rousseau brings to the text could have been gleaned from the poem itself. Heidegger comments on the Rhine hymn, remarking that the reference to Rousseau's name is a later addition: "The original interpretation of the stanza must therefore be kept free of any reference to Rousseau, only the sense of the entire stanza can explain why the poet here is also able to name Rousseau" (*Oeuvres complètes* 39, 278). To the extent that Rousseau "is also able" to name Rousseau, the reference becomes unnecessary. Since nothing would be lost by its absence, it is superfluous and could be deleted without compromising the comprehension of the text. This consequence, not articulated in Heidegger's text, raises questions about the attempt to connect Rousseau to the poem based solely on context. Doing so preserves both the poem's self-sufficiency and the reader's ability to understand it in and of itself, but the foreign name becomes superfluous in that it is explained within the poem's context. Since it cannot be integrated, it becomes a nuisance that cannot be ignored.

The difficulties are no less if the reference to Rousseau is taken to be a necessary addition to the poem as a whole. The reference does not realize itself but opens itself to the foreign text, thereby questioning its own self-sufficiency. But since the reference to the foreign text is assumed to be necessary, the poem's integrity can no longer be preserved by ignoring it. It must be reestablished via a discussion of Rousseau. Such a discussion must enable us to see the names "Rousseau" and "Lake Bienne" so that what is named in them can be meaningfully incorporated into the context of the poem. Any interpretation that attempts to do this aspires to ascertain Hölderlin's view of Rousseau. This is based on the premise that the name Rousseau means something in particular to Hölderlin and that this meaning is incorporated in the Rhine hymn. If we can succeed in reconstructing Hölderlin's interpretation of Rousseau's text, then we can substitute this reconstruction for the name in the poem. If, however, the poem is an interpretation and in turn an appropriation of the foreign text, then the reference becomes superfluous again, because, as an appropriation, it is no longer foreign but integral to Hölderlin's poem, which then replaces it. The integrity of the poem is regained via the foreign by reducing it to its own. It remains incomprehensible why Rousseau is named at all. As an appropriation, he is no longer in need of a name.

In the appropriation of the foreign as well as in its suppression, one senses the refusal to deal with it because it is unsettling. The foreign is unsettling insofar as the foreign cannot be integrated. By referring to the foreign text, the poem admits to being dependent on it and thereby questions its own integrity. The text that opens itself to the foreign and refuses to appropriate it saves itself from the interpreter's appropriation. All inclination to put aside the foreign as foreign is due to the drive to regain the text's domination, something Hölderlin refuses. It would be premature to justify the rejection of such attempts with the notion that the poem speaks of the foreign. The fact that the foreign is discussed, as in "what shall I call that stranger?" and the assertions that accompany these references make the preservation of the poem's integrity possible. The poem by no means delivers itself up to the foreign simply by mentioning it. Rather, the stranger is available as something named and can be integrated into the whole. This is why Heidegger attempts to read the text with reference to the "foreign" and not to "Rousseau." Insofar as Rousseau can be identified as the stranger, he is already integrated into Hölderlin's poem. "The stranger" is not the presence of the foreign as such in the poem but rather its linguistic subjugation. This changes if Rousseau is no longer called "the stranger" but the foreigner is called "Rousseau." As "Rousseau," Rousseau *is* the foreigner, something he is only *named* as "the stranger." The foreign is recognized as foreign in a name. It realizes the foreignness that is only expressed in the word "the stranger." To the extent that the names "Rousseau" and "Lake Bienne" remain expressionless, and as long as they don't speak based on information that can only be gained from outside the poem, the foreign remains present in the poem. The name as the foreign is the name of the foreign in the name "Rousseau." This can explain the later addition of the name in the manuscript as Hölderlin's answer to the question: what shall I call that stranger? The stranger is named with the name, not in a way that makes him familiar or no longer foreign. The stranger is addressed in the otherness of his irreducible individuality. The stranger is not in the name, because the word "stranger" is understood as a foreigner, already subdued and appropriated. The name may hit at the heart of whomever owns it, but since the heart of the other remains distant, the name is incomprehensible. It names the most personal of the other in its foreignness.

The individuality of the foreigner named Rousseau is to a certain extent restricted. The phrase "but he whose soul, like yours, Rousseau" (v. 139) states that everything that the stanza lists holds true for Rousseau, but also for whomever is like Rousseau. Those who are like Rousseau can only exist if some commonality binds them together, in which case they are not foreign. Whatever Rousseau has in common with others, be it only a potential, is not what makes him a foreigner. It is what is understood about him that makes it possible for others to appropriate him. And still we want to read the phrase so that the listed characteristics make Rousseau and those like him become foreigners. The problem can be solved if we recognize that the foreignness is viewed on a new level. Foreign is what is outside the text and what cannot be reduced to the text, the other text. Foreign can also be what is within the text, figures estranged from their surroundings, with long-lived souls and the gift of hearing and speech, such as the poets in *Hyperion*: "Die Guten! Sie leben in der Welt, wie Fremdlinge im eigenen Hauße, sie sind so recht, wie der Dulder Ulyß, da er in Bettlersgestalt an seiner Thüre saß, indeß die unverschämten Freier im Saale lärmten und fragten, wer hat uns den Landläufer gebracht?" (These good souls! They live in the world like strangers in their own house, they are like Ulysses, the enduring, as he sat at his own doorstep while the brazen suitors reveled in the hall and asked, who brought us this vagabond? [3, 155]). Here the foreign element is no longer what is accessible to discourse but what is expressed by it. Insofar as we can talk about the foreigner, he is no longer a foreigner but a relative accessible in his likeness.

The double meaning of foreignness bridges the gap between foreignness and appropriation in the reference of Hölderlin's poem to Rousseau. This tension should not be ignored while attempting to demonstrate the relationship between the two texts. Whereas the appropriation has received plenty of attention, the foreignness has gone unnoticed, even though the addition of the proper names "Rousseau" and "Lake Bienne" is Hölderlin's express reference to the nonappropriated and the nonappropriatable. The requisite recourse to a text of Rousseau is only defensible to the extent that a complete appropriation does not take place, because this would replace the foreign text and make it untenable. Because this replacement does not take place, and the reference to the foreign text allows it to continue to exist, Rousseau remains the foreigner, and his text remains unvanquished. The relationship between Hölderlin and Rousseau cannot be defined and remains open. Hölderlin's notion of Rousseau can only tendentiously exist in this openness. It remains incomplete as long as the text and its relationship to the other text stays open-ended.

The open-ended relationship between the two texts is the conversation between them. It lasts as long as one does not appropriate and overwhelm the other. In that Hölderlin's poem allows Rousseau's text to remain foreign, it does not read it by force. The open-ended conversation is never-ending, and the reader is invited to join in. The relationship between the two texts is thus never defined and must always be established anew. It would therefore be unproductive to want to reconstruct Hölderlin's view of Rousseau—not, however, to construct it. This is the task of the reader, who must become productive to the extent that the texts are open-ended. In the Rhine hymn, the reference to the foreign text invokes the reader's text as a third, the reader being responsible for constructing the dialogue between the other two. It is necessary to continue this conversation because Hölderlin starts it without finishing it. As long as the conversation remains open-ended, it cannot be replaced by affirmative statements. The assumption that it could solidify into hard and fast assertions contradicts the openness of the text, which only exists as long as the conversation continues. Every statement remains subject to foreign objections and thereby to its own doubt. But keeping the text open-ended is not sufficient reason alone to keep the dialogue between Hölderlin and Rousseau going. The text is open-ended precisely because the conversation is unfinished, that is, it breaks off. If it is taken up again, then the hope is raised that some result might be achieved. Wanting to revert to Rousseau's text is in part motivated by the attempt to appropriate it in the name of Hölderlin, even though this would disregard Hölderlin's recognition of the foreignness in the other. For both tendencies to coexist, the reading of the text itself, as the continuation of the conversation, must take place suspended between foreignness and appropriation, the place Hölderlin's poem occupies. Without this tension, there is no conversation.

If the reader is to assume the responsibility of constructing the conversation between texts, then it remains unclear how this can be done. Texts that converse are not subject to any specific hierarchy.

This could be inferred from the chronology that makes Hölderlin's reference to Rousseau possible but does not seem to allow for the reverse. Either way, the one or the other text could be privileged based on this sequence, but only if we want to see texts as something unalterably present and available only once and for all. Hölderlin's reference to Rousseau, insofar as it is not only appropriation, rehabilitates the unavailability of the text by recognizing its foreignness. In that the texts continue to speak as something read, they change. Rousseau's text is not what it was before Hölderlin's poem. It is not enough to read Hölderlin via Rousseau, as if we knew what Rousseau was. We must instead read Rousseau via Hölderlin to let him become the one who actually had an effect on Hölderlin. In doing so we must always consider that Hölderlin does not say what Rousseau is, since it would then seem unnecessary to read his texts, at least as far as Hölderlin's poem is concerned. But the Rhine hymn does provide clues that could be construed as guidelines for a discussion of Rousseau. What is gained by following them is not Hölderlin's interpretation of Rousseau's text but rather an independent interpretation based on Hölderlin's suggestions, measured by its contribution to the understanding of Hölderlin's poem. The relationship between Hölderlin and Rousseau so constructed is a game between two teams that spur each other on. It is not a definitive result but a point in the conversation between the texts.

We might ask in what direction the clues in Hölderlin's poem point. The mention of Lake Bienne has caused those interpreters interested in the relationship with Rousseau to assume that Hölderlin is primarily interested in the experiences Rousseau relates in the Fifth Walk concerning his stay on St. Peter's Island. This track has been supported by the fact that recent literature on Rousseau has taken a similar course, seeking mainly to understand the dreamer's frame of mind as well as Rousseau's existential feeling described in the Fifth Walk. Although this aspect of Rousseau's text is certainly not unimportant for Hölderlin, and his Rousseau's desire to be on Lake Bienne can hardly be directed at anything else, the exclusivity with which Rousseau's meaning for Hölderlin has been sought in this aspect of Rousseau's text rests on a rather inexact reading of Hölderlin's formulations. Important is not only what Rousseau experienced on Lake Bienne.

> Dann scheint ihm oft das Beste,
> Fast ganz vergessen da,
> Wo der Stral nicht brennt,
> Im Schatten des Walds
> Am Bielersee in frischer Grüne zu seyn,
> Und sorglosarm an Tönen,
> Anfängern gleich, bei Nachtigallen zu lernen.

> Then often to him it seems best
> Almost wholly forgotten to be
> Where the beam does not sear,
> In the forest's shade
> By Lake Bienne amid foliage newly green,
> And blithely poor in tones,
> Like beginners, to learn from nightingales.

"Then often to him it seems best": this is not about the one who is at Lake Bienne but the one for whom being there seems the best. Not only the related experiences, but above all their being told, are important. It is therefore wrong simply to want to insert in the Rhine hymn a dreaming Rousseau on the lake shore, however one might interpret the dreamer's frame of mind. Hölderlin's Rousseau is not on St. Peter's but rather in a situation that can be more precisely determined in the context of the poem, where he looks back on his stay as the best. Rousseau is not only the character in the Fifth Walk, but also the one who writes. Hölderlin reads this text not just as information. He is interested in the relationship between the narrator and the narrated. Rousseau, not as someone presently experiencing but as someone who remembers past experiences, is the contemplative introduced as:

> Drum überraschet es auch
> Und schrökt den sterblichen Mann,
> Wenn er den Himmel, den

Er mit den liebenden Armen
Sich auf die Schultern gehäufft,
Und die Last der Freude bedenket;

And therefore it surprises
And startles the mortal man
When he considers the heaven
Which with loving arms he himself
Has heaped upon his shoulders,
And feels the burden of joy;

The Fifth Walk was created out of this consideration, if we take the *Dann* in v. 159 seriously, and this discourse concerns Hölderlin above all in what it bespeaks. It is pointless to try to establish links to the content of Rousseau's text; they are almost entirely missing. The amazing thing about Hölderlin's reference to Rousseau lies in the fact that there are no apparent similarities. Rousseau does not appear in Hölderlin's text in what he says but always and expressly as the speaker. We learn that he articulates the language of the purest and learns from nightingales, but we do not discover what he says and signs. The insight, supported by the wording of the Rhine hymn, that Hölderlin is concerned not only with what is expressed in Rousseau's text but primarily with its expression, tends to reorient a Hölderlin-related reading of the Fifth Walk. The shift away from what is expressed to the act of speaking is the most important guidance that can be gleaned from Hölderlin's poem. Following this guidance leads to a focus not on the same worn-out old passages but on neglected passages that speak of the relationship between the narrator and the narrative and what is narrated. The Fifth Walk was created out of this consideration, if we take the predicted with as little certainty as can its effects on the understanding of the Rousseau passage in the Rhine hymn.

ROUSSEAU'S FIFTH WALK

The simply constructed Fifth Walk is divided into two main parts, the first of which (pars. 1–11) is more of a narrative, the second (pars. 12–17) more of a reflective nature. The first part can again be divided. In an introduction (1–6), Rousseau describes St. Peter's (1–3), tells of the circumstances of his stay there (4–5), and asks wherein the happiness lies that he has found there (6). Looking ahead to an answer to this question, the second half of the first part (7–11) describes the daily routine on the island, and finally (11), the question, in what way this life has become a happy one, is repeated. In the second part (12–17), the question is answered in an explanation of the nature of *rêverie*. After the emphasis on the importance and difficulty of lasting happiness (12–13), *rêverie* is shown to be one possible realization of such a happiness (14–16). In the closing passage (17), Rousseau evokes once again his frame of mind on the island and tries to understand his relationship to it is as one who remembers.

The organization shows that the text is more than just a characterization of *rêverie* as an existential feeling, which some of his readers have restricted it to. Two ways of relating to what is said are examined in narration and explanation, and at the end the relationship between the one who remembers and the remembered, on the one hand, and the experience of remembering, on the other, is, compared to the remembered experience in the text, a theme in itself. The attempt to read the text with Hölderlin's guidelines in mind, the importance of how Rousseau as speaker stands to what he says, is justified by Rousseau's text, because it is not only concerned with *rêverie* but also with its placement vis-à-vis the discourse that bespeaks it. Instead of viewing this existential feeling in isolation, we have to try to understand its place in the whole of the text, because only in this way does the meaning of its being expressed become accessible.

Existential feeling and the circumstances under which it occurs are described in paragraph 9.

> As evening approached, I came down from the heights of the island, and I liked then to go and sit on the shingle in some secluded spot by the edge of the lake; there the noise of the lake and the movement of the water, taking hold of my senses and driving all other agitation from

my soul, would plunge it into a delicious reverie in which night often stole upon me unawares. The ebb and flow of the water, its continuous yet undulating noise, kept lapping against my ears and my eyes, taking the place of all the inward movements which my reverie had calmed within me, and it was enough to make me pleasurably aware of my existence, without troubling myself with thought. From time to time some brief and insubstantial reflection arose concerning the instability of the things of this world, whose image I saw in the surface of the water, but soon these fragile impressions gave way before the unchanging and ceaseless movement which lulled me and without any active effort on my part occupied me so completely that even when time and the habitual signal called me home I could hardly bring myself to go. (*Oeuvres complètes* I, 1045)

What is happening here should not be misunderstood as shutting out the environment and withdrawing to some inner self. The soul may quiet itself, not because the environment no longer exists, but because the environment is of such a nature that it quiets all unrest. The senses are not suppressed but fixed on the external movement ("the movement of the water") that replaces internal unrest ("all other agitation"). The internal unrest that must be eliminated, because it would otherwise obstruct access to related experiences, is passion ("But most men being continually agitated by passions know little of this condition" [1047]). Passion disrupts the cooperation between internal and external. The movement that displaces all internal movement is the back and forth of the waves ("the ebb and flow of the water"). This movement makes sufficient demands to prevent any sense of deficiency from cropping up and keeps the senses occupied but is never sensed so strongly that thinking would need to overcome it. The external is cradling and carrying, and the internal conforms to this rhythm. All objective sense is lost, and all that is left is the pure feeling of being in the world. This existential feeling of being carried through one's surroundings can only come about if the external is experienced not as object but as sojourn. This most likely succeeds where, as on an island surrounded by water, the surroundings are only present in that they surround. This being surrounded is buried underneath overriding change just as it crumbles in the wasteland of complete stagnation. If the environment is unnoticeable enough to be forgotten yet noticeable enough to be remembered, then it allows whomever it encompasses to experience the perfect harmony of being carried and of carrying.

The back and forth of the waves is able to effect this equilibrium between internal and external, provided the soul yields to the soothing evenness of its rhythm as the existential feeling is suspended. But the motion of the waves can only invoke the experience of equilibrium of internal and external in the observer because it is itself already an image of this equilibrium. The external favors most the balance between internal and external, which is in itself balanced. And so the equilibrium is not restricted to the back and forth of the waves but epitomizes for Rousseau the entire Lake Bienne landscape, which makes the experience of the environment as a nondisruptive carrier possible. The importance of the environment's internal harmony is most apparent when it is disrupted. In his description of the lake, Rousseau mentions a second, smaller, and uninhabited island. It is said that it will eventually disappear because all its earth is being transported to the larger island to repair storm and wave damage. "Thus it is that the substance of the weak always goes to profit the powerful" (1041). The mention of this small island is connected with the power vacuum between large and small, which destroys equilibrium (1044). When Rousseau, with the ceremonious participation of the local inhabitants, takes a litter of rabbits to the small island and lets them go, the founding of this colony is to be seen as an attempt to save an endangered equilibrium. The ceremonial crossing represents the back and forth of the dirt transports, which reduce the substance of the island.

The condition of the balanced exchange between internal and external, created by the surrounding nature and at the same time represented in it, can be regarded as the message Rousseau's text attempts to transmit. This transmission transpires on the one hand as narration, on the other hand as explanation, and we must question the purpose of this dual approach. As for the narrative, the text indicates that it fulfills the purpose of the remembered realization. After the description of the island's typical daily routine, we read: "even fifteen years later I am incapable of thinking of this cherished spot without each time being transported by pangs of longing" (1045). And at the end Rousseau preserves the prospect of remembering his stay on the island against those who drove him from his refuge on St. Peter's: "But at least they will not prevent me from transporting myself daily on the wings of imagination and from tasting for several hours the same pleasure as if I were still living there" (1049). The narration aims at reliving past experience. In the realization of the past, the distance to it is overcome, and the lost is reestablished. The narration facilitates an inebriation by means of what is narrated, enabling its language to be forgotten and what is experienced to be rediscovered.

Why do we need to explain the narration? Rousseau himself offers an explanation for the explanation. The narration is provoked by the question of the nature of happiness on the island. "What then was this happiness and wherein lay this great contentment? The men of this age would never guess the answer from a description of the life I led there" (1042). The challenge of explaining happiness based on the narration is repeated at the end of the narration: "I should like to know what there was in it that was attractive enough to give me such deep, tender and lasting regrets that even fifteen years later . . . " (1045). It should, in Rousseau's view, be self-evident that life as it is described is happiness. But it is so uneventful and quiet that his contemporaries ("men of this age"), who seek happiness in the unusual, in the "brief moments of madness and passion" (1046), have no appreciation for it. "But most men being continually stirred by passion know little of this condition, and having enjoyed it only fleetingly and incompletely they retain no more than a dim and confused notion of it and are unaware of its true charm" (1047). Because these people fail to see that and how this life is a happy one, they need an explanation. This justification is unsatisfying to the extent that it is based not on the narrative as something to be explained but on the failings of certain readers.

If the need for explanation springs from the narrative itself, then the narrative only makes what is to be told partially accessible and requires the help of another discourse. The explanation is necessary to the extent that something is missing in the narrative. If we assume that the narrative makes what is told present in a way that allows the experience to be repeated, as Rousseau tells himself, then the fault lies not with the narrative, which delivers all that is expected of it, but with the experience that is retold. But the nature of island life is again and again described as one of complete happiness and lacking nothing: "I look upon these months as the happiest time of my life, so happy that I would have been content to live all my life in this way, without a moment's desire for any other state" (1042). The description of happiness in the second part leaves no doubt as to the perfection of this state.

> But if there is a state where the soul can find a resting place secure enough to establish itself and concentrate its entire being there, with no need to remember the past or reach into the future, where time is nothing to it, where the present runs on indefinitely but this duration goes unnoticed, with no sign of the passing of time, and no other feeling of deprivation or enjoyment, pleasure or pain, desire or fear than the simple feeling of existence, a feeling that fills our soul entirely, as long as this state lasts, we can call ourselves happy, not with a poor, incomplete and relative happiness such as we find in the pleasures of life, but with a sufficient, complete and perfect happiness which leaves no emptiness to be filled in the soul. Such is the state I often experienced on St. Peter's Island in my solitary reveries, whether I lay in a boat and drifted where the water carried me, or sat by the shores of the stormy lake, or elsewhere, on the banks of a lovely river or a stream murmuring over the stones. (1046f.)

This characterization of Rousseau's happy state of mind practically demands a comparison with divine self-sufficiency: "as long as this state lasts we are self-sufficient like God" (1047). How can any explanation be added to this perfect wealth and then be understood as a supplement to something that seems to need no augmentation? This wealth has the fault that it is has no fault to make its perfection discernible. In this wealth's lack of contrast, the ability to recognize its completeness is lost. This only becomes appreciable—or, to use Hölderlin's word, perceivable—when it no longer exists and becomes determinable based on a regained incompleteness as its opposite. In Rousseau's text, the explanation comes from a distance the narration tries to overcome. The narration, even if, especially if, it were to succeed in reestablishing the divine self-sufficiency of happiness through the evocation of island life, could never say this in its perfection, whereas the explanation achieves this by its exclusion from this happiness. The blindness of happiness towards itself is its speechlessness. It disappears in being expressed. Insofar as both the narration and the explanation are ways of expression, the difference between the two is not easily maintained. Perfection is lost even in narration if it can be expressed. Narration strives to overcome its own being in language through the total realization of what is narrated. Explanation remains at arm's length to understand it instead of succumbing to the illusion of its reality. The difference between the tendency of both manners of discourse justifiably remains and allows us to see the strange position of the explanation better. This offers us an understanding of happiness that happiness lacks. Since happiness is the absence of shortcomings, one who is happy does not perceive the lack of understanding to be an imperfection. This only comes into play retrospectively, when it is corrected by the explanation. The explanation bestows this shortcoming on the perfect self-sufficiency of happiness and then constitutes itself as its elimination. Insofar as it adds something that was not previously present, the explanation is necessary. Insofar as what it adds is perfect and complete, it becomes superfluous. It is paradoxically a necessary excess. The second, explanatory part of the Fifth Walk is thus to be incorporated in the entire text, even though it cannot be included. It is an augmentation that comes to the narrative and complements it, even though it should actually be self-sufficient and is not recognizably deficient until it is supplemented.

Narration, as opposed to explanation, is understood as the refer-

ential realization of what is narrated, the complement to perfection
that must be considered superfluous and necessary at the same
time, because it is an augmentation to something that does not
leave room for it and yet still is incomplete. It can be shown that
not only the explanation behaves in this manner towards the
narrative but also the narration to what is narrated. This can be
demonstrated in an exact reading of the final section of the Fifth
Walk. This section is divided in three parts. In the first, Rousseau
thinks back once more to his stay on Lake Bienne and to the
dreamlike life he led. In the nostalgic middle section, he regrets
that he cannot return to St. Peter's and the lifestyle he enjoyed
there. The third section expresses that, despite the impossibility of
returning, no one can stop him from reliving the past happiness in
his imagination.

The third section illustrates the situation of one who remembers
the lost past and in dreaming relives the narrator's situation. His
relationship to the narrative is outlined in a few sentences:

> But at least they will not prevent me from transporting myself daily on
> the wings of imagination and from tasting for several hours the same
> pleasure as if I were still living there. Were I there, my sweetest
> occupation would be to dream to my heart's content. Is it not the same
> thing to dream that I am there? Better still, I can add to my abstract
> and monotonous reveries charming images that give them life. During
> my moments of ecstasy the sources of these images often escaped my
> senses; but now the deeper the reverie, the more vividly they are
> present to me. I am often more truly in their midst, and they give me
> still greater pleasure than when I was surrounded by them. (1049)

The situation of remembering and the remembered situation have
one thing in common: dreaming. Rousseau tended to dream on the
island but now dreams of being on the island. These two kinds of
dreaming are at first equated, even if only in a question: "Is it not
the same thing to dream that I am there?" A differentiation follows.
Dreaming *on* the island appears as "abstract and monotonous
reveries." The deprecating tone of this characterization is surprising, if we consider that we are discussing the faultless condition of

divine self-sufficiency, something that has just been celebrated. The fact that this reevaluation is at first unexplained does not diminish the contrast to the dreaming *of* the island, which is ranked higher because it produces images. This differentiation between pictorial and nonpictorial dreaming already appears in the second-to-last section of the text (1047f.). Rousseau's dreaming on the island was nonpictorial. This imageless dreaming is bound to certain environmental conditions described in the narrative part of the Fifth Walk and generally mentioned in the explanatory part. The environment must be perceivable just enough so that it is sensed neither as defect nor as intrusion. If it is too demanding, there is no dreaming, because the external pulls the soul away from itself and occupies it. Dreaming is possible if the environment is lifeless, for example, in prison, because then the imagination of what is missing externally can always be replaced. "The movement that does not come from outside us arises within us at such times" (1048). This dreaming is no longer imageless, as if internal and external were balanced, but rather pictorial to the extent that the imperfection of the environment is compensated for by the imagined images.

The separation of nonpictorial and pictorial dreaming seems at first to be easily transferred to the entire text. The ideal conditions were present at Lake Bienne, and nonpictorial dreaming was possible. For the narrator looking back, these conditions are no longer present, and he must call on his imagination to regain them as things represented. But the text cannot be read in such a simplistic manner, first because the images not only supplement what is missing, and second because the dreaming on the island, as it is described at the beginning of the last section, is unexpectedly pictorial.

The one who looks back places himself in a dreamlike state that he remembers as past. He dreams that he dreams on the island. The recovery of the past experience requires referential illusion, in which the language of the remembered, which is in this case the dreaminess of the dream, is forgotten, just as the narrative is taken to be the thing itself in the narrative part of the Fifth Walk. The role of images in this recollective dreaming should then consist of creating the conditions for nonpictorial dreaming, which are no longer present through the representation of the past environment. The images would have to disappear to exactly the same extent to which they appear, because imageless dreaming demands an environment no longer experienced in its presence but felt as a supporting structure. Rousseau's text, however, does not allow us to conclude that the environment of the remembered island landscape, reproduced in images, disappears in its pictorialization by freeing the soul for the earlier, nonpictorial dreaming. It is expressly emphasized that the appeal of the earlier dreaming was increased in its repetition when objects that were at first not experienced are added to the experience. This is why dreaming *of* the island cannot be equated with dreaming *on* the island, but is more: "In dreaming that I am there, am I not doing the same thing? I do even more; I add charming pictures that vivify the abstract and monotonous reverie" (1049). Since the condition of nonpictorial dreaming, based on its description throughout the text, is thought to be perfect bliss, the images of the recollective dreaming become an addition to what is already complete. The excess is an augmentation of the whole. Rousseau does not recognize excessive augmentation as such but prefers to accept a contradiction by denouncing nonpictorial dreaming as "abstract and monotonous reverie." Its deficiency is made good by images that can be integrated into a whole that would otherwise be incomplete without them. Regardless of whether the augmentation is added as excess to the whole or as supplement to the imperfect, we are left with the curious conclusion that what is remembered in remembering is more than it was in reality. Contrary to first impressions, the relationship between the remembering narrator and the narrative in the Fifth Walk is not nostalgic. The narrative is superior to what was experienced. Narration is a superior experience to what is narrated. The narration, as a representation of what was, is not a makeshift substitute but an escalation. The linguistic rendering of what was is more than what was.

Pictorial dreaming and the problem of incorporating it into the whole of the text already present themselves at the beginning of the final section. Rousseau seems at first to want to recall the previously detailed description of island life. After considering ways to experience the joys of dreaming in the previous section, under even less fortuitous circumstances, the beginning of the last section sketches the ideal conditions for the dreamer on St. Peter's. It says that the company of the inhabitants of the island was "attractive and pleasing without being so interesting as to constantly occupy me" (1048) and that the guest was able to follow his interests "without care or hindrance." The surroundings correspond to previous descriptions and are defined in that they allow neither too little nor too much. The relationship to the environment is so balanced that any demands it makes are not perceived as such. Although such a relationship with nature was earlier seen as a precondition for imageless dreaming, the dreams that Rousseau claims to have had on St. Peter's are now characterized by their pictorial nature.

> It was without doubt a fine opportunity for a dreamer who is capable of enjoying the most delightful fantasies even in the most unpleasant settings, and who could here feed on them at leisure, enriching them with all the objects that his senses actually perceived. Emerging from a long and happy reverie, seeing myself surrounded by greenery, flowers, and birds, and letting my eyes wander over the picturesque far-off shores, which enclosed a vast stretch of clear and crystalline water, I fused my imaginings with these charming sights, and finding myself in the end gradually brought back to myself and my surroundings, I could not draw a line between fiction and reality; so much did everything conspire equally to make me love the contemplative and solitary life I led in that beautiful place. (1048)

What appear here as "agréables chimères" and "fictions" are images created by the imagination that really have no place in the perfection Rousseau experiences. This is made clear if we question the relationship of the images (*fictions*) to what is really present (*réalités*). It is characterized at first by the verb *concourir*, which appears twice, expressing that reality is shaped in such a way that it contributes to the dream and at the same time can be included in it.

The dream image (*chimère*) and what encounters the senses in the outside world ("ce qui frappot reellement ses sens") are so closely connected that neither can be differentiated. This is demonstrated in awakening, something described as the transition from dream to reality but also as a state where changes no longer take place, because dream and reality are the same, and the borders between the two do not exist: "I could not draw a line between fiction and reality." If, however, what is dreamed is already present in reality, then the dream becomes superfluous, because it is added to reality when reality has no need for addition.

The introduction of the unnecessary pictorial dream makes it difficult, maybe even impossible, to incorporate the final section into the context of the entire text. The assumption that the narration is summarized and retold after the interpretive remarks of paragraphs 12–16 is untenable. Something completely new is reported that does not correspond to the previous narration. It is even more difficult to join the final paragraph (17) to the explanatory section. After it has been remarked under what conditions imagination must become active to make dreaming possible, images are created where they are not needed. In that the pictorial dream takes place under conditions previously associated only with nonpictorial dreaming, the argument falls apart. The beginning of the final paragraph cannot be incorporated into the order of the entire preceding text. It is conversely not difficult to recognize a kinship between the first and third parts of the final paragraph. This correspondence is based on the richness of the image, which does not represent something missing but is added to a complete whole. This similarity of the two text parts is made more interesting in that the one is concerned with recollective narration and the other with recalled narrative. Based on this, we can reconstruct the relationship between the narration and the narrative. The examination of the situation of the narration has demonstrated that dreaming *of* the island is more than dreaming *on* the island, because images are added to objects that were not perceived at the time. This augmentation of the images is now carried over from the situation of the narration to the narrated situation. The first part of the final paragraph tells of the past as if the augmentation of the images, only realized in the recollective retrospective, were already present. It is told as if the present objects had already been represented, that is, dreamed. What is not present until the level of the narration is asserted for the narrative's level. In this way the narration contradicts itself. The situation of the narration reaches into the narrative and destroys its coherence. The narration at the beginning of the last paragraph is wrenched from the context of what is reported, where it seems out of place. It does not allow itself to be incorporated into the order of the narrative and is only comprehensible, as it is presented in the third part of the final paragraph, from the perspective of the narration.

The transfer of the "augmentation of images" from narration to the narrative is an attempt to come to grips with the paradoxical fact that the narrative is complete and the narration is more than just the narrative. It would be more correct to say that the narrative is more than the experience and that the experience is poetically enhanced as something it can only be as narrative. By attributing the augmentation to the experience, Rousseau tries to overcome the gap that separates the narrative from the experience. The scandal of the superfluous remains, only now it has taken effect in the experience, thereby becoming the already narrated. This excessive augmentation is at best representation. In the recollective dreaming of the past, the representation of the real environment is the supplement to the remembered nonpictorial dream. In the subsequent attempt to integrate this augmentation with the recalled dreaming on St. Peter's, the dream becomes the double representation of reality and therefore superfluous, because everything is already present without it.

The problem of narration of the Fifth Walk is the representation of perfection. The problem lies in the fact that Rousseau situates perfection first, where representation no longer exists, and where the unmediated presence of the thing itself is dominant. Perfection is therefore nonlinguistic, and its nonexistence in language can be taken two ways. If it is perfect to be nonlinguistic, then language is a fault that must be overcome to reach perfection. But if language, as the manifestation of perfection, is not a fault, then the absence of language is the fault of perfection, and only language can make it what it is. Both are true: perfection's absence of language allows it to be direct and is also its fault, that is, the impossibility to manifest itself as perfect. In the mediation that included it, perfection is lost. Language, subjected to perfection, is the necessary but superfluous excess. It is excessive because it is added to the nonlinguistic perfection that survives without it. It loses itself in that it must conceal its characteristic directness to be able to appear to itself.

THE BEST AND THE HIGHEST

The section of the Rhine hymn dedicated to Rousseau is divided into the three initially quoted stanzas (10–12). Rousseau is at first the speaker who imparts the language of the purest. He does not impart content but language. Nowhere do we read what is said, but we read everywhere about the way things are spoken. The "foolish, divine, and lawless" manner of speech is that of one inspired, through which more is said than what he himself is. Out of his own limitations, he is placed not in a contralegal but in a prelegal condition, standing open to the divine and passing it on without realizing what he is doing. The speaker is not master of the language he speaks. He may present it but only as the gift given him, the language of the purest. This gift is not received without merit. It "became" to him just as the persevering soul became unconquerable. The perseverance in which the soul became unconquerable is the persistence in hearing's receptivity, connected to a speaking where the speaker breaks through to something greater. In the following stanza, the discourse of the one given over to hearing the divine is interrupted. Thoughtfulness takes the place of effortless reception. This is a pause on the straight path of discourse. In contemplation, the received is recognized as a burden, and being startled by the burden of heaven leads to fear. The selflessness of the speaker in the tenth stanza gives way in the eleventh to the realization of the disproportionate nature of burden and carrier. It is from this perspective of the disproportion between heaven and mortal humans that we are to read the second part of the stanza as Rousseau's answer to the fear in reflection. However we might understand the reference to the Fifth Walk, it leads in any case to a more balanced and less dangerous relationship to the divine, in the twelfth stanza no longer a foreboding burning stream of light but an inviting "softer light."

The question that is now raised concerns the relationship of these three stanzas to Rousseau's Fifth Walk, as I have attempted to read it based on the guidelines in Hölderlin's poem. This should not raise the expectation that everything that is said about Rousseau can or should be related to his text. The theme of the entire passage is the relationship between man and the divine and especially the danger of the divine for those subjected to it. This Hölderlinian theme that dominates the preceding passage (sts. 7–9) does not come from Rousseau. Hölderlin apparently has found in Rousseau a certain, obviously exemplary, way of relating the connection to the divine. The Fifth Walk is mentioned just when the sudden realization of the weight of divine power gives way to fear. Rousseau's text represents the conquering of this fear and the potential of a supportable relationship with the divine. How this relationship is achieved cannot be deduced from Hölderlin's poem, given our general considerations of the reference of texts to each other. The mention of Rousseau and his text is necessary in that Rousseau's text is not appropriated but continues to speak in its own name. I therefore assume that Rousseau's text enables an understanding of Hölderlin's text otherwise not possible. How the relationship to the divine is mastered is not explained in Hölderlin's poem but must be approached via Rousseau's text. But what "Rousseau's text" means is now limited in that I have tried to understand it by way of guidelines found in Hölderlin's poem. The most important clue is provided in the verse "Dann scheint ihm oft das Beste" (v. 159) and precludes a simple reading for content. Overcoming the fear of divine onus is not achieved during Rousseau's stay at Lake Bienne but in thinking back on it, that is, in the state of mind that created the Fifth Walk. This overcoming is neither final nor singular. The word *often* makes it impossible to relate the singular biographical occurrence of Rousseau's sojourn on St. Peter's. Much more important is the repeatable realization of this remembered singularity. The entire development described in three stanzas about Rousseau, if we pay attention to the word *often*, is not meant as an irreversible progression leading to a determined goal. The divine can always become a danger, and if mortal humans are frightened, it always seems best to be at Lake Bienne. Rousseau's text is set in the exemplary course as an exemplary means of overcoming the fear of the divine onus. We are then faced with the task of understanding Rousseau's text based on Hölderlin's guidance as a way to carry the burden of the divine.

It seems at first difficult to make a connection between our interpretation carried out according to Hölderlin's guidance and the Rhine hymn. The second half of the eleventh stanza does not at first seem to allow any connection to what Rousseau expresses about the relationship of the speaker to what he says. The main points of this passage seem instead to indicate that Hölderlin refers to content and interprets this in a particular way. The passage has usually been read so that the one subjected to, then frightened by, the divine burden withdraws to a place where he is no longer directly affected by the divine. The word *vergessen* (v. 160), to be read as active (Böschenstein, 104), points to flight and search for asylum from the divine and means having forgotten rather than being forgotten. Sleep (v. 166), too, seems to guarantee peace from anxiety, and the phrase "Where the beam does not sear" (v. 161) can, in Hölderlin's language, only mean the place where one is spared the merciless directness of divine presence. How this withdrawal is to be understood is, in the framework of this reading, less important than the conclusion that it cannot be Rousseau's stay on Lake Bienne. The word *often* provides the act with a repeatability not befitting the event but only its linguistic representation. This means that Hölderlin's Rousseau does not retreat to St. Peter's but to a special way of speaking about this event. This discourse must, if it is a flight from a danger that threatens the speaker at the time of speaking, be so insistent in what it says that everything else is forgotten. This kind of discourse is nostalgic narration, mentioned in connection with Rousseau's text. It strives to achieve such a complete realization of the narrative that its language is forgotten, enabling the event's repetition. This interpretation of Rousseau's retreat as an escape into the forgetting of language is unsatisfying for both texts in several respects. The realization, gained in anxiety, has in this escape by no means been overcome, only repressed. The flight, occurring as the discourse, would be naive but without divine sanction. We would also not expect an escape to somehow introduce an opportunity for a more tolerable relationship with the divine. Escape would be the negation of the inclination to face up to it. Coming from Rousseau, reduction to a language-forgetting discourse would be untenable as well. It does come up in the Fifth Walk, not as an actual devotion to the narrative, but reflected as language's potential to entice us into what it expresses. But even if Hölderlin's Rousseau could be completely transferred to a referential illusion, he would not escape the divine, because the condition in which he would be placed would be divine. It is hard to believe that Hölderlin overlooked one of the few passages in Rousseau's text where the theme of his own poem comes to bear, even if in a very different way: "as long as this state lasts, we are self-sufficient like God" (1047). Finally, the complex relationship between the narrator and the narrative is emphasized and discussed too much at the end of the Fifth Walk to be limited to a simple flight into what is expressed. On the other hand, there is nothing in the Hölderlin passage referring to the Fifth Walk that could be connected to Rousseau's thoughts on the relationship between discourse and what it expresses. This changes if we include the broader context of Hölderlin's poem.

The clearest mention of the relationship between the divine and the human, shared by the Rousseau passage, is in the eighth stanza.

> Es haben aber an eigner
> Unsterblichkeit die Götter genug, und bedürfen
> Die Himmlischen eines Dings,
> So sinds Heroën und Menschen

Und Sterbliche sonst. Denn weil
Die Seeligsten nichts fühlen von selbst,
Muss wohl, wenn solches zu sagen
Erlaubt ist, in der Götter Nahmen
Theilnehmend fühlen ein Andrer,
Den brauchen sie;   (Vv. 105–14)

But their own immortality
Suffices the gods, and if
The Heavenly have need of one thing,
It is of heroes and human beings
And other mortals. For since
The most Blessed in themselves feel nothing
Another, if to say such a thing is
Permitted, must, I suppose,
Vicariously feel in the name of the gods,
And in him they need;

There exists an earlier, rejected version:

Denn irrlos gehn, geradeblikend die	105
Vom Anfang an zum vorbestimmten End'	106
Und immer siegerisch und immerhin ist gleich	107
Die That und der Wille bei diesen.	108
Drum fühlen es die Seeligen selbst nicht,	109
Doch ihre Freude ist	110
Die Sag und die Rede der Menschen.	111

(2, 726, vv. 22–28)

For they travel aimlessly, gazing straight ahead	105
From beginning to predetermined end	106
And always victorious and the same	107
Are deed and will for them.	108
The blessed do not, therefore, feel themselves,	109
Their joy is, rather,	110
The narrative and discourse of mortals.	111

These verses reflect Hölderlin's thinking going back to his first encounter with Fichte's philosophy and continued in the Homburger Essays. In a letter to Hegel dated January 26, 1795, Hölderlin discusses Fichte's absolute I, which contains all reality:

> It is everything, and outside it is nothing; there is, then, no object for this absolute I, for otherwise there would be no reality within it; a consciousness without object is, however, unthinkable, and if I myself am this object, then I am, as such, necessarily limited, even if it is only a temporal limitation, that is, not absolute; there is, therefore, no consciousness possible in the absolute I; as absolute I, I have no consciousness, and insofar as I have no consciousness, I am (for myself) nothing; therefore, the absolute I is (for myself) nothing. (6, 155)

Hölderlin, and this is meant as a criticism of Fichte, can only imagine the absolute as the unconscious, because it can have no object outside itself. The absolute I is in itself nothing because, having a consciousness of itself and being object to itself, it would no longer be absolute. To have a consciousness of the perfect, there must be imperfection. This is also substantiated by the beginning of the fragment *Hyperions Jugend* (Hyperion's youth), where the concept of self-perception is introduced.

> If we were once perfect and free of all limitations, we would not have lost our all-encompassing sufficiency, the right of all pure spirits, for nothing. We traded the feeling for life, the bright consciousness for the carefree rest of the gods. Just think, if you can, of the pure spirit! It does not concern itself with matter; that is why no world is alive for it; no sun rises or sets for it; it is everything and therefore is nothing for itself. It does not go without, because it cannot desire; it does not suffer, because it does not live.—Forgive me the thought! it is only thought and nothing else.—Now we sense the limits of our existence, and the restrained power wrestles anxiously with its bonds, and the spirit yearns for the clear ether. But there is something in us that gladly endures these bonds; for if the spirit were unlimited by any resistance, we would be unaware of ourselves and others. To not be aware of oneself is death. (3, 201f.)

All these texts speak to the paradox of the imperfection of the perfect, which, in that it is everything and outside itself nothing, is denied the opportunity to compare itself with others and recognize itself as perfect. To be sensed, the perfect must have within itself the drive to create the imperfect. This must not be experienced by the perfect as something outside itself, because perfection would be negated as soon as something were to be assumed outside it. The perfect must therefore create imperfection within itself. It should be separate but at the same time be part of it. In his essay "Über den Unterschied der Dichtarten" (On distinctions of poetics), Hölderlin conceives of the creation of the imperfect out of perfection as the process of dividing the whole into its parts. The part is, inside the whole, separate and thereby the means for the whole to become aware of itself without sacrificing its perfection. It is reasonable to ask, however, how the whole, complete unto itself, can initiate the process of division, since it could stay at rest in its perfection. Hölderlin speaks of an "excess of spirit in unity" (4, 269). There is something beyond the whole, an augmentation, that initiates the division of the whole into its parts. Hölderlin calls it "the necessary discretion of Zeus" (4, 269). Zeus represents a play on the division of the whole as creative act. This act is capricious because the whole in its perfection is not determined by anything and can only act freely out of itself. Nevertheless, this free act is necessary because only through it, that is, through the creation of imperfection, can the whole become aware of its perfection. The whole can only come to itself in that it goes out of itself. The necessary discretion of Zeus is, within the whole, more than the whole that makes it spill over. This overflow limits the imperfect in its parts as it strives to regain perfection in the unified whole and, in the sense of its imperfect partition, senses the perfection of the whole in which it takes part but which it is not.

In the Rhine hymn, the relationship between the whole and the part appears as the relationship between God and mankind. God needs mankind to sense in His name what He cannot feel Himself. Based on the many passages that demonstrate Hölderlin's effort to come to grips with this relationship, it is impossible to understand the relationship as complementary. God is not in need of mankind in the same way that imperfection is in need of what it lacks to become faultless perfection. Mankind is not the complement to God, because He has always been perfect. God does not need mankind because He is lacking something but because of His perfection, which makes it impossible for Him to sense His own perfection. Human perception in the name of God does not fill a void but is added to the perfect as an extension, which seems to be superfluous from the viewpoint of the perfection of what is felt but seems necessary based on the inability of the perfect to be aware of itself. Necessary excess is the foundation without which none of Hölderlin's attempts to understand the sensibility of the divine can stand. The necessary discretion of Zeus and the participating feeling of mankind are both this augmentation, without which the perfection of the perfect could not appear and of which it is therefore both dependent and independent. Necessary discretion is the augmentation seen from above: the excess of the whole, the reason for its division and encounter with itself in its own parts. Human awareness and discourse is the augmentation seen from below: the addition to the perfect, imperfect only because it is felt and expressed.

The third and fourth sections of the Rhine hymn examine ways in which the relationship between mankind and God, characterized in the eighth stanza, can succeed or fail. Awareness in the name of the gods is awareness of the divine. This feeling requires that man be able to participate in place of God, who he is not. Only those who are mortal can sense it, but to do so they have to contrast immortality with their own mortality. In feeling what one is not, there is always the danger of forgetting that one is not what one feels. Those who succumb to the temptation of believing that they are only what they can feel, because they are not, are "defiant" (v. 101). They strive for divinity and lose the sense of their own imperfection. Their presumption is based on forgetting the language of feeling, which can represent the divine insofar as it is different. The contrast to the audacity of the defiant is Rousseau's fear. When the distance between the person feeling divinity and what we feel grows too small, we succumb to hubris. If the distance grows too great, then we become frightened of the immensity we are supposed to sense in our imperfection. In contrast with the audacious, who transgress against the divine and are punished, the frightened are given the chance to overcome their fright through a better understanding of their relationship to the divine. In this understanding, described in the eighth stanza, those who feel must understand themselves to be both superfluous and necessary to the divine. That they are used will save them from succumbing to their own weakness, and being superfluous will prevent them from losing themselves as godlike. Hölderlin does not directly say that Rousseau, among the frightened, attains such a balanced relationship to the divine. He does so through reference to the Fifth Walk. A connection between the two texts is now established. Hölderlin's relationship between mankind and God corresponds to Rousseau's relationship between the narrator and the narrative. Mankind's feeling is an augmentation to the perfection of God, just as narration is an augmentation to the perfection of the narrative. For Rousseau, the narrative is additionally a condition of godlike self-sufficiency that seems not to allow any experience beyond itself and is still heightened in the language of being remembered. From the narrator's insight in the Fifth Walk, his position becomes justified. What is told can be as perfect as it likes, it is still elevated by being told. If Hölderlin's Rousseau, as the narrator of the Fifth Walk, understands feeling in the name of God in this way, then this understanding conquers the fear that results from the disproportion between mankind and God and makes clear the task for which God needs him. This understanding does not belong to all who feel in the name of God but only to those who consider this feeling in retrospect. This is true in Rousseau's text, but also in Hölderlin's poem, where Rousseau seems to think it the Best to be at Lake Bienne; however, in that it seems to him the Best, it really is the Highest.

> bis in den Tod
> Kann aber ein Mensch auch
> Im Gedächtniß noch das Beste behalten,
> Und dann erlebt er das Höchste. (Vv. 199–202)

> but until death
> A mortal too can retain
> And bear in mind what is best
> And then is supremely favoured.

The augmentation of remembering as opposed to what is remembered is understanding the relationship in which those feeling in the name of God stand to God. This knowledge makes it possible to carry the "burden of joy" (v. 158), something granted only to those who are capable of attaining the Highest.

> Nur hat ein jeder sein Maas.
> Denn schwer ist zu tragen
> Das Unglük, aber schwerer das Glük. (Vv. 203–5)

> Yet each of us has his measure.
> For hard to bear
> Is misfortune, but good fortune harder.

Hölderlin grants Rousseau not only the experience of the Best but also that of the Highest. The Best is the self-forgetful sleep of nostalgic discourse, the Highest is the discourse of the Best. In a discourse of perfection where this or that excessive necessity is added, Hölderlin's Rousseau gains, as the one used in his frailty by God, the opportunity to overcome the fear of the divine burden.

This establishes a relationship between the texts of Rousseau and Hölderlin that should not go unconsidered. We should begin with the twofold relationship between the Rousseau passage in the Rhine hymn and the entire context of the poem, on the one hand, and with Rousseau's text, on the other. These two relationships must be integrated into any attempt at interpretation. This was done with a reading of the Fifth Walk, first examined according to Hölderlin's guidelines regarding the relationship of the discourse to what it expressed, and then by the definition of Hölderlin's Rousseau as a figure representative of feeling in the name of the gods. We concluded that the relationship in Hölderlin between God and a mankind that feels for God corresponds with the relationship between the narrator and his narrated memories in Rousseau. In both cases, feeling and expressing perfection are understood as an amplification of the perfect, superfluous and necessary. This correspondence makes it possible to use Rousseau's text, read with Hölderlin's guidelines, for understanding the poem and to concede to Rousseau the insight into the relationship established between mankind and God in the eighth stanza. We should ask, however, how this correspondence came about. It was neither planned nor predictable, and it would be senseless to want to force an answer. The risk that nothing of the sort would happen goes along with the attempt to establish a textual relationship. The method of determining such a relationship cannot be generalized as theory, and it is impossible to develop rules for a process of general text comparison that would guarantee success. This impossibility is predicated on the unpredictability of the reader's performance of his task as a third party. The reader has a freedom vis-à-vis the texts that these cannot take away, because they require the discourse of a third. The proposed correspondence between the texts of Hölderlin and Rousseau cannot be based on any assumed intention of Hölderlin's, even though it was made possible by certain guidelines within his poem. It is the result of my interpretation and thereby bound to it. It can especially not be based on what Hölderlin says about Rousseau. This correspondence is only established if we read the texts in a way that acknowledges tendencies that may be influenced by the other but without thus impinging on their autonomy. The relationship between Hölderlin and Rousseau is the concern of the reader, who recognizes the freedom of his own text within the framework of the other texts' potential. The reader's text is legitimized by laying out the potential of the texts and by doing so intensifies their meaning. This seems to me to exist in our case not only in the fact that Rousseau's place in the Rhine hymn becomes more accessible, but also that the determined correspondence between the two texts allows for a better understanding of the reference to the foreign text as such.

The correspondence between the two texts, required by the reference in the Rhine hymn to the Fifth Walk, is to be found in the augmentation of a perfect whole by the expression of this whole. The status of this augmentation must be determined as both superfluous and necessary. Is this not also true for the reference to Rousseau in Hölderlin's poem? If we assume that the poem is in itself a complete whole, sufficient unto itself, then the reference is unnecessary. If, however, it is necessary, then it manifests the poem's demand to be connected with the foreign text. The reference to Rousseau is, independent of how the relationship to the text is constituted, the necessary discretion of the whole, the means by which it goes beyond itself to return to itself via the foreign discourse. In referring to the other text, the poem makes known that it needs the other discourse, which feels in its name. But now we see that this necessary-superfluous augmentation to the whole, as we understand the reference to Rousseau, is at the same time what makes the two texts correspond. The reference is the call for a discourse to augment and express the whole. The augmentation to the whole is its own expression. The texts of Hölderlin and Rousseau, which determine the expression of the whole as the augmentation of the whole, qualify themselves as this augmentation with reference to the whole they express (the divine, the existential feeling). But these texts are also a whole that must be expressed without being able to express itself. This is why the text, as a perfect whole, pushes beyond itself. It has within it an excess, the reference to the other text. The text flows out in the necessary-superfluous discourse, which it needs although is not lacking. I understand my own discourse in this same way.

THE PART AND THE WHOLE

Even if the reference to the foreign text questions the poem as something complete within itself, thereby ripping apart its closure, the Rousseau passage is still a part of a whole, and we should examine the connection between the two. I would like to establish this connection with the help of the last of the three stanzas concerned with Rousseau. This stanza shows a transition from Rousseau's experiences on Lake Bienne to the universal experience of the wedding feast of mankind and the gods and occupies an intermediate position that can be interpreted from its manner of discourse.

> Und herrlich ists, aus heiligem Schlafe dann
> Erstehen und aus Waldes Kühle
> Erwachend, Abends nun
> Dem milderen Licht entgegenzugehn,
> Wenn, der die Berge gebaut
> Und den Pfad der Ströme gezeichnet,
> Nachdem er lächelnd auch
> Der Menschen geschäftiges Leben
> Das othemarme, wie Seegel
> Mit seinen Lüften gelenkt hat,
> Auch ruht und zu der Schülerin jezt,
> Der Bildner, Gutes mehr
> Denn Böses findend,
> Zur heutigen Erde der Tag sich neiget. (Vv. 166–79)

> And glorious then it is to arise once more
> From holy sleep and awakening
> From coolness of the woods, at evening
> Walk now toward the softer light
> When he who built the mountains
> And drafted the paths of the rivers,
> Having also smiling directed
> The busy lives of men,
> So short of breath, like sails,
> And filled them with his breezes,
> Reposes also, and down to his pupil
> The master craftsmen, finding
> More good than evil,
> Day now inclines to the present Earth.

The stanza has always been connected with Rousseau. There is nothing to contradict this, but, following the previous interpretation, it is no longer clear who Rousseau is: the person staying at Lake Bienne or the one thinking back on his stay. Both are possible. If we read on in the previous vein, then the awakening appears as an emergence from the linguistic amnesia resulting from the rememberer's nostalgic evocation. The sleep of remembering, from which Rousseau awakens, is holy, because this godlike state can be reexperienced. With awakening, the level of insight is achieved where the relationship to the divine becomes transparent. By recognizing themselves as superfluous but still needed, those who feel in the name of God overcome the anxiety over their relationship to the divine. They are now able to approach the milder light of God. If the stanza can be assigned without difficulty to the level of the one remembering, then there is nothing in the text that would prevent its being set on the level of what is remembered. Both the sleep and the awakening, as well as what follows, would then refer to the time spent at Lake Bienne. This possibility is not very fruitful for an understanding of the argumentative context of the poem, but it does open up a path to the problematic tone in which the stanza speaks. The stanza speaks in a curious suspension that makes it impossible to assign a place to the landscape rising out of the words. The "coolness of the woods" seems to take up the "forest's shade" at Lake Bienne, but the day has been personified as a god, which invites us to read the landscape allegorically. The "mountains" and "rivers," which are evoked here in great generalities, seem to disallow any localization. That it is nonetheless possible to integrate this landscape with place names in the previous stanza prevents a complete allegorization and preserves a sense of individuality for this unreal landscape by its association with Lake Bienne, thus thwarting its complete transition to meaning.

The stanza's suspended tone is related to its multiple referentiality. In that it can refer both to Rousseau's stay on St. Peter's and Rousseau's situation as he remembers his stay, all possibilities are not yet exhausted. These verses speak in a way that does not require a connection to Rousseau. The actions of awakening, arising, and encountering follow in subjectless indetermination. Rising from a sacred sleep is wonderful, regardless who is doing it. It is as if the figure of Rousseau fades in the milder light of evening, and his experience loosens itself from him to continue to work in a broader framework. This broader connection, to be inferred from the manner of speech, presents itself if we no longer connect the stanza with what immediately precedes it. Then we can see that many elements of the landscape that unfolds in the eleventh and twelfth stanzas are already familiar from the other landscape in which the poet sees himself at the beginning of the poem.

> Im dunkeln Epheu saß ich, an der Pforte
> Des Waldes, eben, da der goldene Mittag,
> Den Quell besuchend, herunterkam
> Von Treppen des Alpengebirgs,
> Das mir die göttlichgebaute,
> Die Burg der Himmlischen heißt
> Nach alter Meinung, wo aber
> Geheim noch manches entschieden
> Zu Menschen gelanget; von da
> vernahm ich ohne Vermuthen
> Ein Schiksaal, dann noch kaum
> War mir im warmen Schatten
> Sich manches beredend, die Seele
> Italia zu geschweift
> Und fernhin an die Küsten Moreas. (Vv. 1–15)

> Amid dark ivy I was sitting, at
> The forest's gate, just as a golden noon,
> To visit the wellspring there, came down
> From steps of the Alpine ranges
> Which, following ancient lore,
> I call the divinely built,
> The fortress of the Heavenly,
> But where, determined in secret
> Much even now reaches men; from there
> Without surmise I heard
> A destiny, for, debating
> Now this, now that in the warm shade,

My soul had hardly begun
To make for Italy
And far away for the shores of Morea.

The forest, the midday sojourn in the shade, the divinely built mountains are inescapable commonalities of both passages. This introduces a new dimension to the twelfth stanza and the Rousseau passage as a whole. If the poet's stay at the beginning of the poem corresponds to that of Rousseau on Lake Bienne, then the twelfth stanza can be connected not only to the eleventh but also to the first. In it are united two strains. The entire development of the poem since the beginning and the path of Rousseau merge in the single evening awakening. Rousseau and Hölderlin both move towards the softer light. The attribution of the verbs is suspended, because the stanza refers both to the whole of the poem and to this part of the poem. It is valid for the speaker as well as the one spoken about. This suspension of multilayered discourse is an indication that the Rousseau passage repeats the entire progression of the poem and is to be understood as its self-representation. It remains to be shown how this happens.

The situation of the poem's speaker, who appears in the first stanza as *I*, is comparable to Rousseau's. If the entire development of the poem is represented in the Rousseau passage, then it is the development of the speaker in his discourse that is meant. The *I* disappears from the discourse of the poem after the first stanza, but it is important for the desired connection that it appears again at the beginning of the Rousseau passage. The appearance of the Rousseau figure coincides with the retrospection of the speaker. Since Rousseau is introduced into the text as a speaker, this coincidence is confirmation of the view that Hölderlin sees himself in Rousseau as the speaker of his poem. If we want to understand the entire progression of the poem from the standpoint of the speaker, then we must question the connection between the two passages as the speaker refers to his own situation.

Important for the first stanza is the heretofore unnoticed fact that it is written in the past tense. The sojourn portrayed is not of the poet's present as he takes up his pen, rather it is past and remembered. The speaker relates to it as a retrospective narrator in the same way that Rousseau later looks to his sojourn on Lake Bienne. The unsuspected experience of the fate of the Rhine occurred in the past, which is why the following depiction of this fate is to be understood as a subsequent report of something previously experienced. Up to and including the ninth stanza, the poem consists of narration and reflection on the narrative. This changes in the tenth stanza:

> Halbgötter denk' ich jezt
> Und kennen muß ich die Theuern,
> Weil oft ihr Leben so
> Die sehnende Brust mir beweget. (Vv. 135–38)

> Of demigods now I think
> And I must know these dear ones
> Because so often their lives
> Move me and fill me with longing.

It has been questioned whether the *now* refers only to what follows or also to what precedes it. If we read the passage in connection with the beginning of the poem, linked by the renewed mention of the *I* which had receded, then this question seems less important than the observation that the *now* contradicts the past tense of the opening stanza. For the first time, the discourse is not directed to an other about which it reports but to its own present. Important are not only the demigods but also the relationship the speaker has to them. Hölderlin's retrospection on his own discourse is not coincidentally at the beginning of the Rousseau passage, dealing as it does with the anxious hesitation in divinely naive discourse. This parallel confirms the correspondence of the Rousseau passage to the poem's whole. The beginning of the tenth stanza is, in the entire sequence, the concern attributed to Rousseau in the eleventh stanza. The speaker knows the demigods because they often stir his heart. This *often*, which characterizes the repeatability of this realization, corresponds to the *often* in verse 159, where being at Lake

Bienne seems to Rousseau to be the Best. This *often* presumes an awareness of this recurrence. If the life of the demigods stirs the speaker's heart, then it does so in a discourse of actualization, for example, in the narration of the Rhine hymn. Now, however, the demigods are *thought*. Instead of realizing them only in language, the speaker thinks about his relationship to them. By representing this reflection, the Rousseau passage takes its place. It *is* the reflection of which it *speaks*. The speaker's reflection coincides with Rousseau's reflection, and the dual reference of the twelfth stanza becomes transparent, because the discourse that expresses Rousseau's reflection represents what it does by expressing it.

But why are demigods thought in the Rousseau passage? Rousseau is introduced as one who feels in the name of the gods. Whoever feels in the name of a god must to some extent become a god without being one, and it is not farfetched to view the person who feels this way as a demigod.

> Denn über der Erde wandeln
> Gewaltige Mächte,
> Und es ergreiffet ihr Schiksaal
> Den der es leidet und zusieht,
> Und ergreifft den Völkern das Herz.

> Denn alles fassen muß
> Ein Halbgott oder ein Mensch, dem Leiden nach,
> Indem er höret, allein, oder selber
> Verwandelt wird, fernahnend die Rosse des Herrn,
> (*Sonst nemlich, Vater Zeus* . . . ; 2, 226f., vv. 18–26)

> For above the earth move
> Mighty powers
> And their destiny grips
> Him who suffers it and looks on
> And grips the hearts of the peoples.

> For all things he must grasp,
> A demigod or a man, in the way of suffering,
> By hearing it, alone, or being transformed
> Himself, divining from afar the horses of the Lord,

Denn einsam kann
Von Himmlischen den Reichtum tragen
Nicht eins; wohl nemlich mag
Den Harnisch dehnen
      ein Halbgott, dem Höchsten aber
Ist fast zu wenig
Das Wirken   wo das Tagslicht scheinet,
Und der Mond, (*Kolomb*; 2, 244f., vv. 127–34)

For lonely not one
Can endure the wealth
Of the heavenly; for indeed
     a demigod
Can stretch the armour, but
To the Highest
Such working is almost too little
Where daylight shines
And the moon,

In the Rousseau passage, the relationship of the one feeling in the name of a god, that is, the demigod, is thought.

Reconsidering the attempts to connect the Rhine hymn and the Fifth Walk, one notices certain contradictions. Above all, the double-layered composition of the twelfth stanza just proposed is hard to reconcile with the earlier course of the investigation. If the development of Rousseau and the speaker of the hymn come together in this stanza, then the Rousseau passage can be easily incorporated in the whole as the self-characterization of the poem's progression within the poem. But it is questionable how this integration of Rousseau relates to the previously emphasized foreignness of his text, which alone justifies the reference to it. The self-characterization of Hölderlin's poem in the Rousseau stanzas is not dependent on the mention of Rousseau. Why then does it use his name and his text? Is the reference to Rousseau unnecessary, necessary, or both?

A part of the poem is the representation of the whole of the poem. The whole is blind to itself, as is God, who does not feel Himself. To be expressed as what it is, it must depend on the part that can express what it is not. But by expressing itself in its part, the whole is no longer what it expresses itself to be, because the self-expressing whole is more than the whole it expresses itself to be. As this more-than-whole, it is taken away from itself. The self-expression of the whole is a constant motion, and the self-expressing text is always open. Any attempt of the whole to express itself is an attempt to close this opening and come to rest within itself. The self-expression of the whole always takes place in the illusion of being able to reach itself in this self-expression. This is an illusion to the extent that it succeeds, because this success is added to what is expressed as the unexpressed. In Hölderlin's poem, the illusion, according to which the text could have caught up with itself, is shattered by the reference to the foreign text. In opening to the foreign, the poem abandons any hope of ever being able to express itself as a self-expressing whole. This renunciation is necessary because the whole that expresses itself always offers an excess of expression that it cannot express. What any one text cannot do for itself is possible for another. A foreign text can represent one's own text as a self-characterizing text if it represents itself. This is why Hölderlin refers not to any random text but to Rousseau's Fifth Walk. In the juxtaposition of two foreign, self-expressing texts, each is able to cure the blindness of the other to itself, because each can express the other without slipping away from itself, as must occur whenever any text expresses itself. What then, from this perspective, is the reference to Rousseau? Through him the text opens itself, in each of those parts in which it expresses itself, to a foreign text, which likewise expresses itself and thereby the other as self-expressing. If the reference to Rousseau were missing, Hölderlin's poem would say nothing else. But since the poem remains *with* this reference what it would be *without* it, the text to which Hölderlin refers is able to express his poem as self-expressing without changing it. Through the reference to Rousseau, the poem enables its own expression as self-expression without having to express itself and thereby lose itself. Rousseau's text can only express Hölderlin's as self-characterizing if the connection between the two is established. The poem cannot do this alone, because it could then never go beyond its own discourse. It must entrust itself to a foreign and then to a third text, one that reads the two and then makes the connection.

The Sacred and the Word

In his article "Hölderlin und das Wesen der Dichtung" (Hölderlin and the essence of poetry), Heidegger explains why he chooses Hölderlin to demonstrate the essence of poetry. This poet rises above all others as the "poets' poet" (*Erläuterungen*, 34). This distinguishes him from others whose work only realizes "the general essence of poetry." This general essence of poetry is valid for all poetic works, is independent of individual works, and can be brought together "in a general concept." The essence of poetry is, in their case, something that precedes each individual work and is "realized" in it, that is to say, comes to be presented. Hölderlin is the poets' poet because his poetry does not validate some otherwise valid essence of poetry but is "led by a poetic determination to write the essence of poetry itself." Poetry writing its own essence is not preprogrammed but first occurs within it and can therefore not be separated from it or generalized.

Regardless of whether this distinction justifies Hölderlin's privileged position above other poets, one problem which appears in it is characteristic of Heidegger's work on Hölderlin. The general essence of poetry, which is equally valid for all poetry and therefore detached and nonessential, can be conceptually defined and expressed. Conversely, "the essential essence of poetry," as something that only exists as it happens, is inaccessible to a conceptual approach and cannot be formulated. Writing the essence of poetry does not mean expressing it. Expression requires some distance from what should be expressed, by which the transpiring discourse is already separate from what it talks about. For Heidegger, however, the one who writes the essence of poetry is also the one who expresses it. The poets' poet is also the poet *on* poets. Heidegger expressly counters the argument that writing *on* poets is "the sign of confused introspection" and "clueless exaggeration, something late, and an end." The article as a whole considers "five key concepts of the poet on poetry." That writing on the essence of poetry is at the same time a writing *on* poetry is not self-evident. The relationship between the two is instead rather problematic. It could be that the essence of poetry is most likely written where it is not discussed. In Heidegger's writings on Hölderlin, the relationship between writing poetry and writing about poetry is fuzzy, even suppressed. Hölderlin's texts are read as if they were what they themselves express about poetry. Not taken into account is the fact that poetry on poetry can never be what it expresses about itself because it *expresses* it, just as some expression can be reduced to what it expresses. This blindness may have to do with the adherence to the untenable distinction between the poets' poet and other poets. The written essence of poetry begins to share in generalities, to the extent that it is expressed, from which Heidegger would like to keep it distinct. Poetry can only express the essence of poetry insofar as it is no longer only the result of but also the instrument to understanding. Poetry sacrifices its written essence by expressing it. Poetry makes its own essence more accessible by compromising itself. What poetry expresses as its essence is not what is written in it. The tension in which Hölderlin's poems speak is lost in Heidegger, as is apparent in his interpretation of the hymn *Wie wenn am Feiertage* (As on a holiday).

Heidegger reads the poem as "the Hymn of the Sacred" (76). Heidegger's interpretation aims at the relationship between the sacred and the word. The beginning of the third stanza deals with this relationship:

> Jezt aber tagts! Ich harrt und sah es kommen,
> Und was ich sah, das Heilige sei mein Wort. (Vv. 19–20)

> But now it dawns! I tarried and saw it coming,
> And what I saw, the Sacred should be my word.

My investigation must concentrate on these verses, but I will first attempt to examine the progression of Heidegger's interpretation

of the relationship between the sacred and the word based on two
sentences, the first of which determines the sacred, the second its
relationship to the word. They are: "The sacred is the essence of
nature" (59) and "The word is the occurrence of the sacred" (76).

"The sacred is the essence of nature." What Hölderlin calls
nature in this poem "reverberates in the entire poem to its final
word" (52). Nature, which for Hölderlin is ubiquitous and inclusive, is not a sphere of being among others. It is what is effective as
its potential. "It is never encountered anywhere within reality as a
singular reality" (52), because it is present in all reality. It is therefore only accessible but not attainable through reality. As something that precedes all else, it is the unforeseeable. As the basis for
all transmission, it is the immediate that eludes all transmission.
This inexpressibility of nature is evident in the inappropriateness
of all its names. Nature, the sacred, the spirit, the open, the
immediate, the chaotic are inadequate names for something that
remains unexpressed in all of them. The unexpressed is present in
the expressed as the inaccessible. The essence of nature is the
unapproachability of its detached ubiquity. When it is said that the
sacred is the essence of nature, then this connection of two names
is based on the opinion that one concept—"the sacred"—comes
closer to the unapproachability of the inexpressible as the essence
of nature than the other—"nature." The inappropriateness of the
depleted name "nature" is emphasized in two passages (56, 58).
"The sacred" identifies the essence of nature as surpassing what is
present in everything real. It identifies the unapproachability of the
unexpressed in the expressed. It does not identify the unapproachable essence but rather its unapproachability, and it is therefore
itself an inappropriate word, because it identifies what is inappropriate for every word. The inadequacy is not the word "nature,"
simply needing to be replaced with one more appropriate, but
rather the inadequacy of language when faced with the inexpressible.

If, however, no name is sufficient for the sacred, how then is it
put into words? The following sentence provides an answer: "The
word is the occurrence of the sacred." The sacred does not exist in

the word by being named but by happening within it. The word in which the sacred occurs is the song that testifies to both, which Hölderlin calls "the work of the gods and of mankind" (v. 48f.). Song is not just mankind's work. Something works within it that goes beyond mankind. Song is also not the work of God, who is dependent on mankind. Song therefore testifies neither to mankind nor to God but to their inseparability. This is based in a Highest to which both God and mankind are subject and that is now put into words as the sacred. The otherwise unapproachable sacred occurs as the testimony to the inseparability of God and mankind in song. In that song is the work of both God and mankind; nature, the sacred, works as the inclusive potential of this community. The sacred is not evident as something identified in song but is identified by song as what is active and occurring within it. "The words of this song are no longer a 'hymn to' something, not the 'hymn to the poets,' not the hymn 'to' nature but rather the hymn 'of' the sacred. The sacred bestows the word and comes into this word. The word is the occurrence of the sacred" (76). At this point, Heidegger's interpretation is no longer just an attempt to understand Hölderlin's definition of song but infringes on the particular song in which the definition is given. The poem *is* now the song of which it speaks. "The word of *this* song" (my emphasis) is the occurrence of the sacred. Heidegger takes this step within the framework of explaining the *now* that opens the third stanza. This *now* does not identify any specific moment but rather the present, the moment the poem's discourse takes place. Whether this discourse can be shown to be the occurrence of the sacred depends on whether the beginning of the third stanza can be read the way Heidegger does.

The verses "But now it dawns! I tarried and saw it coming, / And what I saw, the Sacred should be my word" are cited three times and read differently each time. The first time reads daybreak as an arrival, the second time as the transmission of the sacred, and the third time as the *now*, as the presence of discourse. First Heidegger takes the daybreak as "the arrival of a previously resting nature. Dawn is nature itself in arriving" (57). The arrival comes second in the word. The end of the article questions how the sacred is put into words as the immediate without being perverted in its essence and becoming something transmitted (72). The arrival remains an arrival and is therefore never present as something accessible to transmission. In that the sacred is always put into words as the arrival, it is not named in the word but occurs within it. Third, daybreak occurs now (75) in the discourse that expresses that it is put into words. Hölderlin's poem is daybreak as the occurrence of the sacred put into words.

This interpretation, in which everything is related to the occurrence of the poem's discourse, fails to consider the temporal structure of Hölderlin's verses, whose expression belongs to three different tenses. I saw it arriving in the past, in the future the sacred should be my word, but now, in the present, it is dawn. Daybreak is the arrival of day, but the arrival that occurs in the text, or better yet, seeing this arrival, is past and precedes the present daybreak. The arrival is not the coming-into-words of the sacred, because it is an unfulfilled wish that the sacred become word. The becoming-word of what was previously seen has yet to take place. The poem speaks *now*, between the having seen and the being-word of the sacred. The presence of daybreak seems to fade in relation to Heidegger's interpretation, because it cannot receive the sight of the arrival, nor does the sacred become word in it. What's more, the relationship between these occurrences has to be newly constructed.

The daybreak makes sight possible, because only light makes things visible. Seeing before daybreak pertains only to something that does not require light to be seen. Because without light there is no sight, what is seen before things become visible can only be light itself: not the light that is already present but the light that is yet to come. The seeing that precedes the daybreak is, as a seeing in the night, the sight of light's arrival. In the specific language of the poem, what has been seen is the *it* in "it dawns." The arrival of light is daybreak, and Heidegger is right to shift this arrival into the present of the ascent of the light (57). But even if the arrival of light and daybreak were simultaneous, the sight would still remain anticipatory. It is the sight of an arrival already begun before dawn, a coming of light that precedes the becoming-light of day. If light is still absent, that is, about to arrive, then the sight of dawn occurs in the dark. Daybreak already appears in its arrival, but it is as if the "it dawns" could only be seen as long as it is absent, as if the daybreak would extinguish this sight as it occurs.

Sight is not simply lost in the presence of speech. It is present in the discourse as something remembered. The sight of dawn's arrival can be expressed because it has become removed. This is how memory justifies its intent to express the remembered: "And what I saw, the Sacred should be my word." If the distance exists now, as it is being spoken, then an identification could follow, and no delay would be required. The poet would simply speak about what he had seen earlier. But the phrase "the Sacred should be my word" should not be read simply as a demand that the sacred be expressed. Instead, the sacred should *be* the word. The word that names the sacred is not itself sacred. In that both are distinct from one another, an identification is made possible. If the sacred is to *be* the word, then the discourse on the sacred must overcome the distance that is the basis for its occurrence. The wish "the Sacred should be my word" requires the discourse to go beyond itself and become what it expresses. Expression and being should coincide. This coincidence is, as long as one is speaking, always in the future and is present in the discourse only as the aspiration to go beyond itself.

The presence of speaking is a privation of the sacred. I saw it coming, and it shall be my word. But I can only say that I saw it coming and that it should be my word because this is no longer true. In the discourse that expresses what happened and what should happen, whatever it expresses cannot, to the extent that it is expressed, occur. The verb forms of the two verses make this clear and make it impossible to set the occurrence of the sacred into the present tense of the now-speaking poem. Heidegger reads as if Hölderlin says: "the Sacred *is* my word." But even if the sentence said this, it would not solve the paradox of the discourse's self-reference; rather it would simply leave us in the dark. The phrase "the Sacred is my word" contradicts itself to the extent that "my word" identifies the discourse in which the phrase occurs. The phrase suspends what it says by saying it, because the word that expresses itself to be sacred is not. By using the subjunctive as opposed to the indicative, Hölderlin avoids the confusion of saying and being to which Heidegger falls victim. The sacred is not the word simply because someone says that the word should be sacred. The poem that speaks of song is not this song but is separated from it by the distance that makes it possible to speak about it in the first place.

Opposing this we have the fact that it is still a song that speaks of song, that the discourse is, despite everything, exactly what it says it is. The discourse that speaks about the poem is not terribly different but is itself poetry. This can only mean that the discourse does occur as what it expresses. If the previous considerations are to be tenable, then they should be more precisely defined. If the poem is not what it expresses insofar as it expresses what it is, then this does not mean that it can't be what it expresses. It only means that it is not by making itself the object of its own discourse that the poem is what it expresses. What the poem expresses itself to be only exists where it does not express itself. "Where" does not mean somewhere else in the poem but on another level of discourse, a level to which we remain excluded as long as we only pay attention to what is expressed.

The "now" identifies the presence of the poem's discourse. But the event that places this discourse in the present is daybreak. "But now it is dawn," that is, the discourse and the dawn occur at the same time. It dawns now that the discourse occurs. But daybreak is not an event independent of the discourse that coincidentally happens at the same time. The poem speaks not only in the morning but whenever it is read and each time it is dawn, because the daybreak does not simply run parallel to the discourse but occurs within it. It dawns in the poem. The discourse itself brings light. But this remains a postulate, just as the phrase "But now it is dawn" remains a simple statement as long as the linguistic dawn cannot be experienced as something actually happening. Verses 19–20 make this possible if we allow them their halting movement and do not jump ahead of the gradual pace of the statement's determination too eagerly. In the phrase "I tarried and saw it coming," there is nothing at first that permits us to understand *it* as the sacred. Even if such an equivalency can be argued retrospectively based on the next verse, it would disregard the linear wording. Hölderlin does not say that he saw the sacred coming, but that he saw *it* coming. It would be of little use to argue that *it* is indeed the sacred, since this connection is made possible by the grammatical order of the sentences. But it is important that *it* in the sentence "I tarried and saw it coming" is *not yet* the sacred, because the sacred is not yet identified. *It*, in this position—disregarding the fact, as already shown, that the *it* from "it dawns" is taken up—is the anticipation of a name that is still missing. It is a pronoun that stands for a missing noun. In this most extreme uncertainty, it is the demand for a name that determines it. This is not immediately forthcoming. In "And what I saw," the uncertainty of *it* is at first confirmed as the unnamed thing that was seen. Not until the second part of the verse is *it* identified as "the sacred." In these verses the sacred is put into words not because it is named, but because, in the progression of the discourse, the gradual arrival represents the dawning of the name. This sequence cannot be seen as a statement. It is the reservation of a taciturn discourse that opens itself as something arriving precisely there, where it reaches for the inaccessible expression.

The poem's discourse is the arrival of the sacred, not because but in spite of the fact that it expresses it. The poem is what it says in its own manner of discourse, where it says the least, in those formulations that hardly seem to contribute to the account. There is, however, a point where the level of occurrence and the level of identification coincide. Where *it* is identified as the sacred, the occurrence merges with the identification. The identification appears from this standpoint as the goal of the linguistic progression. The course of the coming-into-words peaks in the finding of a name. But if the sacred, just put into words, is the named sacred, why then doesn't it say in this moment of fulfillment: "the Sacred *is* my word"? The subjunctive "the Sacred should be my word" changes the fulfillment to a wish. As soon as the discourse's progres-

sion has achieved its goal, the discourse defers it, so as to remain
motion. It must do so because the sacred only arrives in words as
something not yet present in words. With naming, the distance
from which it must arrive is once again decreased. Nevertheless,
identification becomes unavoidable. What is put into words and
arrives in the word always moves towards being named, even
though it sacrifices the character of the arrival, its essence, in its
identification, being fixed as an accessible object of the present.
The impetus to name and the impetus towards dissolution are both
effective in Hölderlin's discourse.

How are these considerations of the opening verses of the third
stanza relevant to Heidegger's interpretation? The reading of the
verses in two different ways has led to opposing results. If we
proceed from the temporal structure of the text, then what is to be
put into words and what was earlier seen as coming are not present
in the speaking that *now* concerns this before and after. Memory
and desire enable what can occur as a contemporary event but
cannot be named to be said. Nevertheless, these verses, as the
second reading has shown, are the occurrence of arrival, not as an
explicit statement but as a discourse that is recognized in its slow
progress as something that feels its way along but is incapable of
naming. The daybreak named in the phrase "But now it dawns" is
withdrawn from itself and can only occur to the extent that it does
not express itself. This silent speech event cannot be named to the
extent that it happens, but nevertheless it happens as the meaning
of the event—the event as past or future—and allows us to establish
a connection to Heidegger's interpretation, in which the poem is
the occurrence of the sacred it expresses. There remains one important difference to consider. Hölderlin's text tells us through its
chronological structure that it cannot be what it says insofar as it
says what it is. Its event characteristics are therefore not to be
gleaned from what it expresses but only from the inexplicitness of
its discourse. The inner tension of Hölderlin's discourse is missing
in Heidegger, who fails to recognize the special manner of discourse and, ignoring the verb forms, simply relates the expression
to what was expressed. Since Hölderlin says that the sacred should

be his word, his word is already the sacred. The word is, for Heidegger, what it says in that it says what it is. Heidegger's understanding of language is different from Hölderlin's, and we should question in what way his discussion of Hölderlin's poetry is influenced by this difference.

The difference between *naming* and *being* is constantly blurred in Heidegger's text. This is clear in the following passage: "Because the daybreak, easily encompassing and wonderfully ubiquitous, has now become *the only thing to say* and *is in the word,* nature 'is now awakened with a clang of arms . . .' But why must 'the sacred' *be* the word of the poet? Because the one standing 'under favorable weather' only has to *name* what he listens to with anticipation: nature" (58, my emphasis). "Being the word of the poet" is here "being in the word," and "being in the word" is "being expressed, named." The sacred is put into words by being named. "The Sacred should be my word" is for Heidegger "my word should name the Sacred." This fusion is not necessarily incompatible with Hölderlin's text and may even be suggested by the ambiguous formulation "the Sacred should be my word." But the subjunctive makes it impossible to overstate the difference between *being* and *naming.* That the word *should* be the sacred can only be said because it is not now the case. The word that demands that the sacred be the word names the sacred without being it. Whereas Hölderlin's discourse continues in this tension, Heidegger, who ignores the subjunctive, sees the named as being present on account of its being named in the discourse. The phrase "The essence of the named is uncovered in the word" (57) expresses this precisely. It is unimportant for Heidegger to distinguish between *being* and *naming,* because to him the word *named* by the word *is* in the word.

The naming of which Heidegger speaks is not signification. The name does not refer to the named as the sign to the signified, as something separate and already present. Naming means to uncover the essence of the named. This essence is not already present but only comes to be by being named. Naming therefore means: to allow the essence of the named to occur. Since this essence can only disclose itself in being named, the named demands its naming.

This is not the reproduction of something already present, but is, as Heidegger says with a word Hölderlin uses, endowment [*Stiftung*]. If the word *naming* has been previously used in the sense of a mediating expression, then this is not in Heidegger's sense, who, on the contrary, understands naming as the process in which the thing named occurs and its essence is exposed. This naming takes place beyond all semantics. It is nevertheless not wrong to mention a more everyday use of *naming*. Heidegger himself works (at least in this article) much less with the eventful expressing of Hölderlin's poem than with what is expressed in it. What is expressed is in this case the eventful expressing, but we should not equate the two. By substituting the expressed event for the event of expression, Heidegger misses the tension of Hölderlin's discourse, which constantly speaks with the awareness that it estranges its own realization by expressing it. It can only express itself—in the everyday sense of naming—if it steps outside itself and confronts itself. Through the silent equation of the expressed discourse with the discourse itself, Heidegger confuses the endowing with the mediating kind of naming. The difficulty lies less in the unclear distinction between the two than with the fact that Heidegger is unwilling to grant the mediating naming any part in Hölderlin's discourse, whereas he himself is constantly forced to refer to the expression of this discourse, that is, to what is mediated by it. This problem can be examined more closely in Heidegger's comments on Hölderlin's fragment *Das Höchste* (The highest), which comments on Pindar.

In connection with Hölderlin's reflections on the inaccessibility of the immediate, Heidegger says: "The immediate ubiquity is the mediation for everything conveyed, that is, for the mediate. The immediate is itself never a mediate, although the immediate is, strictly speaking, the mediation, that is, the mediateness of the mediate, because it enables it with its own essence" (62). Nature affirms itself here as the place where all reality appears and in which it takes part. It "mediates appearances for everything" (62). As the unmediated enabling of all mediation, nature is the immediate. It is said of the immediate that it is the mediateness of the mediate; of the mediate that it is the mediated. In that the mediateness of the mediate is understood as its being mediated, then the immediate is equated with mediation. This equation is the special point of Heidegger's considerations (de Man, 814). The immediate is not only the enabling of mediation but the mediation itself. The distinction between the act and its enabling is thereby eliminated. This means that the act of mediation is self-enabling. If the immediate is the mediation, then there is no preceding opportunity for mediation from which the mediation could be undertaken. The immediate instead exists only as the mediation. The mediation is the occurrence of the immediate. The immediate is, however, by no means what is mediated through this mediation. "The immediate is itself never a mediate." The immediate cannot be mediated but occurs as the mediation of the mediate.

Heidegger's interpretation of Hölderlin's phrase "the Sacred should be my word" must be seen within the framework of this reflection on the immediate. The phrase reads in Heidegger's version: "The word is the occurrence of the Sacred." The sacred as the immediate that makes possible the mediation through the word cannot be separated from the word as mediation but occurs as the mediation through the word. The equation of the immediate and mediation allows Heidegger to say: the sacred is the word. The sacred is the word, just as the immediate is the mediation. But just as the immediate as mediation is never the mediated, the sacred is never what the word says but only the linguistic occurrence of what is said. The sacred occurs in the expression of another as what remains unexpressed in this expression. In the sentence "the Sacred should be my word," the event is not expressed as a contemporary event but as a desire. By expressing the event as something that should be, Hölderlin contrasts his current discourse, to the extent that Heidegger's interpretation is correct, with the word that would be the occurrence of the sacred. The discourse that is not the event but only expresses it, however, is an instrumental, communicative discourse. Insofar as it expresses the desire for eventful discourse, it strives towards its own obsolescence. It opens itself to the eventful discourse by speaking of it. But in speaking about it, it is kept at a distance. In that Hölderlin speaks of the word as the occurrence of the sacred, he strives to do the impossible, that is, mediate the immediate by turning it into its opposite, the mediated. Just as the immediate is lost in its own mediation, a discourse that speaks of the word as the occurrence of the sacred is not necessarily the occurrence itself. This transfer takes place with Heidegger, who continuously attributes what Hölderlin says about the poem to the expression of the poem. It is the same transfer that takes place in the equation of the poet on the poet and of the poets' poet.

We might now see Heidegger's interpretation in a strangely scintillating connection to Hölderlin's poem. This interpretation's goal is to make the eventfulness of Hölderlin's discourse accessible. This is almost exclusively based on what is expressed, even though, according to Heidegger's interpretation, the expression of what occurs in the discourse can never become its own expression. Starting with the expression itself is justified for Heidegger by the fact that in Hölderlin's poem, song as speech event is thematized. But the conclusion that the poem is what it says about itself is completely unsupported. That the poem *is* what it *names* as its task is asserted without presenting any evidence from within the poem itself. Heidegger's attempt is contradictory insofar as he seeks the immediate that occurs in the discourse of the poem, something that cannot be mediated by language, in the expression of the poem, where it cannot exist to the extent that it is named. This does not mean that Hölderlin's discourse cannot be understood as an event in Heidegger's sense. The double-layered interpretation of the opening verses of the third stanza in Hölderlin's hymn has shown that the discourse that expresses the event can at the same time be that event only insofar as it expresses it. Since what occurs in language stops being an event when it is expressed, the event itself remains unexpressed. It occurs in the movement of the discourse that is no longer where it came from and does not yet know where it is going. This discourse speaks to find what it has to say and arrives at its destination by not being there yet. Hölderlin's discourse expresses what it is and is what it expresses. But it is not what it expresses by virtue of its expression but through the way in which it expresses itself. This is what is special about this discourse:

it expresses the event without ceasing to be it. Heidegger's equation of *being* and *naming* is not justified, because it presumes that this coincidence needs no further explanation. Hölderlin, on the other hand, achieves the simultaneity—not the correspondence—of the two from their mutual exclusivity. This tension, the outstanding characteristic of Hölderlin's discourse, has left no trace in Heidegger's text.

Reference Matter

A Note on Translations in the English Edition

Mallarmé

The translation of *A la nue accablante tu* is based on C. F. MacIntyre, *Stéphane Mallarmé: Poems* (Berkeley, 1957) but has been substantially modified; some modifications have been influenced by Robert Greer Cohn, *Toward the Poems of Mallarmé* (Berkeley, 1965). The translations from *Salut* and *L'après-midi d'un faune* are from MacIntyre. The translation of *Une dentelle s'abolit* and those from Mallarmé's correspondence are by Bridget McDonald.

Baudelaire

Many of the Baudelaire quotations are adapted from Lois Boe Hyslop and Francis E. Hyslop, Jr., trans. and eds., *Baudelaire as a Literary Critic* (University Park, Pa., 1964); others are by Bridget McDonald. The quotation from "L'art mnémonique" is from Baudelaire, *"The Painter of Modern Life" and Other Essays*, trans. Jonathan Mayne (New York: 1964). The translation of *Chacun sa chimère* (*To Every Man His Chimera*) is from Charles Baudelaire, *Paris Spleen*. Copyright © 1970 by New Directions Publishing Corporation. Translated by Louise Varèse. Reprinted by permission of New Directions Publishing Corporation.

Rimbaud

All translations from the French are by Bridget McDonald.

Hölderlin

All translations from Rousseau's *Rêveries du promeneur solitaire* are adapted from *Reveries of the Solitary Walker*, trans. Peter France (New York, 1979). Translations from Hölderlin's *Wie wenn am Feiertage* are by William Whobrey. All other Hölderlin quotations are from his *Poems and Fragments*, trans. Michael Hamburger (Cambridge, 1980).

Works Cited

Primary Works

Baudelaire, *Oeuvres complètes* I/II, Bibliothèque de la Pléiade, Paris, 1975/76.

Hölderlin, *Sämtliche Werke*, Stuttgart ed., Stuttgart, 1946ff.

Mallarmé, *Oeuvres complètes*, Bibliothèque de la Pléiade, Paris, 1945.

——, *Correspondance 1862–1871*, Paris, 1959.

Rimbaud, *Oeuvres complètes*, Bibliothèque de la Pléiade, Paris, 1954.

Rousseau, *Oeuvres complètes* I, Bibliothèque de la Pléiade, Paris, 1959.

Secondary Works

Austin, Lloyd J., "L'après-midi d'un faune, essai d'explication," *Synthèses* 258–59 (Dec. 1967–Jan. 1968): 24–35.

Böschenstein, Bernhard, *Hölderlins Rheinhymne*, Zurich, 1959.

Cohn, Robert G., *Toward the Poems of Mallarmé*, Berkeley, Calif., 1965.

de Man, Paul, "Les exégèses de Hölderlin par Martin Heidegger," *Critique* 100–101 (Sept.–Oct. 1955): 800–819.

Documents Mallarmé II, ed. C. P. Barbier, Paris, 1970.

Heidegger, Martin, *Erläuterungen zu Hölderlins Dichtung.* 4th, expanded ed., Frankfurt am Main, 1971.

——, *Hölderlins Hymnen "Germanien" und "Der Rhein."* Complete ed., vol. 39, Frankfurt am Main, 1980.

Mauron, Charles, *Mallarmé l'obscur*, Paris, 1941.

Noulet, Emilie, *Vingt poèmes de Stéphane Mallarmé*, Geneva, 1967.

NOTE   A portion of the original German version of the Baudelaire chapter was first published as "Über die Erinnerung bei Baudelaire," *Symposium* 33, no. 4 (winter 1979): 312–30. It appeared in the German edition by permission.

MERIDIAN

Crossing Aesthetics

Library of Congress
Cataloging-in-Publication Data

Frey, Hans-Jost.
[Studien über das Reden der Dichter. English]
Studies in poetic discourse : Mallarmé, Baudelaire, Rimbaud,
Hölderlin / Hans-Jost Frey ; [translated by William Whobrey ;
translations from the French and Latin by Bridget McDonald].
p.   cm. — (Meridian)
Includes bibliographical references.
ISBN 0-8047-2469-5 (cl.)
ISBN 0-8047-2600-0 (pbk.)
1. French poetry—19th century—History and criticism.
2. Hölderlin, Friedrich, 1770–1843—Criticism and
interpretation.   I. Title.   II. Series: Meridian (Stanford, Calif.)
PQ431.F7413   1996
841'.709—dc20   95-10585   CIP

⊗ This book is printed on acid-free, recycled paper.
It was typeset in Adobe Garamond and Lithos
by Keystone Typesetting, Inc.

Original printing 1996

Last figure below indicates year of this printing:

05   04   03   02   01   00   99   98   97   96